Society in Crisis

The Washington Post
Social Problems Companion

The Washington Post Writers Group

Allyn and Bacon

Boston • London • Toronto • Sydney • Tokyo • Singapore

Editorial Director: Bill Barke
Editor-in-Chief, Social Sciences: Susan Badger
Senior Editor: Karen Hanson
Editorial Assistant: Marnie Greenhut
Cover Administrator: Linda Dickinson
Manufacturing Buyer: Louise Richardson
Cover Designer: Suzanne Harbison

ISBN 0-205-14681-3

This book is printed on recycled, acid-free paper.

Printed in the United States of America

10 9 8 7 6 5 4 3 2 1   97 96 95 94 93 92

Contents

Foreword

Society in Crisis: The Washington Post Social Problems Companion, explores social problems in the United States and around the world, as enacted in real-world events. Written by many of America's foremost journalists, the articles bring timeliness and relevance to the classroom.

In organization, *Society in Crisis* devotes a separate chapter to each major type of generally recognized social problem, making it an ideal companion to any social problems text. Separate chapters include Economy, Politics, Environment, Population/Urbanization/Housing, Social Class/Poverty, Race/Ethnicity, Gender, Sexual Orientation, Family, Aging, Illness/Health Care, Mental Disorders, Education, Work, Crime, and Drugs. Introductions at the beginning of each chapter provide a brief overview and context for the articles that follow.

By studying social problems in United States society as well as problems in societies other than our own, the reader will gain a sense of the strong interdependence among all societies. It is our hope that this understanding will ultimately result in the creation of workable solutions to the myriad social problems facing the world today.

The Publishers

Economy *1*

Economic conditions have a profound effect on many aspects of society. The first article in this chapter explores the impact of the decline in the "service sector" on the current economic recession in the United States.

The next two articles look at issues of interdependence between the U.S. economy and the economies of other nations. United States ambassadors make efforts to boost U.S. trade in Asia, where neglect by many major U.S. corporations, particularly large automobile companies, has made establishing significant economic and trade ties an uphill battle. While the United States slashes foreign aid budgets and rethinks international assistance, Japan develops Third World markets for the 21st century.

The final two articles examine economic conditions in two distant societies. India, with economic problems stemming from huge internal budget deficits and the world's fourth largest external debt load, is considered to be at the "crossroads" of economic development. It could easily become a bankrupt economy like so many countries in Latin America, or a booming economy such as many of those in Southeast Asia.

The final article looks at some of the societal transformations in present-day Moscow, with its new free-market economy.

This Time, A Different Kind of Downturn

Slump in Services Threatens Recession

STEVEN PEARLSTEIN

If this be a recession, it is not like any we've seen.

Its epicenter lies closer to New York than Indianapolis.

Its onset was announced not by a buildup of steel and clothing in warehouses and loading docks, but by a buildup of office buildings with nobody to rent them.

And its severity is likely to be measured not simply by the length of the unemployment line, but also by the sharp drop in prices for stocks, junk bonds and real estate.

Until late this summer, most economists had been reluctant converts to the recession scenario. Their optimism finally gave way after a doubling of oil prices stoked inflation, sent stock markets reeling and sapped consumer confidence. The consensus view now calls for a mild "supply shock" recession that will generate its own recovery by 1992.

"The slump should be short and shallow," predicted Jerry Jordan, chief economist at First Interstate Bancorp in Los Angeles, speaking for most of his professional brethren.

Or will it? While most economists continue to view the current downturn in the context of the past 50 years of economic data stored in their computer models, others question if they are not like the infamous generals who have outfitted themselves splendidly to fight the last war. Is it not logical to question, they say, why a U.S. economy that has shifted so dramatically from blue-collar to white, that has taken on unprecedented levels of debt and that has been dragged kicking and screaming into a newly competitive and interrelated world economy—why this economy would behave just like it did before?

"The faster the world is changing, the less accurate the computer models are likely to be," argued Lester Thurow, dean of the Sloan School of Management at the Massachusetts Institute of Technology and something of an renegade among academic economists. "And the world is now changing very quickly."

Unlike many past recessions, this downturn is not being molded on the factory floor.

Although the economy as a whole has lost as many as 600,000 manufacturing jobs since January 1989, it is merely an acceleration of a process that began 10 years ago. Manufacturing employment has dropped from 22.3 percent of the work force in 1980 to 17.6 percent today. Few doubt it will continue its long-term employment decline. But what is most notable about the last year or so is how those losses are no longer offset by gains in "the service sector"—retail stores, restaurants, hospitals and medical labs, TV and movie production companies, travel agencies, software developers, banks and insurance companies, to name a few.

Consider the states at the cutting edge of recession. Among the nine states that reported virtually no growth in jobs or actual year-over-year job losses in August, seven were clustered in the Northeast: all six New England states, plus New York (Michigan and the District of Columbia were also on the list). These were among the places where jobs and income grew faster than the nation as a whole during the 1980s, largely on the strength of a real estate boom and spectacular growth in service employment.

Even as those economies began to unwind three years ago, with the cooling of the construction and real estate markets, unemployment rates remained remarkably low. Only when the service industries began to decline did the unemployment rates begin to move up—and, in many cases, the reversals were stunning and dramatic.

Connecticut, for example, which had been adding 10,000 jobs a year in insurance and other financial services, by this summer was adding none. Retail and wholesale trade, used to 15,000-a-year job growth, actually began shrinking. Meanwhile, construction and manufacturing, which had begun to slide much earlier, were each down roughly 9,000 jobs.

In New York State, the retail and wholesale sectors had been adding 38,000 jobs a year on average since 1982. This year: down 30,000. Financial services, good for 18,000 new jobs each year during the '80s, were down 12,000.

The slowdown looks a lot different in the states of the Rust Belt. In Ohio and Indiana, for example, construction employment was higher this August than last, while manufacturing jobs were down only fractionally. Meanwhile, service employment was still growing—80,000 in Ohio, 40,000 in Indiana.

Based largely on such state-by-state jobs numbers, the economic forecasting firm DRI/McGraw-Hill now calculates that a dozen or more states are already in a recession; economist Allen Sinai of the Boston Co., a unit of American Express Co., said it's closer to two dozen. But in almost every state at or over the edge, softness in the service sector has tipped the balance toward recession.

"We've had a long period of decline in manufacturing and construction," explains Sinai, "but what distinguishes the last few months is that the service sector is showing up weak and losing momentum. . . . Considering how large the service sector has become, I don't think we can really have a full-fledged recession until service industries begin to slide."

This notion that the service economy might actually lead a recession and operate relatively independently of the goods-producing sectors (manufacturing and construction) is still somewhat foreign to many economists. Traditional theories about the business cycle discount it. And the data on which economists rely—reports from purchasing managers, figures on inventory buildups, capacity utilization and the length of the average workweek, the performance of the Dow Jones industrial average, construction starts, the rise and fall of interest rates—shed little light on the performance of service companies that account for two-thirds of the country's gross national product.

"We don't have a set of accounts to measure the service economy very well," admits Sinai, who has been studying it more closely for the Washington-based Coalition of Service Industries as well as his own employer, service-sector giant American Express. "And analytically, we as economists haven't come to grips with it yet."

There is a growing body of evidence, however—some of it statistical, much of it admittedly anecdotal—that the rhythms and cycles by which the economy grows and contracts do not always track those of the industrial sector.

Commerce Department data reveal that service companies rely on manufacturing and construction for only about a quarter of their sales, while relying on other service companies for roughly half. Put another way, if you're wondering who all those accountants and lawyers and marketing specialists and consultants and computer programmers are doing business with, as likely as not it is with each other. That helps explain why the recession appears to have "spread" from New England along the Amtrak line as far south as Washington—and why it is hasn't "spread" to the Midwest or Southeast, where the service sector is less predominant, or parts of the Pacific West.

Obviously, there are a number of service industries that are closely tied to manufacturing—railroad companies that move finished goods and retail outlets that sell them. But these days it also works the other way around. Among the fastest growing manufacturing industries are some that depend heavily on service-sector customers: aircraft manufacturers that rely on the airlines; medical equipment makers that sell to hospitals and labs; computer makers, whose largest customers include all those banks and insurance companies. Government data confirm that the percentage of business investment in plant and equipment made by the service sector has been increasing steadily.

The composition of the unemployment line today also bears out the general impression that this is more a white-collar recession than we've seen before. Back in September 1982, at the height of the last recession, roughly half of those listed as without jobs were classified as white-collar employees or service industry workers. In September 1990, that figure was 60 percent. By contrast, only 23 percent of the unemployed today fall into the category generally thought of as assembly line and factory workers; eight years ago, it was 34 percent.

Economist Robert Gordon at Northwestern University suggests one additional reason recessions may be less driven by ups and downs of the manufacturing cycle—namely, those ups and downs are becoming less severe. The reason: overseas sales that remain strong even when U.S. sales are weak. Because of a declining dollar and a decade of factory modernization that has made U.S. products more competitive, estimates are that exports now account for 11.2 percent of U.S. manufacturing shipments, up from 8 percent during the high dollar days of 1983.

"To the extent that manufacturing these days is protected by (rising exports) and the economy relies more on the behavior of the consumer, we could have what you might call a service-sector recession," said Gordon.

"The possibility of a service-sector recession cannot be precluded," agreed Victor Zanowitz, a professor emeritus at the University of Chicago Business School and one of the leading scholars on the business cycle. But he quickly added, "I don't think we have seen one yet."

If there were a man-on-the-street explanation for the current economic situation, it might go something like this: The U.S. economy came to be dominated during the 1980s by financial manipulators who made huge fortunes by using borrowed money to run up the price of stocks and real estate so high that it eventually had to come crashing down, bringing the savings and loans and the banks and maybe even the whole economy down with it.

By the end of the decade, public and private debt in the United States rose to the highest point since the Great Depression: 1.9 times the gross national product versus 1.4 times at the beginning of the decade. Nearly half of all the working capital financing American business was borrowed from bondholders and banks, up from one-third 10 years ago. The debt held by the average American household has reached 88 percent of after-tax income, up from 72 percent at the beginning of the decade.

Much of this debt was used to pay for a buying spree that helped fuel the economy of the 1980s, in the process driving up the prices of businesses (stocks and junk bonds) and real estate. Now, as all can see, the bubble has burst.

Nationwide, the price of the average single-family home rose less than 1 percent per year after a decade of spectacular double-digit increases, and prices are actually falling in the Northeast and West. Harder hit has been the value of commercial real estate: According to one widely used index, the value of office buildings in the last three years has fallen 15 percent nationwide. Stocks are off 20 percent from their highs this past summer. And junk bonds—bonds that have become the moral equivalent of stocks because they are so risky—as a group have lost 35 percent of their original value, most of it in the last year.

Most forecasters are at something of a loss to say precisely what this steep decline in asset values means for what is called revealingly, the "real" economy. Few would say that the run-up in debt and asset prices actually caused or triggered the current downturn. And while a number of analysts say that the high level of debt and the rapid fall of asset prices could make a recession longer and deeper, they admit they have no good way to quantify that notion or incorporate it into their computer models. That is one reason that most are standing by their prediction of a recession that is short and shallow.

Not Gary Shilling, who as far back as 1987 was predicting a sharp decline in asset prices and serious recession. Shilling said the problem with most economists is that they keep looking for signs of an "income statement recession"—one in which profits and sales dip for a few months—when they should be tracking the coming "balance sheet recession" in which investors and lenders simply get wiped out, companies fall into bankruptcy and banking is strained to its limits.

"We don't have any experience with this kind of recession (since the Great Depression)—that's why those guys with the computer models can't pick it up," Shilling said.

"Maybe it will start when a money market fund—which most people think is like a bank account but isn't—actually declines in value because some Japanese bank can't roll over its commercial paper. And then a couple of big LBOs go belly up just as a few more Third World countries forfeit on their loans and the (bank insurance fund) finds itself in need of a bailout. People are going to say, 'Good grief, when is this all going to end?' Confidence just evaporates—and then watch out."

Just last week, economist Henry Kaufman warned that it would be folly to view the recession that he believes is now underway as just a garden variety version because of the high levels of debt and the extreme "fragility" of the U.S. financial system. In other words: Don't count on short and shallow.

While Shilling and Kaufman are viewed as doomsayers by many economists, more mainstream forecasters admit they haven't factored any sort of financial sector shock into their computer models or published economic projections.

Earlier this year, the Brookings Institution published a paper by economists Ben Bernanke and John Campbell, whose computer model showed that corporate debt payments now consume such a large share of corporate cash flow that even a moderate recession could send 20 percent to 25 percent of big U.S. manufacturing firms into insolvency.

While not predicting that will happen, Bernanke, a professor at Princeton University, said the high level of debt and the inflated values at which some assets are being carried on company books will certainly make a recession shock "significantly worse."

One way that the problems of high debt and declining asset values are transmitted to the rest of the economy is through the banking system, and clearly that has already begun to happen.

Largely as a result of falling real estate values and tougher accounting rules imposed by federal regulators, the value of problem loans and foreclosed property on the books of the nation's banks and thrifts has gone from about $60 billion at the end of 1985 to roughly $150 billion today (including the $45 billion or so of those loans now in the hands of the government).

To deal with the crisis, many banks have had to trim staff and reduce the amount of lending they do—not just to real estate developers, but increasingly to other kinds of businesses that are reporting difficulty in securing what used to be routine loan approvals. The Federal Reserve recently reported that overall bank lending had declined $5 billion so far this year, to $315 billion, and Chairman Alan

Greenspan has said that the central bank is worried that a credit crunch may be developing that could trigger a recession.

But declining asset values also can work their way into the "real" economy by way of the consumer. "For the first time since anyone can remember, housing values are falling," said MIT's Thurow, a reversal that "strikes right at the middle class, which, in effect, has used the family home as a savings account all these years."

Geoffrey Moore, who heads the Center for International Business Cycle Research at Columbia Business School and is among the most respected students of business cycles, conceded it is difficult to predict how the problems of the financial sector will work their way through to the real economy.

"There comes a time when the speculative excesses have to be corrected by a recession or even a depression," he said. "It happened that way in 1929, of course, and during several of the great panics of the 19th century, and it could happen this time, too.

"But right now," he was careful to add, "I'd have to say it looks more like an average type of downturn."

November 4,1990

U.S. Ambassadors Making Business Their New Business

Effort Planned to Boost American Trade in Asia

WILLIAM BRANIGIN

Years ago, American cars were a fairly common sight in Southeast Asia. Now, except for the wheezing relics that still ply the roads of such relative backwaters as the capital of Myanmar and southern Vietnam, they are hard to find. And even in those places, they are rapidly being replaced by shiny new Nissans and Toyotas.

The abandonment by American automakers of potentially lucrative markets in Southeast Asia reflects a mindset that U.S. government officials and businessmen say is shared by many American companies: a preoccupation with domestic sales at the expense of exports. At the same time, they say, efforts to remedy the situation by prying open the Japanese market may amount to barking up the wrong tree.

"The growth market in Asia for automobiles is Southeast Asia, not Japan," said Michael Dunne, an American automotive consultant at the Bangkok-based Southeast Asia Management and Investment Co. "Between 1988 and 1990, Thailand's auto market grew by 40 percent per year." Compared to growth in the U.S. car market in the range of 1 percent to 2 percent during that period, he said, "that's phenomenal."

Indeed, said Robert D. Orr, the U.S. ambassador to Singapore, "we spend so much time trying to open up the Japanese market that we almost totally overlook the fact that the Japanese are everywhere selling their products. They consider the world as their marketplace."

In an effort to awaken American companies to trade opportunities around the region, Orr and four other U.S. ambassadors are making an unprecedented tour of the United States this month. The group, including the envoys to Indonesia, Malaysia, Thailand and the Philippines, is to visit Portland, Chicago, Detroit, Atlanta, Houston and Washington during the 11-day trip starting Saturday.

"We hope it will have a consciousness-raising effect," said a U.S. official in the Philippines. "The ambassadors will be the barkers to get people into the tent."

At the core of the trip is a perception that the United States needs to increase its competitiveness in the world marketplace.

"It's so difficult to talk American business people into exporting," said Orr, a former governor of Indiana. "They're so addicted to our great big beautiful market."

Although U.S. exports have been rising in recent years, he said, they accounted for only 7.2 percent of GNP in 1990, compared to an average of 19 percent among major competing nations.

"If we were to double our exports, there wouldn't be a recession right now," Orr said.

Together, the countries that make up the Association of Southeast Asian Nations (ASEAN)—Indonesia, Malaysia, Thailand, the Philippines, Singapore and Brunei—represent a market of 320 million people with a growth rate that has averaged 7.25 percent over the last two years. And the market is relatively open.

"Market access is just not the problem that it is in Northeast Asia," said one U.S. commercial officer in the region. Whereas non-tariff barriers and other protectionist mechanisms often discourage U.S. companies from trying to penetrate markets in Japan and South Korea, he said, "it's not that difficult to do business here."

Still, he added, developing trade relationships with Southeast Asia requires an investment of time and effort that some American firms seem to ignore.

"We still get a lot of U.S. companies that think they can do it all by mail," the official said. "The good news is that the market is open. The bad news is that it's not an automatic sale. if you want a long-term relationship, you have to build it."

Generally, U.S. government and corporate officials say, it is not the American industrial giants such as IBM and Exxon that need coaxing to venture into the Far East, but the smaller "middle class" of corporate America.

According to Jack Hanlon, co-chairman of the Investment Promotion Committee of the American Chamber of Commerce in Thailand, 80 percent of U.S. foreign investment is done by no more than 100 major firms. "The rest have no inkling or interest in foreign investment in the exotic tropics," he said. "I think it's just xenophobia on the part of the U.S. businesses. It will take a tough, uphill fight to get small businesses to take advantage of their opportunities here."

A prime example of lost opportunity is what many U.S. businessmen regard as Detroit's neglect of its export markets. With economic prospects looking fairly bleak after the communist takeovers of South Vietnam, Cambodia and Laos in 1975, General Motors and Ford virtually pulled out of Southeast Asia, leaving the field open for the Japanese.

"Years and years ago, you used to see American cars all over the place," a U.S. business executive in manila said. "Where did they all go? The American automakers concentrated on the U.S. market and they neglected the rest of the world. It's their own fault."

Certainly, the U.S. auto market dwarfs those of Southeast Asia. The United States produces 6.5 million new units a year, compared to about 300,000 in Thailand and Indonesia, 200,000 in Malaysia and 50,000 in the Philippines. However, Dunne said, "if you look at the whole region, it's a very attractive place for investment." China's market is about 700,000 new cars a year and Taiwan's is another 500,000, he noted. "Add all this up, along with the vast potential for growth, and there's every reason for American automobile manufacturers to be more aggressive out here," Dunne said.

Today, Japanese companies control about 90 percent of the market for commercial vehicles and 85 percent for passenger cars throughout Southeast Asia, Dunne said. U.S. companies have less than I percent of the market share, with European manufacturers making up the rest.

"American automakers always have an excuse for not competing," Dunne said. "Meanwhile, the Japanese just eat it up. Local partners are not thrilled about being dependent on the Japanese. They'd like to work more with Americans."

Part of the problem is that, like the Japanese, most Southeast Asians drive on the left side of the road. The exception in ASEAN is the Philippines, but even in that former U.S. colony the automobile market has long since succumbed to the Japanese onslaught.

Dominating the protected Philippine market are car and truck assembly plants controlled by Nissan, Toyota and Mitsubishi. The latest entry is a South Korean firm, Kia, which has begun assembling a model called the Kia Pride.

In Malaysia, a Mazda model called the Telstar is assembled by Ford, which owns 25 percent of Mazda. But the bulk of the market is held by a Malaysian car, the Proton Saga, the only indigenous auto in the region. Although it uses a Mitsubishi Lancer chassis, the body is Malaysia's own design and about 60 percent of the content is locally made.

Ford's strongest presence in the area is on Taiwan, where the company eventually hopes to make cars for export to mainland China.

Other U.S. automakers also are starting to take a second look at the region. Chrysler opened an office in Thailand in 1990 and hopes to launch its Jeep in the country in 1993.

In an effort to boost its meager market share, General Motors has set up offices in Hong Kong and Thailand, a joint venture in Shenyang, China, and wholly owned subsidiaries in Taiwan and Indonesia.

According to American officials, some of the best opportunities for U.S. business in Southeast Asia lie in such sectors as computers and peripherals, food processing and packaging machinery, aircraft and avionics, telecommunications gear, health care and pollution-control technology, management services, and oil and gas equipment.

Relatively low labor costs and a growing pool of technicians and middle managers make the region attractive for foreign investment. However, new investments by U.S. firms in recent years have been lagging behind those of Japan, Hong Kong and Taiwan.

The major obstacle to increased American trade and investment in Southeast Asia, U.S. officials say, is intellectual property rights. The worst offender in the region is Thailand, where the counterfeiting of everything including designer watches, videotapes and computer software is a growth industry. But problems exist elsewhere as well. In the Philippines, for example, it is estimated that only 5 percent of the software sold in the country is legal.

For many companies, the new frontier in the area is Vietnam. Government efforts to attract foreign investment, a cheap and relatively well-educated labor force and the prospect of new offshore oil discoveries have fueled intense interest by Asian and European businessmen. American firms have been lobbying Washington to lift its economic embargo on the country so that they can compete, especially in the oil sector.

Within ASEAN, the United States has been running trade deficits with every country except tiny, oil-rich Brunei. But the total deficit with ASEAN of nearly $7.4 billion for the first 11 months of 1991 is small compared with the $66 billion deficit in U.S. trade over the same period with the rest of East Asia and the Pacific. The figure includes negative balances of $9 billion with Taiwan, $11.6 billion with China and nearly $39 billion with Japan.

In its efforts to promote exports, the U.S. government maintains foreign trade offices that offer various services to American firms at nominal cost. But the facilities are relatively modest compared to those of some foreign competitors.

"The South Koreans have as many trade offices overseas as we do," a U.S. commercial officer said. "Worldwide, we are generally outgunned by our trading partners."

Southeast Asia Sketches

Thailand

Economy and trade: The kingdom's economic boom—9 percent real GNP growth in 1990, 7.9 percent last year and up to 8.5 percent projected for this year—has put a strain on infrastructure that has somewhat slackened the pace of foreign investments. In the first 11 months of 1991, Thailand ran a trade surplus with the United States, importing nearly $3.4 billion worth of U.S. goods and exporting $5.6 billion.

Investment climate: Still, the projects keep rolling in. In 1988 and 1989, Japanese investment reached nearly $10 billion a year. New U.S. projects in 1991 were valued at $1.1 billion.

Malaysia

Economy and trade: Gross domestic product grew by 10 percent in 1990, 8.6 percent in 1991 and is forecast at 8.5 percent this year. In the first 11 months of 1991, the country ran a trade surplus with the United States of $1.9 billion.

Investment climate: In recent years, the top investors have been Taiwan, Japan and Singapore.

Products: The country is the world's largest exporter of semiconductors—and one of the world's top exporters of room air conditioners and videocassette recorders.

Philippines

Economy and trade: After zero growth in 1991, the economy is projected to expand by 3 percent this year. Trade with the United States showed a surplus in the Philippines' favor of $1.1 billion.

Investment climate: A liberalized foreign investment law took effect late last year, but kidnappings of Americans tend to discourage new U.S. investors. The bulk of U.S. investment came from companies already established in the Philippines.

Labor costs: While still cheap by U.S. standards, labor in the Philippines has become costlier than in some competing countries, with basic blue-collar wages in Manila now starting at $5.12 a day.

Singapore

Economy and trade: America's leading trading partner in Southeast Asia, the city-state bought $8.1 billion worth of U.S. goods in the first 11 months of 1991 and exported $9 billion worth to the United States. Economic growth reached 8.3 percent in 1990, but dipped to 6.5 percent last year and is forecast at 6 percent this year.

Investment climate: With labor in increasingly short supply in the island state of 2.8 million people, Singapore has been moving into high-tech investments and a "triangle of growth" concept with Malaysia and Indonesia.

Indonesia

Economy and trade: Economic growth last year reached 7 percent and is projected at 5.5 percent this year. U.S. exports to Indonesia have risen from less than $1 billion in 1985 to $1.9 billion in 1990.

Investment climate: Indonesia is the giant of ASEAN and has been attracting massive investments, an estimated $70 billion from 1989 to 1991. U.S. private investments have grown from less than $1 billion to about $2 billion.

Special correspondent Mary Kay Magistad in Bangkok contributed to this report.

March 20, 1992

Japan's Hands-on Foreign Aid

As U.S. Slashes Assistance, Tokyo
Develops Markets for 21st Century

STEVE COLL

At dawn in this remote and smoky industrial town, a steel skeleton rises in the half light, the beginnings of an $850 million, 1,000-megawatt electric power generating station being constructed by Mitsui & Co., the Japanese trading giant. The plant, which will pump power across India's densely populated north, was made possible by a record $600 million, low-interest-rate loan from the Japanese government.

To Japanese officials, the plant is a symbol of Tokyo's new place as the leading philanthropist in the Third World, a position it assumed at Washington's urging. But to some resentful Western aid officials, the symbolism is very different.

While the United States slashes its foreign aid budget and rethinks its international assistance, they say, Japan is using its bountiful aid coffers to develop Third World markets for the 21st century—in many cases using development aid explicitly to promote Japanese companies against Western competitors.

As it did with the power plant under construction here, Japan often links large loans and grants to poor countries with procurement of Japanese equipment and technology, an approach that not only enriches Japanese firms in the short run, but also provides them with a strong marketing edge once an aid program is finished.

Japan's seemingly clear-eyed emphasis on its economic self-interest contrasts with a U.S. aid program that appears to be in a state of confusion, shrinking in size and uncertain of its purpose.

Nowhere is this more obvious than in South Asia, a poor but steadily developing region with more than 1 billion people and a growing penchant for market capitalism. In the region's three largest markets—India, Pakistan and Sri Lanka— Japanese bilateral assistance now far outstrips that of the United States, amounting to more than $2 billion annually.

The vast majority of Japan's aid comes as low interest rate, or "soft," loans for big infrastructure projects such as power stations, telecommunications systems, and energy and transport, and the Japanese loans have strings attached: U.S. and European companies are largely excluded from participation in the projects, permitting Japanese firms to make immediate profits, establish their technologies in nascent industries and develop future markets.

As one Western aid official noted: "Once a user becomes familiar with Japanese equipment and technology, they'll keep using it."

It is a self-interested aid philosophy that "is skewed in a manner to promote Japanese interests to the great detriment of the development needs of the recipient country," said another Western aid official.

In the U.S. approach, on the other hand, this official argued, "There is a dimension that goes beyond self-interest . . . that is altruistic. This is an important part of American values."

In private, Japanese businessmen and officials scoff at American attempts to hold the moral high ground on aid.

They point out that "altruistic" programs, such as U.S. food donations to India, are protected in Washington by corporate farm and shipping lobbyists, whose clients reap millions of dollars annually from the program. They note that among developed Western countries, the United States is virtually alone in not linking economic aid to the explicit interests of its own companies. And they argue that the thrust of Japan's aid program promotes the goals articulated by the Reagan and Bush administrations: to encourage recipient countries to solve their problems of poverty and development through capitalism.

U.S. aid officials acknowledge that their own house is in a state of relative disorder. "Probably over the years we've had (on) a bit too many rose-colored glasses," said a Bush administration official. "We have to see that it's a different world and we have to adjust. . . . I think we should be prepared to meet the competition in whatever form it takes."

Meet Fukuo Yamanaka

Here is the competition: a round, bespectacled, unusually friendly Japanese executive named Fukuo Yamanaka, chief representative in India of Mitsui & Co., the Japanese trading giant. Yamanaka knows the United States—he worked there for nine years—and he remembers his time fondly. But his career provides a microcosm of how the nexus between government aid and private trade has changed in Japan and the United States during the past three decades, and how those changes are reshaping international economic competition.

Yamanaka's business is power—the manufacture, sale and maintenance of electric power generating stations and their assorted industrial components. He first came to the United States in the early 1960s, when "made in Japan" was synonymous with "cheap and shoddy" and when the international electric power business was dominated by U.S. firms, particularly General Electric Co.

As an engineer and salesman, Yamanaka's job in those days was to acquire and sell GE power turbines to Japanese users, often municipal governments and other utility authorities. No company in Japan could make turbines as well as GE, so Mitsui in those days made its money brokering American exports to Japan.

Because of the huge sums involved in building a power plant, and because governments are almost always involved in the business, it is typical for large deals to be supported by government credits or low-interest loans. Back in the 1960s, Yamanaka's job was made easier by the favorable financing he arranged with the U.S. Export-Import Bank. In those days, Japan was a big recipient of U.S. economic aid designed to rebuild its war-shattered infrastructure and to reinforce prosperity, democracy and political stability.

When Yamanaka returned to the United States during the 1970s for his second tour as a salesman, Mitsui had redefined his responsibilities somewhat. Now Japanese companies allied with Mitsui made some turbines and other heavy industrial equipment in competition with U.S. manufacturers. Yamanaka still used Ex-Im Bank credits to sell GE turbines to Japan, but he also sold Japanese products to U.S. companies, taking advantage of favorable public and private financing arranged by Tokyo.

By his third and final tour, during the mid-1980s, the tables had turned completely. Now 95 percent of Yamanaka's time and energy was absorbed by selling Japanese turbines and industrial equipment to U.S. users. It was a good business, and many of the Japanese products were considered superior.

As for GE's business in Japan, Yamanaka notes dryly that, "These days, Japanese customers don't need any economic aid."

Today, Yamanaka is posted on Mitsui's next frontier: the developing world, where demand for electric power far outstrips supply, and where governments are anxious to build plants quickly on favorable terms. GE is still one of Mitsui's competitors, but in India and elsewhere in South Asia, the contest isn't very close.

One big reason: Japanese government aid, in the form of "soft" loans from its bulging Overseas Economic Cooperation Fund (OECF), has made Mitsui pretty much unbeatable by U.S. companies in South Asia.

Mitsui's biggest project in India today is the construction of the two 500-megawatt electric generating facilities at Anpara. Mitsui won the lead position on the contract after outbidding a single Japanese competitor.

The deal was clinched by a $600 million OECF loan carrying a 2.5 percent annual rate of interest, a 10-year grace period and a repayment period stretched over 30 years.

Like many Japanese, Yamanaka is sensitive to any implication that Japan is cynically using its aid budget to a poor country like India to promote the prosperity of Japanese corporations. The OECF loan restrictions excluding Western companies from competing "is of course a mixture, the political decision, the business decision."

As for Mitsui's goals, they are twofold, he said: to make immediate profits by winning contracts, and to build for the long run by using government-financed deals to introduce technologies and find partnerships with Indian companies.

Virtually all OECF loans to this region bar U.S. and European companies from competition, as was the case with the Anpara loan, but companies from developing countries are permitted to compete. In the rare instances where they beat out a Japanese competitor, negotiations later still often result in a tie-up with a Japanese company.

There are dozens of deals pending or underway in South Asia where Japanese firms have won contracts to build infrastructure projects using restrictive OECF loans or outright grants from Tokyo. Grants require 100 percent procurement from Japan.

A particularly vivid example of how such assistance promotes Japanese exports is visible in Sri Lanka, the island nation off India's southern tip. In the early 1980s, Sri Lanka had virtually no television facilities. With soft loans and grants, Japan donated state-of-the-art broadcast and transmission equipment, constructing a powerful network.

Today, Japanese manufacturers dominate Sri Lanka's booming market for color television sets—a market that hardly existed 10 years ago.

Despite a gradual relaxation of the exclusive conditions, Japan's aid to developing countries retains "a very, very close connection with private business," said a Japanese source who asked not to be further identified. This situation arises in part from a shortage of government staff devoted to managing the huge aid program overseas. As a result, "the role in identifying projects is played by the big trading houses in Japan, and they encourage the (recipient) government to submit a proposal."

The system "is not necessarily a bad thing," this Japanese continued. "Our companies are very efficient and are able to identify projects that will help the recipient countries. But our companies can make money under our system."

In India, where the government tends toward xenophobia even in the best of circumstances, there is a voluble debate about whether the Japanese aid system is as good for India as it is for Japan. Some accuse Japanese firms of taking advantage of their quasi-monopoly status in big projects to charge exorbitant prices. Others worry that Japan doesn't do enough to involve Indian companies in development work.

"One thing is very clear: The bulk of the OECF money ultimately goes back to Japanese companies," said Naresh Minocha, an Indian financial analyst. "And the Japanese companies quote higher prices than they would in full global competition."

Rethinking the Purposes of Aid

It now is clear that Japan's aid program in South Asia and much of the developing world dwarfs that of the United States and helps Japanese companies secure a toehold in markets where they might otherwise be left behind. But these truths do not necessarily mean that the United States will be less competitive than Japan in Third World markets during the 21st century, some economists and business officials say.

That is one reason specialists in Washington are today unsure about what the purpose and character of U.S. aid to poor countries should be.

U.S. aid policy remains driven by diverse impulses: to shore up friendly governments in strategic regions, to promote the spread of democracy and capitalism generally, and to provide direct relief to those living in the depths of Third World poverty.

The promotion of economic competitiveness has joined that list of goals during the Reagan and Bush years, but some U.S. aid workers say the idea has been slow to take root in an aid bureaucracy populated by people who see their careers as being devoted to altruism, not economic nationalism.

Some economists and government officials say the United States should try to best Japan not by imitating its approach to foreign aid, but rather by exploiting U.S. "comparative advantages" against Japan.

The biggest of these advantages, they say, is a relatively open U.S. immigration policy that encourages the development of international family-run businesses with a strong anchor in the United States.

For example, there are now about 26,000 Indians attending U.S. colleges and universities, according to U.S. officials. Presumably, some of them will start trading and making money on their own when they are finished with school, as thousands of Indians before them have done, building up two-way trade that totals billions of dollars annually.

Still, some U.S. officials argue that Washington should do much more to integrate the specific needs of U.S. businesses into its foreign aid budget, particularly in areas of the world where markets are young and Japanese and Europeans are working aggressively.

"If the Japanese companies have been so successful [in South Asia], it is because of the close linkage between industry, banking and the government," said V. Krishnamurthy, former chairman of the Steel Authority of India and a key architect of Japan's aid and trade relationship with India. "If you had gone to the American embassy in [New] Delhi, or to the government in Washington with a proposed deal, they would not" have provided much guidance or assistance.

The U.S. government is trying to change that, but the pace is slow. U.S. embassies now have instructions to integrate more closely the work of Commerce Department officials and representatives of the Agency for International Development (AID), which administers most U.S. aid to poor countries.

Last year, AID established for the first time a $300 million "war chest' to help U.S. companies arrange competitive soft loan financing against Japanese and European firms. But the amount available for such loans is relatively paltry. And during the same period, Congress defeated, at AID's urging, a bill that would have directly linked U.S. aid donations to procurement from U.S. companies.

"The goals remain the same—to improve the quality of life for poor people in developing countries," said a U.S. aid official. "We're also interested in developing an environment conducive to U.S. investment abroad . . . but we're not the instrument for U.S. business."

Krishnamurthy, recalling the days of the Kennedy and Johnson administrations when India was plagued by famines and the U.S. government boldly led a rush of charitable donors onto the subcontinent, said the U.S. aid philosophy has been well-intended but ultimately unprofitable. "Looking back, U.S. aid was directed in the right places" to alleviate poverty, he said. "But it was not aid that had a commercial future."

January 13, 1991

Third World Crossroads

Two Tales of Hope and Worry; India Faces Questions about Debt, Reforms

STEVE COLL

Buried in borrowings and short of hard cash, India may become the world's next victim of the debt crisis that already has crippled developing economies in Africa and Latin America, according to a growing number of finance specialists here and abroad.

Even though it is stumbling under the weight of huge internal budget deficits and the world's fourth-largest external debt load—$63 billion and rising—India's economy nevertheless has continued to lurch ahead at an admirable rate of growth. But planners and international financiers are beginning to worry that without politically painful reforms, India's economic bubble could burst during the early 1990s, with devastating consequences for the country's impoverished and rapidly expanding population.

"India is at the crossroads, and its decisions could take it either toward the bankrupt economies of Latin America or the booming economies of East Asia," said Gene Tidrick, chief economist of the World Bank here.

Runaway inflation or a deep recession—the calamities that lurk for economies overloaded with debt—would cause widespread suffering in India, where an estimated half of the country's 820 million people live in poverty. In addition, military planners and diplomats have begun to worry about what would happen in populous and friction-ridden South Asia if India, the bastion of stability in the region, experienced a serious economic crisis.

It may be three years, it may be five, but an [economic] crisis is going to hit our policy makers in the face," predicted Surjit Bhalla, an economist and political scientist at a private New Delhi research center. "The potential loss to India for inaction now is very high."

Such fears about India's immediate future are based on signs of disturbing imbalances in the economy. The most obvious is the rapid rise of external debt—money owed to international lenders such as the World Bank and International Monetary Fund, commercial banks in Europe and the United States, and to private citizens. Not only has the absolute amount of India's external debt tripled since 1980, but the country's debt-service ratio—a key economic measure that depicts how much available cash is needed each year to pay off existing obligations—is reaching levels comparable to such crippled debtors as Brazil and Nigeria.

India's overseas debt load is exacerbated by two other emerging problems: a spiraling internal budget deficit twice as large as that of the United States relative to the size of the economy, and a cash crunch due to a trade deficit now running between $5 billion and $6 billion annually.

While India used to have a comfortable reserve of foreign exchange with which to pay for necessary imports—products ranging from oil to artillery to industrial machinery—it now has only enough hard cash to cover two months of imports. India's currency, the rupee, isn't convertible on world markets and thus can't be used to pay for imports from abroad.

These complex and difficult problems loom at a time when India is being led by a minority government backed by an unusual array of political parties, ranging from Communists on one side to Hindu conservatives on the other. The new prime minister, V.P. Singh, a former finance minister, is regarded as an informed economic thinker, but his cabinet includes a potpourri of agricultural populists, unbending socialists and political opportunists.

A number of senior economic planners in Singh's administration concede privately that the problems are serious, but most dismiss the fears of an impending crisis. They argue that the country can use its continuing industrial growth to muddle through the early 1990s without undertaking drastic budget reforms and trade liberalization measures recommended by commercial bankers and international agencies such as the IMF.

Some Indian economists also say that comparisons with such debt-laden countries as Mexico and Argentina are not justified because a large amount of India's debt burden is fixed at concessional interest rates by international lenders, meaning that India is less subject to the whims of commercial bankers and is better able to manage repayment schedules.

Since it achieved independence in 1947, India has been a vocal champion among developing nations of economic self-reliance and what Indian politicians call "the middle way" between capitalism and socialism. With a high savings rate and an ancient culture that emphasizes frugality and adaptability, it has maintained remarkable political and social stability despite regular droughts, wars and other catastrophes. While some in Singh's cabinet support a gradual shift toward free markets, none calls for a radical departure from the country's historically cautious path.

India's economic policies of heavy public ownership of industry, centralized planning, big domestic subsidies and some of the world's highest tariff barriers have produced some notable successes, such as the virtual elimination of famine. The country's relative economic stability also has allowed the government to implement an array of poverty-abatement, health and other social programs, while at the same time building a strong defense capability.

Nonetheless, India's economic problems are formidable. Poverty remains deep and widespread. High tariff protection for domestic industry has produced a surfeit of shoddy consumer and industrial goods—nails that bend upon hammering, tape that doesn't stick and cars that belch and rumble at a maximum of 50 miles per hour. Government intervention in the economy, in the form of an impenetrable thicket of regulations and required licenses, has led business to institutionalize payoffs.

India's politicians apparently believe the country can carry on this way indefinitely. But the country's growing debt load, combined with political and economic changes at home and abroad, have led a growing number of Indian economists and international finance specialists to question whether the "middle way" is viable any longer.

For example, India's economic balancing act during the 1970s and 1980s depended in considerable part on its close relationship with the Soviet Union, particularly on a series of trade agreements that allowed India to import Soviet military hardware and export consumer and industrial products without spending any of its precious hard currency. New Delhi's so-called "ruble account" with Moscow permits India to account for all of its Soviet trade in rubles and rupees, currencies that are not recognized on world financial markets.

Soviet President Mikhail Gorbachev is under pressure to change this system, and if he does, India will face a series of major problems during the early 1990s.

Last fall, the Soviets floated a proposal that constitutes an Indian economic nightmare—that india start paying for its huge Soviet military imports in hard currency, not rupees. This would put enormous pressure on New Delhi's balance of payments at a time when its trade deficit is already badly out of whack.

The Indian team that heard the Soviet proposal at a November meeting in Moscow rejected it adamantly, saying it was not part of the two countries' most recent trade agreement. But the Indians came away with a sinking feeling that the change was inevitable, according to S.B. Chavan, the former finance minister who led India's delegation at the talks.

"They are bound to ask for it again. The question is how long can you resist," said Chavan.

Other economic challenges loom at home.

Expectations among the country's growing middle class are rising and there is an increasing awareness that in terms of the quality and availability of most consumer goods, India lags badly behind its Asian neighbors, including China, whose xenophobic Communist leaders have, ironically, done much more to liberalize their economy and to import foreign technology than have democratically elected politicians in India.

Socialist and free-market economic planners alike agree that the best way to keep India out of the international debt trap would be to reduce its massive budget deficits, easing the country's appetite for foreign funds.

But the budget promises made by Singh's new administration, including continuing large agricultural subsidies, waiving loans to small farmers and businessmen and instituting massive public employment schemes, offer the minority government little room for political maneuvering. Analysts say that whatever programs emerge from India's parliamentary budget session this spring, they will be a far cry from the austerity programs recommended by international lending agencies.

March 25, 1990

Reinventing Russia

Moscow, from Church Bells to Cheeseburgers

ROBERT G. KAISER

Driving out of the center of Moscow on Prospekt Mira at 8:10 p.m., I see a strange, bright light 200 yards ahead. It looks like the light of a welder's torch, but who in this land of notoriously lazy workers would still be welding at 8:10 p.m.? Drawing closer, I see the welder, wearing a mask, coming into view—in the courtyard of a Russian Orthodox church. He is working on a huge, cast-iron church bell.

This Moscow is the capital of free Russia, a land where workers work past 8 p.m., and church bells—banned for decades by the Communists who lately ruled here—are legal again.

Returning to Moscow for the first time since the demise of the Soviet Union and the Communist Party is a confusing experience for an old hand. The set is familiar, but the play is dramatically new—as though the Globe Theater were being used to stage a Sondheim musical. Massive changes are occurring at breakneck speed. A rigid political and economic culture is suddenly so elastic that it sometimes seems to be stretching out of control. A great country is reinventing itself.

Amazingly, the first three months in the history of free Russia have gone quite well. No mass starvation, no riots. On the contrary, the markets of Moscow have not been so well stocked in early spring for years, probably decades. (Nor have prices ever been remotely so high in Russian history, an important reason why the stores are well-stocked.) Not that the future is assured, or even visible. From the highest government officials to the most humble working men and women, no one in free Russia will predict a rosy future, but very few are wallowing in despair, either. "These are anxious times," observed Mikhail Litvinov, an old friend, now 75 years old, whose lifetime neatly spans the Bolshevik era. Very anxious, but also very exciting.

It would be hard to exaggerate the dislocations now upsetting the lives of nearly all Russians. To get a sense of what is happening, imagine how Americans might react if they had watched the price of their groceries go up by a multiple of 10 or 15 in the past three months—and that is just the most obvious source of discomfort and confusion. This society, so tightly organized around a political and bureaucratic structure, a centralized economic plan and 70 years of ideological traditions, has suddenly shed all of them, without waiting for replacement structures or beliefs to emerge. Russian society is now dangling between two realities, one that shaped the outlook and habits of every Russian but is now fast disappearing, the second still indistinct over the horizon.

Gennadi Burbulis, President Boris Yeltsin's principal aide and deputy prime minister of the Russian government until Yeltsin shifted him out of that job on Friday, has set himself up as the philosopher of the new situation. "No one has ever confronted such a formidable task before, because communist empires did not exist prior to the 20th century," he observed in a conversation in the old headquarters of the Communist Party's central committee. "And nobody has ever been able to move out of a totalitarian regime right into full-scale democracy."

"We are not in a position to choose a better history," he added, sitting in the huge office once occupied by the party's chief ideologists. "Our task now is to survive in our specific conditions, with our specific people, with the distorted economic system and its unique features [that we inherited] . . . "

There's the rub. The transformation now under way will succeed only if millions of people can traverse an enormous distance from old ways to new. Workers must learn to work, managers to manage. A woman who teaches English at the Pushkin Institute of foreign languages in Moscow complained that "now we'll have to work all the time. To tell you the truth, I don't like to work all that much. It's boring." Hers is a profoundly typical attitude.

Can they do it? Yes they can—which doesn't mean they will. Carnations and tulips can stand as an early sign of success. They are available in great profusion in the subway stations of this city, stacked on card tables by newly minted entrepreneurs who are selling three blossoms for 25 rubles. Not so long ago 25 rubles was considered a lot of money. It's still a lot for pensioners living on 200 to 300 rubles a month. But for others, it is obviously a manageable amount. The flower-sellers are doing a brisk business.

Flowers are hardly a necessity. A strong demand for such a frivolous and expensive item suggests that the economic reforms are working, at least for some people. (No one knows how much money the "average Russian" has. Wages have risen rapidly since the first of the year, and savings are enormous. While some Russians are living on 200 rubles a month, others have many thousands.)

Another sign that reform is working is the famous Yeliseyevsky food store on Tverskaya Street (Gorki Street under the Communists), Moscow's main thoroughfare. This was a famous pre-revolutionary emporium, converted under communism to "Moscow Gastronom Number One," though Muscovites always called it Yeliseyevsky's. It is now operating as an independent business and is filled with fresh and exotic food, from chickens and eggs to fancy chocolates and salami from the Cherkizovsky meat-packing plant in Moscow, famous for its wares. A kilogram (2.2 lbs.) of the best salami costs 180 rubles, a staggering sum, but on a recent morning there were dozens of people lined up to buy it.

Lined up for the second time, amazingly. Yeliseyevsky's is transformed, but it still uses the traditional Russian system: one line at the cashier to pay the exact amount of one's purchase, a second line to hand over the receipt and receive what you've bought. (A third wait is required if you have to first pick out what you want and have it weighed and priced.) The survival of this inefficiency is a reminder of the complexities ahead.

Across Tverskaya Street and a couple of blocks to the west is Moscow's mammoth McDonald's, a beacon of decadence and hope at the same time. Before prices were freed at the first of the year (and the cost of a Big Mac soared to 65 rubles—or $.60 at the current free rate of exchange) the line to get it could take hours. Now there is almost no line, though business is brisk.

This is the biggest McDonald's in the world, nearly the size of an American supermarket. There are so many scrubbed and eager young helpers behind the counters that a first-time visitor wonders if two or three shifts have come to work at the same time. These youngsters try to outshout one another to get a new customer's attention, hoping to be chosen to fill his order. They have learned to be polite, efficient, clean, orderly—all qualities never observed in the restaurant help in the old Soviet Union. There is more service here than in any American McDonald's, including busboys and girls who won't let you throw out your own trash.

These youngsters are learning skills and attitudes that just may carry them into a prosperous free-market future. At least they know how to work, how to please a customer, how to maintain a clean establishment. At the other extreme is the giant Roselmash enterprise in Rostov that remains Russia's only producer of harvester combines. "It's a terribly inefficient factory that produces more harvesters than America does," according to Yegor Gaidar, the young economist relieved Thursday as finance minister but still deputy prime minister in charge of economic reform. In an interview in his office, also in the old central committee building, Gaidar described how the enterprise had decided to increase prices by 1,500 percent, while jacking up salaries and benefits.

The result, Gaidar said, was that "nobody would buy harvesters." With virtually no sales since the first of the year, "they are near bankruptcy, pleading with the state to save them." He indicated that this might happen but said the factory would have to concentrate for some years on producing spare parts, to keep the existing stock of harvesters in operation instead of making new ones.

Breaking up such monopolistic enterprises will be the most difficult aspect of reform. There is no way to create a second manufacturer of harvesters, yet a single producer will inevitably enjoy undue economic power. There are situations as bad, or nearly so, in many different industries, and Gaidar has no short-term plan for dealing with them. He concedes that the government will have to control monopolistic enterprises directly to prevent them from abusing their power.

Gaidar has other plans for more immediate progress toward a real market. For one, he is calculating that the failure of inefficient industrial enterprises will result in a significant movement of population back to the countryside, where new opportunities to raise food and make money will suddenly seem attractive. For many years, he noted, "the best possible strategy for a clever boy from the countryside was to migrate to the city." He wants to reverse that now, and bring some talented, ambitious people back to the farms.

It is tempting to hope that the huge losses—as much as 20 or even 30 percent of every harvest—that typified Soviet farming will now be stopped. Certainly rural residents now have powerful new incentives not to let grain and potatoes rot in the fields, as they often did in the past. The greatest transformation must take Russians from a totalitarian psychology to a free one. Generations of Russians grew up believing that government was all-powerful and would take care of everything. Now Yeltsin and his people talk constantly about their inability to solve all problems, about the need for Russians to take responsibility for their own fate.

Interestingly, many of Russia's best-educated citizens, members of the old intelligentsia that helped keep ideas of freedom alive during decades of communist rule, are now the most pessimistic about their country's prospects. The academics and writers who for years helped outsiders understand their country have now been shunted aside, and they are afraid of the future. Ironically, the old system protected them, even gave them comforts and luxuries, but the emerging market economy here has not yet found a way to reward artists and intellectuals.

At the same time, tens of thousands of ordinary Russians have thrown themselves into the new commercial arena. In just three months an extraordinary new culture of sidewalk entrepreneurship has grown up in this huge city. On some streets, it is impossible to walk through the teeming crowds of buyers and sellers. Kiosks offering "everything for you," featuring perfume and cognac, electrical appliances and apples, books on "biznes" or the new Russian-language edition of "The Joy of Sex," have sprung up outside most subway stations in the city.

With this commercialism has come corruption on a massive scale. There are no effective laws governing business, and gangs the Russians call "mafias" control much of the street commerce. Bribery and corruption of officials are commonplace. All of this profoundly offends many Russians.

"What is important is that Russians have shaken off the communist ideology rather painlessly," said Burbulis, Yeltsin's key aide. This was possible because communism "was so unnatural, so hypocritical and repressive," he said. By all appearances he is right. Democracy has caught on. Every faction has its own newspaper, from "For the Motherland, For Stalin!" to the tabloid "Sex in the Life of a Woman." Even the unreconstructed old Communists have learned to stage a street rally, as they did here a fortnight ago.

"We are living in an interesting time," said Alexander Yakovlev, the co-author with Mikhail Gorbachev of the failed reforms that led to the collapse of communism and the Soviet Union. Yakovlev is now working with Gorbachev in the former president's new think-tank. He had just spent an hour speaking critically of the Yeltsin government's policies, but he wanted to leave a different final impression on American visitors:

"We are moving in the right direction. I believe that we'll make it, although I am always afraid of stupidity. I am trying to be an optimist, but I always remember . . . [Nikolai] Gogol, the most Russian writer, who observed that Russia is rich in fools and bad roads."

April 5, 1992

2 *Politics*

The articles in this chapter explore the social impact of United States political decisions in our country and other countries.

The first article deals with the Los Angeles riots in late spring 1992. Both Republicans and Democrats argue about the causes and consequences of the new wave of urban disorder, and whether the 1990 riots will play the same role with respect to political and societal changes as the 1960 riots.

The next two articles deal with problems in the United States government. The first explores possible conflict of interest problems with key Bush campaign aides serving both the White House and outside business interests, including domestic and foreign clients. The second examines the impact of political decision making by exploring some if the problems the "peace dividend" is causing, namely, the loss of jobs.

The final articles discuss the impact the end of the Cold War is having in other countries. With the former Soviet Union no longer supplying billions of dollars in aid to countries such as Ethiopia and Angola, and the United States no longer supplying massive amounts of aid to countries such as Sudan, Liberia, Zaire and Somalia, the political landscape in Africa is changing dramatically. Similarly, the end of the Persian Gulf War is causing European politicians to reassess their own national security and defense policies.

Los Angeles

Images in the Films—This Time, America Must Learn the Right Lesson from the Rage in the Streets of its Cities

JUAN WILLIAMS

Two images now compete for the nation's attention: The first is of a black man being brutally beaten by officers of the law; the second is of rioters looting and destroying homes and neighborhoods. The nation must choose which of these images will shape its sensibilities and guide its policies over the years to come. Twenty-four years ago, it did not understand this choice and it made the wrong one.

In the decades following the death of Martin Luther King Jr., many Americans let their fear and revulsion at the ensuing riots overcome their concern about the social decay that spawned them. Despite the immediate expressions of commitment, the appointment of commissions and the launching of well-meant but often short-lived programs, the enduring legacy of the 1960s riots has been the dominance of conservative Republican administrations supported by voters who fled to the suburbs and of "law and order" as the prevailing theme in our national political life.

"The most interesting question," said Kevin Phillips, the conservative political analyst, "is whether 1990s dislocation—and this won't be the last—will play the same role 1960s dislocations played."

"In the '60s," said Phillips, "there were riots because of rising expectations. Blacks wanted more things more quickly as opportunity dawned. Now we have outbreaks in a decade of diminishing expectations. This time they are frustrated that prospects for a better life are disappearing, for blacks in particular."

The reality behind those diminished expectations is nowhere more evident than in California, long the symbol of unlimited American promise. Increasingly the state is populated by sharply contrasting classes of people: wealthy suburban communities growing richer but with populations shrinking as young people are driven out by the high real-estate costs; crowded cities full of poor people who strain local budgets and services; middle-income communities shaken by the job losses produced by upheavals in aerospace, real estate, banking and other once-steadily growing industries.

This should build a case against the Republicans, who have inhabited the White House for the last 12 years and pursued now-failed economic and social policies. Thus far, though, the Democratic Party has failed to advance a convincing alternative vision of America. And now, when a new opportunity might have presented itself, many political professionals think the case may never be articulated.

For now, when the widely unpopular Rodney King verdict (most white as well as black Americans say they disagree with it) might shame ruling-class America into facing the nation's widening economic and racial divisions, public attention is being diverted. Flames and violence are, in the mind of affluent America, reinforcing threatening stereotypes of poor blacks in the inner city, obliterating what seemed an opportunity for a national awakening to the brutal reality of life on the margins of American society.

The case against the Reagan and Bush administrations is undercut, according to Phillips, by "the behavior of the rioters. It is not justified by the Rodney King situation. It is a matter of which angle comes to dominate: The case against social and economic policies that have been apathetic and said, 'everything is okay'; or the anger at the people taking part in the dislocation."

Alan L. Keyes, the black conservative who is running for the Maryland GOP nomination for the U.S. Senate, thinks that politicians will find it easy to play the anger angle. "They are playing on a society torn by fear. Some people say it's racial, but I think it is a matter of people fearing the government won't protect them from crime. Politics is going to respond to that situation where people feel they have no control of their neighborhoods or their lives. In poor neighborhoods the only people who have a sense of power are the gangs and the drug-dealers." Any society must have effective mechanisms for dealing with crime. Liberal thinkers have failed to offer credible proposals for dealing with crime and that has undermined attempts to build a consensus of compassion for the poor. So it would not be surprising if middle-class America—both white and black—responds to politicians' renewed attempts to play on their fears. When jurors in the trial of the Los Angeles policemen accused of beating Rodney King deny that racism played any part in their not-guilty verdicts, they are speaking the truth -their truth. It is a limited gospel, a constricted vision from frightened Americans of all colors who have increasingly sanctioned police to do whatever it takes.

In this case, the threat was embodied in a drunk, hulking black ex-convict driving his car down Interstate 210 at high speeds while ignoring police orders to stop. Perhaps that view of Rodney King will be softened in the minds of many Americans by the rough eloquence of his televised appeal for calm on Friday. But in recent years the threats have taken other forms: muggers who make dark streets dangerous; "wilding" teenagers attacking joggers and shoppers; crazed drug users; insistent beggars demanding money.

"Every day, everywhere in this country, there is a certain amount of winking and nodding directed to the police to tell them to do what is necessary to keep 'those' people under control," said Drew Days, a law professor at Yale University and former assistant attorney general for civil rights. "We tell the cops, 'Just do it—just don't tell me how you do it.' We want the homeless off the benches in Grand

Central Station, and we want the cops to do it. But we don't want them to tell us how they do it."

The major issue of "confrontation between black and white, rich and poor in this country," is crime, said Lawrence Sherman, a professor of criminology at the University of Maryland and president of the Crime Control Institute. "There is frustration with the lack of penalties and punishment for criminals in this country.... Many people are satisfied when cops beat up Rodney King, an armed robber, because people like him put guns in the face of middle-class people at the teller machine. A guy like King did that to my wife."

These reactions are understandable, but they are not sufficient to our purposes and objectives as a nation. They lead in only one direction—a future in which an affluent minority lives, even as the residents of Los Angeles's wealthy suburbs now live, in hilltop enclaves guarded by fences and electronic guard systems, cut off from the lives of the desperate masses in the teeming urban lowlands. It is a life familiar to the now-besieged white minority of South Africa and to the wealthy landowners of South America. It is not a pleasant life, nor is it a future worthy of America's heritage.

There is also the danger that the black community—which in recent years had come increasingly to rediscover its own sense of responsibility for the fate of black families and communities—will again, as in the aftermath of Martin Luther King's assassination, focus blame solely on the transgressions of the larger society. Avoiding that future will require that affluent Americans—of all races and ethnic backgrounds—confront both the direction in which the country is headed and its unexamined attitudes toward the less fortunate among their fellow citizens.

"The divisions between suburban whites and urban blacks are growing," said Elijah Anderson, a professor of sociology at the University of Pennsylvania, "because many white Americans feel distant from black people in general, and poor blacks in particular. When somebody like Rodney King is in custody they (white suburbanites) feel the police have to do something about him. And never having known any poor black people they assume that 'these people' have to be controlled by any means necessary and therefore the police are justified in doing what they have to do."

This psychological divide of "us-versus-them," does not break neatly on racial lines in a society where access to good education, health care and housing are closely tied to the availability of jobs at decent wages. Poverty rates in America are high, at 30 percent for blacks, 26 percent for Hispanics and 10 percent for whites (a far larger group), according to 1990 Census Bureau numbers. But the disadvantage of poverty is acute for young black and Hispanic Americans.

In 1988, 60 percent of black Americans 15 to 24 years old lived in poverty, as did 25 percent of those 25 to 34 years old. Poverty gripped some 40 percent of Hispanics 15-to 24 years old, and 26 percent of those aged 25 to 34. Young whites are not excluded: Nearly a quarter—24 percent—of whites aged 15 to 24 lived in poverty. By now these numbers have surely increased.

But young black Americans are far more likely to come from broken homes: Nearly two out of three black children are now born to unwed mothers. An added racial factor, correlated with their high incidence of poverty, is the disproportionate number of black Americans involved with crime. According to the 1990 Sourcebook of Criminal Justice Statistics, blacks account for 46 percent of arrests for rape; 56 percent for murder and 65 percent for robbery, even though blacks are about 11 percent of the population. These numbers came alive on March 3, 1991, in the person of Rodney King, then 25 and three months out of prison where he had been serving a 2 1/2-year term for an armed-robbery conviction. King was scared and drunk. On the famous videotape, King seems to come out of the car in a hurry; the police said he lunged at them and they feared he was on PCP, a drug that could make him dangerous and impervious to pain. The policemen told the jury they were frightened of King.

Their lawyers played on this fear. Attorney Michael Stone told the jurors, "These officers don't get paid to lose street fights. . . . If we as members of the community demand they do that, the thin blue line separating the law-abiding from the not-law-abiding disintegrates."

Was the jury listening to a racist appeal or a description that fits a Hispanic policeman dealing with poor folks in Miami, a black cop dealing with poor folks in Dallas as well as a white cop dealing with poor folks in L.A?

Judging by the explanation offered by an anonymous juror after the trial, the jury made an effort to convince itself that its deliberations were not corrupted by racial considerations. For example, the juror noted that Bryant Allen, a passenger in King's car, testified that he had asked King to stop the car and begged him to obey the police. Allen said he had never "seen him [King] act like that before." Allen and another passenger in the car, both black, were unharmed by police during the attack on King.

But even if the jurors did not consciously make their decisions in racial terms, that does not mean that racism was not a latent factor—just as it is latent in many of the everyday actions and assumptions of mainstream American life.

"I do think there is an element of racism in the verdict but I don't think it was calculated racism on the part of the jury," said William (Chip) Mellor, president of the Institute for Justice, a conservative Washington public interest law firm. "The racism was manifest in the various assumptions that have gone into their deliberations," Mellor explained. "A large black man is viewed as much more threatening by whites who live in the suburbs than by people who live in South Central Los Angeles."

Perhaps even more to the point are the observations of George Mallory, former president of the Langston Bar Association, the association of black lawyers in Los Angeles. "I see it as a matter of life experience and class structure more than race," said Mallory. "What the jurors saw happening there they could not fathom as happening to them. They couldn't imagine themselves being beaten like Rodney King. And that's correct. They never will be."

"I know from my experience prosecuting those cases that police officers who are inclined to be brutal pick their victims fairly carefully," said Yale's Drew Days. "They know who they can beat on without being called to justice. They beat on people who are not going to be credible to the upstanding, middle-class people on juries. They go after poor people, homosexuals, homeless people and racial minorities. Police officers don't go around beating up on middle-class white folks or even middle-class black folks, although they make mistakes sometimes and beat up a power forward for the Lakers."

Politicians, no less than lawyers and policemen, can play a dangerous game with the law-and-order issue, walking a thin line between expressing legitimate concern for the maintenance of public order and capitalizing on the mainstream public's deep-seated if unarticulated fears. Both President Bush and his Democratic challenger, Arkansas Gov. Bill Clinton, have been teetering along that line in recent days. Both must do better. They must challenge the country to confront its racial and economic divisions—and to recognize the ugly future toward which these divisions have propelled us. Otherwise America may again choose to remember the wrong image to guide its future policy.

May 3, 1992

The Uncertain Intersection

Politics and Private Interests—Key Bush Campaign Aides Serve White House, Clients

CHARLES R. BABCOCK AND ANN DEVROY

Several top officials of President Bush's reelection campaign team, with access to high-level White House policymakers and in some cases participation in policy meetings, continue to maintain outside business interests and to serve as paid consultants to domestic and foreign clients.

Recognizing what one aide acknowledged is a "sticky new era" in the ethics of presidential campaigns, White House and Bush campaign lawyers have issued "Guidelines for Avoiding the Appearance of Conflict of Interest." Seven campaign officials have made voluntary internal disclosures of their outside clients and financial holdings, from corporate giants such as Ford Motor Co. and investment banks to the ruler of Abu Dhabi.

White House counsel C. Boyden Gray said in an interview that he would not disclose client lists of the officials, however, or the policy areas they have agreed to avoid because they are private citizens and such disclosure "is not required."

Among the campaign officials who continue to represent clients or retain relationships with businesses are Robert M. Teeter, the campaign chairman; Frederic V. Malek, the campaign manager; James Lake, a deputy chairman; and Charles Black, a senior adviser. In addition, former commerce secretary Robert A. Mosbacher, the campaign's general chairman, and former Cabinet secretary James Cicconi, now in a law firm and serving as a senior issues adviser, have filed disclosures.

Democratic presidents also have had campaign advisers with private clients, but the practice has grown in recent years, along with the numbers of GOP consultants and lobbyists whose client lists are based in part on their access and political ties to the Republican presidents they helped elect.

Bush's decision to install what one aide called "Corporate Inc." in his 15th Street NW campaign headquarters is in sharp contrast to the hierarchy there in 1984, the last time an incumbent president ran for reelection. That effort was run by Edward J. Rollins and Lee Atwater, who left their White House political jobs for the campaign and had no outside business interests.

Bush challenger Patrick J. Buchanan has aired television ads naming two of the campaign's private businessmen, Black and Lake, whose firms have foreign clients. "No wonder Michigan has lost 73,000 jobs," the commercial says.

White House and campaign officials said White House Chief of Staff Samuel K. Skinner "defers" to Teeter in numerous policy and political areas because of Teeter's influence, long-standing relationship with Bush and two decades of presidential campaign experience.

Teeter was heavily involved in crafting the president's State of the Union proposals, in last month's health care initiative and in many of the speeches Bush has given in recent weeks around the country. An aide said that because Teeter is a consultant to Ford Motor Co., he took no part in preparing the president's trip and speech to Detroit Friday, which featured a plan to free auto manufacturers of some environmental regulations.

Teeter and Malek have the highest-level access to administration policymakers, meeting each morning at the White House with Skinner; his deputy, W. Henson Moore; Cabinet Secretary Ede Holiday; White House press secretary Marlin Fitzwater; and other key aides. These "funnel" meetings have been set up to provide coordination between the campaign and White House policymakers, although Fitzwater said they rarely include policy discussions.

Teeter also routinely meets with Skinner outside the daily meetings, sources said. He has attended legislative strategy sessions at the White House and specific issue-discussion sessions, and has acted as a go-between for Cabinet members, elected Republicans and others to get their policy proposals into the White House discussions. Lake periodically attends communications meetings at the White House.

Mosbacher also attends some policy discussions at the White House, but is not allowed to attend any meeting with his former Cabinet colleagues because of "revolving door" rules, officials said.

While campaign aides routinely discuss policy options with White House officials, Gray said, "They do not make policy. Policymaking is in the province of the White House."

Teeter owns Michigan-based Coldwater Corp., which provides "strategic advice" to a range of American corporate clients, including Ford. He also sits on four corporate boards, including United Parcel Service and Browning-Ferris Industries.

Bobby Burchfield, general counsel for the campaign, said that Teeter has a clause in all his consulting contracts "that says he will not be called on to do lobbying work or to contact government officials."

Teeter declined in an interview Friday to reveal his corporate clients. "I'm not going to get into specific clients except to say that Fred (Malek) and myself, along with the White House, wanted to make absolutely sure we didn't violate any laws or give the appearance of violating any and we have been following these guidelines scrupulously."

Table 2–1 • Selected List of Bush Team Links to Corporate World.

Bush Campaign Official	Clients or Companies Where Official Serves as a Director
Robert M. Teeter Chairman	Ford Motor Co. Browning-Ferris Industries Detroit and Canada Tunnel Corp. United Parcel Service Durakon Industries Inc.
Frederic V. Malek Manager	American Capital & Research Corp. American Management Systems Inc. CB Commercial Holdings Inc. Manor Care Inc. National Education Corp.
James Lake Deputy Chairman	Abu Dhabi Sheik Zyed bin Sultan Nahyan California Prune Board Mitsubishi Electronics America Inc. Atari Games Corp. Japan Auto Parts Industry Association
Charles Black Senior Adviser	Aetna Life & Casualty Allied-Signal Inc. Bethlehem Steel Corp. Casino Association of New Jersey Clark Construction Group; (Bethesda, Md.) Commonwealth Edison Co. Johnson & Johnson Tobacco Institute Trump Organization Union Pacific Corp. United Way of America

Note: List is partial.

Sources: 1991 Washington Representatives, Congressional Lobby Registration reports, Disclosure, Inc.

Gray said the "internal" disclosure goes beyond what campaign officials in earlier years were required to provide. "We are doing a great deal more, in terms of internal disclosure and disqualification, than any prior campaign has done," he said. To require private citizens to disclose their financial interests, he added, would set an "unwieldy precedent" for future campaigns.

Malek said he has resigned as a senior official for Northwest Airlines, although he retains a major financial interest in the company. But he said in an interview that he has "disassociated himself" from Northwest and from the Carlyle investment group in Washington. He sits on nine corporate boards, but said in an interview that "98 percent" of his time is devoted to the campaign, not business interests. Teeter also said he spends nearly all his time now on the campaign.

Besides the team of consultants already in the campaign, Malek is in discussions with Stanton D. Anderson, a prominent Washington lobbyist for Japanese interests, to serve as his top deputy. And a handful of other Washington lobbyists and consultants serve in lesser campaign roles.

Lake and Black are officials in public affairs and lobbying firms. Lake said he too is spending most of his time on the campaign, with his primary duty to work on appearances by Cabinet members and other "surrogates" for the president. He said his private activities center on providing advice for dealing with the news media, not lobbying.

Buchanan has attacked Lake's work for the Japanese auto parts industry and called the president's campaign staff "a wholly owned subsidiary of Japan Inc." Lake responded that the Japanese firms have 400 plants in the United States, providing jobs for Americans.

Another Lake client, the ruler of Abu Dhabi, is a major shareholder of the collapsed Bank of Credit and Commerce International.

Black said in an interview that he is splitting his time about "50-50" between the campaign and his job managing Black, Manafort, Stone and Kelley, which has about 50 domestic and foreign consulting and lobbying clients. He said he "occasionally" contacts executive branch officials for his clients. "I always start by saying 'My firm represents client X' so it's clear this is not a social call or a political call and that I'm not calling for the president."

The administration's first attempt to deal with potential conflicts came in a Feb. 13 memorandum from Gray to heads of all government departments and agencies limiting their contacts with campaign officials.

It ordered campaign aides to disclose to paid clients that they are not working for the campaign whenever they contact government agencies for clients. The practice will "protect against any appearance that these officials are using their campaign positions to benefit special interests," the memo said.

The memo also established the "funnel" system, under which all "communication between the campaign and officials in the administration" must be directed through Skinner and his designated aide, Holiday.

Asked, for example, if Teeter and one of his oldest friends, Secretary of State James A. Baker III, could not talk without Skinner's approval, Gray said, "It must have some prior blessing from Skinner. Seriously." He added, "We might break the rules sometimes. We are in a shakedown period here but, seriously, he's not supposed to do that. We are dramatically reducing the access the campaign has to the government. That is the principle."

Gray said the goal is not to bar campaign officials from policy discussions but "to make sure that in terms of intersection with government that they do not have the power to execute anything . . . they are not making policy. They may discuss it but there is nothing they can do to execute policy."

In another memo, dated March 10, Gray and Burchfield outlined the guidelines for the voluntary financial disclosures by top campaign aides and noted that campaign officials would not discuss specific issues about "an identifiable client or fiduciary" if the official had been involved with the issue in the past year.

If a White House discussion of transportation policy occurred when he was present, Malek said, he interpreted the guidelines to mean "I would have to leave" the room. Gray, asked if Teeter's relationship with Ford would allow him to discuss, for example, airbag regulations, said, yes, as long as Teeter was not specifically advising the automaker on that issue.

Published Corrections The public affairs firm of Bush-Quayle campaign deputy chairman James H. Lake represents the Abu Dhabi Investment Authority, not Sheik Zayed Sultan Nahyan, the ruler of Abu Dhabi, as a story and chart reported Sunday. (Published 3/17/92)

March 15, 1992

With Cold War Won, Jobs Are Being Lost
Hill, Military Face 'Peace Dividend' Irony

HELEN DEWAR

For as long as most lawmakers can remember, Congress dreamed of the day it could declare the long-awaited "peace dividend," showering a grateful nation with the fruits of victory from the nearly half-century-long Cold War.

Now the moment is at hand, and there is little joy on Capitol Hill.

"The truth is we are not prepared for peace in the world," said Rep. Julian C. Dixon (D-Calif.).

The reason for the dismay—and second thoughts about defense spending cuts that are gripping doves and hawks alike—is jobs, especially jobs during a recession.

As many as 2 million civilian and military jobs will be lost by 1996 even if Congress goes no further than President Bush has proposed in cutting the defense budget, Senate Armed Services Committee Chairman Sam Nunn (D-Ga.) has concluded.

Aside from suggestions by Nunn and a few others, there is no short-term or long-term plan for conversion of these jobs, skills and resources to domestic purposes, a failure of foresight that the United States shares with the former Soviet Union, lawmakers note sardonically.

Without such planning, Nunn said in a speech last week, 'we may not only inhibit recovery from the current recession, we may also lose our best opportunity that recovery can lead to long-term economic growth."

The Electric Boat Division of General Dynamics Corp., largest employer in Rhode Island and second largest in Connecticut, has announced layoffs of up to 4,000 employees by year's end because of planned termination of the Seawolf nuclear submarine program. Without Seawolf, General Dynamics has said it would pare back its Groton, Conn., work force of 20,000 over the next five years until work was finished on 15 other submarines on its order book.

Across the country in southern California, Northrop Corp. announced elimination of 1,500 jobs when Bush proposed to phase out the B-2 "stealth" bomber program after adding five more planes, stopping at 20 instead of the 75 advocated earlier by the administration. Ultimately, nearly 40,000 jobs could be lost on the B-2 project, sooner rather than later if Congress rejects the five new planes. In all, 200,000 defense industry jobs in California are believed imperiled by planned defense cutbacks.

Since the height of the Reagan administration's defense buildup in 1985, spending authority for new weapons has declined precipitously: from nearly $100 billion a year to $59 billion this year. Bush's proposal for fiscal 1993 would slice it further, to less than $55 billion, cutting, delaying or terminating programs ranging from cruise missiles to tanks.

It was easy to strike heroic poses when the issue was guns vs. butter and the threat was the military-industrial complex or a hostile Soviet bloc, said a House Democratic aide. "It's not so easy when all the devils are gone, and the issue is some average guy's job on an assembly line . . . especially if he's in your congressional district," the aide added.

"Congress is caught between a rock and a hard place," said Gordon Adams, director of the private Defense Budget Project, which has pushed for a leaner military program. "The rock is the desire for a peace dividend. The hard place is jobs in your district."

As Nunn put it, "The real irony is that . . . these people are not losing their jobs because they failed, they are losing their jobs because they won," Nunn added.

For Democrats like Sen. Christopher J. Dodd, who is running for reelection this year in economically reeling Connecticut, desperate times give rise to what once would have been regarded as heresy. "For the first time since the '60s, Democrats can talk about defense from a position of strength," he said. "Instead, they're trying to outbid the president on how deep to cut. . . . The people they're kicking in the teeth are pipe fitters, welders, drafters, middle-class working people who are traditionally considered Democratic supporters."

A new fault line has emerged in congressional politics, obscuring all others, according to House Armed Services Committee Chairman Les Aspin (D-Wis.). "The major split in Congress right now is not between hawks and doves, or Republicans and Democrats, but between those who have military facilities and plants in their districts and those who don't," Aspin said. "The first group wants to keep what they have, and the others want to take the money and spend it on something else."

For Congress, the critical decisions about cancellation of weapons, force reductions and base closures come when other jobs are shrinking rather than growing and when Americans are pessimistic about their economic future. In some areas, a military base or defense plant is the foundation on which the local economy rests.

Initial decisions also must be made during an election year marked by bipartisan expressions of concern for the middle class, which includes the vast majority of rank-and-file defense workers.

Because of the high costs of terminating projects and because defense savings start small and build up slowly over the years, Congress will have little to show in the short-term for the pain it is causing. The political cost will come before the elections, the political benefits later.

Moreover, many who have characterized employment as the best social program that a free-market economy can offer are asking how they can justify laying off people in the name of expanding social welfare programs to take care of people without jobs. Defense jobs, especially military service, are also important paths of opportunity for poor, especially minorities, they note.

As a result of these and other considerations, powerful pressures are building in Congress for a slowdown, or stretchout, of military spending cutbacks to allow more time for conversion of defense plants or development of alternative jobs. It is not so much what will be cut but when, lawmakers said.

The range of debate appears to lie between savings of at least $100 billion that Senate Majority Leader George J. Mitchell (D-Maine) has proposed over the next five years and the five-year, $50 billion savings Bush has advocated. Many Democrats are predicting a compromise closer to Bush's number than Mitchell's.

A key question is whether lawmakers with imperiled defense installations will pull together to vote for a military spending program that is fat enough to accommodate them all and then vote for each other's programs in a kind of giant logroll.

More likely, many say, is a narrower, every-district-for-itself approach. Some also suggest regional warfare, pitting the high-tech weapons makers of the two coasts against military bases of the South, to say nothing of shootouts between producers of submarines and surface vessels for shrinking shipbuilding dollars.

"People won't vote for someone else's program. . . . The money you spend on something else means less is left for what you want," said Rep. Sam Gejdenson (D-Conn.), who is concentrating on saving the Seawolf. A B-2 supporter dismissed the Seawolf by scornfully suggesting that "it leaks," a reference to welding problems that Seawolf backers say have been corrected.

But some believe a marriage of convenience could come on what is expected to be an early vote on breaking down the budgetary "wall" that prohibits transfer of resources from defense to domestic accounts through the rest of this fiscal year.

To the surprise of many lawmakers, the Senate last month voted 53 to 45 against a nonbinding proposal by Sen. Timothy E. Wirth (D-Colo.) to break down the wall to permit use of defense funds for education and other domestic programs. Four of the six senators from the principal B-2 and Seawolf states opposed the proposal; only Sens. Alan Cranston (D-Calif.) and Claiborne Pell (D-R.I.) supported it.

Retaining the wall will not necessarily save any weapons program, but any breach would make the job much harder, both sides agree. Mitchell, who wants to break down the wall, said last week he is uncertain whether the votes are there to do so. "My guess is the votes are there . . . but I wouldn't bet on it," Aspin said.

As Aspin, Nunn and other defense planners prepare initial recommendations, unofficial caucuses are developing around the B-2 and Seawolf, laying the groundwork for major rescue efforts.

The roughly 20 California lawmakers who claim at least some B-2 workers, including liberals and conservatives who rarely agree on anything else, are uniting to assure production of the five additional planes.

Dixon and Rep. Jerry Lewis (R-Calif.), strategically placed on the House Appropriations subcommittee on defense, have set themselves up as a bipartisan task force to win the $3.6 billion that Bush has requested for the planes.

The Californians acknowledge they face an uphill fight in light of Congress's fading support for the plan even before Bush moved to cut production, although they and others say the jobs issue could make the difference. "The jobs issue will determine whether it's 20 planes . . . it could be 20," said the Defense Budget Project's Adams. Aspin noted that it became easier to win support for the last few MX missiles during the 1980s after agreement was reached to cap production at 50.

Saving the Seawolf is expected to be more difficult, even though the Connecticut and Rhode Island delegations are working even more feverishly than the Californians. Sen. Joseph I. Lieberman (D-Conn.) has produced a spiral-bound "white paper" on the Seawolf's future; Dodd becomes almost lyrical about the history of Electric Boat.

Lawmakers from the two states meet frequently as a united delegation and talk almost as one, hawks and doves alike, about the need to maintain the nation's industrial base, especially the capacity to produce submarines, which they describe as the cutting edge of the nation's defense in a post-Cold War world.

Bush not only opposed more Seawolfs but proposed to reach back and rescind $3.4 billion in funding for two boats that have been authorized by Congress, leaving only one submarine as the Seawolf fleet—"Lone Wolf," it is being called. Dodd contends it could cost $2 billion in contract termination costs to kill the program, with no boats to show for it. But key lawmakers say the Seawolf is probably beyond saving.

For the B-2 and Seawolf crowd, a gift sent by one Senate staffer to another summed up the mood. The first staffer, employee of a senator who supports the B-2, got an electric-pink Northrop cap, emblazoned with the image of the bat-wing aircraft, and sent it to the second staffer, who works for a senator opposing the B-2. Attached to the cap was a handwritten decal reading: "Peace is the pits."

February 14, 1992

From Angola to Ethiopia, End of Cold War Transforms Africa

NEIL HENRY

From Angola to Ethiopia this week, the end of the Cold War is transforming the political landscape of Africa at a breathtaking pace.

What a difference a decade can make. Just 10 years ago, competition between the superpowers was a preeminent force shaping political events and economic development in Africa.

The Soviet Union was busy supplying billions of dollars in aid to nominally Marxist client states such as Ethiopia and Angola in pursuit of its dream of international communism, while more than 50,000 Cuban troops were stationed there to support shaky regimes against insurgencies.

The United States, for its part, was funneling hundreds of millions of dollars in military and economic aid to African countries it perceived as vital to protecting American interests against Soviet and radical Arab threats—Sudan, Liberia, Zaire and Somalia among them.

The roll call of African events in 1991 describes a different political landscape.

The Soviets are preaching the virtues of peace in the Third World and establishing contact with the once reviled state of South Africa.

The last contingent of Cuban proxy troops has packed up and flown home to Havana, as part of an Angolan peace accord that is expected to be signed Friday in Lisbon.

And the United States is playing the unlikely role of a political traffic cop in Ethiopia, ushering to power a rural insurgency that once idolized the example of Joseph Stalin.

What in the world is going on in Africa?

"I see a number of factors, not least a growing demand for political pluralism and democratization," said Richard Joseph, a fellow at the Carter Center of Emory University in Atlanta, which mediated Ethiopian peace discussions in the past.

"But there is also the geopolitical aspect. . . . We are living in a unipolar world. The bipolarities of the past have ended and the U.S. has emerged as the lead player. Whether this is good or bad remains to be seen, but it is clear that it has become a critical factor in Africa." U.S. mediation of Ethiopia's civil war, which culminated in Tuesday's rebel capture of Addis Ababa, represents the latest in a number of

Table 2–2 • Africa: The Changing Continent

Nation	Recent Political Changes
Ethiopia	Rebel soldiers stormed the capital on Tuesday, just a week after former Marxist president Mengistu Haile Mariam fled the country.
Angola	An agreement to be signed today between the government and U.S.-backed rebels could end 30 years of nearly constant warfare.
Somalia	War, social and political anarchy plague the country abandoned by president Siad Barre more than three months ago.
Zaire	Long a staunch ally of the U.S., Zaire faces profound political and economic crises that may threaten President Mobutu Sese Seko.
Congo, Cameroon, Togo	Authoritarian regimes in these nations have been forced to accept pluralistic reforms.
Benin	Economist Nicephore Soglo became president last month, after defeating dictator Mathieu Kerekou in the country's first free elections.
Mali	A coup in March toppled president Moussa Traore after 22 years in power and established a multi-party democracy.
Ivory Coast	President Felix Houphouet-Boigny, Africa's longest-serving leader, faces increasing pressure for democratization.
Liberia	Remains a divided country months after its government collapsed. Capital is controlled by a West African peace-keeping force; the rest of the nation by the National Patriotic Front.
Cape Verde Islands	The republic's first freely-elected president took office earlier this year.
Sao Tome and Principe	Held its first multi-party presidential vote in March.

remarkable events in Africa that, although unrelated directly, are resulting in a redrawing of the continent's political map.

The end of superpower contention, the drop-off in foreign military aid that has weakened longtime dictatorships, and popular pressures for civil liberties and more accountable governments have all played a role in these changes.

Like a pressure cooker relieved of its top, many of Africa's ethnic tensions and political and regional struggles—some up to 30 years old—are exploding.

The end of the Cold War "has meant that factions and governments in Africa cannot count on the consistent support of anybody, no matter what," said Claude Ake, a fellow at the Institute for African Studies at Columbia University in New York who has written extensively on democracy and political change in Africa.

"This has not only undermined people in authority, but it has given confidence to people fighting that authority. . . . Africa is entering a period of fluidity that may last some time."

Many of the recent events in Africa are devastating and still unresolved. Starved of American aid, Liberia collapsed into war last year and is still divided along battle lines.

Finally spurned by the United States, the Somali regime of Mohamed Siad Barre fell apart and the nation is still in the throes of anarchy and war.

Other long pent-up pressures are leading to new borders and even new nations founded along ethnic and regional lines. Northern Somali rebels, for example, have broken with their brethren in the south and announced the formation of the nation of Northern Somaliland.

On Wednesday, in the northern Ethiopian province of Eritrea, victorious rebels proclaimed a provisional government for the region, separate from the control of Addis Ababa. The Eritreans do not hide their desire for secession.

"It is quite likely there will be more signs of disintegration," said Ake; who explained that "such pluralism, which should have expressed itself long ago in Africa, is finally doing so."

Still another momentous event was the agreement reached to end years of civil war in Angola and to start a democratization process, a prime reflection of greater international cooperation between the United States and the Soviet Union.

In this, Soviet President Mikhail Gorbachev's open-mindedness in foreign affairs, shattering the Soviet rigidity of the past, has had a profound influence.

"It took the Soviet Union almost 30 years to recognize that much of what was happening in Africa could not be fitted into the grand ideological design," wrote Leonid Fituni, a director of the Institute for African Studies of the Soviet Academy of Sciences, in a recent article published by the Center for Strategic and International Studies in Washington.

Instead, Fituni wrote, the Soviets have designed a policy for Africa that abandons the confrontations of old in favor of cooperation in more pragmatic concerns.

The regime of Ethiopia's former ruler, Mengistu Haile Mariam, arguably suffered more than most Third World client states from this sea change in foreign attitudes. After receiving more than $10 billion in Soviet military aid during the 1980s, the Ethiopian ruler found himself starved for aid and under increasing pressure to liberalize the political and economic system—pressures that only added to the eventual disintegration of his government.

The United States has moved into the political vacuum of this Soviet ideological retreat, as was underscored by Assistant Secretary of State Herman Cohen's efforts this week to mediate among Ethiopian parties that have all expressed favor for Marxism in the past.

But what is America's interest in Africa now that the Cold War is over?

U.S. officials argue that economic development and humanitarian concerns play a part, particularly at a time when an estimated 7 million Ethiopians are threatened by famine.

American policy makers are also concerned about containing anarchy and chaos—such as that in Liberia and Somalia—as the continent struggles for political change.

And while, as Joseph said, "Europe and the Soviets are willing to let America take the lead," geopolitical factors certainly still play a role.

Western analysts say U.S. officials remain concerned about the influence of Libyan leader Moammar Gadhafi in Africa and are particularly worried by his close ties to the victorious rebels in Eritrea.

But perhaps most important, shorn of more pressing geopolitical concerns, American interests may finally be linked as never before to a true development of political pluralism in Africa—and, by extension, to human development.

Ake termed this an 'American hegemony' in Africa, but it doesn't worry him for now, he said.

"This flexibility is giving room for a political realignment and renewal that Africa needs," he said. "It is improving the consciousness of ordinary people that things can change. . . . I don't think Africa's lived through a period in modern times when its collective consciousness has changed so much."

May 31, 1991

Europeans Rethinking National Security Policies

GLENN FRANKEL

The end of the Persian Gulf War has sent European strategists, planners and politicians back to their drawing boards to wrestle with basic questions about national security and defense policy that many believed had been put to rest with the end of the Cold War.

For many policy-makers, it is a time of soul-searching and upheaval. French Foreign Minister Roland Dumas derides his country's long-standing policy toward the Arab world as "a series of illusions," while Volker Ruehe, general secretary of Germany's ruling Christian Democrats, calls for major changes in his country's approach to foreign affairs. "Once again history is at our door," said European Commission President Jacques Delors.

The questions they are raising include: What kind of armed forces and weapons do European nations need for future conflicts; how should they deal with "out-of-area" threats; and should they pool their resources and create a common defense policy?

Beyond these are even more fundamental questions about exactly what constitutes security in the last decade of the 20th century and what are the best means of ensuring it in a world where the rigid, ironclad certainties of the East-West conflict have been replaced by a new, more fluid and in some ways more dangerous set of circumstances.

"It is extraordinary how a picture which seemed so clear has become clouded and ill-focused after seven months of crisis and war in the Middle East," wrote Max Hastings, former defense correspondent and now editor of the *Daily Telegraph*.

As Delors pointed out in a recent speech at the International Institute for Strategic Studies here, the very definition of security is up for grabs. It includes not only maintaining militarily defensible borders but also providing a livable environment, economic prosperity and protection from terrorist threats. And the locale where threats to security can arise is unpredictable: one moment it is the Persian Gulf, the next it could be Eastern Europe or the Soviet Union.

With one superpower in an advancing state of collapse and the other set to contract militarily even after its triumph in the gulf, the Europeans are left to ponder a future in which they may be forced to make decisions and take steps many tried to avoid during the crisis.

"We are left preparing for a series of uncertain contingencies that are all very different," said Lawrence Freedman, chairman of the war studies department of King's College here. "We have to work with others because there's no way we can plan for all of them—but with whom and why?"

When the gulf crisis began, Britain and France were in the midst of programs of major defense cuts, based in part on the assumption that their past emphasis on heavy armor and artillery was a Cold War relic. The future appeared to lie in developing lightweight, flexible and highly mobile units that could move quickly to quell "out-of-area" threats.

But the gulf war contradicted that strategic concept by requiring massive air power and armor. Both Britain and France found their forces stretched to the limit, with the French particularly caught short. They had always treated distant conflicts as "brush-fire wars" extinguishable by a few thousand lightly armed Foreign Legionnaires. Without the United States providing the bulk of forces, many defense analysts agree, neither country could have coped.

Some leaders have argued that the inability of the European powers to sustain such a conflict on their own makes a good case for a joint security policy. Delors in his speech called for the European Community to "exercise pooled sovereignty" on defense matters, just as it does on economic ones.

But skeptics argue for a very different lesson. They contend that the deep divisions in policy and approach among EC nations revealed by the gulf crisis make unrealistic the kind of joint policy Delors is pressing for. After all, they argue, if Britain and France had been committed to a pan-European security policy in which other EC member states wielded a veto, chances are no European troops would have been sent to the region.

"Those who said we should have a common defense and security policy because we basically agree on everything have found their positions were mistaken," said a senior aide to British Prime Minister John Major.

The differences among Europeans over the conflict were not just over the use of force but over fundamental issues of policy and approach, Freedman said. In a recent talk at the Center for Defense Studies in London, he outlined four European approaches—and flaws in each:

Britain stuck the closest to America's position during the crisis, a reflection not only of its view that Washington must continue to take its advocacy of what it views as on its experience in the 1982 Argentina, Britain saw Iraq as a clear transgressor that should be dealt with firmly and defeated.

The problem, Freedman noted, is that the British approach invariably involves double standards—it tackles issues like the Iraqi occupation of Kuwait but ignores others. And some principles contradict others. In the case of Israel's occupied territories, for example, where the lead in security issues but also of international principles. Based in part war to regain the Falkland Islands from Palestinian right of self-determination clashes with Israel's right to secure and defensible borders, Britain's approach offers no guidelines.

Germany, by contrast, relied on what might be labeled pocketbook principles. "As soon as you come across a difficult problem, you pull out your wallet and with a deep sigh say, 'Okay, how much?'" Freedman said.

Besides being expensive, such an approach at best only buys time and ignores the deeper problems that lie at the heart of conflicts. One good example, Freedman said, is Bonn's attempt to assist Moscow with emergency financial aid that is likely to do little to solve the structural weaknesses at the heart of the Soviet Union's economic crisis.

Italy revealed its preoccupation with institutions, calling for a Middle Eastern equivalent of the Conference on Security and Cooperation in Europe. Foreign Minister Gianni De Michelis, in a recent article, said the new system should codify "a set of rules and principles" and provide for "a regional security system, encouraging the establishment in the area of a real balance of power, underpinned by a strong legal basis and guaranteed by international support."

The drive to create new structures stems from a belief that world problems are caused by lack of understanding and communication and that those problems can be cured if countries would discuss them and sign codes of conduct. But Freedman said there is no reason to believe new organizations would be more effective than existing ones such as the United Nations. Since Iraqi President Saddam Hussein has repudiated virtually every international accord he has signed, the ultimate control over conduct of countries like Iraq remains the willingness of other countries to oppose them, even with force.

France, by contrast, pursued the art of the deal. For months before the air war began in January, French diplomats searched for a way to satisfy Saddam's demand for linkage of the gulf crisis with the Palestinian question—even though many experts argued that Iraq was merely using linkage as an excuse for its continued occupation of Kuwait.

All four approaches were flawed, Freedman concluded, yet all offered elements needed for a workable policy. "The challenge for European security policy is to put all four elements together," he said.

March 23, 1991

3 Environment

The articles in this chapter explore some of the social impacts of environmental problems in the U.S. and around the world.

The first article examines the economic impact faced by U.S. companies and individuals if the Clean Air act is strengthened. The second article deals with the controversy over logging on virgin forest land in the Northwest, home to the endangered spotted owl.

Environmental problems are world-wide. The third article explores problems and possible solutions for Mexico, where factories contaminate water sources along the U.S.-Mexico border, and this same water is then sold to water-starved companies within Mexico. Ultimately the water trickles down to be used by poor families without plumbing. The fourth article explores problems with polluted water in Poland, where people live in an environment fouled from years of neglect and disruption by a totalitarian political system.

The final article discusses what the Worldwatch Institute calls a "sustainable society" by the year 2030, one which "satisfies its needs without jeopardizing the prospects of future generations."

Breathing Easier Has its Price

Consumers will Ultimately Pay for Cleaner Air

JOHN M. BERRY

Like an earthquake ready to rumble along a California fault, the coming extension of the 20-year-old Clean Air Act is about to shake up some parts of the American economy.

It is difficult to say for sure what the impact will be as the nation begins to pay the price for intensifying the cleanup of dangerous chemicals and acids from its air. For the most part, pictures will just sway on the walls. But in certain pockets of the economy, buildings are likely to come crashing down with some workers' lives changed forever.

There is general agreement among economists that strengthening the Clean Air Act will pose no significant threat to the overall U.S. economy, which this year will produce goods and services worth well over $5 trillion. After all, the United States already spends some $90 billion a year controlling pollution. And the Bush administration is determined that the new legislation, once the House and Senate work out their differences, should add no more than $22 billion to that figure. Environmental groups say the costs may be significantly less.

Still, such cost estimates are extremely imprecise and in some ways understate the likely impact the legislation will have on scattered companies, communities and individuals. Few bills out of Congress carry with them the potential to cut through so many industries with new rules that will change the way products are manufactured, where they are made, by whom and with what materials.

Among those that will pay the heaviest price are the oil, auto, steel, chemical, dry cleaning, paint and furniture industries and electric utilities dependent on high-sulfur coal. In certain communities, the changes brought on by the legislation could be devastating.

The cost of compliance for some factories will be so high that plant closings could likely result. Some mines producing environmentally damaging high-sulfur coal used to produce electricity will close in West Virginia and Ohio—and in parts of those states where there are few other jobs paying comparable wages.

In other cases, American companies will find it easier and cheaper to import products rather than meet stringent new pollution standards.

The effect in some cases might be similar to that on American factories in the 1980s when a soaring U.S. dollar made their products too expensive to sell abroad.

Most workers found new jobs, but some workers' incomes never rebounded, according to Robert Z. Lawrence of the Brookings Institution.

American consumers should encounter changes, too. The cost of driving a car, getting a suit cleaned, turning on the lights and painting a house probably will go up. While much of the actual cost of compliance will be paid initially by industry, consumers ultimately will pay the bill that comes with making the air cleaner.

It is impossible to predict the precise cost that will be incurred as the nation tries to reduce acid rain in the Northeast, slash emissions of toxic, often cancer-causing substances and cut smog in the nation's cities. In some cases, there is not even a clear sense of whether the proposed standards can be met at all, or whether the standards will be enforced if the costs of compliance are too high. After all, the rules have on occasion been relaxed under the present Clean Air Act, and few cities have ever had to pay the specified penalties for failing to meet the law's standards.

There will be positive entries on the balance sheet to offset some of the costs, but those benefits are equally difficult to calculate. As a whole, the nation should expect to see lower health costs, reduced damage to buildings and streams and forests where the effects of acid rain have been etched, a boost to industries that produce cleaner burning fuel and jobs created by pollution control.

The money spent to control pollution "doesn't go down a rat hole," said David Doniger, senior staff attorney with the Natural Resources Defense Fund. "It gets spent on goods and services that produce pollution control."

Political Questions

Nevertheless, most of the debate in Congress has focused not on whether the Clean Air Act should be strengthened but on what the costs are and who will bear them.

"What is notable," Frank Press, president of the National Academy of Sciences, said last week, "is that this year they argued mainly over questions of economics and equity, rather than about science. Who should pay for scrubbers in Ohio? What should be done about mountain resorts in New England whose forests are harmed by acid rain? These are political questions. We may not like the economic implications of some of the answers."

When President Bush first proposed that the Clean Air Act be strengthened, the Environmental Protection Agency admitted that it had no firm idea how about one-fourth of the required reductions would be accomplished, much less their cost.

But the administration says now that the estimated cost should peak at $22 billion—calculated in terms of dollars with today's purchasing power—in 2005 when the economy should be considerably larger than it is today. At that level, the cost is quite manageable, administration officials maintain.

"Unless we are seriously wrong, there should not be" any major impact on the overall economy, said Richard L. Schmalensee, a member of the president's Council of Economic Advisers who is partially overseeing compliance costs for the legislation.

Schmalensee sees the impact on productivity, not jobs: Some workers could find themselves producing fewer goods because their employers are spending more money on pollution control equipment instead of new machines to boost productivity.

The bottom line, said Schmalensee, is that workers will be spending time doing things that benefit the environment but don't necessarily show up on the economic scorecard.

Nevertheless, additional costs will have to be borne—either by consumers who will pay more for the things they buy, workers whose real wages will be lowered if the more costly products cannot be sold or, possibly, business owners whose profits may be reduced.

A business lobbying group, the Clean Air Working Group, estimates that the legislation that passed the Senate with the president's blessing will cost not $22 billion a year but $45 billion. The key difference in costs was the result of assuming that a number of U.S. cities' air would remain dirty enough to require extremely costly cleanup measures to bring them into compliance.

"There will be investments hither and yon throughout the economy, in autos, oil, utilities and so on," Schmalensee said. Equipment used to reduce plant emissions "are fairly costly little items. There will be some tooling investments in automobiles . . . a lot of this stuff is capital intensive."

Out of the thousands of individual factories facing tighter standards, some undoubtedly would close rather than invest in expensive new equipment.

The steel industry, for example, has warned that proposed restrictions on plant emissions could force it to stop making coke from coal in the United States. If the firms can't make coke, a key ingredient in the steelmaking process, they would have to import it or go out of business, the industry argued.

Indeed, the issue of cooking hard coal in huge ovens to make coke is an example of a technological problem no one now knows how to solve. No one knows how to make steel without coke, though in theory it might be done, and no one knows how to make coke without violating the proposed air pollution standards. And if a new technological fix were found, no one has any idea what it would add to the price of steel.

Conceivably, such a new technology might even be cheaper than today's steelmaking process. Industry experts believe that is unlikely, but possible.

Cleaner Car Exhaust

In the auto industry, a large part of the added economic burden associated with the legislation involves making car exhaust cleaner—either by making engines burn more cleanly or by switching to new fuels. Recently, tests of a new type of catalytic converter similar to those now in use indicate there might be a far cheaper way to meet the new standards without resorting to alternative fuels. Again, no one knows whether the new catalytic converter will do the trick.

Such uncertainties have caused the administration and even some environmental groups to insist that the version of the Clean Air Act that Congress passes set standards but not specify how they should be met.

Just as the administration wants to leave industry as much flexibility as possible to reduce air pollution at the least possible cost, it also wants to avoid providing special benefits for workers, companies or communities that might suffer from the law's passage. In particular, Schmalensee said, the administration opposed an amendment added in the House that would pay extra benefits to workers who lost their jobs because of the law. "That would have a terrible precedential effect" that could apply to military base closings or just about any federal action that affected the economy, he warned.

Maybe symmetrical treatment would be in order, he joked: "My response to such proposals is to suggest that we should place a surtax on anyone who gets a job as the result of the law."

Tomorrow in Washington Business: The Clean Air Act's effect on utilities will be felt by households and businesses alike.

June 10, 1990

As Northwest's Ancient Forests Dwindle, Policy Questions Remain

JOHN LANCASTER

Freshly felled trees lay like matchsticks on the hill overlooking Windfall Lake, a small, clear jewel that brims with cutthroat trout and once was flanked by towering stands of Douglas fir.

To Forest Service managers, the 35-acre timber sale was a routine part of business in the Willamette National Forest, a sprawling, New-Jersey sized preserve that is the largest timber producer in the United States.

But to Forest Service wildlife biologist Ken Kestner, it was a mistake. Last summer, Kestner identified the area as the "center of activity" for a pair of northern spotted owls—a rare, nocturnal species uniquely dependent on the Northwest's virgin forests—and recommended against the cutting.

"I would assume that whatever tree they used for nesting has probably been harvested out," Kestner said while touring the site recently. "I see it as making a significant impact."

The division within the Forest Service is symptomatic of the broader debate over the future of the Northwest's dwindling ancient forests, a mountainous, fog-shrouded realm that stretches from northern California to British Columbia.

The controversy entered the national political arena after lawsuits by environmental groups on behalf of the spotted owl limited timber sales throughout the Northwest, prompting loud protests from logging towns and the timber industry. But the compromise that emerged from Congress in September was only a yearlong stopgap, leaving unresolved basic questions with profound implications for national forest policy, the environment and the economy of the Pacific Northwest.

On one side are the multi-billion dollar wood-products industry and hundreds of towns that depend on the timber harvest for their economic lifeblood. On the other are environmentalists, many scientists and a mounting body of evidence that "old-growth," or virgin, forests play a key role in the maintenance of wildlife populations, soil quality and biological diversity.

Because the forests constitute the last remnants of temperate rain forests in the continental United States, the debate has also assumed international significance in light of U.S. efforts to curb the destruction of rain forests in Brazil and elsewhere in the Third World.

Although Northwest forests are replanted or grow back on their own, scientists say that generations will pass before they assume the characteristics of those they replaced.

"Besides the aesthetic value, old-growth forests represent a reservoir of biological diversity and nutrient recycling that is essentially irreplaceable," said C.J. Ralph, a Forest Service research ecologist.

Concentrated for the most part in 12 national forests on the western slope of the Cascades, these giant evergreen stands of spruce, hemlock and Douglas fir—some more than 500 years old and taller than a 30-story building—once covered an estimated 19 million acres. Today scientists say only 2.5 million to 3.5 million acres of old-growth timber remain and that is disappearing at the rate of 67,000 acres a year. About 900,000 acres are permanently protected in parks or wilderness areas.

Environmentalists have tried for years to slow the logging in the Northwest, but they acquired the mechanism to do so only after the U.S. Fish and Wildlife Service agreed to consider listing the spotted owl as an endangered species. Under intense Pressure from logging interests, members of the Northwest's congressional delegations fashioned a compromise that forced environmentalists to lift some of the injunctions in exchange for reducing the overall timber harvests for 1989 and 1990.

Contrary to assertions by some politicians that the lawsuits had shut down mills throughout Oregon, the injunctions would not have had a significant impact until next year. That is because the injunctions blocked timber sales, which typically take place a year or two in advance of harvesting, and loggers are still cutting trees from timber purchased in 1988 or before.

"The cutting is going on fiercely," said Mike Kerrick, supervisor of the Willamette. "The market's been real hot."

Timber industry spokesmen assert that further restrictions will jeopardize jobs and communities. Moreover, they say, adequate amounts of old-growth timber already are protected in parks and wilderness areas, while modern forestry practices ensure a sound environment in harvested forests.

"It isn't an all or nothing situation," said Chris West, a forester with the Northwest Forestry Association, an industry group. "We may not have as many spotted owls, but the biological diversity will be there."

Although the matter is far from settled, few people expect the record harvests of recent years to persist. The Forest Service is preparing long-term management plans for the Northwest, and officials have indicated that old-growth and spotted owls will figure prominently in their calculations.

Last month, Associate Chief George Leonard announced that the service had adopted a policy that would preserve about half the remaining unprotected old growth in the Northwest. Environmentalists were skeptical, noting that the Forest Service has yet to decide precisely which forests fall into the category.

Nevertheless, even the agency's harshest critics concede that the Forest Service's traditional focus on timber production is changing. Publicity brochures emphasize recreation and wilderness not tree farms. more significantly, pesticide use is down, and loggers often are required to leave branches and other tree remnants for the benefit of soil and wildlife.

"We are very capable of altering our management systems to protect more of the kinds of ecological values associated with old growth," said Jerry Franklin, the service's chief plant ecologist and a frequent critic of past logging practices. "Right now the rate of change is just breathtaking. And it's very hard to see where it's going to end."

Perhaps nowhere are competing pressures more acute than in the 1.7 million-acre Willamette, which sprawls across Oregon's western Cascades like a giant throw rug.

Like other national forests in the Northwest, the Willamette remained largely undisturbed until the post-war building boom. Even now, 'scenic buffers" along major roads shield many logged-over areas from public view.

But from the air can be seen a checkerboard of bald hillsides and mountains laced with logging roads. Spotted owls and environmentalists notwithstanding, timber still drives the regional economy and accounts for 85 percent of the Willamette's management budget, according to Kerrick.

About 500,000 acres of old-growth remain in the Willamette, and 90,000 of that has been permanently protected as designated wilderness. Management plans call for setting aside an additional 207,000 acres for at least the next 15 years, Kerrick said.

"The environmental community would have you believe that the last of the old-growth is on a logging truck, and that's not the case," he said.

Rangers such as Karen Barnett emphasize recreation—hiking, rock-climbing, fishing, boating. "Sweet Home probably has more opportunities [for recreation] than other districts," Barnett said. "We have significant stands of old-growth left."

But many government scientists remain concerned that the Forest Service's shift in priorities may come too late for some species, particularly the spotted owl. Some scientists estimate that a single pair of the rare nocturnal birds, which grow to about 15 inches tall, require about 4,000 acres of old-growth forest to ensure an adequate food supply.

"If you cut down the old trees, you will drive the bird to extinction," said Charles Meslow, an Oregon State University professor of wildlife ecology who has studied the bird since 1975. Biologists estimate that the bird's population, now at about 3,000 pairs, is declining at the rate of one percent to 2 percent a year.

But forest managers in the Willamette and elsewhere still are obligated to provide timber at the levels specified by Congress. As a consequence, they frequently find themselves at odds with their own biologists.

The most recent conflict has occurred in Oakridge, a traditional Oregon timber town where local officials have been trying to diversify the economy through tourism. The effort got a boost last summer, when the local sawmill shut down after running out of timber on adjacent private lands.

"Obviously, you can't sell yourself as a recreational paradise if you have no trees," city administrator Wes Hare said.

Last summer, Hare and the supervisor of the local recreation center, Norm Coyer, learned of the Forest Service plan to allow logging at Windfall Lake, their favorite trout fishing spot. "I've been to hundreds of lakes in this part of Oregon and I've never seen one quite like it," Coyer said. "It was a very special place."

The two raised the matter with Kestner, the Forest Service biologist, who agreed that it should not be logged. Situated in a remote basin reached after a grueling scramble down a steep mountainside, the lake in reality is a tiny pond, formed when a natural landslide dammed a creek.

With its high elevation and girdle of old-growth forest, the area constituted "a mini, little wilderness," Kestner said. Moreover, Kestner determined that the area was being used by a pair of spotted owls, although he was never able to find the nest. But the district ranger overruled his request, explaining that no "substitute" timber was available elsewhere.

Kerrick said he is sympathetic to Kestner's concern but that a timber sale, once made, is very difficult to undo. "That's hard for biologists to accept," Kerrick said.

November 12, 1989

Expanding Waste Line along Mexico's Border

EDWARD CODY

For the last 15 years, Armando Beltran has been pulling up in his green-and-white tanker truck and connecting to a six-inch pipe that gushes with free—and chemically polluted—drinking water.

Along with dozens of other pipers here, Beltran has made a business of trucking the municipal water around a city struggling with an exploding population and an outstripped water system. The contaminated output from Nogales's Tomatera well, he said, goes to water-starved local factories, where it runs through faucets, sinks and toilets, and into the city's sprawl of plywood-and-cinderblock shacks, where thousands of poor families without plumbing store it in metal barrels to drink and wash with.

Although Beltran professes not to know it, his daily trips to the Tomatera pipe have come to symbolize a legacy of filth and toxicity along Mexico's border with the United States. The water that comes out there was found more than a year ago to contain potentially dangerous industrial solvents. But hard-pressed city authorities have yet to cut off the flow.

All along the 2,000-mile frontier with the United States, Mexico's municipal, state and federal governments have been similarly slow to react to the accumulation of environmental horror stories that have become an important part of life in a string of dingy factory towns, industrial parks and slums from Matamoros on the Gulf of Mexico to Tijuana on the Pacific Ocean.

A week-long trip along that string made evident a tragic despoiling as industry—much of it American-owned—sprang up without effective enforcement of environmental controls. The new factories also have attracted hundreds of thousands of new workers, submerging the border strip's infrastructure and turning the Rio Grande from a river where children used to swim into a gently flowing cesspool.

As a result, the south side of the U.S.-Mexican border has become a picture of neglect, of factories leaking foul-smelling effluents into brackish green and yellow canals, of muddy lanes connecting rows of slapdash huts where workers' children drink polluted water from drums that used to hold toxic chemicals, of culverts spewing human feces into rivers and ditches while garbage and chemical leftovers putrefy nearby in open dumps.

As Mexico and the United States negotiate along with Canada for a North American Free Trade Agreement, environmental activists have voiced alarm that similar deterioration could occur in the Mexican interior over the coming decade unless environmental controls are enforced. Although comparatively low Mexican wages are the main attraction for American and other investors here, they have warned, some companies have moved plants to Mexico—and may again in the future—partly to take advantage of traditionally lax antipollution enforcement.

"Once these problems take place in the interior, no one will be able to do anything about them," said Richard Kamp, a longtime environmental militant who monitors border pollution as head of the Border Ecology Project in Naco, Ariz.

President Carlos Salinas de Gortari, who has made the free-trade accord his top foreign priority, repeatedly has pledged to get a grip on Mexico's environmental mess, in the smog-infested capital as well as along the border. He enacted tough new antipollution laws soon after coming to office and has set aside $460 million for his Ecology and Urban Development Secretariat (known by its Spanish acronym SEDUE) to strengthen enforcement over the next three years.

Mexico's enforcement practices to date are likely to provide ammunition for U.S. congressional opponents of a free-trade accord.

In part to meet environmental fears in Congress and bolster a free-trade accord, Mexico's ecology secretariat and the U.S. Environmental Protection Agency also have negotiated an Integrated Border Environment Plan due for publication late this month. Officials of the two environmental agencies have described the document as the first comprehensive survey of border pollution and recipe for cleaning it up.

Local activists on both sides of the border have dismissed the plan as a public relations ploy, however, asserting the governments are putting on a display to assuage congressional concerns and assure passage of the trade agreement once negotiations are completed, probably later this year. The critics have made their assessments on the basis of nearly complete drafts of the plan made available last week by SEDUE officials in Mexican border towns.

"I don't think there's any meat to this, how do you say, this circus between Mexico and the United States, between SEDUE and the EPA," said Fernando Medina, who heads the Civic Committee for Ecological Disclosure in Mexicali.

Campaigning for Change

On both sides of the border, vocal environmental groups have expressed skepticism on promises from environmental officials because of what they say has been a historical refusal by Mexican authorities to move from declarations of good intent to actual enforcement.

"We don't trust the authorities to monitor this enough to know that we will be safe," said Laura S. de Durazo, part of a group opposing a seaside toxic-waste incinerator due to begin operation soon on the outskirts of Tijuana.

On the other side of Tijuana, in a ravine filled with ramshackle houses along muddy streets without drainage, Maurilio Sanchez Pachuca also has concluded that getting authorities to deal with pollution can be difficult. Since 1983, he has been leading a petition-writing campaign, visiting offices and inviting officials to visit—all without response.

The 25,000 families of his Chilancingo neighborhood have been frightened by what happens when rain falls heavily on the Otay Mesa industrial park, a flat hilltop just above their homes where a number of American-owned factories have gone into operation over the last decade. A 48-inch drain pipe serves the mesa, Sanchez said, but it overflows during heavy downpours, sending factory wastes into three gulleys that lead directly into Chilancingo's rutted streets, past a kindergarten and on to the Canon del Padre River.

Sanchez said he started his campaign to eliminate the pollution by writing Tijuana health authorities. For three years he wrote and waited for answers, fruitlessly. Then he started writing to health authorities in the Mexican state of Baja California, also fruitlessly, and to the state governor.

"We didn't get an answer from him either, nothing," Sanchez said, flipping through a file of his letters.

Finally, after four more years of letter-writing, Sanchez was told President Salinas planned to come and see for himself. Local residents prepared for his visit. But it never happened, and they still do not know why.

"He could at least fly over in a helicopter, because I am sure he doesn't know about our case," Sanchez said. "We have confidence in the president. If he knew, we could get something done."

In his correspondence file, Sanchez also has a copy of some pages from a sampling he said was done by the Autonomous University of Baja California showing that the wastes flowing into Chilancingo contain lead, copper, zinc, cadmium and chrome, all presumably from the factories up on the mesa and all presumably dangerous to the neighborhood's health.

Partly because of a tradition of confidentiality in the Mexican government and partly because Salinas's antipollution orders are only now beginning to take effect, shortage of official data has plagued cleanup efforts along the entire length of the border.

Kamp said, for example, that the 1990 binational study of Nogales drinking water remains the only comprehensive look at what has happened to city water since the rise of factories alongside a highway south of the city.

City authorities closed down two water wells after the study, he said, but have refused to accept the unofficial data as conclusive. The Tomatera facility was closed for several days, but reopened to whoever wants to draw water there even though it lies near the polluted Nogales River waters that run through town. After the river crosses into the United States, however, the garbage-lined wash has been posted by U.S. health authorities with a sign saying: "Danger, Keep Out, Polluted Water."

Rise in Birth Defects

Carmen Rocco, a physician and medical director at the Brownsville, Tex., Community Health Center, has encountered similar frustration in her efforts to determine why an unusually high number of babies are being born without brains in the city's Valley Regional Medical Center and Brownsville Medical Center hospitals, just across the Rio Grande from a zone of factories in Matamoros, Mexico.

She said her research has shown that 42 births troubled by neural tube defects, including 28 anacephalics, took place between November 1989 and January 1991. This is about six times the U.S. average, but nobody knows why, Rocco said.

She and some colleagues have an idea, however. They have begun pursuing the chemical wastes that she said regularly turn Matamoros canals into "orange and brown rivers" that empty into the Rio Grande and nearby lagoons that flow into the Gulf of Mexico.

Along the broad avenues of Matamoros's Finsa industrial park, where brightly painted factories are flanked by lawns and soccer fields for employees, the extent of filth has long been difficult to discern with scientific certainty.

Shampoo-like bubbles foamed one recent day, for instance, where wastes flowed directly into a canal from a concrete trough leading from an electrical-components factory. Juan Nicolas de Leon, an architect who until last week ran the local SEDUE office, said the factory has its own pretreatment plant for water-borne wastes that should make them "crystalline" when they pour into the canal.

Another, nearby plant that finishes automobile bumpers recently received certification from SEDUE that its operations are environmentally harmless, de Leon said. But a sampling taken just downstream from its discharge for a report last May by the U.S. National Toxic Campaign Fund showed 23.2 million parts per billion of the chemical xylene—which the researchers said is 52,700 times the U.S. standard for drinking water.

Xylene was identified as a solvent that has been connected to respiratory irritation and damage to the lungs, liver and kidneys. The discharge sampled for the report is released into a series of canals that eventually flow to the Rio Grande and the Gulf of Mexico.

The Baja California state SEDUE representative, Cesar Ruben Castro, said the problem with treatment equipment in many factories is that it is only partly effective, removing all waste in some cases but only half the waste in others.

Sights for Sore Eyes

Monitoring wastes has been easy at some spots along the border. The Mexican city of Nuevo Laredo, for example, with a population of more than 600,000, discharges about 27 million gallons of raw sewage a day directly into the Rio Grande at more than 25 points. Fecal matter can be seen floating in the current as the river curves southward—toward towns down river that pump their drinking water from the same stream.

A new sewage-treatment plant has been scheduled for construction. But Nuevo Laredo's population has been growing so fast the plant's capacity will be inadequate even before it is completed, said Adolph Kahn, a retired veterinarian and environmental activist from Laredo, Tex., just across the river.

As Kahn looked on, pigs rooted contentedly in an open Nuevo Laredo dump only a few hundred yards from the river. Oily black residue covered some patches of the dump. Chalky yellow residue covered others.

Guillermo Giron, president of the environment committee of a national assembly-plant association, estimated recently that some 260,000 tons of toxic wastes produced by American-owned firms are dumped illegally in Mexico every year. U.S.-Mexican accords since 1986 have obliged assembly plants to return to the United States any toxic material brought into Mexico. In fact, authorities on both sides acknowledge no one has kept track of how much comes in or how much goes out, and the officials suspect much of it is dumped after use.

The U.S. General Accounting office estimated that of the 1,449 assembly plants along the border, about 800 create hazardous wastes. Of these, only 446 have registered with authorities to allow tracking of incoming and outcoming materials as required by the U.S.-Mexican accords, the GAO reported.

Salinas, as part of his environmental push, has pledged to quadruple the number of inspectors along the border to 200 as part of the three-year binational plan.

In Matamoros, for example, SEDUE recently hired three university-trained inspectors to visit plants. When Castro took over SEDUE's Baja California operations two years ago, the state had 23 inspectors; it now has 43 and is recruiting 40 more.

Also as part of the new get-tough rules, the Matamoros SEDUE office ordered closure of Productos de Preservacion, an American-owned pesticide factory, and the Mexicali office closed Quimica Organica last month. Both factories had been cited for dangerous leaks of chemical gases.

These were among some 700 such closures, most of them temporary, ordered by SEDUE in the last year under the campaign by Salinas to crack down on offenders.

February 17, 1992

Poland Faces Communist Legacy of Pollution

Water That Burns Skin is Reminder That Freedom is No Quick Cure for Fouled Environment

BLAINE HARDEN

It spurts yellowish-brown from the tap, laced with heavy metals, coal-mine salts and organic carcinogens. It stains the sink, tastes soapy and smells like a wet sock that has been fished out of a heavily chlorinated swimming pool.

Given a few weeks, it will eat a hole in a steel pan. Better to wear rubber gloves while washing the dishes. Better to boil it before cooking. Best not to drink it.

Tap water drips daily into the collective consciousness of Warsaw as part of the pernicious legacy of four decades of communism. The water is a long goodbye from a totalitarian system that scorned environmental common sense and poisoned people in the name of the masses.

More than two years after Polish voters dumped communism, each morning's grungy dribble from the tap is a dispiriting reminder that political freedom and free-market economics offer no quick cure for a catastrophically fouled environment. Wretched tap water sends the same dismal message in Prague and Budapest.

Residents of these capitals need go no farther than their kitchen sinks to see— indeed, to taste and smell—that the old Eastern Bloc remains a poor, polluted and unhealthy appendage of the new Europe.

"When I washed my face with tap water, it caused little red blotches. My skin felt stretched and itchy. I felt like it might crack or split open if I spoke or laughed too much," said Barbara Matusevicz, 36, a secretary at Warsaw University's department of law.

Like many Warsaw residents whose skin hurts after washing with tap water, Matusevicz has experimented for years with boiled water, bottled water, skin lotions and home remedies. She finally settled on a cheap, if unorthodox, cure.

"I started making a facial mask out of porridge, the same stuff I serve my son for breakfast. It moisturizes and makes my skin feel smooth," Matusevicz said.

Jan Dojlido, head of the department of water chemistry and biology at the Polish Institute of Meteorology and Water Management, does not smear porridge on his face—but neither does he drink Warsaw water directly from the tap.

Strictly speaking, Dojlido said, the tap water is not "toxic." The water's tendency to irritate human skin, he said, is caused by its high concentration of chlorine, and heavy chlorination is required to de-fang the noxious cocktail of industrial and human waste that is present in river water as it is sucked into the Warsaw's water-treatment plants.

For his own family's supply of drinking and cooking water, Dojlido runs tap water through an activated carbon filter and then boils it. He advises mothers to bathe their babies only in tap water that has been boiled for a full 15 minutes; this rids the water of cancer-causing organic compounds that he regularly measures in tap water at concentrations he said are more than twice as high as minimums set by the World Health Organization.

As a scientist who has been studying water quality for much of his adult life, Dojlido has a difficult time talking about Warsaw tap water without occasionally resorting to an unscientific adjective like "horrible."

"I came to Warsaw in 1948 and the water here is steadily getting worse. Warsaw is very unlucky when it comes to water," said Dojlido.

The causes of the pollution are many but the problem begins with Warsaw's principal source of drinking water, the Vistula River.

That river, Poland's longest, flows clean and drinkable out of the Carpathian Mountains in the south of the country. But about 150 miles before it reaches Warsaw, the Vistula soaks up the runoff from Silesia, Poland's industrial heartland. Few areas of the world are more polluted.

Using the river as a lifeline and a toilet, Communist central planners concentrated the nation's steel, chemical, fertilizer and pulp-and-paper plants in Silesia. People who live there have significantly higher rates of cancer, along with circulatory and respiratory diseases, than other Poles, according to recent studies. Rates of mental retardation in Silesia have been described as "appalling" by the Polish Chemical Society.

Over the years, the Communists' central plan did not insist that Silesia's toxic waste be kept out of the river. The Ministry of Environmental Protection reported last month that about a quarter of Poland's big industrial plants either have no waste-water treatment or use devices of insufficient capacity. The ministry said half of the country's small industrial plants use no waste-water treatment.

Silesian factories seed the Vistula with pollutants including ammonia, phosphates and heavy metals such as lead and mercury. For example, the average concentration of mercury in the Vistula in 1990 was nine times higher than the Polish norm for safe drinking water.

Existing water treatment technology in Warsaw can do little to remove heavy metals from river water, according to Robert Latawiec, central waterworks manager.

Coal mines in Silesia are the biggest polluters of the Vistula. They dump about 6,600 tons a day of chlorides and sulfates into the river, according to the Ministry of Environmental Protection. These corrosive salts are the reason why Warsaw tap water can eat a hole in a baking pan and why rusted-out water pipes have to be dug up and replaced every 10 years. The ministry says corroded water pipes leak about one-third of the water they are supposed to carry.

The river is going to get even saltier. According to the Ministry of Environmental Protection, the amount of such salts in the river will increase by about 70 percent over the next decade as coal mines continue to be exploited. Lacking oil, natural gas or nuclear-power plants, Poland needs the coal to produce electricity.

Salts are the major reason why 57 percent of the Vistula is classified as unfit for any purpose.

Polish cities and towns also contribute. About 40 percent of the country's sewage is untreated. A large proportion of it goes straight into the Vistula, both up-stream and downstream from Warsaw. This city treats only about one-third of the waste it pumps into the river.

"The Vistula is a sewer for half the country," said Dariusz Jan Stanislawski, a scientist at the Polish Department of Water Economy and an adviser to the minister of environmental protection.

Cleaning up a national sewer that also happens to be Poland's main source of drinking water is a complex and costly project that environmental officials say will take at least 20 years.

The World Bank, along with Sweden and the Polish government, is paying for studies of a comprehensive cleanup of the Vistula. Sweden is keenly interested be-cause the river is the largest single source of pollution in the Baltic Sea.

Poland has put together an ambitious cleanup program. Nearly 3,000 new waste-water treatment plants are to be built. Desalination plants are also proposed. Some of the worst-polluting industrial plants have been closed, and others are being forced to pay heavy fines. Excepting salts, pollution is no longer getting worse.

But the Warsaw government, already running a deficit and struggling with a free-market economic transformation that most Poles no longer support, cannot pay for cleaning up the entire river using modern technology. Nor are foreign donors rushing in to pick up a tab estimated at tens of billions of dollars.

Environmental officials here said that the fastest and cheapest way to improve the quality of tap water is for Poles to stop wasting it.

The average resident of Warsaw, for example, uses about twice as much tap water as the average resident of Western Europe—about 98 gallons a day per per-son in Warsaw compared to 53 a day in the West. The average Pole produces four times as much waste water as West Europeans.

"In Poland, like all of Eastern Europe, there was no economic incentive to save water. Nobody thought of charging for water. Houses don't have water meters," said Bronislaw Kaminski, president of Poland's National Fund for Environmental Protection and Water Management.

Kaminski said technocrats from his water fund have been rushing around Poland in the past year preaching conservation and ordering a halt to the construction of 50 water-treatment plants "that are too big, too expensive and which use old technology."

Kaminski is the father of a nationwide crusade to cut back on water usage by making consumers pay a market price for the water they consume and the sewage they create.

"In a market economy, the money for good water has to come from taxpayers. If we reduce consumption and make consumers pay for water, we will have resources to build smaller, more efficient plants that use the best technology," said Kaminski.

Warsaw residents will probably have to wait several years before conservation, higher water bills and new treatment technology can purify water drawn from the Vistula.

Even then, the Vistula may prove a poor source of good-tasting drinking water. As Robert Latawiec, manager of Warsaw's waterworks, explained, "From this quality, you can't make miracles."

In the meantime, there is a less polluted alternative, a man-made reservoir north of the capital. Warsaw already draws more than a third of its drinking water from the reservoir, which is called Zegrzynskie Lake.

Still, as water chemist Dojlido likes to point out, Warsaw is very unlucky about water.

"The rivers that flow into Zegrzynskie Lake drain wetlands where there is something called humic acid. It makes for a bad color. When this water is treated with normal amounts of chlorine, it can produce very toxic haloforms," said Dojlido.

The most common haloform in Warsaw tap water, Dojlido said, is chloroform, a known cancer-causing agent when its concentration in drinking water exceeds 30 parts per billion.

"It often happens that the concentration of chloroform is over the permissible limits. In fact, it happens that the level is more than double the limits set by the World Health Organization. The water is not safe then for drinking," said Dojlido.

Warsaw does have one other option—underground water. The city lies on an artesian basin, with clean drinking water lying at a depth of about 650 feet.

During the Communist era, the city drilled a small number of public wells and made water available to residents willing to line up outdoors with plastic jugs. Over the years, as the quality of tap water has deteriorated, the lines for well water have grown longer. Huge plastic jugs, along with portable rollers, sell briskly in local markets. The usual wait for good water is about half an hour.

As part of the government's low-tech cure for the capital's clean-water crisis, scores of new wells are to be dug throughout the city in the next few months. The wait for underground water should soon disappear. Unfortunately, according to water experts, so will the good water.

December 15, 1991

Rising Third World Energy Demand Imperils Economies, Environment

Report Outlines Dilemma of Poorest, Most Crowded Nations

THOMAS W. LIPPMAN

A rapid increase in energy demand in developing countries threatens to undermine their fragile economies and negate environmental gains in the industrialized nations, according to a new analysis by the congressional Office of Technology Assessment.

The report dramatizes the dilemma facing many of the world's poorest and most densely populated nations: the more their people gain access to motor vehicles, mechanized farm equipment and modern appliances, the more they have to spend on power plants and imported oil and the greater the risk of environmental degradation.

"Energy services are essential for economic growth (and) improved living standards," said the report, part of a study of Third World energy problems requested by several congressional committees.

But providing those services means buying oil and building power plants in countries already burdened by debt, damming rivers and inundating farmland for hydroelectric facilities and burning more coal.

Unrestrained use of coal, especially in China, along with increased urban bus fleets and the burning of wood for fuel in the poorest countries, contributes to the worldwide emissions of greenhouse gases believed to be responsible for global warming, according to the report.

The global warming debate has begun to focus international attention on energy and environmental problems in the developing countries. Delegates from more than 100 nations will gather in Chantilly, Va., on Feb. 4 to begin negotiations on an international agreement to limit greenhouse gas emissions.

"This will be one of the focuses of any global warming treaty," said Alden Meyer, director of the climate change and energy policy program at the Union of Concerned Scientists. "You can't ask these countries to forgo development, so you have to make it possible for them to develop in a more environmentally friendly way . . . . You don't want them to follow the fossil fuel model."

"Concern about this was deader than dead when we were formed in 1984," said Deborah Blevis, executive director of the Washington-based International Institute for Energy Conservation. "All the arguments we have been making since '84 are coming out now."

Blevis said most projected growth in energy consumption "is disproportionately going to occur in the developing countries or Eastern Europe. They can least afford an out-of-whack energy system."

Jessica Mathews, vice president of the World Resources Institute, said the problem of Third World energy demand is "a deeply neglected area" because the World Bank has not made energy efficiency part of its development loan policy and because "American energy policy analysts have a little bit of a credibility problem. We ought not to be offering energy policy thinking when we don't have an energy policy of our own."

According to the OTA report, however, the issue of energy use in the Third World and its effect on the global environment can no longer be ignored. The increasing consumption helps to drive up oil prices, adds to air pollution and undermines the international banking system through energy loans that cannot be repaid.

Developing countries accounted for 17 percent of world commercial energy consumption in 1973, the report said. That figure is now 23 percent and is expected to rise to 40 percent by 2020. But among the countries classified as developing by the World Bank, the rate of consumption growth is vastly uneven.

The 50 countries of Africa consume less than 3 percent of world commercial energy. China, India and Brazil account for 45 percent. China alone will account for more than one third of the expected increase in the next 30 years, according to the report.

Meeting projected growth in electricity demand will require investment of $125 billion a year, twice the current level, the report said, citing World Bank estimates. In countries that cannot provide enough electricity to meet demand for heat and light among their fast-growing populations, consumers will be forced to use more and more "biomass"—wood, crop wastes and animal dung—with potentially devastating environmental and social consequences, the report warned.

"Overuse of biomass already contributes to environmental degradation" through soil erosion and smoky emissions, the report said. "Moreover, gathering traditional supplies of fuel wood is time-consuming, exhausting work frequently undertaken by women and children, who are thus diverted from other activities (education and farming) that could eventually improve their productivity and living conditions."

A later OTA report will make recommendations about policy and technology for dealing with the Third World energy problem.

January 21, 1991

'Sustainable' Society Urged By Year 2030

Research Group Warns of Global Degradation

JOHN LANCASTER

Solar energy will power most homes and factories. Commuters will get to work on bicycles and mass transit as others work from home on computer terminals. Industry will rely on recycled goods for basic materials, while shoppers carry home their groceries in reusable canvas bags.

That is how the Worldwatch Institute pictures a "sustainable" society in its latest "State of the World" report, a global environmental roundup that otherwise warns of food shortages, environmental degradation and spreading social chaos if mankind does not mend its ways in the next 40 years.

The authors of the report, published annually by the Washington-based research institute and released yesterday, acknowledge that there are many obstacles along the road to a sustainable society, defined as "one that satisfies its needs without jeopardizing the prospects of future generations."

Among other things, their model assumes that society will wean itself from fossil fuels such as coal and gasoline, not to mention the automobile. Basic assumptions about economic growth—that human progress depends on the rising output of goods and services—would be supplanted by an emphasis on other qualities, such as durability and environmental protection.

"It's a definition" of what a sustainable world would look like, said Lester Brown, president of Worldwatch and the report's principal author. "It's not a prediction."

Even now, the world according to Worldwatch is not a pretty place. The authors claim that the economic gains of the past four decades are largely illusory, predicated on polluting industries, overcut forests and reckless agricultural practices that lose 24 billion tons of topsoil to erosion each year.

The report cites evidence that environmental degradation already has cut into food production, and it warns of mounting threats to human survival posed by the accumulation of "greenhouse" gases in the atmosphere and a population that is projected to reach 9 billion in the next 40 years.

The report relies heavily on government data and scientific studies. But like the computer models that project a sharp rise in global temperatures in the next century, its bleak predictions are far from universally accepted.

Last week, for example, White House Chief of Staff John H. Sununu criticized what he termed "a tendency by some of the faceless bureaucrats on the environmental side to try and create a policy in this country that cuts off our coal, oil and natural gas. I don't think that's what this country wants. I don't think America wants not to be able to use their automobiles."

But the report suggests that Americans may someday have little choice. It warns that unless society achieves "sustainability" by the year 2030, "environmental deterioration and economic decline are likely to be feeding on each other, pulling us into a downward spiral of social disintegration."

Technology could provide much of the answer, according to the report. In the institute's vision of the sustainable world of the future, la typical urban landscape will have thousands of [solar] collectors sprouting from rooftops, much as television antennas do today." Third World villages will get their electricity from photovoltaic cells, while wind generators help light Denver and Kansas City.

Recycling will be the rule instead of the exception. "Bottlers will simply clean the container, steam off the old label and add a new one," the report said. "The steel mills of the future will feed heavily on worn-out automobiles, household appliances and industrial equipment."

One doesn't need to look 40 years into the future for examples of sustainable technologies. Already, the report notes, steel mills in the United States produce one-third of all steel from scrap in super-efficient electric arc furnaces, while the city of Shanghai uses recycled sewage to grow vegetables.

But the report acknowledges that its sustainable society cannot be achieved without fundamental shifts in human attitudes and behavior. "Sustainability will gradually eclipse growth as the focus of economic policy-making," the report said. "Materialism simply cannot survive the transition to a sustainable world."

In the sustainable world, the report said, "it will become unfashionable to own fancy new cars and clothes."

February 11, 1990

4 *Population, Urbanization, and Housing*

The rapid increase in world population affects virtually all aspects of society.

The first article in this chapter explores how the world population could be stabilized by the next century if government spending on family planning programs were drastically increased now. The second article discusses how the increase in energy demand in developing countries, due to their growing populations, threatens to undermine their economies and environmental gains. The next article discusses how in spite of India's "Green Revolution," whereby the country is self-sufficient in food, roughly half of its people are still undernourished. Millions of the rural poor have seen little benefit from the technological advances, and are caught in a cycle of being underfed and overworked.

The next two articles deal with urban woes in the United States. Brought to the forefront by the 1992 Los Angeles riots, the first article points out the dramatic transformation of the cities in recent years—an exodus of the middle class; more concentrated and persistent poverty, increasing racial dynamics driven by growth of numerous ethnic groups, and fewer good jobs available for unskilled workers. The following article discusses aspects of our current urban problems, from welfare to housing to schools to neighborhoods and crime. Finally, as a symbol of the current housing and employment crises, the final article provides a close-up view into the homeless situation in New York City.

Costs of Stabilizing World Population Tallied

$10.5 Billion a Year Needed, Report Says

SUSAN OKIE

The world population, now 5.3 billion, could be stabilized at 9.3 billion by the end of the next century if governments and international organizations increase annual spending for family planning programs from the current $3.2 billion to $10.5 billion over the next decade, according to a report published today.

Without such a spending increase, world population is expected to grow to more than 14 billion by the year 2120, according to United Nations projections.

"What we as a society of nations do in this decade will determine population trends for the next century," said Sharon Camp, vice president of Population Crisis Committee, a nonprofit organization advocating family planning programs that prepared the report.

The added funding would be used for efforts to increase worldwide use of birth control by the year 2000 to approximately 75 percent of all couples of reproductive age. According to the report, that frequency of birth control use would result in an average family size of two children per woman and lead to population stabilization by the end of the 21st century. Recent projections of a near tripling of population by 2120 have alarmed many experts, who fear such explosive growth would strain the planet's capacity to produce food, irreparably deplete natural resources and damage the environment.

Camp said the report is the first attempt to determine, for 125 countries, what level of birth control use would be needed to modify the current pattern, and what it would cost to achieve that level. The calculations estimated it costs $16 per year per couple to provide family planning services.

By the year 2000, the U.S. government's annual contribution to family planning programs should be $1.2 billion, according to the report. Camp said the U.S. government contributed about $227 million to international family planning efforts in 1988, roughly half of it to individual nations and the rest to institutions.

The report said 29 countries have achieved an average family size of two children or less and have either stabilized their populations or are expected to do so. They include the United States, Japan, South Korea, Australia, most West European countries and several in East Europe. More than 70 percent of couples in the majority of these countries use some form of birth control, the report said.

Another 12 countries were rated as having "good" family planning records, with between 61 percent and 75 percent of couples using contraceptives and with an average of 2.6 children per woman. Among the countries in this category were China, Thailand, Sri Lanka, Colombia, Chile and Brazil.

The Chinese government's family planning policies have been widely criticized in recent years as coercive. The United States has not contributed to the U.N. Population Fund since 1985 because part of the money goes to China, where 74 percent of couples use birth control.

Twenty-one countries were rated "fair," with rates of contraceptive use ranging from 43 percent to 60 percent of couples and with an average of 3.9 children per woman. Included in this category were Ireland, Mexico, Zimbabwe, South Africa, Indonesia and the Philippines.

Eighteen countries were rated "poor," including the Soviet Union, India, Bangladesh, Egypt, Kenya and Guatemala. Family size in these countries averaged 4.3 children per woman, and contraceptive use rates ranged from 15 percent to 42 percent of couples.

Forty-five countries were rated "very poor," with fewer than 15 percent of couples using contraceptives and with family size averaging 6.4 children per woman. Camp said it is unlikely that many of these will achieve the goal of 75 percent of couples using contraceptives by the year 2000 but said lack of progress in some countries could be offset by better-than-expected gains in others. She said countries in the "very poor" category make up only 14 percent of the world's population.

Currently, 80 percent of family planning costs in developing countries are paid by the governments and consumers in those countries, Camp said. The plan would require most developing countries to at least double their family planning budgets over the next decade. It proposes that by the year 2000 slightly under half of the projected $10.5 billion annual cost of family planning should be paid by developing countries.

February 26, 1990

India's 'Green Revolution' Leaves Many Poorer, More Poorly Fed

STEVE COLL

In this dry district of southern India, where about 2 million people scratch a living from sandy soil, the government is trying to overcome the most vexing paradox of India's development since independence: Although the country is now self-sufficient in food, roughly half its people are undernourished.

The victims of India's chronic malnutrition are disproportionately peasant farmers and rural laborers who have been left out of the 'green revolution' that retrieved Indian agriculture from the brink of disaster and turned it into a rare success story in the developing world.

These hundreds of millions of rural poor have seen few benefits from the technical advances of the green revolution. Many have seen their lives worsen as India grows less traditional food high in protein and vitamins and more cash and export crops with limited nutritional value.

Yam Appayah, a peasant farmer who labors to feed a family of 11 from three-quarters of an acre of land, stood in a field of potatoes one recent afternoon and explained that while he has obtained a number of things his parents didn't have—limited access to irrigation water, higher-yielding seeds and free bags of insecticide handed out by the state government—he cannot keep his family fed. "It is nowhere near enough," he said, waving at his modest plot.

Across the way, members of his family squatted in a patch of radishes under the supervision of a wealthy landlord who hires them as day laborers for as little as 60 cents a day. The landlord also receives irrigation water, seeds and supplies from the government—and because he farms on a large scale, he makes profitable use of them, Appayah said.

Peasants such as Appayah's family used to try to feed themselves by growing protein-rich crops known as pulses, including lentils, and cooking them as the popular Indian staple food, dal. Now Appayah plants potatoes, sells them for cash and buys his food at the market—where there are few pulses because most farmers have quit growing them. The repetition of Appayah's story hundreds of millions of times across India has kept the subcontinent's nutritional levels among the lowest in the world, worse than some countries such as China with comparable per capita income, according to nutritionists and agricultural economists.

The reasons are not mysterious. India's declining staple, dal, has four times the protein, hundreds of times more vitamin A, three times the iron and five times the calcium of rice. Yet rice is one of the most common crops in the Kolar District, in part because of the spread of green revolution seeds and irrigation.

It was only 20 years ago that many in the West and in India predicted a tragic food shortage on the Indian subcontinent. The U.S. Agency for International Development and United Nations agencies warned that tens of millions of Indians might die in famines caused by overpopulation and lack of basic foods during the 1980s.

Instead, as the decade passes, India has become a net exporter of wheat and rice. Through the green revolution's intensive agriculture development—which was designed and implemented by Indians and assisted by money and technology from abroad—states such as Punjab fast produced huge surpluses of food, enough to feed residents of poorer states and still export abroad.

Yet here in the south and in the poorer states of eastern India, vast areas remain untouched in crucial ways by that success. "It is now clear that, contrary to predictions, the major factor that underlies India's problems of undernutrition is not overall shortage of food grains but low purchasing power . . . by vast sections of people," said C. Gopalan, one of India's leading nutritionists. Nor does the fundamental problem appear to be one of distribution. In Kolar and most rural areas, there is food in the markets but not enough money among the poor to buy it.

Few would call the green revolution a failure because it did not solve all of the economic imbalances in the countryside. But some economists worry that the gap between rural rich and poor may be growing. And the disparity in rural incomes is turning into an issue not only of nutrition and health, but of politics.

In November, Prime Minister V.P. Singh's National Front coalition was voted into office with massive support from peasant farmers and landless laborers eager for rapid change in their living conditions. Independent peasant farmer movements also have grown in recent years.

In the Kolar district, the farmers' movement hasn't been very active, but that may be because at least 60 percent and perhaps as much as 80 percent of the district's population is undernourished, according to state nutrition director N.G. Dandin. Underfed and overworked, the district's farmers and laborers have little energy left for politics.

In that and other ways, Kolar is typical of the areas of India left out of the green revolution. Only 11 percent of its land is irrigated—the rest depends on whether the monsoon rains come. Most of the district is planted in cereals, with protein-rich pulses now taking up less than one-fifth of the area under cultivation, according to government statistics.

Both New Delhi and the state government of Karnataka are trying to address these problems by encouraging poor farmers to grow more pulses. The government gives away tens of thousands of bags of seeds and fertilizers each year in an experimental program. But the program's impact has been marginal largely because farmers can earn more cash growing other crops.

A shift to more lucrative cash crops would not be a problem if the farmers and laborers used their increased income to buy nutritious food. But few do, local officials say, in part because there is a shortage of pulses at the stores. So the government also has launched an education program about what to eat and how to cook it. Still, the program has reached only a scant minority of the district's residents.

A booming silkworm industry in Kolar has caused overall agricultural revenue to rise dramatically here since the green revolution began. But the paradox remains: While the agricultural economy gets richer, many Indians in Kolar and elsewhere remain both poor and poorly fed.

January 10, 1990

Urban Recovery Impeded by Changes of Past Three Decades

BARBARA VOBEJDA

From the smoldering ruins of last week's riots have come conflicting strains: a cry for help for America's inner cities, and bleak predictions that revival will be more difficult than ever before.

City officials, policy experts and scholars, conservative and liberal, cite a continuing, dramatic transformation of the nation's cities that makes the task of healing formidable: an exodus of the middle class; more concentrated and persistent poverty; an increasingly complex racial dynamic driven by the growth of numerous ethnic groups; and fewer good jobs available to unskilled workers.

"We're working with more difficult and complicated problems than we were in the late '60s," said Paul Soglin, mayor of Madison, Wis. Soglin, who was active in anti-poverty programs two decades ago, served as mayor in the 1970s and returned to office three years ago. "There was a sense of optimism," in the '60s. Now, he said, "I just see it's going to be a difficult and more protracted struggle. . . . I'm talking years."

The obstacles to recovery stem from several sources, urban experts say, including sweeping demographic and economic changes that make the cities a very different place than they were a generation ago.

The middle class, both black and white, has left central cities for the suburbs in large numbers, leaving behind a more concentrated poor and predominantly minority population. That exodus has reduced the tax base in many places and left fewer stabilizing forces that might encourage businesses to come in and stay.

More and more, suburbanites are not even going into the city to work, shop or see a movie, said William Frey, a demographer at the University of Michigan. "There is much less identification with people who live there," he said.

At the same time, massive immigration has brought large numbers of Hispanics and Asians into the cities, complicating racial interactions. The recent antagonism between blacks and Koreans in New York and Los Angeles illustrates the competition that can stem from that new mix.

"There are a lot of turf wars that still need to be played out," Frey said.

The nation's stagnant economy is also engendering less public willingness to spend money on social problems, said Douglas Massey, a sociologist at the University of Chicago.

In the 1960s, he said, the common expectation was that personal economic fortunes would continue to improve. "It's easier to be generous then," Massey said. "The whole mindset has changed. The attitude is not one of rising expectations, but trying to hold on to what you've got."

Even in a more favorable set of circumstances, those who struggled to rebuild Washington, Detroit, Los Angeles and other American cities after the riots of the '60s were surprised and frustrated at the slow progress. And vacant, burned-out buildings in many of those cities still loom today as reminders of that era.

Gilbert Hahn Jr., a Washington lawyer appointed to chair the city council a year after the 1968 riot, said he mistakenly believed at the time that homes and stores would simply be rebuilt with insurance funds. But in many cases, businesses chose never to return to those locations, forcing inner-city residents to travel long distances to shop for basic goods.

"Looking back, I can see that there wasn't ever a chance," he said.

Richard P. Nathan, who worked on the presidential commission appointed to study the riots of the late 1960s, said an "ebullient spirit" at the time allowed many of the commission's recommendations to be put into place.

At the same time, the civil rights movement ushered in great improvements, including the dismantling of segregated neighborhoods. But today, "the tough, residual underclass areas are something new and more serious than they were 25 years ago," said Nathan, who went on to serve in the Nixon administration and now is director of the Rockefeller Institute of Government at the State University of New York.

Carl Horowitz, a policy analyst at the Heritage Foundation, argues that some progress has been made in American cities. Many of the worst problems of the past—lack of plumbing facilities and electricity in the homes of the poor, for example—have been virtually eliminated.

But he agreed that the road ahead will be extraordinarily difficult. Business investors will hesitate to move back into neighborhoods where they have already been burned out, he said. "The rioters in a few days managed to create a situation where it may take 20 years to get back to where we were."

The loss of businesses in the riots exacerbates the long-term decline in manufacturing jobs available to unskilled workers in the cities. While many downtown areas have seen office construction, the result has been mostly white-collar employment out of reach to city residents without education, said Richard Forstall, a demographer at the Census Bureau.

Urban experts also cite as obstacles the increase in guns on the street, drug trafficking and gang activity. And there is a critical change in attitude, they say: By comparison to the 1960s, America in the 1990s seems hard-bitten and cynical.

Sterling Tucker, who headed the Washington Urban League in the late 1960s, remembers flying into National Airport after the assassination of the Rev. Martin Luther King Jr. and seeing the city in flames. In the following days and months, he said he came to see that, even with the commitment of government, the impoverished neighborhoods would never really be rebuilt.

"I don't know of any city that's better off in its neighborhoods because it had riots," said Tucker, who later served in the District government and now runs a consulting business. There is always a burst of determination to bring these neighborhoods back, better than ever, he said. "But I don't know anyplace where that has happened."

May 8, 1992

Disorder Puts Search for Answers to Urban Woes at Top of Agenda

MARY JORDAN

"The time really has come to try a new way," President Bush said, as he arrived in Los Angeles Wednesday night to tour the wreckage of the nation's worst riots this century. "There must be no return to the status quo."

After more than a decade of inattention to the problems of the nation's cities, the Los Angeles disturbances have created a new urgency among policymakers to craft new solutions.

"All of us know [the conditions that bred the riots]," President Lyndon B. Johnson declared after the 1967 Detroit riots. "Ignorance, discrimination, slums, poverty, disease and not enough jobs."

The root causes have hardly changed, but with hindsight, many leading policymakers say the solutions must.

Policy shapers on both the left and the right agree, for instance, that big, cinderblock public housing was a mistake. Government should step up incentives to business to build less dense and less concentrated apartment buildings and town houses for the poor.

Welfare, too, is now widely thought of as too dispiriting, too anti-family and too lacking in incentives for recipients to find jobs. Remodeled versions of welfare and other tried programs—including a new public jobs program and teachers corps—are suddenly getting widespread attention. And, new ideas—from a new transportation system to bring city workers to suburban jobs, to offers of free college tuition to those who pledge to be police officers or inner-city teachers—are being discussed at higher levels and in more impassioned tones than at any time since Johnson called on the country to fix America's "cities [that) can stimulate the best in man and aggravate the worst."

"What happened in L.A. is not unique to problems in the inner city," said Bertha Gilkey, president of the Cochran Gardens Tenant Management Corp. in St. Louis and a national public housing advocate. "For the last 10 to 15 years this has been building. What happened in L.A. was inevitable."

That kind of thinking is prompting coast-to-coast meetings with a common agenda: Something must be done.

Some believe, as does Walter Williams, professor of economics at George Mason University, that the root causes 'are beyond the ability of government to solve."

"If [women) would say I'm not going to have babies until I'm married and both parents are working, we wouldn't have a poverty problem," Williams said. "But what can government do to make people hold off, what can government do to make people study? God can't even solve that kind of problem."

But even the Bush administration, which like the Reagan administration before it, has been criticized for a hands-off approach to worsening family, poverty and violence problems, is talking a new urban agenda.

Bush and a more vocal Housing and Urban Development Secretary Jack Kemp support creating new enterprise zones in inner cities, where job-generating businesses would get tax breaks. Democratic presidential contender Gov. Bill Clinton also supports this idea.

To improve city schools, Bush favors "choice," a plan that would allow parents to use a federal voucher for perhaps $1,000 to pay for private school tuition. Supporters argue that the "choice" system would create much needed competition for bad and bloated public school systems, forcing them to shape up.

Clinton, as do many others, opposes federal vouchers for private schools, saying they would drain much needed money from already hurting neighborhood schools.

"As someone once said, 'Civilization is a sequence of new tasks,' " said Charles M. Haar, a Harvard Law School professor. "We now have a new task." As the debate over possible solutions grows louder, the prime problem areas being focused are jobs, welfare, housing, schools, neighborhoods and crime.

Jobs and Transportation

Many conservatives and liberals favor a public jobs program that would put poor people to work building bridges, parks, schools, libraries and hospitals—particularly those in the inner cities. While correcting infrastructure problems, the program would also create badly needed job histories for thousands of inner-city residents.

Haar, a former assistant secretary of metropolitan development at HUD under Johnson, said new transportation solutions are critical because of the mismatch between where jobs are and where people live.

In the 1970s, Haar said, "barely a majority of jobs" existed in the suburbs. Today, two-thirds do. "We need to get people to the jobs in the suburbs," he said. "There is not enough of a concentration of people to support mass transit [in the suburbs], so we have to come up with a new transportation system—minivans, buses—some other way."

Subsidies for low-cost car rentals would also help transport inner-city workers, said Anthony Downs, senior fellow at the Brookings Institution. Suburban companies could provide transportation to low-skilled workers from the inner city.

Glenn Loury, a Boston University economics professor, is one who touts a job corps. "It's worth a shot at trying to intervene with troubled youngsters," he said.

"It's expensive to give them that boot camp sort of experience, but it might be the only hope for saving some of these youngsters."

Welfare

The idea that single mothers who work can support their families without any government help, should be abandoned said Christopher Jencks, Northwestern University professor of sociology and urban affairs.

"A large percentage of welfare mothers could get jobs paying $5 or $6 an hour, but they can't live on that alone," said Jencks, who believes the country should encourage these women to take the jobs by allowing them to buy Medicaid coverage for, say, 5 percent of what they earn, and provide subsidized child care and Section 8 housing certificates. "If we did those things, taking a $5 an hour job would pay, and you would see a dramatic decline in the number of women collecting welfare," he said.

Nearly half of all black families are headed by single women and 27 percent of all births occur to single women.

Isabel Sawhill, senior fellow at the Urban Institute, advocates channeling many dollars currently going to welfare into creating jobs. And critical to providing jobs for welfare mothers, she said, is "putting much more emphasis on developmental day care for 2- to 5-year-olds."

Housing

Many policymakers agree that the old-style cinderblock public housing units that sprang up after World War II and were initially designed as short-term housing have become unmanageable and crime-ridden. Smaller buildings, scattered in different neighborhoods and built with the help of private industry, have seen more success. But the political will to force subsidized housing into middle-class neighborhoods has been weak, at best.

"The major need is rental housing," Haar said. "The way to go is public-private partnerships."

Through incentives such as below-market interest rates and tax-exempt bonds, Haar said, the government could induce more private industry to build the much needed apartment buildings. Bush could also pressure the banks and insurance companies to set aside money for housing, as Johnson did in the Great Society, he said.

Both liberals and conservatives applaud the practice of resident management of public housing units and new incentives for home ownership. The Kenilworth-Parkside property in the District, which is managed by its residents, is projected to save the District government $5.7 million over the next 10 years.

Schools

High on many lists are greater funding for the popular Head Start program for low-income preschoolers, and mentor programs to try to give individual attention to those likely to quit school. So are college tuition incentives to draw bright young students interested in teaching in the inner cities, and teacher retraining programs to better those currently in the classrooms. high on many agendas.

More controversially, Gary Orfield, a Harvard professor and expert on deseg-regation, supports opening up school districts so that inner-city children could attend neighboring middle-class class schools in the city or suburbs. As long as seg-regation exists, he said, so will unequal education.

Orfield, like many others, also favors building on "successful" programs, Pell grants for needy college students and the Upward Bound College preparation program, for example.

Neighborhoods and Crime

Robert L. Woodson, president of the National Center for Neighborhood Enterprise, located here, believes that the bureaucracy of government poverty programs—which he said absorbs 70 percent of federal dollars spent—must be dismantled.

"The bloated 'industry-poverty pentagon' has a proprietary interest in treating the problem of poverty as opposed to solving the problem," he said. "This industry thrives at the expense of low-income people. As an alternative, the nation needs to invest in the capacity of low-income people to solve the problems they face."

Gilkey, the national housing advocate, agrees.

"The money is going to these traditional groups of outsiders who have high administrative costs and salaries." Instead, she said, the money should not be fun-neled, as it is now, into "outside organizations who make their living off the poor, but given to people from within the community, who know the community, who care about the community," she said.

Downs, of Brookings, said more emphasis should be placed on discouraging drug consumption than on restricting its supply. He also believes that drug-related violence that has turned American neighborhoods into so-called Dodge Cities, would ease if consumers were prosecuted more severely and community policing programs—where residents participate in the patrol—were stepped up.

Staff writers Malcolm Gladwell and John E. Yang contributed to this report.

May 8, 1992

Calcutta on the Hudson

We New Yorkers are Learning How to Escape from the Giant Army of Homeless People

MICHAEL SPECTER

She was beautiful and so was her son. In one hand she carried the umbrella that comes from a generous donation to National Public Radio. Her child, who was about 4, held onto the other hand. Together, they watched in silence as a grubby man slowly made his way up the movie line.

"What does he want?' said the boy, as he tried to learn from his mother's face whether or not to be scared. "Doesn't he have a ticket?" "No dear," she said, clearly worried about what would come next. "He's homeless. He doesn't have anything."

"Yeecchh," said the child without a moment's hesitation. "Get rid of him."

The ticket line erupted in laughter and cheers. The outraged mother, however, was not part of the fan club. She yanked her bewildered child out of line, gave him what appeared to be an extremely brutal lecture on the virtues of compassion and then hauled him away, presumably toward home.

The woman's immediate and appropriate response made me feel like a fool. For while I was not among the cheering section, I certainly did smile when the boy made his comments. These days it is very difficult to do anything else.

Homeless people live on my street. They stand in the bank lobby around the corner and watch as the cash machine spews out money on demand. They are at every movie theater every day. Three times a week, they rip through my trash looking for an old shoe, half a meal or some tin they can recycle.

We know all that, I guess. New York has a huge homeless population, possibly more than 70,000. As a percentage of residents, it may be smaller than the District's, but in a city of houses, such as Washington, the homeless can become almost invisible. Not here. Here we all live on top of each other so that no matter who you are, the problem never goes away. They are mentally ill, they use drugs, they have no hope. They are the dark reflection of a sick society. They symbolize the housing crisis and the jobs crisis and the uncomfortable Darwinian reality that the strong rarely do help the weak.

When I came back here last fall after five years in Washington, I couldn't believe how many people were living in the street. But eventually I came to accept it. The homeless live in every neighborhood, not just the bad ones. In my relatively affluent area, it is not hard to find window signs that say "NO CRACK, NO

MENUS, NO HOMELESS." The signs certainly don't scare away crack dealers or the homeless.

There is really nowhere to scare the homeless to. Unless you travel exclusively by limousine, you cannot pass a day in this city without seeing a man wearing a cardboard sign that says "Please Help This Vet With AIDS," or "I Would Do Anything for a Clean Place to Sleep." City shelters have become an abomination. Welfare hotels are much worse. Many prefer to risk freezing to death than go to either.

So they live on milk crates over steam vents, sweating in the icy weather. Plastic-wrap shanty towns have arisen in nearly every city park. Dumpsters and abandoned cars have proven to make nice homes. At Columbus Circle each night, a quiet and organized army of street people assemble with shopping carts full of tin cans and paper they can recycle for money. Dickens could not have invented this vision of hell, as they sift through the city's rubbish, piling up pennies for food.

The police gently try to move them along, but as one cop said to me at the Port Authority Bus Terminal during a patrol on a bitterly cold day, "I don't care what my orders are. I am not going to be the one to send these people into the street to die." So they live in corners, under buses, in the stairwells. One day not long after I got here I decided to walk to work and give a dollar to every person who asked me for money. Fifty blocks: $48. The first time we found somebody sleeping in our foyer last fall, I thought that making it available as shelter might be a good way for us to help the homeless. The next day a psychotic vagrant stabbed somebody around the corner from our apartment. Now I lock the outer door every night.

Slowly, inexorably, I have became acclimated to ignoring the plight of others. I stopped carrying extra quarters. I avoid certain blocks and parts of Central Park. Not out of fear, really. It's just escapism.

I began to detest the hopeless wretches who constantly occupy the benches at my subway stop. I have never been on a street, a subway or in a train station here without some person accosting me. There is a woman who lives with her two children on the steps of Carnegie Hall. I don't go there. Others hang around the parking garage that costs more each month than any of these people could possibly see in a year.

After a while, I befriended a couple of the guys who live, literally, on my street. I thought maybe if I had some contact with one or two of them, I would feel less guilty about ignoring the rest.

One is handicapped and says he is a veteran. He is quiet, Hispanic and in his forties. He calls himself Ralph, but who knows what his name is?

Ralph works the Citibank cash machine at 94th Street and Columbus Avenue. He told me he never asks for anything. He just sits there, in his wheelchair with a paper coffee cup on his lap, waiting for someone to walk by with a handful of stiff, new bills. He says he wants to move to Florida or California where it is warm and he has friends, but he doesn't think he'll make it.

"I don't know," he told me with a shrug of resignation. "I'm kind of set up here. And anyway, it would be tough to leave the city."

He meant that. He really did.

The other guy I talk to a lot is considering legally changing his name to Nameless.

"It sort of goes with the anonymity of my situation," he said. "It's not as if my name really matters." He is one of the wizened street people who could be 30 years old or 50. He doesn't want to say. In fact he reveals little about himself. He has been after me to show him some of my stories ever since I told him I was a newspaper reporter. He reads the local papers pretty carefully and says he has heard good things about *The Washington Post*.

But I haven't been able to force myself to show him my work. Don't ask me why, but giving out quarters was a lot easier than talking to these two perfectly nice men each day. Probably more useful too. Seeing the homeless always puts me on edge now. That means I'm always on edge. It would be simplistic to call it conscience, but it's hard to read the presence of a vast horde of semi-clad street people as anything other than a constant cloud of anguish that even wealthy New Yorkers must confront each day. It has become like Calcutta, the price you pay to live in the most interesting city in America. The only way to make the problem go away, I am convinced, would be to leave, and who would want to do that?

One morning, a black man in a ripped T-shirt and very little else started to motion at me on the subway. I paid no attention, but he kept flicking his wrist at me. Still, I ignored him.

He started for me and just as I was deciding whether to run for it or stomp on his barely covered foot, I heard him speak. "Your color is twisted man," he said to me. "It's all messed up."

Oh God, I thought, not this. "Your color," he repeated. "Fix it." A nut, a vicious racist nut.

Suddenly, he reached for my neck and smoothed the crinkled collar of my suit jacket.

"There," he said as he turned to walk away. "Now you're looking good."

March 3, 1991

5 *Social Class, Poverty*

Poverty is a universal phenomenon, even in the most industrialized nations. The first three articles in this chapter explore various aspects of poverty in the United States. The first article examines the sizeable underclass in the United States. The next article talks about the shrinking middle class in the United States and some of the related problems in light of the recession. The third article questions our assumptions about poverty among children in the United States, and perhaps most alarming, the inability of government programs to lift poor children out of poverty.

The next article probes some of the problems of the current welfare system and discusses "universalism," an alternative approach which seeks to combine social insurance with reciprocal obligation.

The final articles explore poverty and social class in other societies. In India, crushing poverty has forced millions of child laborers into the workplace. In South Africa, Operation Hunger is trying to help the growing ranks of jobless and destitute people. Because of prolonged economic recession and the governments privatization of major state companies and service, tens of thousands of jobs of black and white workers have been cut.

Poor People in Rich America

HOBART ROWEN

"I need my job, I want my job back—I'm the only one in my family who has a job," moaned a distraught nurse's aide at a New York City hospital, one of 6,300 municipal employees fired over last weekend. As she wept, the painful scene was recorded on national TV.

My sense of pride is marred on this Day of Independence, as we pledge allegiance to the flag and reflect on the nation's accomplishments. There is much to be thankful for, and I join with other Americans in our annual ritual.

But despite constitutional guarantees, the opportunities for health, happiness and economic security available to most seem an increasingly remote prospect for too many.

America is really two countries, one in which a privileged middle class and the wealthy have access to education, wealth and medical care that Roman emperors could only dream of. As recession fades, it means for them a gradual resumption of business profits and gains in the value of invested wealth.

In the other an underclass America of mostly blacks, Hispanics and poor whites millions have inadequate health insurance or none at all. Huge numbers are homeless. The bipartisan Jay Rockefeller Commission affirms that one out of five American children is brought up in poverty. For this part of America, the end of recession, when it comes, will be a statistic without meaning.

Poor people in rich America live in a cruel Third World of their own. The ugly side of our affluent society was recently reaffirmed by a Supreme Court ruling that effectively denies poor women the option of an abortion, easily available to richer women.

In his book, "The Work of Nations," Harvard economist Robert Reich demonstrates that the gap between managers and workers in America is getting wider. In 1960, the salary of chief executive officers at America's 100 largest corporations averaged $190,000 or, after taxes, 12 times a factory worker's pay.

By the end of the Reagan era, however, Reich says, these CEOs averaged $2 million in annual salary, and, given the benefit of tax cuts slanted to the upper brackets, the CEOs' multiple of factory pay skyrocketed to about 70.

In the 1960s under presidents Kennedy and Johnson, the Democratic Party articulated some goals to promote what might roughly be called social justice. One was a commitment to reducing unemployment to 4 percent or less, assumed to be the rough definition of an economy with "full" employment.

Now, Democrats want to appear as safely conservative as their Republican counterparts. Therefore, they accept 6 percent unemployment as the proper standard, because anything under 6 percent might trigger inflation. In today's single-party atmosphere, control of inflation has a higher priority than worries about recession and unemployment.

Find the Democratic leader in House or Senate who would repeat what Kennedy's labor secretary, W. Willard Wirtz, told me in 1962:

"Maybe I do get emotional about the unemployment problem. Maybe I am overconcerned by the fact that there are 4 million people unemployed in this country, people who are denied the essential right to work—using that term in the only true sense it should be. But I think the situation is so deplorable in human terms that it warrants an indignant intolerance of any explanation for it in terms of any kind of economic analysis."

As of the end of May, the unemployment rate was close to 7 percent, meaning there were 8.6 million people seeking jobs and unable to find them. Many losing their New York City jobs worked in hospitals, street maintenance or as garbage collectors, surely not the dream jobs to which college-educated, middle- and upper-income young people can aspire. They are filled mostly by nonwhite Americans trying to make an honest buck with which to put food on the table.

What's happening in New York is a microcosm of distress in scores of other cities and states that are struggling to meet added costs forced on them by the recession and shrinking federal outlays. In this bind, compromise is necessary, and union "give-backs" on wages will be needed to save jobs.

I have recently seen citizens at my local drugstore laboriously count out $60 or $70—sometimes in one-dollar bills—for a tiny vial of prescription drugs. It may be that they will recover most of the cost from Medicare, Medicaid or private insurance. But even if they are reimbursed, laying out the cash must be a hardship.

I have also seen citizens at the local supermarket watch as the cash register adds up their grocery bill, then carefully return one or two items because they can't pay the total.

Something's gone sour in this great country of ours, and it makes me sad as I contemplate Independence Day.

July 4, 1991

America's Middle-Class Meltdown

While Few Escaped Poverty, More
Fell into it—And it's Getting Worse

RICHARD MORIN

America's vast middle class, the undervalued force that has stabilized and moderated American society and politics, is shrinking right before the worried eyes of economists.

During the 1980s, the rules that govern the economic fortunes of Americans were quietly and perhaps permanently rewritten. Economists now report that the boom years of the 1980s were a bust for fully half of all Americans. At the same time, the safety net of social programs for the nation's poor was replaced by a safety net for the rich, speeding the decline of the middle class.

The result: an extraordinary 20 percent shrinkage in the proportion of middle-income Americans during the 1980s, according to a new analysis of two decades of data that track the changing fortunes of American families.

These trends are already influencing the politics of the 1990s. From Pennsylvania to Louisiana, and from Capitol Hill to the White House, politicians have suddenly discovered the plight of the increasingly beleaguered middle class.

A look at data collected annually since 1968 by the University of Michigan's Panel Study of Income Dynamics reveals social change that is nothing short of startling. While three out of four Americans could claim to be in the middle class just 15 years ago, barely six out of 10 could make that claim by the end of the 1980s.

"And it's still falling," said Timothy Smeeding, professor of economics at Syracuse University and one of those who analyzed the data. "What we are looking at is a permanent (proportional] decline in the size of the middle class."

The panel study began in 1968 with a random national sampling of 5,000 families. For every year since, the economic fortunes of those families—and the new families that formed from parts of the original sample as children married or couples divorced—have been carefully measured by researchers. Since 1968, more than 40,000 people have participated in the project. This year, researchers obtained data about 20,000 individuals in 7,300 families.

Researchers say that the makeup of study participants mirrors the demographics of the country as a whole. The results of these annual checkups are accepted by economists as a highly reliable indicator of the relative economic health of Americans.

What Syracuse's Smeeding and Greg Duncan, a Michigan economist who directs the panel study, saw when they looked at 22 years of accumulated data was little change—until the 1980s, when the middle class began shrinking at an alarming rate.

They found that the percentage of Americans living in households earning $18,000 to $55,000 in 1987 dollars adjusted for inflation fell from 75 percent in 1978 to 67 percent in 1986. By the end of the 1980s, Smeeding estimated that only six out of 10 Americans fell in this income range, a standard economic definition of the middle class.

The abruptness of the drop startled researchers. "Between 1950 and the 1980s, income distribution was ho-hum," Smeeding says. "But with 1980, it changes, and now it's a brave new world out there."

Two factors sharply winnowed the ranks of middle-income Americans during the 1980s. And the implications of these ongoing changes are ominous.

The good news is that a larger proportion of the rich stayed rich during the 1980s than in the previous decade. And slightly more middle-income Americans moved into the higher-income group than moved up in earlier years. Together, those factors produced a 50 percent increase between 1978 and 1987 in the proportion of Americans earning more than $55,000 a year, Smeeding said.

While the rise in the number of affluent Americans is significant, other economic factors were also at work nearer the bottom of the income ladder. A smaller proportion of Americans moved out of poverty during the 1980s, compared to earlier years. Also, a larger share of the middle class slipped into the poorest category.

Those factors combined to swell the ranks of the poor and near-poor by more than one million men, women and children during a decade of unparalleled economic expansion.

"The elevator isn't working anymore," Smeeding said.

Among the study's key findings:

Between 1967 and 1980, 35.5 percent of the poor moved into the middle-income group. But during the 1980s, only 30.4 percent graduated to the middle class.

During that 13-year period ending in 1980, 6.2 percent of the middle-income individuals typically fell into the lower class. After 1980, the proportion increased to 8.5 percent.

Before 1980, 6.3 percent of the middle class became wealthy. During the 1980s, 7.5 percent of middle-income families made the transition to the high-income group.

These changes, the researchers noted, produced a dramatic 50 percent increase in the proportion of relatively wealthy Americans, which grew from 8 to 13 percent during the 1980s. "It was a dismal picture unless you happen to be part of the 20 percent who are well-to-do; they did and are doing quite well, thank you," Smeeding said.

Most studies do show it truly was the rich who got richer during the past decade. For example, the median net worth of high-income panel-study families grew from $167,700 to $305,400 between 1984 and 1989—an 82 percent increase—while the wealth of those in the lowest income group declined 16 percent, from $3,700 to $3,100.

"The expansion of the 1980s lifted all of the yachts but none of the tugboats or rowboats," Smeeding said.

Part of the reason why the rich are getting richer is that the rich had friends in high places during the 1980s. The tax cuts of 1981 and 1986 let more affluent Americans keep more of their money, constituting a safety net of sorts for the rich. A capital-gains tax cut, some arguer would provide another layer of protection for the wealthiest Americans.

"What you've got during this period in question is obviously a government in which the public policy was biased toward the upward bracket," said Kevin Phillips, a political analyst and author of the such-praised book, "Politics of Rich and Poor: Wealth and the American Electorate in the Reagan Aftermath." "Take George Bush now, not wanting to disturb the bond market with a tax cut for the middle class. . . . It's fair to say the administration has been very solicitous of the upper-bracket investor and speculators."

Some economists have a more sanguine view of these changes. "To the extent that the middle class has shrunk because people have moved up, that's a good thing," said Marvin H. Kosters, director of economic policy studies at the American Enterprise Institute. "It is also true that there has not been such movement from the lower into the middle class and that is a cause for concern. But on balance, I believe what occurred in the 1980s was a net positive change."

To others, these are ominous changes. They fear the growing concentration of Americans in the high and low income ranges threatens to further exacerbate class and racial animosities.

"People are going to become angry with the small group of people at the top with the capital skills and education," Phillips said. "It's the Europeanization of American politics, a more class-oriented politics, a politics that produce a Harris Wofford on the one hand and a David Duke on the other." Phillips believes that these two faces of populism will play a major political role in this decade, and perhaps beyond.

The study by Duncan and Smeeding, as well as recent work by other economists crunching other data, also takes such of the bloom off of the economic boom of the decade just past.

Despite the lingering buzz about those Golden '80s, half of all America saw their incomes erode, not improve, during the past decade. "For those in the bottom half of the income distribution, the 1980s were one long recession," Duncan said.

Other economists also have noted that the wage gap between high and low earners, which had narrowed during the previous two decades, reopened in the 1980s.

Using data collected by the federal government, Gary Burtless, an econouist with the Brookings Institution, reports that the hourly wage rates of men in the bottom fifth of the income distribution "have fallen by about one percent a year" between 1979 and 1989.

"Among men in the second fifth, their wage rates declined by a little more than one percent a year," Burtless said. "But in the top fifth, hourly wages for men have risen about six-tenths of a percent each year." (The numbers for women show roughly the same pattern, with those in the bottom fifth of the income distribution losing ground while those at the top flourished.)

It doesn't even pay to be young any more.

"Being young used to be a facilitator for moving from low- to middle-income groups," Duncan said. "This was part of a normal progression that occurred as an individual moved from their twenties into their thirties and gained enough training, or seniority, or perhaps married and acquired a second income and moved into the middle class. But in the 1980s, being young conferred no economic advantage at all." These changes in income patterns have little to do with demographic or cyclical economic factors. "Rather, it appears that technological changes in the workplace have led to the stagnation of real earnings among the young and less educated, and growth in earnings among better and more experienced workers," Duncan and Sueeding reported.

The recessign may further worsen these income trends. Although the recession will slow the upward mobility of middle-class workers, it may also be wiping out many white-collar jobs—perhaps forever.

"Recessions tend to reduce upward mobility," he said. "This recession has been described as a white-collar recession, and I fear that these white-collar jobs that have been lost aren't going to come back. That's going to cause more people to fall from the middle class. The well-educated will still do well."

Economists do believe the elevator up from poverty can be fixed.

One approach is to tax those who benefited most from the fat years of the 1980s. "There's room to raise income-tax rates and start talking about a wealth tax," Smeeding said. "Federal taxes on estates and gifts, possibly to fund things like long-term care for the elderly" and increased education and training programs, are needed to extend the chance for upward mobility to all income classes.

"Basically, we have to make some investments in people," he said. "We're not doing that."

December 1, 1991

Children in Poverty—Who Are They?

Private Study Takes Aim at Stereotypes

PAUL TAYLOR

Today's quiz is about America's poorest group, its children. There will be two questions.

1. Of all the poor children in America today, what percentage conforms to the following stereotype: a black child living in the inner city with a nonworking welfare mother who was a teenager when that child was born?

   A. 30 percent
   B. 20 percent
   C. 10 percent
   D. 5 percent
   E. 2 percent

   Answer: (E). Most poor children are not black. Most poor children live outside central cities. Most live in families that have a wage earner. Nearly half live in families that do not receive welfare payments. Roughly half were born to mothers who were 20 or older when they had their first child. Mix it all together, and just one poor child in 56 fits the stereotype.

2. In order to provide the cash assistance needed to lift all 12.6 million poor children in the United States out of poverty for one year, what percentage of taxpayers would have to give up one year's worth of the net tax breaks they have received from tax legislation enacted since 1977?

   A. The richest 50 percent.
   B. The richest 25 percent.
   C. The richest 10 percent.
   D. The richest 5 percent.
   E. The richest 1 percent.

   Answer: (E). Based on Census Bureau calculations, it would have taken $28 billion in 1989 to lift every poor family with children to just above the official poverty line. According to the Congressional Budget Office, if the richest 1 percent of Americans were taxed in 1990 under the tax laws that were in effect in 1977, they would have paid $39 billion more in taxes in 1990.

Table 5–1 • America's Poor Children

A Profile for 1989

Percentage of Poor Children Who Were:	
White, non-Latino	41
Black, non-Latino	35
Latino	21
Asian or Pacific Islander	3
Rural	26
Suburban	29
Central City	46
In married-couple families	38
In female-headed families	54
In male-headed families	4
Percentage of Families with Poor Children Which Had:	
At least one worker	63
One worker	43
Two workers	7
Three workers	3
Household head who worked in 1989	54
Worked full time, year-round	18
Worked part time, year-round	5
Worked for only part of the year	31

Source: Children's Defense Fund

The answers are taken from a stereotype-busting report, "Child Poverty in America," to be released today by the Children's Defense Fund, that depicts childhood poverty as a more demographically diverse and less intractable phenomenon than often perceived.

"In all societies, there is a tendency to stigmatize the poor as not being like the rest of us—it makes it easier for the majority who aren't poor to ignore the problem," said James D. Weill, general counsel of the child advocacy group. "This report illustrates that families with poor children, while not identical to the rest of society, are a lot closer to home than most people think."

The report acknowledges that "lasting solutions to the problem of child poverty are more complex" than a straight transfer of $28 billion a year to poor families, but it says that "the size of this cumulative poverty deficit does demonstrate that the problem is manageable, and not beyond our means to tackle and solve."

Rather than tackling the problem of childhood poverty, however, the drift of government policies over the past two decades has been to exacerbate it, the report states. While large tax breaks were being enacted for the wealthy, Aid to Families

With Dependent Children (AFDC), the principal cash transfer program to poor children, was losing 39 percent of its value in inflation-adjusted dollars from 1970 to 1990.

Because of this erosion, government cash transfer programs now lift only about 10 percent of all poor children out of poverty. In 1979, government cash benefits lifted 20 percent of all poor children out of poverty.

The contrast in the government's anti-poverty efforts toward children and toward elderly Americans is especially stark, the report notes. Because the principal cash transfer program to the elderly—Social Security—has been indexed to inflation, 76 percent of all elderly who would have been poor are lifted out of poverty by government cash transfers.

Not only are children nearly twice as likely as adults to be poor—in 1989, 19.6 percent of all children were poor, compared to 10.2 of all non-elderly adults and 11.4 percent of all the elderly—but the poverty of children has grown deeper than it was just a decade ago.

In the late 1970s, less than a third of all poor children lived in families that had incomes less than half the official poverty line. By 1989, 4.9 million children— more than two poor children in five—lived in such families. At half of the official poverty line, a family of three has an income of $4,943 a year, or $412 a month.

Nearly one-fourth of all black and Puerto Rican children live in these families that are in deep poverty, while only one in 23 white non-Hispanic children lives in such families.

The official definition of poverty has long been a source of dispute among conservative and liberal groups. Conservatives say that the government overcounts the poor by at least 10 percent because it does not include non-cash benefits, such as food stamps, in its family income measures.

Liberal groups counter that the government undercounts the poor (at least in a relative sense) because it has not adjusted the poverty standard to reflect changing household economics and rising standards of living in society as a whole.

If the ratio of the poverty line to the median income line were the same in 1989 as it was in 1959, the Children's Defense Fund report notes, the child poverty rate would have been 30 percent in 1989, not 19.6 percent.

The conservative view is that the combination of AFDC, food stamps, Medicaid and housing programs have "all but eliminated material poverty in this country," said Kate O'Beirne of the Heritage Foundation. "The average poor family in America is better housed than the average family in Western Europe. But we are now confronted with a more serious problem here, behavioral poverty—the failure of poor people to complete their education, to have children inside of marriage, to stay regularly employed." This behavioral poverty, she argued, is in part a perverse byproduct of the government's very effort to eradicate poverty.

O'Beirne called for poverty programs that condition the award of benefits on socially acceptable behaviors—such as work, marriage and education.

The Children's Defense Fund report calls for creation of a refundable children's tax credit and a government-insured child support payment system as a way to provide a more reliable income floor for low-income families with children. It also calls for an increase in the minimum wage and unemployment insurance coverage, passage of the Family and Medical Leave Act, increases in job training programs and better access to health and child care for low-income families.

June 3, 1991

Revamping Welfare With "Universalism"

Alternative Approach Seeks to Combine Social Insurance Function, Reciprocal Obligation

PAUL TAYLOR

During the recession-weary 1990s, the war on poverty has given way to a war on welfare, and the high ground has been seized—at least for the moment—by strategies that purport to help the poor by punishing them.

A half-dozen states have unveiled or implemented proposals that reduce benefits to the poor who don't work, stay in school or get health checkups. Dozens of other states have cut or frozen welfare payments across the board, without any pretext of inducing behavioral change. These cuts seem popular because, in addition to saving money, they resonate with the widespread view that welfare does as much harm as good by rewarding dependency, illegitimacy and sloth.

With less fanfare, an alternate approach to revamping welfare is beginning to take shape.

It, too, seeks to undo the perverse incentives and debilitating stigma built into the dole. But rather than slashing benefits to the poor, this approach tries to preserve a safety net while it recasts welfare into a program of social insurance coupled with reciprocal obligation. And rather than being targeted to the poor alone, it tries to broaden political support by spreading some benefits around to the working poor, the middle class and even the wealthy.

Hugh Heclo, a professor of public affairs at George Mason University, has dubbed this more universal approach "helping the poor without talking about them." There is already one successful program that combats poverty in this manner, and it owes its political inviolability largely to the fact that it is rarely thought of as an anti-poverty program. It is called Social Security.

A child in the United States today is nearly twice as likely to be poor as a senior citizen—the most extreme age bias to poverty anywhere in the world. At the heart of this disparity lies the popularity of Social Security, which has been indexed to keep pace with inflation since 1972, and the unpopularity of Aid to Families with Dependent Children (AFDC), which has been cut by 42 percent, in real terms, since 1970. Social Security lifts more than eight of 10 senior citizens out of poverty who would otherwise be poor without government transfers. AFDC lifts out of poverty less than one in three children who would otherwise be poor without government transfers.

The leading advocates in Congress who are trying to do for children what Social Security does for the elderly are Sen. John D. "Jay" Rockefeller IV (D-W.Va.), chairman of the National Commission on Children, and Rep. Thomas J. Downey (D-N.Y.), acting chairman of the Ways and Means subcommittee on human resources.

Last week Rockefeller introduced the Family Income Security Act of 1992. one of its components would provide a $1,000 per child refundable tax credit for all of the nation's 64 million children, rich and poor alike. (Downey and Sen. Albert Gore Jr. (D-Tenn.) introduced a similar bill last year.) Another would expand the Earned Income Credit, which now offers a cash wage supplement of up to about $1,235 to working parents with earnings of less than $21,250. A third proposal, a child support insurance demonstration project, would couple tougher enforcement of child support laws with a guaranteed government payment of $1,500 per child to custodial parents in cases in which the noncustodial parent cannot be made to pay.

"This is long term, this is big picture, this is a revolutionary change in our income and welfare policy," said Rockefeller, who said that if all of the pieces were in place, the AFDC program would be vastly reduced.

The refundable tax credit would go to all families with children, but it differs from the increased child exemption recently proposed by President Bush in a fundamental way—its value would be three times greater for poor parents than for rich ones. (Bush's plan offers twice as much tax relief for rich parents as for middle-class parents, and nothing for poor parents.)

Harvard sociology professor Theda Skocpol has called the unadvertised redistribution built into Rockefeller's approach "targeting within universalism" and argues that, given the public's antipathy to welfare, it is the most politically promising way to channel income support to America's poorest citizens.

The framers of Social Security understood this sort of sleight of hand quite well. They sold Social Security as an earned benefit program, and their rhetoric freed the program from associations with welfare. However, while there is an earned benefit element built into Social Security, there are also large doses of income redistribution and social insurance. An elderly person who earned a minimum wage all his or her life replaces a much higher percentage of income in retirement through Social Security than does someone one who earned the median wage.

Most industrialized nations use child allowances—both universal and targeted—to defray the costs of childhood in a similar fashion. The United States does not. As longtime social insurance specialist Elizabeth Wickenden has pointed out, "Poor children in this country have a political problem—they come attached to parents who aren't very popular."

Those who want to overhaul welfare doubt they can do much overnight for the reputation of the parents of the poor, but they do believe they can make welfare less unpopular by making it more rational.

A refundable tax credit, for example, would go to a parent regardless of earnings, and therefore would avoid the "earn a dollar/lose a dollar" trap that a welfare mother currently faces if she tries to join the labor force.

The earned income tax credit, similarly, is a reward for work, endorsed in Congress by liberals and conservatives alike. Canada has a similar program, and is about to experiment with a massive, fourfold increase in its cash value to see if it would induce greater work effort from the poor.

Child support insurance would go to all custodial parents, at all income levels, whether they work or not—and again, there is no work disincentive. It also would extend the notion of reciprocal obligation for the first time from the welfare mother to the welfare father. Downey estimates that 80 percent of all welfare children have an absent father who works, averaging $15,000 a year in earnings, but only 15 percent receive child support payments from these fathers. He wants to stiffen enforcement, with the threat of jail for nonpayers. And he wants the insured benefit to go to the custodial parent if that parent (usually a woman) helps in tracking down the noncustodial parent.

Other universal strategies are being studied. Child development specialist Edward Zigler of Yale University is crafting a plan that would enable young parents—no matter what their income—to take a credit against their Social Security "account" of up to $5,000 a year in the first few years of their child's life, to make it affordable to stay home or pay for high-quality child care.

Some of these approaches are expensive; the price tag on the refundable child tax credit is $40.3 billion per year. Some will be criticized as welfare by a different name. But as another generation of children sinks further into poverty, and another generation of parents deeper into dependency, the proposals are not going to disappear. "It might take us 10 years to get all of these pieces into legislation," said Downey, "but it's the only way to make the system rational."

Percent Change in Caseloads, July 1989 to November 1991

After remaining relatively stable throughout the 1980s, food stamps and Aid to Families with Dependent Children—the biggest voucher and cash welfare programs—began to rise sharply in mid-1989, an early indicator of the current recession. Both are now at record highs, with nearly one in every 10 Americans receiving food stamps and one child in every seven receiving AFDC. States are ranked below by percentage of increase.

Table 5–2 • Food Stamps

Rank	State	Percent Change
1	New Hampshire	133.7%
2	Florida	90.6
3	Nevada	75.9
4	Connecticut	69.3
5	Arizona	61.6
6	Delaware	59.1
7	Washington	54.7
8	Indiana	51.1
9	Vermont	50.9
10	New Jersey	50.7
11	Rhode Island	49.9
12	Maine	49.5
13	Georgia	49.1
14	North Carolina	49.1
15	Alaska	.47.4
16	Texas	44.3
17	Virginia	43.2
18	Oklahoma	40.9
19	District of Columbia	40.5
20	South Carolina	40.0
21	New Mexico	39.0
22	California	36.3
23	Massachusetts	34.5
24	Maryland	34.3
25	Tennessee	33.9
26	Missouri	31.6
27	New York	28.6
28	Kansas	27.6
29	Utah	25.0
30	Alabama	23.9
31	Oregon	23.8
32	Pennsylvania	23.5
33	Idaho	21.9
34	Minnesota	21.2
35	Colorado	20.3
36	Arkansas	20.2
37	West Virginia	18.9
38	Illinois	17.7
39	Montana	16.3
40	Kentucky	15.7
41	Iowa	14.3
42	Ohio	14.1
43	Wyoming	13.9
44	Michigan	12.3
45	Nebraska	11.6
46	Hawaii	11.2
47	Mississippi	8.5
48	South Dakota	8.5
49	Wisconsin	8.2
50	North Dakota	7.1

Rank	State	Percent Change
51	Louisiana	3.9
52	Virgin Islands	1.7
53	Guam	7.0
54	Puerto Rico	n/a
	UNITED STATES	31.8

Table 5–3 • Aid to Families with Dependent Children (AFDC)

Rank	State	Percent Change
1	New Hampshire	98.1%
2	Arizona	64.1
3	Florida	63.0
4	Nevada	51.4
5	North Carolina	47.6
6	Connecticut	45.4
7	Georgia	41.8
8	Vermont	41.4
9	Kentucky	40.3
10	Texas	40.1
11	Delaware	39.7
12	Rhode Island	38.2
13	Alaska	37.0
14	New Mexico	36.8
15	South Carolina	36.3
16	Oklahoma	35.6
17	Maine	33.9
18	Oregon	33.3
19	Tennessee	32.4
20	Indiana	30.6
21	California	29.1
22	Massachusetts	26.1
23	Virginia	25.6
24	Maryland	25.6
25	District of Columbia	24.9
26	Wyoming	24.0
27	Missouri	23.7
28	New Jersey	22.6
29	Idaho	22.4
30	Washington	19.8
31	Colorado	19.6
32	Utah	18.2
33	Ohio	17.2
34	Montana	16.7
35	New York	16.2
36	Illinois	15.2

continued

Table 5–3 continued

Rank	State	Percent Change
37	Hawaii	15.1
38	Pennsylvania	14.5
39	Nebraska	13.5
40	Kansas	13.4
41	West Virginia	13.1
42	Alabama	11.7
43	Minnesota	11.4
44	Virgin Islands	11.1
45	Arkansas	10.0
46	North Dakota	9.3
47	Guam	9.1
48	Iowa	8.0
49	South Dakota	7.6
50	Michigan	7.3
51	Wisconsin	4.1
52	Mississippi	3.4
53	Puerto Rico	3.2
54	Louisiana	0.0
	UNITED STATES	24.1

Source: American Public Welfare Association.

February 26, 1992

Life Offers Little to India's Child Laborers

Millions Find Future Restricted
by Crushing Poverty, Ignorance

RICHARD M. WEINTRAUB

The knot of boys sat in the shadow of a small brick building, shielded from the blistering June sun but not from the 100-degree heat it generated.

For eight hours a day, six days a week, they sit, their faces and ragged clothes blackened by polishing agents, turning out the shiny nickel-covered plates and cups that are the staple of the Indian table.

Aftab Aziz is only 16, but already he is a veteran of the polishing crew. He began work at 14, as did many of the others. Two of their crew appeared to be 10 or 12. For their work, they can expect to start at 200 rupees, or $12, a month, technically a few rupees over the 134-rupee poverty line, about $8.10. But the poverty line here is too low for families to live on, and these children rarely make much more.

All across this vast country of more than 800 million people, ignorance, tradition, and, above all, a crushing poverty, have forced millions of children, some as young as 5, into the workplace. Some are virtual slaves, bonded to a farmer or handicraft artisan or small shopkeeper by parents so desperate that, in effect, they sell their children so the family can eat.

In the carpet-weaving region of central India near Varanasi, for example, as many as 150,000 children work weaving the carpets that go primarily to homes in Western Europe and the United States. Of these, according to one expert in the region, at least 15,000 are bonded labor working without pay.

Child labor is a fact of life in many Third World countries, from the dump pickers of Mexico City, to the carpet weavers of the Middle East, to migrant field hands in farming societies around the world.

But nowhere is the problem greater than in India, if only because of this country's huge population. By official count of the last census, there were more than 11 million children under the age of 14 in the labor force. Other studies by non-governmental groups have put the figure at 40 million or higher.

For many of these children, school is something only for the offspring of the privileged. Playtime for the poor, if there is any, is squeezed into the only free hour or two they have each day. The future for these children is circumscribed by a poverty so pervasive that few even know it is possible to dream and fight for a better life.

A small number, perhaps 10 percent, work in the hellish heat of glass factories, the choking dust of slate mines or gem-polishing factories, or at the cramped looms that produce fine carpets.

Most, however, are in what is called the "unorganized" sector of the economy, as dishwashers, street hawkers, tea boys, tire or motor repairmen, cleaners of floors and toilets. The vast majority work as agricultural laborers in a country that still is 80 percent rural.

It is one of the striking contrasts of contemporary Indian society that for every child of the newly emerging middle class—the pride of the country and a mark of its battle for a better standard of living—there are four who remain at or below the poverty line.

One of those still at the bottom is Soraju, a studious-looking 13-year-old who, along with his older brother, provides the only support for their family in Jehangirpuri, a densely packed neighborhood on the northern edge of New Delhi, about an hour from the broad lawns and wide boulevards around Parliament and major federal buildings.

Soraju is a ragpicker, the name here for dump scavenger. Every day, Soraju and his brother start out at 6 a.m. or earlier and make their way by foot, bus or bicycle rickshaw to one of the more affluent areas of the sprawling metropolitan area. There, they pick through the trash, searching for bottles, plastic, pipe, wiring, old shoes, belts -anything that can be sold to scrap dealers for recycling.

"I've been doing this for six or seven years. I used to earn about five rupees (30 cents) a day, but now it is 15 (90 cents). I give it all to mother. My older brother makes trouble sometimes, though, and doesn't give the money. He fights with mother," Soraju said.

Many of the 700 families in Jehangirpuri make their living by ragpicking, one of the few jobs open to the group of poor Bengali Moslems who came to New Delhi in the early 1970s.

They initially settled in makeshift slums east of the city, but the New Delhi administration moved them to the newly built Jehangirpuri, where they could buy tightly packed, two-room brick huts on narrow but paved lanes for about 200 rupees, or $12, a month, paid out over 10 or 12 years. There is a water tap for each lane and community latrines every 100 yards. Drainage ditches are filled with fetid water, but they exist.

Every morning, sometimes as early as 3 a.m., the children of Jehangirpuri spread out across the city. They generally have to walk or ride bicycle rickshaws with little carts attached because the public buses will not allow them and their smelly bags aboard. For their 10 or 15 rupees a day, they undergo constant harassment from the police and suspicion from residents of more affluent communities.

"The biggest problem we have is with the police. We get beaten up all the time. If there is any robbery, they blame us, and if we end up at the station, we have to pay ta bribe of) 200 or 300 rupees to get out. On the buses, they don't let us inside, but sometimes we can ride on the roof," said an articulate 19-year-old named Salim.

Speaking with the street smarts gained over six years as a ragpicker, Salim added: "There's a lot more trouble making it these days than when we were younger. Things are so expensive now, people don't throw as much away."

Despite the millions of working children in Indian society, the government has passed only limited legislation dealing with the issue. The vast majority of working children are not protected at all. Others find the conditions of their work theoretically regulated, but not prohibited.

Officials have admitted enforcement of legislation is difficult.

"The Child Labor Act has as its first goal the prevention of hazardous work and then the alleviation of work conditions in other areas. But how do you enforce it? Parents need money and children will go to work," said an official for an international organization.

"Many have child labor in their own houses and don't see it. Why is it just in hazardous industries? It is in people's homes, in tea stalls, everywhere."

Under the Child Labor Act of 1986, employment of children under the age of 14 is prohibited in certain hazardous industries, such as mining, construction and transportation. In other industries, work is limited to six hours with an hour of rest and is banned between 7 p.m. and 8 a.m.

At best, however, the act covers only about 20 percent of the child workers in India, and it has spawned a debate in which critics charge that by regulating work conditions for some children, the government is actually sanctioning child labor.

Government officials say they are in a bind. "if you ban all child labor as of today, you have to see that it is enforced. There must be enforcement machinery and it may not be possible," said Meena Gupta, a key policy-maker in the Ministry of Labor.

One of the main problems is coordination between the government in New Delhi and state governments that have to enforce laws and run federal programs.

"If you have a state official who is committed, you can get something done," said one expert, while noting that very few are committed to the issue of child labor when there are so many other pressing problems.

Gupta said the government in New Delhi is developing experimental programs under which inspectors will be appointed to deal only with child labor.

With special funds from international organizations, the government also is developing model schools and welfare programs in 10 cities around the country known for high levels of child labor. Critics have charged, however, that the programs are slow to get off the ground and only touch a limited number of children.

For most of the children of Jehangirpuri, as for most of the child workers of India, the future holds little but ragpicking. However, for a few, like Soraju and Salim, a slim avenue of hope for something better has been opened.

For the past year, a Moslem named Akbar Ali has been holding an evening literacy class for ragpicker children in a small classroom. With limited backing from the archdiocese of New Delhi and with some government funds, Ali has shown that the children of Jehangirpuri want to make more of their lives.

Soraju has been at Ali's school for a year and now reads haltingly from his small copybook.

"I go out at 6 a.m. and come home at 3. Then there is school at 7. In between, I go to scooter training. I also study at home some," said Soraju, sitting surrounded by his classmates.

"I want to study more," he said quietly.

"He would be good, if he had the chance," Ali whispered.

Others, like Salim, are placing their hopes in a small motor-scooter repair school also run by Ali. The motor scooter is to the Indian middle class what the car is to the American, and as the number of motor scooters rises, so do the number of shops needed to repair them.

But there are still powerful forces working against the children. While India's constitution requires compulsory education, and compulsory education has been cited in recent studies as being important in reducing the level of child labor, it is not yet a reality. Implementation of programs providing it have been postponed, and the official goal now is the year 2020.

In addition, many poverty-stricken parents remain skeptical even when educational opportunities exist. The country's highly regimented system of education has been criticized by experts for turning out large numbers of children who will not be able to find jobs.

Given the cost of books and uniforms—not to mention income lost to families—there often is cynicism about children of the poor going to school.

"Why send the child to school when you can get him to learn a trade?" said the father of a youngster who had been put to work in the gem industry of Jaipur, according to a recent study done for UNICEF.

"After all, educated or uneducated, he will be in this line. There are no great advantages in education. But if the child starts learning young, he will start earning young," the father said.

Muhammed Asim went to school in his native Moradabad in nearby Uttar Pradesh state until the third grade, attending classes from 7 a.m. until noon, then working at a tailor's shop until 8 p.m. He then got a chance to work in a small brassware factory, stopped school and began work as an apprentice-trainee along with two other children. He got no salary, a common practice by which shopowners use children to get cheap labor, but was given five rupees a day for food.

"That was a good place to work, and once I became trained, I could have earned 700 rupees [$42] a month," he said, adding that he was confident he would have finished his training in a year. "It depends on your intelligence, nothing else."

But when there was a theft in the shop, two boys blamed him, Muhammed said, so he had to run away to New Delhi. Now he sells tea at the railroad station, and on a good day will make between 20 and 25 rupees, or about $1.20, plus a 10-rupee stipend from his employer.

He said his family has no idea where he is.

Special correspondent Siddharth Dube contributed to this article

July 5, 1989

Poverty Lurks Beneath Veneer of Cold

As Economy Founders, South Africa Grapples with Swelling Jobless Ranks

DAVID B. OTTAWAY

Deep in the misty mountains of Kwazulu in Natal Province—far from the gold and diamond mines that once made the name South Africa synonymous with wealth and riches—unemployed Zulu miners are returning home by the thousands.

As they attempt to eke out a subsistence living on the stony hillsides and dry lands of their home villages, they are joining the ranks of the country's 2 million jobless and destitute people -testaments to a new economic reality affecting both blacks and whites.

The South African government, long reluctant to acknowledge the existence of poverty in its own backyard, has begun taking drastic measures to combat what it now admits is a massive and steadily growing problem.

The government has allocated $78 million to provide food for the "ultra poor" and for tens of thousands of black and white workers whose jobs are being cut because of a prolonged economic depression here and the government's privatization of major state companies and services.

"It's the first time the government has acknowledged poverty," said Ina Perlman, the outspoken executive director of the U.S.-assisted Operation Hunger, the biggest private relief organization involved in aiding the poor here. "It's a hell of a change from nothing."

Operation Hunger is now providing food assistance to 1.8 million destitute people—200,000 more than last year. Perlman said her waiting list of people seeking help is growing rapidly. By next year, she said, "I can see a situation where . . . 2 million will be needing food aid."

The government's own estimate is even higher: About 2.3 million people are in need of "nutritional assistance," according to a recent National Health Ministry study of the poor and needy. But that was based on two-year-old statistics.

Among those now lining up for help from Operation Hunger are 50,000 poor whites, the victims of rampant inflation, economic depression and the privatization of state-run services.

In the latest Operation Hunger bulletin, Perlman wrote that South Africa was facing a "tidal wave of destitute, hungry people" as unemployment escalates in the gold and other mines and scores of other depressed industries, with the specter of 600,000 more jobless on the horizon by 1992.

Already 16 million people—as much as 43 percent of the population—are estimated to live below the minimum subsistence level, according to government statistics. But the government prefers to measure poverty in terms of nutritional standards, bringing its figure down to 2.3 million.

Rina Venter, minister of national health and population development, said the poverty crisis facing the government today is much worse than that caused by the Great Depression of the 1930s. This spurred the ruling white Afrikaners, the descendants of the original settlers, to launch massive state welfare programs and state-run companies to employ their own people. The system was dubbed by some critics as "Afrikaner socialism."

"The extent of the problem that we have to deal with now is much bigger than the one we had to deal with at that stage," she said in an interview.

The current government response is also much bigger, she said. It is selling off 1 billion rand ($357 million) in strategic oil reserves this fiscal year and spending the proceeds on 667 social welfare projects, including construction of housing, clinics, schools and rural roads.

The government also has established a $714 million Independent Development Trust to invest in similar projects of what it calls 'social upliftment" in black communities.

The government's acknowledgement of serious rural poverty seems to date back only to 1989, when it produced a report on the development for a food and nutritional strategy that, according to Venter, led to the government decision this year to launch a nationwide feeding program through the state schools and 1,300 private welfare and nongovernmental organizations.

Here in Natal Province, however, government programs are virtually nonexistent. Operation Hunger is helping with the cultivation of 84 communal vegetable gardens and other programs to assist 1,600 dry-land farmers scattered across Natal. It is the only organization seeking to cope with returning migrant laborers.

A visit to a half-dozen projects during a 650-mile tour of the Kwazulu homeland found mostly women hauling water and tending to the gardens. Two women working in the hot sun of the hillside Ekuthuleni Garden here said their husbands had recently lost their jobs in mines near Johannesburg. Asked where the men were, one replied, "They are home sleeping."

"Do the men really want to do it or, like everything else, will it become women's work?" Perlman asked a smiling Martha Kanyile, chairwoman of the communal garden at another village near here.

"The men want to do it," replied Kanyile. "If they don't do anything else, they will do the plowing."

Perlman said she found it strange that farming was today considered "women's work," since black farmers had been successful in Natal before various land acts passed around the turn of the century forced them off their plots and into the mines in search of work.

The government has discovered it badly needs Operation Hunger, particularly in the rural areas, because of its extensive rural coverage. The government effort so far has appeared disorganized and has tended to focus on urban rather than rural areas.

The attitude toward rural poverty still seems highly ambivalent.

"We do not want to embark upon a . . . scheme where you hand out food to any person who approaches you. We believe this is the way to make people dependent on the state," said Venter.

On the other hand, "the state has got the responsibility to see to it that nobody dies of hunger," she said. "We are doing exactly that, making [food] accessible to people, bring them to the clinics and hospitals. The criterion is the nutritional status of the person, not to focus so much on the handout."

The focus of the government's feeding program, Venter said, will be the "poorest of the poor," particularly pregnant women, breast-feeding mothers, children under age 5, the elderly and the newly unemployed. The government will probably more than double the size of the program next year to $178 million, she said.

Perlman said her organization had been wary of taking any government money up to now because of its fears that strings might be attached or that the organization's U.S. grants might be affected. One stipulation of the U.S. Comprehensive Anti-Apartheid Act passed by Congress in 1986 was that no money could go to any organization receiving South African government funds.

The U.S. Agency for International Development has just provided Operation Hunger with a $500,000 grant to expand its community self-help program, which has been operating for years now. The Office of U.S. Foreign Disaster Assistance also has been providing about $500,000 annually.

But Perlman said Operation Hunger has come to the conclusion it badly needs more than the $11.8 million it now has in its budget to cope with the deepening poverty crisis. It had the organization and infrastructure to double its emergency relief program. Cash was "the sole limiting factor," she said.

The decision had been taken, she said, to apply for "interim assistance" from the government until it became clearer whether there were any strings attached.

"We could not live with ourselves if we did not clutch at every opportunity that would enable us to meet the need that confronts us," she explained to her donors in the latest Operation Hunger bulletin. "We must pull out every stop we can in our response to this national crisis."

October 14, 1991

Race and Ethnicity 6

Racial and ethnic inequality know no boundaries. The United States has witnessed alarming increases in racial and ethnic disparity, and international issues such as immigration and apartheid are alive and well.

The first three articles in this section deal with the aftermath of the Los Angeles riots in the spring of 1992. The first article presents some results from polls taken immediately after where majorities of African-American and whites rejected the jury's finding in the Rodney King beating case and demanded federal actions against the police officers involved. While gaps among African-American and white remain persistent, these results perhaps gave a glimmer of hope that American wants to confront racially motivated injustice and violence. The second article explores the reactions and uneasiness of people of variety of racial and ethnic backgrounds in Los Angeles immediately after the riots. The third article gives a personal account of being an African-American in America and the some of the preconceived perceptions that go along with being an African-American in the United States.

The fourth article explores race-based discrimination in mortgage lending. The fifth article explore the idea of environmental racism, whereby minorities are the ones most affected by pollution.

Looking at race and ethnic relations globally, the next article explores the increase in ethnic strife among Asian Americans, in part based upon the U.S.-Japanese tensions. The final article talks about the changing ethnic face of the heartland of America, where immigrants arrive in near-record numbers, African-Americans, Asians and Hispanics. The migration of minority groups into new communities has a vast effect on economic and human factors—job opportunities, social networks, and schooling—to name a few examples.

Polls Uncover Much Common Ground on L.A. Verdict

RICHARD MORIN

Smoke from fires continued to smudge the sun-washed Los Angeles sky, and looters carried off the last of their plunder as the first opinion polls reported initial public reactions to the verdict in the Rodney G. King beating case and to the violence that followed.

Such quick polls often are exercises in survey quackery. This time they were not. These polls were a public service, replacing hurtful conjecture with healing facts about the pain and disbelief that most Americans, black and white, shared over the verdict and the violence.

"The polls presented facts rather than pundits' theories about how people were thinking," said Jim Norman, polling coordinator for *USA Today*. "They answered some very important questions."

Such as: Did whites and blacks react oppositely to the verdict? Many politicians and pundits were saying yes, and saying it loudly.

The earliest polls, most conducted within three days of the verdict, suggested otherwise, as majorities of blacks and whites rejected the jury's findings and demanded federal action against the four police officers.

86 percent of the whites and 100 percent of the blacks interviewed by *USA Today* said the verdict was "wrong."

73 percent of the whites and 92 percent of the blacks questioned for *Newsweek* said the verdict was not justified.

64 percent of all whites and 92 percent of all blacks questioned told *Washington Post*-ABC News interviewers that the officers in the King case "should have been found guilty of a crime."

62 percent of all whites and 92 percent of all blacks interviewed for *Time* magazine and CNN said they would have voted to convict the officers.

Closer to the terror, a *Los Angeles Times* poll of area residents last week found that by wide margins, blacks, whites and Latinos condemned the King verdict and felt the violence was unjustified. Even in the jurors' home county—predominantly white and suburban Ventura County—seven out of 10 persons surveyed said they disagreed with the trial outcome, and eight in 10 said they sympathized with blacks who were angered by the verdict.

All the surveys showed Americans overwhelmingly wanted federal action taken against the police officers charged in the King case.

"The question was, did the verdict just surprise . . . some of us, or did it surprise the public too?" said Harold Quinley, senior vice president of Yankelovich Clancy Shulman, which conducted a post-verdict survey for Time and CNN. "We had civil rights groups and politicians saying they couldn't believe the verdict. The vast majority of the public could have reacted differently. In fact, they didn't."

Pundits and politicians also predicted that the riots had torn open old wounds and pushed whites and blacks farther apart.

The correct but less newsworthy view is that it is much too early to tell. But it is encouraging to note that researchers were surprised when the first poll numbers suggested that whites and blacks were closer together on some issues than they were before the verdicts were announced.

"Our survey (for *Newsweek*) was done to measure initial reaction to the verdict and the violence, and to see if there had been polarization on racial issues," said Larry Hugick, managing editor of the Gallup Poll. "In fact, we found the opposite. What might have led to increased polarization instead seemed to show that whites and blacks were coming closer on a number of things."

For example, Hugick noted that "both blacks and whites are saying black suspects are treated more harshly by police. In 1988, 66 percent of the blacks and 34 percent of the whites said blacks are treated more harshly. After the rioting, 75 percent of the blacks and 46 percent of the whites said that.

"The major effect is to see an increase in understanding among whites for the black perspective on that issue," Hugick said.

Nor had the verdict and the violence initially appeared to increase racial hatred, though many Americans feared that it would.

"The result that surprised me the most was that blacks did not express significantly more negative views of whites," Hugick said. "Just a month ago in a Gallup poll, 28 percent of the blacks interviewed said most whites want to see blacks get a better break; after the riots, it was 31 percent. And 20 percent a month ago said most whites want to keep blacks down, and now it's 18 percent.

"It seems to me that one might have expected that there might have been a whole lot of resentment toward whites, and we didn't pick it up. The survey did reflect the fact that blacks do have a very different view of racism than whites do. But it didn't get any worse."

With luck, these encouraging results are something more than mere flashes of tolerance and shared concern. Hugick, for one, said, "People are seeing each other's point of view, and people want healing . . . though it certainly is possible for it to go the other way, depending how it is played by the campaigns."

None of this should suggest that whites and blacks now think as one on racial issues. Just the contrary. The racial divide is, in the main, as deep and as wide and as troubling as it was before the King verdicts. While the days of overt racism sanctioned by law are gone forever, blacks and whites remain suspicious and uncomfortable with each other. And each group has very different views of the role race plays in society.

For example, when the *Post* and ABC asked if the King case "shows that blacks cannot get justice in this country," 78 percent of the black respondents but just 25 percent of the whites agreed. Similar results were obtained by other polling organizations.

And the next few weeks are critical, as political leaders and policymakers continue to announce their own verdicts on the verdict and the violence, further shaping and perhaps altering the magnitude and even the direction of public attitudes on these issues.

For now, the story told by the early polls is remarkably hopeful as America again confronts injustice and violence, the twin fruits of past and present racism.

"The polls put these issues back in front of us," said Yankelovich's Quinley. "It sensitized people to the differences between whites and blacks that have never gone away, that there has remained a wide gap between blacks and whites that is real and . . . has a human toll." "It was disquieting . . . that there are these racial divides over whether the system works," said *USA Today's* Norman. "But at least it is all out there, in the open, and being looked at. And that's always to the good."

"I do hope these polls sent out a message of reassurance."

Early Polls Show Broad Agreement among Blacks and Whites USA Today

People of both races who say the King verdict was wrong.
    100% Blacks
    86% Whites

Newsweek From what you know of the Rodney King beating case, do you think the verdict finding the policemen not guilty was justified or not?

	Whites	Blacks
Justified	12%	4%
Not justified	73%	92%

Post—ABC News Q. Based on what you know, is it your opinion that the police officers in the Rodney King case should have been found guilty of a crime, or innocent of a crime, or don't you know enough about it to say?

	Guilty	Innocent	Don't Know
Whites	64%	31%	5%
Blacks	92%	7%	1%

Time If you had been on the jury, how would you have voted?

	Whites	Blacks
Guilty	62%	92%
Not Guilty	4%	2%
Not Sure	34%	6%

July 11, 1992

A State of Siege State of Mind

In Los Angeles, Grappling With Race and Fear

MARTHA SHERRILL

Things seem strangely calm, cleaned up—over—until you look closer. A Hispanic boy stands out on a south-central street with his friends in the sunshine. He's wearing no shirt and smiling and talking, and then you notice the 15-inch kitchen knife in his hand. A beautiful young black girl, wearing a tight black dress with spaghetti straps, is having her picture taken in front of a burned-out FedCo. At another intersection where the signals aren't working, two black teenagers with very serious faces are conducting traffic. They are wearing crisp cotton shorts, but instead of white gloves, they've got long white athletic socks over their hands and arms.

There are police cars accelerating around with huge dents in the sides, and broken windows. You're staring at one, and then realize there's a gun barrel staring back, from the passenger side. Even in a somewhat safe neighborhood, Silverlake, a couple of guys in their mid-twenties—an engineering student and a movie business wannabe—show you something in their jackets: a Beretta 92F compact and a Colt Python.

"The people who sat at home watching TV for three days think it's over," says Eugene Yee, the guy with the Beretta. "That L.A. mentality will take over. Everybody will shrug it off and be laying out in the sun. Hey, man. It's cool. But nothing's over, and I've seen things in the last few days that will stay in my head forever."

Like everybody else around, Yee looks worn out. There are tired, stressed, nervous airport-faces way beyond the airport. It might be from watching all that television, but maybe not. A sour, burnt-plastic smell comes and goes with the wind, along with the sound of helicopters—the ones far away sound like bugs, and the ones up close like huge vacuum cleaners sweeping over your roof. The voices you hear are hyper and quickened—Californians turning into New Yorkers—probably from the residual adrenaline.

"I saw that graffiti that said 'Bloods and Crips and Mexicans together, 4/30/92,' " says one white guy, "and I keep thinking, what about 1993 and 1994?"

Everybody is feeling conscious of his race these days. A Korean man says he gets "hate looks" from blacks everywhere. A white woman, driving around south-central, says she hopes the back of her head "looks Latino." A white man in a car looks over at two classic L.A. types in a black Nissan 300ZX—they are blonded and overtan—and says, "Even I'd like to throw a beer bottle at that car." At a Korean rally and march through the city Saturday, there were signs that said "WE ALL BLEED RED," but it seemed nothing more than a sad observation.

The blacks stuck in south-central feel very stuck—their grocery stores are demolished, the gas stations are gone or have lines around the block. They keep saying in interviews that they don't like driving into other neighborhoods for provisions, because they think their presence scares white folks.

"My girlfriends and I usually go out every weekend," says Renee Kyle, a black woman and a bus driver at Los Angeles International Airport. "We're a mixed group—not all black, you know—but since all this trouble, I don't think it's such a good idea for us to go out together. I mean, I wouldn't want something to happen to them and not to me, because I'm black. Can you imagine how that'd make me feel?'

That L.A. mentality. There's this wonderful thing about Californians: They just want to be happy, to look on the bright side, to move out of the shade. The jacaranda trees are in bloom, their delicate purple blossoms dropping all over Hollywood. And hey, Peter Ueberroth, who did such a wonderful job with the 1984 Olympics, is going to come and fix everything. Not just fix, but make it "a blueprint for inner cities."

A green Jaguar drives down Western Avenue, and a middle-aged black guy is videotaping the demolition while standing through the sunroof. He passes by one bombed-out street corner, where Anna Garcia and her husband, Eduardo Abundiz, have set up their bright blue, homemade lemonade stand under two beach umbrellas. The motels in Malibu are full of people who could afford to flee the city, and the beaches farther south have been crowded—the weather's been so beautiful. The Newport Harbor Yacht Club annual open house went on in Orange County, no problem. Weirder still, Mikhail and Raisa Gorbachev will visit the Ronald Reagan Library in Simi Valley Monday, after having flown in on the Forbes Inc. plane called the "Capitalist Tool."

At the Lucky market on Los Feliz Boulevard, people turn up in convertibles and shorts and sunglasses, buy a few things and leave -with their groceries loose in their arms because they don't believe in either paper or plastic. Oh yes, 'the healing process' has started. Paradise cannot be troubled for long, and even an earthquake—no matter how huge—doesn't last more than a couple of minutes. The rest is mop-up.

Curfews come and go—the sun sets and rises—and with each one the city seems better and better, if you're not looking too carefully. The 24-hour-open-all-night feeling that Los Angeles has always had is gone now—the grocery stores close at 5 or 8—and it's as though the city is trying to repair itself through sleep. You keep hearing gunshots in the distance, but farther and farther away, until you think the war will move to some other place, some other state, some other country, and whatever the fight is about, it won't be in our faces.

"This isn't a race war, it's a class war," says Luca Gratton, an Italian American who grew up in the Miracle Mile district, which has been integrated for decades. "The middle class has been appalled -blacks, whites, browns, greens, everybody— at what's been going on." You notice that soot is sitting lightly on every table top and hibiscus bush in the city. At many intersections in south-central, all four corners are charred, black holes of rubble. After a while, you get used to the aftermath—the melted security fences, the Dumpsters full of broken glass, the caved-in roofs and fallen walls. You get used to the humvees, and personnel carriers full of marines pointing military assault rifles in every direction. You get used to the smell of fire and water, the wet ash and grease and plastic. You get used to the X's burned into the intersections downtown, where flares were lit for three days.

You try not to be obsessed with ironies, but you keep looking above the torched shopping strips and seeing movie billboards: Danny Glover and Mel Gibson are all over town, head to head, gun to gun, for "Lethal Weapon 3." Harrison Ford points his gun all over south-central in a teaser for "Patriot Games" that says "6/5/92. The Games Begin." on the Hollywood Freeway, some tall, blackened stumps line the lanes of traffic. Thursday night the palm trees were so elegant-looking, aflame and bright, the ultimate Tiki Torches.

Driving around, you see stores left standing that say "Black Owned" in spray-paint on the sides. Not just one or two, but block after block. "You can't blame blacks for trying to save their businesses," says one Korean man, "but what is 'Black Owned' really saying exactly? It's saying, 'Destroy the Korean place next door.'"

The animosity between blacks and Koreans has grown steadily over the years in these neighborhoods, and more recently flared with the trial last fall of a Korean shopkeeper who shot and killed a young black girl, Latasha Harlins, after accusing her of stealing a bottle of orange juice. The security video camera in the shop taped the incident, and the gruesome black-and-white footage was seen over and over here. When the shopkeeper—Soon Ja Du, a woman—was given no jail time after being convicted of voluntary manslaughter, blacks protested and rioted.

"You'd think that the blacks and the Koreans would get along," says Jay Yun, a 25-year-old engineer raised in L.A. and now moving to San Diego. "But we are both very emotional people—very—and don't always respond in a collected, rational way to every situation. As far as I could tell, talking to my Korean friends, nobody seemed to think that Korean shopkeeper should have gotten off. It didn't seem at all like self-defense on the video."

"I've been amazed by the ignorance on both sides," says one Japanese American. "The juror [in the Rodney King trial] who talked about 'These people would have rioted no matter what the verdict was'—well, she was obviously talking about black people. And then, I saw this black guy on TV whose store had been burned down, and he was asked who he blamed for the fire, and he says, 'I blame the fire department, because if this weren't a black neighborhood, they would have been here sooner.' "

The fire department. The LAPD. Daryl Gates. Tom Bradley. George Bush. The Crips. The Bloods. Rodney King. Everybody seems to have somebody to blame for the $550 million in damage and the death toll approaching 50 and the 2,000 injured and the 9,000 arrested. Eugene Yee, a Korean American raised in Hancock Park, has spent three nights outside Gun Heaven, a gun store at Fairfax and Olympic where he works part time, holding an assault rifle and defending himself and the store against wave after wave of gang members. They've been driving up with tape stuck over the last three digits of their license plates.

"We called the police the very first night," says Yee. "We told them we had a thousand weapons and maybe 90,000 rounds of ammunition, that we needed some protection. They told us to handle it ourselves."

"Word spreads quickly here," says Renee Kyle, the LAX bus driver, "and everybody heard right away that the police were doing nothing... I never see Mayor Bradley come on TV and say anything until he's already up in flames. He moves too slow for me—and now I think he's called in too many troops."

Way up on top of his apartment building in Koreatown, between Hollywood and south-central, John Hunkele, an out-of-work white actor in his late thirties, sat and watched the rioting. From a crows-nest tower on the roof, he had a 360-degree view of all kinds of things. On Wednesday night, he could see the downtown skyline beyond the red glowing spots and pillars of smoke from countless fires. By midnight, the skyline just disappeared under the soot and smoke, and it wasn't until the breeze on Saturday that patches of blue showed up again. No matter what, you just can't seem to keep the good weather away.

Cartons from looted goods sat around the city right in front of people's houses—empty Sony TV boxes, empty Mitsubishi boxes—waiting for the weekly trash pickup. There were 20 or so scattered shopping carts outside Hunkele's apartment building by Thursday evening. His neighbors had been looting. Down the block, he noticed another apartment building where the carts had been very neatly pushed together in a row, like at the Safeway.

"Why were those carts out there?" asks Hunkele. "No guilt. It was a gift to them, not a crime. All of us can sit around appalled by the looting, but there were open stores with smashed windows and smashed frozen-food section doors. . . . You don't know how much a dollar means to these people, how little they have. And then George Bush comes on TV and says it was 'mob rule.' Well, he just doesn't know what being poor is like."

Looters made their way into the grand old Bullock's Wilshire department store, now boarded up with pale plywood like the black-and-gold deco May Company and countless Circuit Citys and Radio Shacks and Payless Shoe Stores. The sidewalks in front are swept. "Your Circuit City will be open soon," says one marquee. The National Guard is guarding the big stores still standing—the troops sweating under their helmets and camouflage and canteens and guns—but it's hard to know whether there's anything left to guard. Nobody is saying. Nobody wants to say.

"Some of the store owners just opened up their doors," says Mary Yen, a Taiwanese who has lived in Koreatown for 20 years. "The store owner said, 'Let me help you take stuff—just don't burn my place down. This store is all I got.' "

Street corners in south-central are populated by crowds of neighborhood do-gooders of every color, and volunteers both obscure and famous: Sean Penn, Anjelica Huston and Edward James Olmos turned up. The First African Methodist Episcopal Church organized groups of volunteers at sunrise on Saturday, and they fanned out across the city, working in silence and looking like chimney sweeps by afternoon. "Everybody knows what to do," said Scott Kreeger, a 29-year-old short-story and screenplay writer who lives in Santa Monica. "We're just trying to get debris off the sidewalks."

"I saw small Latino children—about 6 or 7 years old—playing with pieces of glass this morning," said Carmen Rico, who lives in Beverlywood and works at UCLA Medical Center. "I just got a shovel and came out here." Rico hadn't even gone home to change—she was wearing a bright green Mexican dress, jewelry, a black bandanna—and was covered in ash and dirt. "At first I felt so sad," she said. "I was alone out here, sweeping. But then somebody else stopped, and then somebody else. I just got some momentum going. People came from all over the city."

"The City." Suddenly that's what people in Los Angeles are calling it, where before it was just Hawthorne and Inglewood, Baldwin Hills and Hancock Park—the wide spread of many places slowly drying out under the sun. Now, after this sad, confusing weekend of civil war, Los Angeles has magically become one place.

The bizarre emotional democracy of it: Almost every neighborhood in Los Angeles felt the troubles. Fires burned at the edge of Beverly Hills. The houses up in the hills above Hollywood looked down through the smoke at the spinning red lights of fire trucks and ambulances and squad cars. People kept saying it was "just like Beirut" or "just like the Persian Gulf," but they'd only seen that stuff on television. It was a little like watching the smart bombs dropping on Baghdad. Here though, there were more close-ups.

The city's poor, more used to facing gunfire and violence, were by far the greatest victims of the riots, but they weren't the only ones sleeping with baseball bats and scissors and knives, worrying about defending themselves. "We were about to bug out to Burbank, where my brother lives," says Mike McCourt, who lives with his wife in the Los Feliz area. "I mean, we were pretty spooked, pretty nervous. And then my neighbor came home with a Beretta and a stun baton and some Mace, and we felt much better."

"Television changed everything," says Scott Arundale, an independent film producer. "You'd think that revolution would have to happen in some tight little space, but people were all watching stuff on TV and getting riled up."

"The TV sucked," says Eugene Yee. "The first night all the action was down south, but then the TV showed interviews with blacks complaining about the damage to their own neighborhoods, then the next day the action started moving all over the city."

People are media-savvy here—they talk about how the newspapers and local television got tired of all the negative stories out of south-central, and how they started to reprogram by Thursday afternoon, reporting "the upside" and "the good-neighbor human interest" stories. People here also talk about the news like it's another movie project. They mention something reminding them of "Road Warrior" or "Fort Apache, the Bronx" or "The Omega Man"—that '70s end-of-the-world fantasy set in Los Angeles and starring Charlton Heston. They rave about the "incredible helicopter shots" that sweep over the city and make people look like ants, and "the fabulous live footage" of looters mugging for the cameras, laughing and giving the thumbs-up sign or saying hello to their mothers.

The movie studios, meanwhile, closed early on Wednesday. At lunchtime, there was a private screening at 20th Century Fox of a rough cut of a new picture called "Unlawful Entry," a Largo Entertainment project starring Ray Liotta as an LAPD officer who befriends a yuppie couple, makes a play for the wife and then turns out to be psychotic. (This kind of thing has proved successful recently—the evil terminator in "Terminator 2," after all, wore an LAPD uniform.) According to one movie exec, the word is that "Unlawful Entry," still in post-production, will be rushed out soon. July is just too long to wait.

May 4, 1992

Coming Home to Los Angeles

Facing the Hurt, When You're Squeezed by the 'Shoe' of Racial Perceptions

LYNNE DUKE

Three generations of our family grew up in this city, so it was understandable that my mother was deeply shaken by riots that ruined so many signposts of our life here.

The day after the Rodney King verdict, I dropped by her apartment in the Fairfax section to make sure she was all right. We talked briefly, and out spilled her set of rationales for the devastation that came so close she could see it from her bedroom window. She said things like, "The system wanted this to happen." And, "It wasn't just blacks. Whites were rioting too."

I heard these kinds of statements over and over while reporting on the riot and its aftermath. They are a response, I believe, to the stigma that many blacks feel is placed on them by society. That is why my mother and so many others would like to see the blame for the riots spread around.

The riots and the way people talk about them remind me of what a black man told Studs Terkel in his book "Race": that being black in America is like being forced to wear an ill-fitting shoe. It squeezes, it pinches, it cuts off circulation and sometimes it drives people to varying forms of distraction. It is not blackness that does these things, the man said, but society's perceptions and expectations of what blackness represents.

The shoe squeezes different people in different ways. It is less severe for those whose educational and economic success can act as a salve. Those without such means scratch and tear away at the shoe any way they can. Or they just give up and let the pain rule them. But whoever you are, the shoe is still on your foot.

I got my shoe during the Watts riots of 1965, when the race line that had seemed sort of fuzzy to me became crystal clear. I happened to be at the home of a white playmate, another 10-year-old, while riot coverage was on TV. As we watched, her parents expressed disgust with what they saw. They spoke of "them" and "those people" and "that neighborhood," which would not have pierced me so had I not understood, somewhere deep in my young mind, that they were talking about me.

Part of my family came from Watts. In fact, while we had only recently moved to Windsor Hills, my grandparents and several aunts, uncles and cousins still lived in Watts. My grandfather helped my dad build our first house there. Our church was there. My Brownie troop was there. The kooky man who dug a bomb shelter in his front yard on my street was there. And Peewee, the funniest kid on the block, was there.

So what my white friend's parents were condemning was a huge part of me. It was an awakening I won't forget.

And today, even as I am repelled and frightened by the wanton violence and bloodletting, I know that the destruction is in part rooted in the rage of people who believe they see all around them evidence of a society that for generations has divided its citizens into "us" and "them"—and then treated "them" as less than the rest.

That is the shoe. It is a uniquely American creation.

To be poor and black—or Hispanic, for that matter—often means that the shoe squeezes so constantly that pain becomes the reference point of life and escape from that pain becomes the main goal. In time, experiencing this pain corrodes the psyche. The man in Terkel's book describes it as a kind of race madness: The tighter the socioeconomic and racial shoe, the deeper you are driven to distraction. And what the brothers of the ghetto and the barrio do to each other and to their communities seems to bear this out.

They kill each other and derive a sense of manhood from it. They peddle drugs, make some money, and derive a sense of control from it. They become legends in their own minds.

With enough provocation, such as that provided in the travails of Rodney King, they may go wild. Those baton blows and kicks that King suffered at the hands of four whites became a metaphor, across class lines, for the pain inflicted in varying degrees by a shoe that never stops squeezing. And the beating by blacks of white truck driver Reginald Denny has likewise become a symbol—of the uncontrolled rage of the inner city.

For this analysis, I will be called an apologist. In our racial discourse, it seems, there are many who view explanations and analysis as excuse-making.

I know this not only from what I hear from some commentators and writers on the subject, but from the mail I receive. And I know this from opinion surveys showing that many whites believe blacks and Hispanics tend to be lazy, dependent and prone to violence.

Enough real-world evidence exists to provide the kernel of truth in these arguments. Blacks are disproportionately represented on the welfare rolls and in the criminal statistics. Such statistics are what keep America's sociologists, think-tanks and universities so engaged in analyzing the root causes of the problem. Meanwhile, a common attitude seems to be that what is happening to the inner-city poor is their fault and their fault alone. It is as if people exist in a vacuum, detached from the social context that shapes their fortunes. "The reservoir of sympathy for blacks on the part of whites just isn't there any more," Charles Murray of the

American Enterprise Institute recently told the *Los Angeles Times*. "They do not accept the premise that blacks are still unfairly disadvantaged."

I am not attempting here to absolve the inner-city poor of the responsibilities that citizenship in this country entails. Rather, I am talking about root causes—that old shoe, well-worn by time, of race. Consider these commonly recited truths: that 45 percent of the nation's prisoners are black, though blacks constitute 12 percent of the total population; that half of all black children live in poverty; and that much of the civil unrest that has rocked American cities has been perpetrated by blacks. Then consider that all of these things involve people who are the descendants of slaves.

The shackles came off long ago, but we are still stuck with this damn shoe.

There is much talk now about rebuilding Los Angeles's devastated communities and bringing more jobs and economic opportunity to areas bereft of both. But there is wide agreement that something more is needed from both black and white. For example, Claude M. Steele, a social psychologist at Stanford University, recently wrote in the Atlantic Monthly of society's devaluation of black children. Their educational prospects are limited, he wrote, because the educational establishment does not expect them to succeed; devaluation by race, he continued, is endemic to our society.

At the same time, blacks often devalue themselves. Last week, I met Howard Barnes, a tow-truck driver and church worker who was among the black men helping to clean up the riot-torn neighborhoods. At one point, he looked at the rubble and said, "The blacks didn't care. If the blacks cared, they wouldn't have done this." When I was 10 years old, I began to understand these pressures. As an adult who regularly butts heads with racial perceptions, I've come to know them well.

As I wandered through the wasteland that has been made of many neighborhoods here, I thought of that ill-fitting shoe, always squeezing.

May 10, 1992

Race Factor in Mortgage Lending Seen

Study Finds Blacks Rejected More Often

JERRY KNIGHT

Banks are much more likely to approve mortgage loans for whites than for blacks and Hispanics, and even poor whites get mortgages more easily than well-to-do minorities, according to a study released yesterday by the Federal Reserve Board.

Documenting widespread racial differences in mortgage approval rates, the study showed that minority home buyers were turned down for home mortgages two to three times more often than white home buyers.

Federal Reserve officials acknowledged that this comprehensive national survey of mortgage lending practices had shown "discriminatory results," but they stressed that more information would be needed to prove that lenders are practicing racial discrimination, which is forbidden by federal law.

"I find these data very worrisome," said Federal Reserve Board member John LaWare, who promised that the Federal Reserve will tell its examiners to look carefully at the mortgage lending practices of specific banks where there is a wide disparity in the rejection rates of blacks and whites.

In the Washington metropolitan area, the rejection rate on all mortgage applications was 6.3 percent for whites, 8.7 percent for Asians, 8.9 percent for Hispanics and 14.4 percent for blacks, according to a breakdown of 19 major cities also released yesterday by the Federal Reserve Bank of Boston.

The rejection rate for black borrowers in the District was the lowest in any of the 19 cities. The overall rejection rate here, 8.2 percent, was second-lowest in the country.

The nationwide study of 5.3 million mortgage applications made in 1990 showed that whites were approved for mortgages more often than blacks and Hispanics in every city and every income group, in predominantly black neighborhoods or white, in rich communities or poor. The study covered all banks and savings and loans in the country.

Federal Reserve officials said some of the disparity in mortgage approval rates is due to the differences between the financial resources and incomes of the applicants rather than racial discrimination. But senior Fed economist Glenn Canner pointed out the one discrepancy that is hardest to explain on any other basis: White borrowers in the lowest income category were approved for mortgages more often than black borrowers in the highest income group.

The highest income borrowers are families with incomes more than 20 percent above the median income in their community. The lowest income borrowers as measured by the study are those whose family income is more than 20 percent below the median. The median is the midpoint in prices, the level at which half the homes are more expensive and half are less expensive.

In the Washington area, for example, where the median family income is $55,000, the high-income group would include families making more than $66,000 a year and the low-income group those earning less than $44,000.

The study found that low-income whites nationally were approved for 69 percent of their conventional loans, while blacks in the richest group of buyers were approved for only 65.7 percent of conventional loans. Low-income whites were approved for 76.5 percent of FHA and VA loans, while higher-income blacks got approvals on 68 percent of government-backed loans.

Among the most affluent applicants, the rejection rate for conventional mortgages was 21.4 percent for blacks, 15.8 percent for Hispanics, 11.2 percent for Asians and 8.5 percent for whites.

LaWare, the Federal Reserve Board's bank regulation specialist, said, "It may be discrimination. It may be something entirely different. I'm not prepared to say there is discrimination going on here until we have gotten into it further."

But David Glenn, president of the Federal Home Loan Mortgage Corp. (Freddie Mac), the nation's second-largest provider of funds for mortgages, said the report is only the latest of many studies to show "definitive patterns of discriminatory lending practices in the mortgage industry."

"Whether these patterns are deliberate or inadvertent is not important. Whether the statistics and data are perfect or flawed is not important. The pattern of discrimination that these separate studies have found must be reversed," said Glenn in a speech to a group of mortgage bankers in New Orleans.

The American Bankers Association, however, released an academic study for which it paid, contending that the Federal Reserve study does not prove discrimination because it does not take into account the financial resources and credit history of the more than 5 million mortgage applicants. Only by looking at every application can it be determined whether lenders are discriminating, the ABA study argued.

This view drew immediate criticism on Capitol Hill.

"It matters not whether the discrimination is intentional. Discrimination by ignorance is just as hurtful and just as destructive as discrimination by design," said House Banking Committee Chairman Henry B. Gonzalez (D-Tex.), who cosponsored the legislation that required the study.

The other author of the bill, Rep. Joseph P. Kennedy II (D-Mass.), said the study "portrays an America where credit is a privilege of race and wealth, not a function of the ability to pay back a loan."

Gonzalez and Kennedy tacked a provision onto the 1989 savings and loan cleanup bill that for the first time required the government to collect information on mortgage applications and approvals by race, sex, income and other demographic data. Until then, the government had only gathered data on loans that were approved by lenders, not loans that were rejected or withdrawn by applicants before a decision was made.

The Federal Reserve released national summaries of the study yesterday. Later lending data will be made available for every bank, savings and loan and mortgage company in the country on a neighborhood-by-neighborhood basis.

The results of the Fed study show that rejection rates were higher for conventional home loans than for government-backed mortgage programs such as Federal Housing Administration and Veterans Administration loans.

On conventional mortgages, 14.4 percent of white applicants were turned down last year, compared with 33.9 percent of blacks, 21.4 percent of Hispanics and 12.9 percent of Asians. On FHA and VA loans the rejection rate was 12.1 percent for whites, 12.8 percent for Asians, 18.4 percent for Hispanics and 26.3 percent for blacks.

Some banks rejected black applications as much as four times as frequently as whites, the data show. The disparity between the rejection rates for blacks and whites varies widely from city to city and from bank to bank.

In Boston, Chicago and Minneapolis, blacks were turned down at three times the rate of whites, while in Los Angeles and Miami the rejection rates for blacks were only about 50 percent higher than for whites.

October 22, 1991

Minorities' Pollution Risk is Debated

Some Activists Link Exposure to Racism

MICHAEL WEISSKOPF

A tour of the most polluted U.S. communities is certain to include the industrial corridor of Chicago's southside, the pesticide bowl of central California farms and settlements along the dioxin-laced Columbia River.

All three communities are populated by minorities—black, Hispanic and American Indian, respectively. Are they victims of "environmental racism," as some minority activists charge, or casualties of poverty?

The Environmental Protection Agency posed the question to a task force in 1990, and in the final draft of their report, the 30-member group concluded that minority communities experience "greater than average" exposure to some environmental poisons, including lead, air pollutants, toxic waste and tainted fish.

But, the authors said, race is not as significant a factor as poverty in determining which communities face the highest risk. "Is there systematic racism out there?" asked Robert Wolcott, an EPA official who chaired the study group. "I don't think so. It's more economic class. It comes down to resources to locate oneself in jobs and homes that avoid exposure. In many cases, racial minorities don't have the capital to exercise that mobility."

The conclusions are expected to be controversial. A growing number of minority scholars and activists contend that industry consciously locates its most polluting plants in low-income minority areas and that government willingly approves and goes easy on regulating them.

"It's definitely racial discrimination," said Benjamin F. Chavis Jr., head of the United Church of Christ Commission for Racial Justice. "I'm not saying that whites aren't exposed. I'm saying the disproportionate exposure to minorities has been the result of systematic policymaking, not a factor of historical coincidence."

The report, titled "Environmental Equity," was assigned 18 months ago by EPA Administrator William K. Reilly after a conference at the University of Michigan raised the issue of whether low-income minority communities faced disproportionate exposure and health risks from pollution.

A task force of EPA staff members—a third of them black or Hispanic—combed government and scholarly reports to determine the extent and source of risk to minority areas, said Wolcott, who heads the EPA's water and agriculture policy division.

The report is scheduled for released late this month. A copy was obtained by The Washington Post.

Although there are clear differences in death and disease rates among ethnic groups, the task force was unable to document how much environmental factors contributed to that rate. Nor were data available that categorized people suffering from environmentally caused disease by race.

The one exception was childhood lead poisoning, caused by a variety of sources, including lead paint chips. Among urban children 5 years old and younger, the percentage of blacks who have excessive levels of lead in their blood far exceeds the percentage of whites at all income levels, according to the report. For families earning less than $6,000, 68 percent of black children have lead poisoning, compared with 36 percent of white children. In families with incomes exceeding $15,000, the ratio spread to 38 percent of black children and 12 percent of whites, the study found.

Wolcott said black people suffer a higher rate of lead poisoning because many live close to sources of the toxic metal. In communities near highways, for example, the fallout of leaded gasoline—burned for decades before it was phased down in the late 1970s—contaminates the soil of playgrounds and fields.

The percentage of blacks and Hispanics who live in areas where air pollution violates federal standards exceeds that of whites, the report showed. For example, a third of the nation's white population is exposed to excessive levels of carbon monoxide, a pulmonary irritant generated by the incomplete combustion of oil and coal. Forty-six percent of blacks and 57 percent of Hispanics are exposed to the pollutant, according to the report.

But the authors attributed the difference to residential patterns. More minorities live in urban settings where air pollution is concentrated.

American Indians who live near waterways such as the Columbia River in Oregon may be exposed to high levels of cancer-causing dioxins and PCBs in fish. But the study attributes the higher risk less to race than their heavy consumption of fish and its traditional importance in their diet.

The report played down race as a factor in minority communities' proximity to sources of pollution and said the differences are "complex and deeply rooted in many aspects of society," ranging from local land use to political power.

"It doesn't seem to be the result of any venal intent," said Wolcott of the disproportionate risk. "Real estate markets play themselves out." Among those who disagree is Robert Bullard, professor of sociology at the University of California at Riverside. In his study of toxic waste sites in five southern cities, he said, "race was a big factor in determining where these facilities go."

In Houston, for example, every municipal landfill and six of eight municipal incinerators were located in black neighborhoods in 1983, when blacks made up fewer than a third of the city's population, Bullard said.

"If it was a class thing, you'd expect some level of random distribution" of the facilities, he said. "To say race has nothing to do with distribution of environmental risk and decision-making when it comes to land use is to ignore institutional racism."

He asserted that the planning and zoning boards that decide where to site landfills and incinerators "have systematically excluded people of color."

According to the task Force report, EPA managers have a "strong commitment" to address issues of environmental equity and some programs already have been launched to deal with high exposure risks in minority communities. Pesticide regulators, for example, take into account the risk to agricultural workers, many of whom are Hispanic, before deciding to license a chemical.

The task force recommended the development of new data systems to assess risk by race and income, improve procedures for identifying highly polluted areas, to look for ways to reduce risk in hard-hit communities and to review permits and enforcement practices to assure that all communities are treated fairly.

January 16, 1992

Ethnic Strife Amid U.S.–Japan Trade War

Some Asian Americans Smarting from Rude Remarks and Gestures

STEPHEN BUCKLEY

Vandals painted the word "Chinks" in front of a Korean family's home last week in Ellicott City. Graffiti in a women's restroom at George Mason University in Fairfax orders Japanese companies to "go back to Japan." As a Japanese American woman walked along the mall recently, she was called a "Japanese pig."

Such incidents have left local Asian Americans saddened and disappointed about U.S.-Japanese tensions. As they listen to politicians bash Japan and read about people of Asian ancestry being physically harmed or threatened by other Americans, they say they hope the two countries haven't launched a new era of bad feeling.

The fear that U.S.-Japanese relations will continue to sour is felt most powerfully by people such as K. Patrick Okura, who endured six months in a California internment camp with his bride, Lily, during World War II.

"A red light goes off," said Okura, 80, a former national president of the Japanese American Citizens League who lives in Bethesda. "Things can happen. People die. People get beaten up. It's alarming. After 50 years, I thought we'd progressed more than we have."

Police departments said they haven't seen a rise in hate incidents aimed at the area's more than 200,000 Asian Americans. Yet Asian Americans say they're acutely aware of rude comments and gestures communicated to them sometimes in subtle—or not-so-subtle—ways.

About two weeks ago, for example, Sen. Ernest Hollings (D-S.C.) joked about dropping the atomic bomb, telling factory workers: "You should draw a mushroom cloud and put underneath it, 'Made in America by lazy and illiterate Americans and tested in Japan.' "

His remark came several weeks after two of Japan's top politicians said U.S. workers are "lazy" and questioned whether U.S. commitment to "producing things and creating value has 'loosened' too much in the last decade." "I think the Japanese are wrong because I know Americans work hard," said Sayoko Ballgodajan, 42, manager of a Japanese restaurant in Northwest Washington. Referring to both countries' leaders, she added, "It is just the fools opening their mouths. The regular people, the small people, do not think that way."

Yet it was no world leader who accosted Ann Yonemura, 44, on the Mall. "I was somewhat shocked. No one had ever been so explicitly hostile," said the museum curator, who has lived in the Washington area for 18 years.

Specialists in international relations note that, historically, anger toward ethnic groups swells during economic hard times. And, those scholars said, Asian Americans have become an obvious target of abuse during the recession because of Japan's economic success.

They add that, because the world views Japan and the United States as the leaders of today's global economy, the timing of these tensions couldn't be worse.

"None of this is very desirable," said Masaru Tamamoto, director of the Center for Asian Studies at American University. "I think the fundamentals of the relationship are strong, but we are losing sight of those fundamentals. The trees have become everything. We're not looking at the forest."

Tamamoto said Japanese nationals living in this country generally hold Americans in high esteem. Yet in recent months a series of events—from President Bush's much-maligned visit to Japan to U.S. industry's push to "Buy American"—has "really shattered the sense of America as a country of fair play," Tamamoto said:

Kenji Yamaguchi exemplifies the ambivalence of many Japanese nationals here. Yamaguchi, 32, arrived in Washington four years ago, received a master's degree in business administration at George Washington University and now teaches Japanese for the Japan America Society.

"America is one of Japanese people's favorite countries. We love this country," said Yamaguchi, who lives off Dupont Circle. "Some people may say strong words against Japan, but it doesn't mean all American people are all like that."

However, asked whether American workers are lazy, he said, "In general, Japanese people have better attitudes toward work. They have better-quality products, better-quality service. They work harder. I speak only in general."

Like Yamaguchi, many Japanese Americans—who like to stress that they are Americans first—are troubled by pressure to purchase only American-made goods.

They see it as a simplistic solution to a complex, long-term problem. "The companies should spend time talking about how to improve our products," said Mona Rook, 29, who lives in Annandale. "I'm not against buying American. But in and of itself, it's just too pat."

Rook, whose mother is from Hiroshima, said she is disturbed when she hears derogatory remarks about Japan. "I understand how Americans feel when they speak that way about Asians," the South Carolina native said with a soft southern accent, "but it irritates me to hear someone speak that way about any group of people."

For some Japanese Americans, these times have raised unsettling questions about what it means to be American.

They say they're troubled that, despite their use of "we" and "us" when they speak of the United States, neighbors and colleagues often see them as Japanese.

They're distressed that many other Americans assume that they speak poor English, drive Japanese-made cars and hail from well-to-do backgrounds.

"It would be very good if we could understand that we are a nation made up of people from every part of the world," Yonemura, the curator, said. "We are all Americans equally. Don't make assumptions based on how we look."

Yonemura also observes that most Americans can't tell apart the various Asian ethnicities. Other Asian Americans, making the same point, said they're afraid that they'll suffer physical harm if they're misidentified as Japanese.

They recalled the murder of Vincent Chin, a Chinese American beaten to death in 1982 in Detroit by two unemployed steelworkers frustrated with the rise of Japanese car sales in the United States.

"I think a lot of people are on edge," said Sonya Chung, a Korean American who works as assistant director of the D.C. chapter of the Japanese American Citizens League. "Things have gotten very emotional, very visceral. During a time like this, all Asian Americans get caught in the cross-fire."

Meanwhile, Japanese nationals and Japanese Americans fear that the Asian nation will become the new Evil Empire if the hot rhetoric of politicians and corporate executives goes unchecked.

"Right now, what they're doing is mutually destructive," said Midori Yanagihara, 32, a free-lance researcher on Asian issues who lives in Fort Washington. "They should quit their bilateral bickering. That would be helpful to the entire world."

March 15, 1992

The Heartland Pulses with New Blood

BARBARA VOBEJDA

Every weekday morning, the booths at the Grant Avenue Diner fill with balding white men, most equipped with hearing aids and hard opinions. For years they have kept this ritual, leaning back against the padded seats, their fingers clasped around their coffee cups, chewing through the gossip and politics and crop prices that affect their lives.

The Formica table tops and vinyl benches form a kind of enclave, an elite circle of the powerful and formerly powerful in town. Little about that has changed, even as the community around them has moved through an extraordinary ethnic metamorphosis.

On the dusty streets outside the diner, their town has a new look and feel: Tornado warnings are posted in three languages, Vietnamese, Spanish and English. The police department is under pressure to hire Hispanics, and farmers look forward to the Asian dragon dance at the Cinco de Mayo parade.

The old-timers can't pronounce the name of the new Vietnamese restaurant, Pho-Hoa, but they know they like No. 38 (barbecue pork and noodles).

And on Thursdays, when the paychecks arrive, Juan Andrade's variety store, El Remedio, is crowded with shoppers. He stocks Mexican products from pottery to pinatas, and on that day, fresh tortillas from California.

Garden City has always had a larger share of Hispanics than many neighboring towns. "Now," Andrade said, "it's like you're in Mexico." But you're not in Mexico. You're in Kansas, square in the middle of the American heartland. A giant beef-packing plant opened here one day in 1980, and the town swelled virtually overnight with newcomers eager for work, many of them immigrants from Mexico and Southeast Asia.

Garden City today is something new, a striking example of the extraordinary racial and ethnic changes that are transforming both U.S. coasts and pushing across the hinterland. This Great Plains town of 24,097, settled a century ago by cattle ranchers and farmers, reflects the newest face of America.

The nation's face is strikingly different from 10 or 20 years ago. Immigrants have arrived in near-record numbers. Black, Asian and Hispanic populations have grown at rates several times that of whites. Minorities have appeared in many communities that, until recently, were homogeneous and white.

America is still an overwhelmingly white country, and minority groups continue to concentrate in a handful of coastal states. But the white majority is slipping: Non-Hispanic whites made up 76 percent of the population in 1990, down from about 80 percent in 1980.

And the expansion of minorities into cities, suburbs and towns away from the traditional ports-of-entry has created an altogether new cultural map. The result is a nation more diverse than at any time in history.

A *Washington Post* analysis of 1990 census figures underscores the extent of that change: The proportion of whites declined in 72 percent of the nation's 3,137 counties. While the changes appear minor in many places, more and more communities are becoming home to what academics call a "threshold" population of minorities, sufficient numbers to support businesses and activities. In other words, these new groups change the cultural feel of a place.

Nationally, the proportion of Asians increased in 80 percent of the nation's counties and the proportion of Hispanics increased in 64 percent of the counties over the past decade, *The Post* analysis showed. Blacks comprised a larger share of the population in 60 percent of the counties, while the proportion of American Indians increased in nearly nine of 10—87 percent—of the counties.

While the black population grew about three times faster than the non-Hispanic white population, it was the rapid growth among Asians and Hispanics that most altered the nation's ethnic makeup. For the black population, the most dramatic changes were geographic, with increased movement to the South and West and entry into metropolitan areas where relatively few blacks have lived in the past.

Behind the migration of minority groups into new communities is a web of economic and human factors: job opportunities, social networks pulling immigrants to new areas, refugee resettlement programs and suburbanization of minorities. Together, these forces are moving many cities away from the traditional white-black polarity to a racial mix that erases any dominant majority. They are also stirring new and more complex competition between groups.

In Santa Clara County, Calif., Asians and Hispanics grew from a quarter of the population to nearly 40 percent, boosted by thousands of newly arrived Asian immigrants settling in with families and friends.

In Texas, home to nine of the 23 counties where minorities became the majority in the past decade, the addition of 1.4 million Hispanics has set up a new political clash: Hispanics are challenging a redistricting plan in Dallas drawn by black state legislators.

And in Finney County, Kan., where Garden City is located, the white share of the population fell faster than in all but five other counties. The changes that descended here in the 1980s were rooted as far back as the '50s, when new irrigation techniques made it more profitable to raise feed grain, which spurred an expansion of feedlots and drew the giants of the meatpacking industry.

When IBP Inc. opened its plant and a second big company, Monfort, expanded its packing operation, the word went out that there were thousands of jobs that could not be filled by the local work force. The result was a wave of new arrivals to town, many of them without skills, many unable to speak English, all of them desperate for work. A New Economic Vitality in Town

Gene Rudd, the former owner of a local savings and loan, offers this shorthand for the town's new demography:

"There are the old-timers, the Texicans and the wetbacks." The "Texicans," he said, are longtime Mexican-American residents who moved to Garden City before the recent immigration wave. The "wetbacks" are undocumented immigrants from Mexico, a term he and his coffee mates use routinely but not, he insists, pejoratively.

"It's a name," he said, over coffee at the Grant Avenue Diner. "I ask my tenants, 'Do you have a green card or are you wet?' They say, 'I'm wet.'"

He does not mention the influx of Southeast Asians, but laughs that, out at the trailer parks, which are occupied heavily by Asians, "I think there's just three televisions out there, and they just keep stealing them" from each other.

The talk at the diner is a reminder of a time in Garden City when Hispanics were barred from the swimming pool and relegated to the movie theater balcony.

There is racial tension still, although Rudd's friends around the table and others in the coffee shop acknowledge that the packing plants and the thousands of workers they have drawn have brought a new economic vitality to the community.

Jim Fishback, a clothing salesman, argued that the Vietnamese children in local schools have "shown the American kids it can be done. They are good students."

"There's only one good thing about the good old days," said Tony Geier, 83, who has lived here since 1925. "You could trust people. You could leave your doors unlocked." Today, he said, "you can't trust anybody."

Geier is not the only old-timer to mention increased crime. Local police statistics show that the number of serious crimes—including murder, rape and major thefts—increased 51 percent from 1983 to 1990.

Some in town blame the increase in crime on the new transient population, others assign it to poverty among minorities.

Only a handful of blacks has ever lived in Finney County and Garden City, although Hispanics have been part of the community for as much as a century, drawn by railroad and farm jobs plentiful when the town was known for its sugar beet production.

But during the 1980s, the county's Hispanic population more than doubled, from 3,459 to 8,353. The Asian population rose even more dramatically, from just 100 in 1980 to 1,203 in 1990. And the county's population overall grew by half, to 33,070.

But the figures do not reflect the true ferment in the community, wrought by turnover rates at the plants ranging from 75 to 96 percent annually. The town has become accustomed to a stream of families coming and going; a third of the students in the local school district move in or out over the course of each year.

Despite the social problems associated with the rapid change high dropout rates in the high school, poverty and language barriers there are many in town who say the newcomers have made their community a more interesting place to live.

"It feels very different, but I like the difference," said Mary Warren, who was raised in Garden City and now runs the county historical society. "To me, it's very stimulating."

University of Kansas anthropologist Don Stull, who conducted research and lived in Garden City for 16 months as part of a Ford Foundation study, concluded that despite some problems, the community has adjusted very well to the influx of minorities.

He attributed that to the small size of the community, a shared ethic honoring hard work and the lack of competition for jobs.

"Yes, there were some problems, but the community was really trying to respond . . . to accommodate the newcomers. It has a small-town mentality in the good sense of the word," he said.

Not everyone shares that assessment. Hispanics argue that the local police are much more likely to crack down on drinkers outside their bars than on those at the mostly white country club. And Hispanic parents say their children are reprimanded for speaking Spanish at school.

"When the kids get in fights, the ones who get suspended the most are the Mexicans," said Maria Zapata, a cook at the Grant Avenue Diner.

Southeast Asian immigrants are less likely to complain, local residents say.

Dieu Vo, who arrived with his wife and three children last December, told of the friendly welcome his family received, including a party held by other Vietnamese in the trailer park. The women prepared traditional Asian dishes, he said, and the men drank plenty of American beer. The other families donated $200 so Vo could buy a 1976 Chevrolet.

Vo, who had been a major in the South Vietnamese Army and a political prisoner for nine years, and his wife, Thuy Huynh, a former teacher, had never heard of Kansas before their refugee resettlement program brought them here. Now, they concede, they have little interaction with town residents, other than with the Vietnamese families who live nearby.

Both are employed at the IBP plant for $6.60 an hour. Vo trims the fat from hunks of beef moving along a conveyor belt; Thuy Huynh seals the meat in plastic, then hoists it into a bin.

For $300 a month the couple rents a sparse trailer, situated with scores of similar drab units on a treeless, windy plain outside town. The family spends money only on the basics, no restaurants or new furniture. They save between $500 and $600 a month, Vo said, which they will use for their children's education.

"My life is over," he said through an interpreter. "I cannot join the army. I cannot be a major any more. My future is nothing right now. I'm just only trying to establish the future for my children."

At the same time, Vo, who is 48, said he appreciates the benefits of American freedom. "If you don't violate the law, you're a free man," he said.

On a recent weekday, the family sat around their metal kitchen table, sharing a meal of vegetables and noodles.

Thuy Huynh asked if she might show off for her visitors a traditional Vietnamese dress, then modeled it with a child's pride, walking through the small trailer, shy and beaming. A few minutes later, she had to travel to the packing plant, cover her head with a hardhat, strap on a protective belt, pull on steel-toed boots and go to work on the bloody production floor.

Recruiting Laotians on Welfare

Roger Vilaysing, a Laotian immigrant who runs a social service agency in Garden City, is scheduled to visit California this week, his third trip there since November.

These are recruiting journeys: Using contacts through a Laotian Air Force veterans association, he gathers a group of welfare-dependent immigrants in a community hall in Fresno. Vilaysing, who is financed by a federal grant, said he speaks in his native Lao, telling the audience of the benefits of Kansas. He brings along a videotape on Garden City and its meat packing industry, borrowed from the Chamber of Commerce.

Then he promotes the nobility of self-sufficiency: You can get off welfare, he promises, if you are willing to take a job at the packing plants.

Since last fall, eight families have taken up his offer. Vilaysing packed their belongings in a rented moving truck and drove 1,640 miles to Garden City. A caravan of families followed in their cars, a modern-day wagon train.

Upon their arrival, the newcomers moved into trailers arranged by Vilaysing, rested for a few days, then started to work in the plants. For 45 days, their expenses were paid, enough time to put several paychecks in the bank.

But once on their own, Vilaysing argues, they would do well to save their money and move on.

"They are very glad they got the job," he said. But he most admires those who have saved $100,000 in five years, enabling them to buy a business or a fishing boat in Louisiana or Texas. "This," he said of Garden City, "is not a good place for living for five, 10 years. . . . The packing house is not a good place to live for the rest of their lives."

Still, Vilaysing said, he will retrace the route back to California as often as necessary, hoping to bring 18 families this year, 50 next year, on this unlikely passage to middle America.

Polling director Richard Morin contributed to this report.

August 11, 1991

Gender 7

Another pervasive social problem in our society is that of gender inequality. The first article in this chapter explores bias against girls in tests, textbooks, and teaching methods. An NCAA task force finds that women are still playing catch up in sports in the second article, from participation in sports programs to positions on coaching staffs.

The next articles discuss the widespread experience of sexual harassment, and an increasingly commonplace occurrence, date rape.

The final article explores communication differences between men and women and how the lack of good communication contributes to breakdown in family structures, for example.

Wide Gender Gap Found in Schools

Girls Said to Face Bias in Tests, Textbooks and Teaching Methods

MARY JORDAN

The most comprehensive report to assess the gender gap in American schools found widespread bias against girls in tests, textbooks and teaching practices—findings that set off an immediate controversy among educators.

"The bias that exists in how girls are taught is no longer blatant, but they experience it on a daily basis," said Sharon Schuster, president of the American Association of University Women (AAUW), which commissioned the report.

The Education Department, which last month proposed eliminating the only federal program aimed at promoting educational equity for girls, said the new report lacked perspective and hard data and maintained yesterday that gender-equity programs were no longer needed.

"You have to look at the larger context, at all the great strides women have made," said Diane S. Ravitch, assistant secretary for educational research and improvement at the Education Department. "This is a period of history in which there have been the most dramatic strides for women."

Ravitch cited statistics showing the percentage of female high school graduates enrolling in college is now larger than males and that the number of women who become lawyers, doctors and other professionals is rapidly increasing.

In 1970, 5 million college students were male and 3.5 million were female, a vastly different composition than in 1989, when 7.3 million were female and 6.5 million male. Likewise, Ravitch noted that only 8 percent of medical degrees were awarded to women in 1970, but 33 percent went to women in 1989.

"But quantity does not make quality," countered Mary Lou Leipheimer, co-chair of the National Coalition of Girls' Schools, who endorses the AAUW report, which is to be released today.

Leipheimer, who runs the Foxcroft School for girls in Middleburg, recited the other side of the statistical battleground: lagging pay for women compared with men, and underrepresentation of women in leadership roles in education. Women earn 69 cents on the dollar compared with equally educated men, according to a Labor Department analysis. And, while the overwhelming number of public elementary and high school teachers are women, more than 95 percent of the nation's school superintendents are men and 72 percent of its principals are men.

However, much of what the report "How Schools Shortchange Girls" focuses on is more difficult to quantify: little encouragement for girls to pursue math and science, few female role models in textbooks, and subtle teacher practices, such as calling on boys more often or gearing school and play activities more to the males.

The report by the Wellesley College Center for Research on Women is largely a compilation of existing studies by well-known researchers at Harvard, American and other universities and is believed to be the most thorough documentation of the gender gap in American schools.

Research by Myra and David Sadker, professors at American University, shows that boys in elementary and middle school called out answers eight times more often than girls. When boys called out, teachers listened. But when girls called out, they were told to "raise your hand if you want to speak."

Even when boys did not answer, teachers were more likely to encourage them to give an answer or an opinion than they were to encourage girls, the researchers found.

The study, noting the disparity between males and females in standardized math and science tests, said teachers often steered more boys than girls to those fields.

From 1978 to 1988, female scores on the SAT increased by 11 points while male scores increased by four points. However, males still outscored females 498 to 455.

In science, the gap is wider, and some studies indicate it might be increasing. On the 1988 SAT achievement test in physics, males averaged a 611 score out of 800, 56 points higher than females' average score of 555.

The scores are noteworthy because girls often received better grades than boys, leading some researchers to suggest bias in the tests, which often determine college admittance and scholarships.

Several studies have suggested that teachers encourage male students to work with laboratory equipment, especially in the more complex sciences. For instance, one study found that 51 percent of boys in the third grade had used a microscope, compared with 37 percent of girls. In 11th grade, an electricity meter had been used by 49 percent of males but by only 17 percent of females.

The study also shows that vocational education programs are often geared to males despite the fact that 45 percent of the work force is female. It also showed that since the early 1970s, the participation of girls in interscholastic athletics has increased dramatically, but that boys still participate in them at twice the rate.

The report, timed to be released at the AAUW National Education Summit on Girls, is drawing the attention of many of the most influential education groups in the nation, including the head of the largest teachers union.

The report says some progress has been made since the enactment of Title IX, the landmark 1972 legislation banning sex discrimination in federally funded education programs. Yet, it says stereotypical images still appear in textbooks, the overwhelming number of authors and role models studied in class are male, and problems confronting women, including sexism, the higher rate of suicide among women, and eating disorders are often all but ignored in the curriculum.

"I think you can look at any situation and see the progress or see the way we have to go," said Susan McCee Bailey, director of the Wellesley research center. "But I think it's dangerous to say that because one-third of our medical students are now women" the struggle for gender equality is over. "There is a great deal more to be done."

February 12, 1992

Report Affirms Women Still Playing Catch-Up

Schultz Gives Survey to NCSS Task Force

KARL HENTE

Twenty years after the passage of Title IX, the federal regulation barring discrimination on the basis of sex in college education, more money is spent on men's intercollegiate athletic programs than on women's, according to a study conducted and released yesterday by the NCAA.

The report attributes the difference to men's participation exceeding women's by a 2-to-1 ratio, much of that because of the "dramatic effect" of football and the lack of a comparable sport for women.

NCAA Executive Director Richard D. Schultz said in the report that although "institutions of higher learning have made positive strides since the enactment of Title IX . . . to enhance competitive athletics opportunities for women, additional work must be done to ensure gender equality." Schultz commissioned a task force made up of NCAA members to develop recommendations on how the organization should respond to the findings.

The report concluded that since offering football meant greater participation opportunities for men, it is also likely to "increase the number that must be offered to women to accommodate equivalently their athletic interests and abilities."

The study used a confidential survey of NCAA member institutions during the second half of 1991, in response to a request by the National Association of Collegiate Women Athletic Administrators.

Since Congress's enactment of Title IX in 1972, NCAA members have been responsible for the creation of equitable men's and women's athletics programs.

"While I was disappointed to see the disparity in funds spent on recruiting," Schultz said, "I was pleased to see that" on average, the colleges have substantially met the Title IX standard with respect to the proportion of scholarship assistance going to women."

In Division I, males in athletics programs outnumbered females by a ratio of 2.24 to 1. The ratio for recruiting expenses was 4.8 to 1, and for scholarship expenses—as to which Title IX requires that expenditures closely parallel participation rates—it was 2.28 to 1. The ratio for average operating expenses for men's sports over women's was 3.42 to 1.

The study found the total coaching expense per participant (average per institution) was $3,162.78 for men's sports and $2,503.30 for women's. The average base salary for head coaches in men's programs was roughly equivalent in most sports to that for women's, with the clear exception of basketball (see accompanying chart).

Schultz also blamed financial pressures on athletic departments for disparities in men's and women's programs. Budget cuts have resulted in reductions in scholarships, coaching staffs and recruiting.

Schultz said he hoped administrators would "analyze the data and ask themselves if men and women student-athletes on their own campuses are indeed treated equitably.

"We have to look for new, innovative ways to expand programs and resources for women in an environment that is dictating overall cuts. I continue to believe that those alternatives exist."

Table 7–1 • Division 1-A Coaching Salaries Average Base Salaries

Sport	Men's Coach	Women's Coach
Base/Softball	$43,466	$30,781
Basketball	$88,984	$45,847
Cross-country	$22,183	$18,412
Fencing	$13,306	$12,361
Field Hockey	N/A	$4,492
Football	$99,429	N/A
Golf	$27,772	$22,672
Gymnastics	$31,340	$32,187
Ice Hockey	$53,597	N/A
Lacrosse	$35,204	$24,453
Rifle	$14,111	$8,211
Skiing	$17,570	$17,200
Soccer	$31,095	$21,660
Swimming	$27,026	$25,590
Tennis	$26,612	$23,802
Track	$32,406	$27,841
Volleyball	$32,739	$32,200
Water Polo	$24,623	N/A
Wrestling	$33,152	N/A
Other	$34,889	$22,345
Avg. per school	$396,791	$206,106

Average coaching expense per athlete:
Men, $3,162.78;
Women, $2,503.30.

March 12, 1992

Between the Sexes, Confusion at Work

Harassment is Widespread, and its Effect are Long-Lasting

ABIGAIL TRAFFORD

She was 15 years old and worked after school in a dry cleaners store. In a few months, she would take her earnings and go to college on a scholarship—then on to medical school and a distinguished career in medical science.

But in 1934, Estelle Ramey worked from 8 p.m. to 11 p.m., cleaning dresses for 39 cents an hour. Her aunt had gotten her the job. The owner was a family friend from church. Every night, he came by the store to pick up the money earned that day. He also put his hands on her shoulders, on her arms. He touched her wrists. She would inch away from him, and he kept coming closer and closer. Although he never assaulted her, she was devastated by the feelings he provoked in her.

"I would have died rather than tell my mother," said Ramey, who today is Professor Emeritus of Georgetown University and a distinguished endocrinologist. "I was ashamed . . . For 60 years, I've carried this inside me."

Following the allegation of sexual harassment against Supreme Court nominee Clarence Thomas, unrelated stories suddenly are everywhere. Sexual harassment is one snapshot experience that binds working women together—and separates them from male colleagues.

While there is confusion over what exactly constitutes sexual harassment, there is no confusion about how it feels. The memories are vivid. So is the shame, fear and despair.

The problem is not just a legal issue in the workplace. Sexual harassment can have profound social and psychological consequences. It usually occurs when women are in their most vulnerable period—when they are young and not yet established in the workplace or in their private lives. In most cases, sexual harassment is never reported—never even talked about. The woman may not be aware of all its effects.

But sexual harassment early in a career fuels two devastating emotions: self-doubt and distrust of others.

It also aggravates the ambivalence of many women—and many men—about the role of women in the workplace. With the flood of women into the labor force since 1960—especially women with small children—the rules of acceptable social behavior between the sexes have changed. But just about every woman who drops her toddler off at day care or has a teacher conference because a teenaged child is doing badly in science feels that twinge of guilt that maybe she doesn't belong in the working world. Maybe she should listen to those internal ghosts held over from times past that tell her she should stay at home. Even if her MBA and her mortgage tell her she can't NOT work.

Sexual harassment, whether it's a crack about her breasts from the janitor or a leer from the vice president for sales, reinforces the self-doubt with the notion that women don't really belong in the workplace.

What is stunning is how widespread various forms of sexual harassment are, ranging from unwanted fondling and lewd propositions to hitting on women for sexual favors in return for job security. A federal study found that more than 40 percent of working women had endured behavior that fits the legal definition.

Some forms are obvious. To get personal, *The Post's* Health Section with 10 women staffers is a microcosm of the typical harassment encountered on the job. Some of the experiences, recounted by nearly every woman, occurred 10 or 20 years ago.

One of us, early in her career, worked for a man who kept pressing her to go out with him, to sleep with him. She rebuffed him. And then he gave her a poor performance rating in her annual evaluation. She never reported it. The situation resolved itself when her supervisor went on to another job. Experts call this the "put out or get out" category.

Another, early in her career, had a co-worker, senior to her, who kept propositioning her and making sexual remarks. She told him to stop, but he continued to bother her. She found that he was doing the same thing to another female employee. They both went to their supervisor to complain. The supervisor took the co-worker aside and told him to stop bothering the two women. The overt actions stopped, but the tension increased, and one of the women moved to another department.

Another one of us, also early in her career, was in the middle of the newsroom when an editor, who had been drinking, came up to her and thrust his head between her breasts. Stunned, she pushed him away and pretended nothing had happened. A supervisor who had seen the incident later complimented her on how well she handled it; the editor received no official reprimand.

Sometimes, it's not so clear that any harassment has taken place. One of us, early in her career at another organization, caught the eye of a senior editor. He liked her work, told her she had talent and encouraged her to write a book. He also had a reputation as a womanizer, so when he repeatedly asked her out for lunch, she felt uneasy. Was he taking her to lunch because she was good or because she was pretty? Or both?

Another *Post* colleague remembered her first boss and how excited she had been to work on special projects with him. It was natural for him to take her to lunch. And then one day, he leaned over, took her hand, and said: "Let's have an affair." She was devastated. It was easy to say no. What was not easy to handle were the doubts now raised in her mind. What about the bonus he gave her, the glowing evaluation? Was it because she was good or because she was pretty?

In quid pro quo cases of sexual harassment, it is usually a male superior who promises a promotion or some kind of reward in return for sexual favors. In academia, it's known as an A-for-a-lay. Or sometimes it's an Important Person who can help advance a career. One of us in the Health Section remembers the head of a federal agency who early in her career squeezed her hand and said that he could only give her a good interview if they had dinner together.

The problem is that women—particularly young women—often cannot tell what is going on. Sometimes, the offer to help a younger woman is simply that. In the real world of the workplace, communication between men and women is subtle and not always straightforward. The language of power and the language of sex often use the same words and there is room for innuendo, mixed messages, misunderstanding.

And what about romance? In recent years, the workplace has become the most effective meeting ground for men and women. Is sexual harassment to one person sexual opportunity to another? In the microcosm of the Health section, two female employees met their future husbands at work.

"Sex is always there," said Babette Wise, a social worker in the department of psychiatry at Georgetown University. "Freud was right. You can't deny the sexual component when you have males and females together."

For most professional women, it is a man who holds the door to advancement, who reinforces the professional self-image. of course, both men and women frequently depend on mentors who pick them out, train them and recommend them for assignments that will further their career. But the experience is vastly different. For instance, a male colleague remembers the first time when the city editor noticed his work, at another newspaper. The man came over to his desk, clapped him on the back, hinted about a promotion. It never would occur to him that the boss's interest was anything but a professional blessing of his talent.

This is why men "don't get it" about sexual harassment, don't seem to understand what all the fuss is about.

A bad evaluation, attempted rape, a bonus for being bedded—men understand that. But this other, this uneasy feeling some women have, this twilight zone of what's user-friendly behavior in the workplace, this shadow of fear and distrust—men generally have a hard time figuring out what the new boundaries are between the sexes. What do women NOT want?

And women don't tell them. Women usually don't let on what sexual harassment is, when it happens or why it hurts, what devastating psychic damage it can do.

The way most women deal with sexual harassment is to ignore it. Only 3 percent of the women in the federal study who experienced harassment ever reported it.

"Most people do nothing," said psychologist Louise Fitzgerald at the University of Illinois. "They basically try to deny it. They pretend it's not going on. They'll minimize the situation—it's no big deal, it was probably a joke, he doesn't mean anything by that."

Sometimes, women succumb to the "red dress" syndrome and blame themselves: If only I hadn't worn a red dress, he wouldn't have said that. Observed Fitzgerald: "These are all internally focused responses—to deny, to distance and finally to blame yourself. Women lose their self-confidence. They feel they didn't handle it right. There probably is no best way to handle it. We tell women who have been sexually harassed: "You did exactly the right thing for you at the time."

Sometimes, women feel guilty because on some level they like being the object of sexual attention. Psychologists call this the "daddy's girl" syndrome. These women want to be the apple of the older man's eye. Many have been galvanized to succeed by adoring successful fathers.

"Harassers can be terrific men," said Washington psychologist Martha Gross. "A woman in her twenties feels complimented. She wants older men to find her sexually attractive. That's how insidious sexism is."

Part of the solution is not just increased sensitivity to these issues by men but the growing confidence of women as they mature in the workplace.

Estelle Ramey, for example, landed a prize job on the faculty of a large university after finishing medical school. Forty years later at a reunion, she asked her old mentor, the eminent chairman of the department, why he chose her over the hundreds of male graduates.

He told her she was the smartest in the class; she was ambitious and hardworking. "And you know," he added, "you were nice to look at."

Professor Ramey smiled at her old mentor and thanked him. But what if he had told her this at the time?

"It would have reinforced my uneasiness as the only woman in the science department," said Ramey. "At 19, 20 or 25, my self-image was so fragile, I had to be reinforced all the time."

October 15, 1991

Date Rape

CHRIS SPOLAR AND ANGELA WALKER

He was her friend. So the 26-year-old real estate agent agreed when he asked to come over after work one night in May 1987. Around midnight, she unlocked the door to her one-room apartment overlooking Connecticut Avenue. She listened indulgently to her friend, a former lover, complain about his job managing a local restaurant. Finally, she asked him to leave. He seemed to ignore her, so she decided to lie on her bed, fully clothed. She dozed off as her friend droned on. At one point, she slipped under the comforter on her bed and wriggled out of her jeans. Sometime in the next hour, she was aware that he was sitting on the bed. Suddenly she awoke with a start, as she realized he had climbed on top of her.

She screamed and tried to push him off the bed. He shoved her back, wrenching her neck and pinning her down. She began to cry. He placed his hand tightly over her mouth and penetrated her. Sobbing and unable to breathe, she began to choke. Blood vessels around her eyes popped from lack of oxygen.

Then she stopped fighting and went limp, psychologically retreating to a place where he could not hurt her. His hand slipped off her mouth; she gasped: "Just get it over with."

With that, he stopped. He rolled off her. He apologized. He swore at himself. He said he had made a mistake and threatened to kill himself. Then he ran out of her apartment carrying his clothes.

She picked up the phone, dialed 911 and reported she had been raped.

Three years later, the man who had been her friend pleaded guilty to one count of sodomy and was sent to jail.

Date Rape Underreported

Women are most often raped by someone they know, not by a stranger who leaps out of the bushes or climbs through a bedroom window in the middle of the night. Acquaintance or "date" rape remains one of the most underreported violent crimes and may account for 80 percent of sexual assaults.

Victims are especially reluctant to report date rape because of the murky circumstances that frequently surround a crime involving two people who may have had a sexual relationship in the past. When the victim knows the assailant, it fuels suspicions that she in some way encouraged or consented to the attack.

Victims face other formidable obstacles as well. Police are often dubious about what really happened, and prosecutors fear no jury will convict. A 1983 study of more than 900 sexual assault complaints filed in Indianapolis showed that men often were not charged when the victims' behavior raised the question of consent.

The author of the study, Gary D. LaFree, a sociology professor at the University of New Mexico, found that charges were rarely filed if the victim delayed in filing a report, if she had a prior relationship with the suspect and if no weapon was involved.

Those same obstacles confronted the Washington real estate agent. Her three-year odyssey through the legal system at times left her feeling abandoned by her friends and family and paralyzed by self-doubt. What makes her case unusual and noteworthy is the fact that she persevered and was successful in pressing her case.

At her request, only the victim's first name, Donna, is being used in this story. Although her case is a matter of public record, The Washington Post does not publish the names of rape victims without their consent.

Jeffrey Darrell Smith, the 36-year-old man who assaulted her, has been confined to the mental health unit of the D.C. Jail since May.

His attorney Steven Kiersh said Smith is being held there because he is a recovering alcoholic and has a recurring psychiatric problem that must be treated with lithium, a drug commonly used to treat manic depression.

Corrections officials and Smith's lawyer declined to allow Smith to be interviewed.

This story is based on court records as well as interviews with Donna, her counselors, police, Smith's lawyer, and U.S. Attorney Jay B. Stephens. Judge Warren King, who presided over the case in D.C. Superior Court, did not return several telephone calls requesting comment about the case. And Stephens declined to permit Paul Howes, the assistant U.S. attorney who prosecuted the case, to be interviewed.

Smith was indicted on one count of rape and one count of sodomy. As part of an agreement made during the first day of his trial last February, he pleaded guilty to sodomy, which carries a maximum prison sentence of 10 years. Rape, a more serious charge, carries a prison term of 15 years to life.

Since 1987, the case has dominated Donna's life. "I thought about the rape, about what to do about it, every single day," she said. "I needed to do something."
Would Anyone Believe Her?

From the beginning, Donna wondered whether anyone would believe she had been raped.

Several hours after she reported the assault, she said, the detective who questioned her at D.C. police headquarters asked whether she really wanted to put her "boyfriend" in jail.

A week later, her father accused her of provoking the attack by having a man in her apartment and by being sexually active. Several male friends advised her to forget the rape: She was sexy, they said, and had to expect trouble.

Donna typifies many young women who gravitate to the Washington area after college, eager to establish their careers. She grew up in a small town in upstate New York, graduated from college and worked in Boston and Denver before deciding to move to the District, then in the midst of a real estate boom.

When she arrived in 1986, she knew virtually no one. In order to meet people and save money, she moved into a group house in Bethesda. Through a housemate, she met Smith, the son of an administrative law judge who lived with his parents in Potomac. Tall and slim, Smith was a restaurant manager and Donna thought he was "kind . . . a nice guy."

In January, five months after they met, they began dating and had sex. After a month, Donna broke off the relationship, saying she just wanted to be friends. After that, they saw each other infrequently but amicably. The night of the attack, May 15, 1987, was the first time Donna had seen Smith in a month.

During her initial interview with the detective assigned to the Sexual Assault Unit, Donna talked about her prior relationship with Smith. "The detective kept saying, 'You don't want to send your boyfriend to jail for life, do you? Because that's what's going to happen' . . . I kept saying: 'You know, he's not my boyfriend,' " she recalled.

The detective declined to be interviewed.

The next morning, hours after the attack, Donna drove to the emergency room of Suburban Hospital in Montgomery County. Hospital records show that a doctor found bruises around her mouth and hemorrhaging around her eyes. The doctor, noting on the hospital chart that Donna said she had been raped, told her that the eye injury was a result of blood vessels that burst, a condition that results from a lack of oxygen.

The following day, Donna said, Smith called her at home. As she later testified in a deposition, Smith told her he wanted to apologize for his behavior. He said he had been drinking. He said he didn't know what had come over him; he did not use the word rape.

The following weekend, Donna's parents drove down for a visit. Her relationship with her father, always tenuous, quickly deteriorated. During an argument, Donna began crying and blurted out that she had been raped.

His response left her feeling rejected. If Smith had really raped her, she said her father asked, why hadn't she had him arrested?

To her amazement, Donna heard herself making excuses for Smith: He was her friend, he had threatened to kill himself, she didn't want to send someone she knew to jail for life.

Her sense of reality was slipping, she realized later, a phenomenon psychologists say is not uncommon among date rape victims. While medical evidence—the bruises around her mouth and eyes—indicated she had been assaulted, Donna said she felt "a little scared I had done something wrong. Why had I let him in my apartment? It was like I was half asleep at the time. I thought, 'Did I lead him on?'"

Getting Angry, Taking Action

The first person who believed Donna was Peggy Speaker, a colleague at the real estate office where Donna worked and on whom she relied for motherly advice.

A few days after the attack, Donna told Speaker about the assault. A petite, dark-haired woman who usually came to work meticulously dressed and manicured, Donna that day "looked awful," Speaker recalled. Her hair was limp, she wore no make-up and looked like she had just dragged herself into the office.

Speaker was most alarmed by Donna's demeanor. Usually vivacious, she seemed frightened and withdrawn. "Somebody had to say, 'You're okay,' and allow her to get angry . . . instead of feeling that she deserved it," Speaker said.

Speaker pushed Donna to do something. She urged her to call the U.S. Attorney's office, to follow up on the police report and to track down information during the investigation that could strengthen her case. The two frequently discussed what Donna could do.

A week later, Donna returned to the police sexual assault unit and filed a formal complaint against Smith. Because the first detective had been promoted, she was assigned a new detective.

Detective Michael Sullivan said he interviewed Donna for hours; her account never varied. With her help, Sullivan contacted another woman Smith knew. Sullivan said she told him she had been sexually assaulted by Smith months before Donna was attacked but had never reported it because she was an illegal alien. Sullivan said by then he was convinced Donna had been raped.

Kiersh, Smith's lawyer, disputed the allegation that Smith had attacked another woman. "That case was never presented to a grand jury and was never presented for a criminal charge. If the U.S. Attorney's Office wanted to move on it, it could have. But it didn't, so there must not have been enough evidence," he said.

Speaker also urged Donna to seek counseling at the D.C. Rape Crisis Center. At first, she resisted. But she began feeling frightened, especially at work whenever she had to show a house to a male client.

Home was no refuge. "I was afraid," she recalled. "I'd look under my bed. I'd look in the closets. I lived in a first-floor apartment then, and I was scared." Most of all, she was terrified that she would run into Smith on the street.

Two months after the attack, Donna made an appointment to see a counselor at the rape crisis center, which operates out of a church near Dupont Circle.

From the outset, Donna told counselor Debbie Aubinoe that she wanted Smith to be prosecuted. Even if he were not convicted, Donna told Aubinoe, she would feel that she had done everything she could.

"She kept saying that she trusted [Smith]," Aubinoe said. "It was a real violation of trust. The physical abuse and the rape itself were horrendous, but I think the breaking of trust was just as devastating. You expect a total stranger to rape you, not someone you know."

Going to Court

In most rape cases, prosecutors say, there are usually two successful defenses: either the police arrested the wrong man, or the woman agreed to have sex and changed her mind after the fact. In Donna's case, they were worried that Smith would contend that she consented.

Donna waited more than a year before her case went to the grand jury. For months, prosecutors in the U.S. Attorney's office debated whether to seek an indictment. The same issues Donna faced during the initial police interview were paramount: She had admitted Smith to her apartment, she had had sex with him previously and he hadn't used a weapon during the attack. In August 1988, more than a year after she reported the rape, assistant U.S. attorney Paul Howes presented her case to the grand jury, which voted to indict.

Every month for the next year, Donna called Howes and detective Sullivan to ask when Smith would be charged and when her case would go to trial. But resistance was building within the prosecutor's office to spending time and money on a trial that, experience had shown, was a poor risk.

Sullivan said that the case bogged down over the same questions that threaten any date rape prosecution: Would a jury find fault with a former boyfriend who demanded sex? Was the case winnable? Had Donna really been raped?

"There's a big problem with date rape. And it's a really big problem when it's brought into the court system. People are always going to question what happened and what her motive is in bringing the case to trial," Sullivan said recently.

As the months dragged by without a court date, Donna, like many victims of date rape, felt tremendously ambivalent.

"So many times, I would cry about it and say he should go to jail. But I really can't stand the thought of jail. I don't believe it does anyone any good. I think anyone who goes to jail ends up worse off," she said.

Crisis center counselor Karen Erdman said the internal struggle Donna faced is typical. "Even if the police and the district attorney are being as helpful as they can be, there's a struggle through each step of the process. The amount of discouragement that [Donna] had would have discouraged most survivors. She was more persistent than most."

Donna kept pressure on the U.S. Attorney's office with visits and phone calls. After nearly a year, she decided to drive from her Northwest Washington office to talk to Howes about the status of her case. As she was rounding the corner near the U.S. Attorney's office, she saw Stephens, the U.S. Attorney, walk out the door and climb into a cab.

She followed him for blocks. At the Willard Hotel, the cab stopped. She quickly double-parked and ran after him as he walked toward the hotel. "Are you Jay Stephens?" she recalled asking. "Because if you are, I want to talk to you. I'm a rape victim and want to know why you won't prosecute my case."

Stephens, surprised but polite, talked to her for a few minutes. He promised to call her back.

And he did. In a recent interview about Donna's case, Stephens said "doesn't usually get involved in individual cases," but her case highlighted a potential problem with the way his office handled the approximately 125 rape cases it prosecutes annually.

"Experience leads you to believe these are very difficult cases to prosecute," Stephens said. "But that alone should not preclude prosecution."

Stephens would not comment on the internal discussions in his office about the case or permit Howes to be interviewed. He said that Donna's demeanor, which he called "very genuine and credible and victimized" plus the strength of the evidence led him to believe in the case.

Because more than a year had elapsed since the first grand jury voted to indict, a new grand jury reviewed the case. On Aug. 16, 1989, it issued indictments and this time, the U.S. Attorney's office moved for a trial.

A trial date was set and then postponed. Finally, on Feb. 20, 1990, the first day of the trial before opening arguments in D.C. Superior Court, Smith pleaded guilty to one count of sodomy.

Prosecutors and defense attorneys say that plea bargaining is common in criminal cases and is, in fact, a necessary part of the judicial system. In many cases, such dispositions save money, ease the already swamped court docket and ensure punishment. About 1,800 trials were held last year in D.C. Superior Court, in which 20,000 felony and misdemeanor cases were filed. Roughly 90 percent of these cases were settled by plea bargain agreements.

In rape cases, the percentage settled without trial is even higher, according to Stephens. In Donna's case, however, the plea was a bit unusual. Prosecutor Howes and Kiersh, the defense lawyer for Smith, asked the judge not to sentence Smith to jail.

Both lawyers requested that he be placed in the John Hopkins University Sexual Disorders Clinic or a similar program to receive counseling, including treatment for alcohol abuse. Maryland Department of Transportation records show Smith was arrested by Montgomery County police and convicted of drunk driving in 1983 and again in 1986.

"It's not common," Stephens said about the plea agreement. "But a disposition of a case tries to take into account as many interests as it can . . . these were two people who knew each other, and [Donna] expressed concern about his health. The disposition reflected her concern and interest in him."

On May 9, King listened to the participants in the case: Howes, Smith's attorney Kiersh, and Smith himself.

According to court records, Smith told the judge that he agreed with the prosecution's statement that he "used force . . . and in the course of the encounter had sexual intercourse with [Donna] and forced her to commit oral sodomy."

By accepting the plea, Smith said, he was making "an act of contrition in the only way that I know how, to the victim in this case."

But it turned out that King was not willing to accept all the terms of the plea bargain agreement. According to the transcript, he said that he viewed the issues raised by Donna's case "a bit differently" than either the prosecution or the defense did.

"I see a serious assault committed by you," the judge said to Smith. "It strikes me that the conduct in this case calls for a period of incarceration."

As Donna watched in astonishment, Smith was handcuffed and sent to jail for a term not less than 2 1/2 years and not to exceed 7 1/2 years. He is eligible for parole in 2 1/2 years.

Smith's attorney has now asked the court to reduce the jail sentence on grounds that Smith was receiving treatment for manic depression at the time of the assault and had stopped taking his lithium a month earlier.

Donna has moved five times since she was raped. She has trouble trusting men who want to know her better. She has dated a few men for months at a time and has had sexual intercourse since the rape. But she often ends up crying afterward.

Donna talks confidently, however, about the future. Like many people who have survived traumatic experiences, she wants to help others who are coping with the same ordeal. She has been able to reconcile with her father about the rape. "We kind of made up," she said. "I think at the time he thought he was supposed to be protecting me and instead he took it out on me."

"I feel like I've been in an emotional coma for the past three years," she said. "Sometimes I think, I just want to be normal. And I try so hard."

September 4, 1990

Sex, Lies, and Conversation

Why is it So Hard for Men and
Women to Talk to Each Other?

DEBORAH TANNEN

I was addressing a small gathering in a suburban Virginia living room—a women's group that had invited men to join them. Throughout the evening, one man had been particularly talkative, frequently offering ideas and anecdotes, while his wife sat silently beside him on the couch. Toward the end of the evening, I commented that women frequently complain that their husbands don't talk to them. This man quickly concurred. He gestured toward his wife and said, "She's the talker in our family." The room burst into laughter; the man looked puzzled and hurt. "It's true," he explained. "When I come home from work I have nothing to say. If she didn't keep the conversation going, we'd spend the whole evening in silence."

This episode crystallizes the irony that although American men tend to talk more than women in public situations, they often talk less at home. And this pattern is wreaking havoc with marriage.

The pattern was observed by political scientist Andrew Hacker in the late '70s. Sociologist Catherine Kohler Riessman reports in her new book "Divorce Talk" that most of the women she interviewed—but only a few of the men—gave lack of communication as the reason for their divorces. Given the current divorce rate of nearly 50 percent, that amounts to millions of cases in the United States every year—a virtual epidemic of failed conversation.

In my own research, complaints from women about their husbands most often focused not on tangible inequities such as having given up the chance for a career to accompany a husband to his, or doing far more than their share of daily life-support work like cleaning, cooking, social arrangements and errands. Instead, they focused on communication: "He doesn't listen to me," "He doesn't talk to me." I found, as Eacker observed years before, that most wives want their husbands to be, first and foremost, conversational partners, but few husbands share this expectation of their wives.

In short, the image that best represents the current crisis is the stereotypical cartoon scene of a man sitting at the breakfast table with a newspaper held up in front of his face, while a woman glares at the back of it, wanting to talk.

Linguistic Battle of the Sexes

How can women and men have such different impressions of communication in marriage? Why the widespread imbalance in their interests and expectations?

In the April issue of American Psychologist, Stanford University's Eleanor Maccoby reports the results of her own and others' research showing that children's development is most influenced by the social structure of peer interactions. Boys and girls tend to play with children of their own gender, and their sex-separate groups have different organizational structures and interactive norms.

I believe these systematic differences in childhood socialization make talk between women and men like cross-cultural communication, heir to all the attraction and pitfalls of that enticing but difficult enterprise. My research on men's and women's conversations uncovered patterns similar to those described for children's groups.

For women, as for girls, intimacy is the fabric of relationships, and talk is the thread from which it is woven. Little girls create and maintain friendships by exchanging secrets; similarly, women regard conversation as the cornerstone of friendship. So a woman expects her husband to be a new and improved version of a best friend. What is important is not the individual subjects that are discussed but the sense of closeness, of a life shared, that emerges when people tell their thoughts, feelings, and impressions.

Bonds between boys can be as intense as girls', but they are based less on talking, more on doing things together. Since they don't assume talk is the cement that binds a relationship, men don't know what kind of talk women want, and they don't miss it when it isn't there.

Boys' groups are larger, more inclusive, and more hierarchical, so boys must struggle to avoid the subordinate position in the group. This may play a role in women's complaints that men don't listen to them. Some men really don't like to listen, because being the listener makes them feel one-down, like a child listening to adults or an employee to a boss.

But often when women tell men, "You aren't listening," and the men protest, "I am," the men are right. The impression of not listening results from misalignments in the mechanics of conversation. The misalignment begins as soon as a man and a woman take physical positions. This became clear when I studied videotapes made by psychologist Bruce Dorval of children and adults talking to their same-sex best friends. I found that at every age, the girls and women faced each other directly, their eyes anchored on each other's faces. At every age, the boys and men sat at angles to each other and looked elsewhere in the room, periodically glancing at each other. They were obviously attuned to each other, often mirroring each other's movements. But the tendency of men to face away can give women the impression they aren't listening even when they are. A young woman in college was frustrated: Whenever she told her boyfriend she wanted to talk to him, he would lie down on the floor, close his eyes, and put his arm over his face. This signaled to her, "He's taking a nap." But he insisted he was listening extra hard. Normally, he looks around the room, so he is easily distracted. Lying down and covering his eyes helped him concentrate on what she was saying.

Analogous to the physical alignment that women and men take in conversation is their topical alignment. The girls in my study tended to talk at length about one topic, but the boys tended to jump from topic to topic. The second-grade girls exchanged stories about people they knew. The second-grade boys teased, told jokes, noticed things in the room and talked about finding games to play. The sixth-grade girls talked about problems with a mutual friend. The sixth grade boys talked about 55 different topics, none of which extended over more than a few turns.

Listening to Body Language

Switching topics is another habit that gives women the impression men aren't listening, especially if they switch to a topic about themselves. But the evidence of the 10th-grade boys in my study indicates otherwise. The 10th-grade boys sprawled across their chairs with bodies parallel and eyes straight ahead, rarely looking at each other. They looked as if they were riding in a car, staring out the windshield. But they were talking about their feelings. One boy was upset because a girl had told him he had a drinking problem, and the other was feeling alienated from all his friends.

Now, when a girl told a friend about a problem, the friend responded by asking probing questions and expressing agreement and understanding. But the boys dismissed each other's problems. Todd assured Richard that his drinking was "no big problem" because "sometimes you're funny when you're off your butt." And when Todd said he felt left out, Richard responded, "Why should you? You know more people than me."

Women perceive such responses as belittling and unsupportive. But the boys seemed satisfied with them. Whereas women reassure each other by implying, "You shouldn't feel bad because I've had similar experiences," men do so by implying, "You shouldn't feel bad because your problems aren't so bad."

There are even simpler reasons for women's impression that men don't listen. Linguist Lynette Hirschman found that women make more listener-noise, such as "mhm," "uhuh," and "yeah," to show "I'm with you." Men, she found, more often give silent attention. Women who expect a stream of listener noise interpret silent attention as no attention at all.

Women's conversational habits are as frustrating to men as men's are to women. Men who expect silent attention interpret a stream of listener noise as overreaction or impatience. Also, when women talk to each other in a close, comfortable setting, they often overlap, finish each other's sentences and anticipate what the other is about to say. This practice, which I call "participatory listenership," is often perceived by men as interruption, intrusion and lack of attention.

A parallel difference caused a man to complain about his wife, "She just wants to talk about her own point of view. If I show her another view, she gets mad at me." When most women talk to each other, they assume a conversationalist's job is to express agreement and support. But many men see their conversational duty as pointing out the other side of an argument. This is heard as disloyalty by women, and refusal to offer the requisite support. It is not that women don't want to see other points of view, but that they prefer them phrased as suggestions and inquiries rather than as direct challenges.

In his book "Fighting for Life," Walter Ong points out that men use "agonistic" or warlike, oppositional formats to do almost anything; thus discussion becomes debate, and conversation a competitive sport. In contrast, women see conversation as a ritual means of establishing rapport. If Jane tells a problem and June says she has a similar one, they walk away feeling closer to each other. But this attempt at establishing rapport can backfire when used with men. Men take too literally women's ritual "troubles talk," just as women mistake men's ritual challenges for real attack.

The Sounds of Silence

These differences begin to clarify why women and men have such different expectations about communication in marriage. For women, talk creates intimacy. Marriage is an orgy of closeness: you can tell your feelings and thoughts, and still be loved. Their greatest fear is being pushed away. But men live in a hierarchical world, where talk maintains independence and status. They are on guard to protect themselves from being put down and pushed around.

This explains the paradox of the talkative man who said of his silent wife, "She's the talker." In the public setting of a guest lecture, he felt challenged to show his intelligence and display his understanding of the lecture. But at home, where he has nothing to prove and no one to defend against, he is free to remain silent. For his wife, being home means she is free from the worry that something she says might offend someone, or spark disagreement, or appear to be showing off; at home she is free to talk.

The communication problems that endanger marriage can't be fixed by mechanical engineering. They require a new conceptual framework about the role of talk in human relationships. many of the psychological explanations that have become second nature may not be helpful, because they tend to blame either women (for not being assertive enough) or men (for not being in touch with their feelings). A sociolinguistic approach by which male-female conversation is seen as cross-cultural communication allows us to understand the problem and forge solutions without blaming either party.

Once the problem is understood, improvement comes naturally, as it did to the young woman and her boyfriend who seemed to go to sleep when she wanted to talk. Previously, she had accused him of not listening, and he had refused to change his behavior, since that would be admitting fault. But then she learned about and explained to him the differences in women's and men's habitual ways of aligning themselves in conversation. The next time she told him she wanted to talk, he began, as usual, by lying down and covering his eyes. When the familiar negative reaction bubbled up, she reassured herself that he really was listening. But then he sat up and looked at her. Thrilled, she asked why. He said, "You like me to look at you when we talk, so I'll try to do it." Once he saw their differences as cross-cultural rather than right and wrong, he independently altered his behavior.

Women who feel abandoned and deprived when their husbands won't listen to or report daily news may be happy to discover their husbands trying to adapt once they understand the place of small talk in women's relationships. But if their husbands don't adapt, the women may still be comforted that for men, this is not a failure of intimacy. Accepting the difference, the wives may look to their friends or family for that kind of talk. And husbands who can't provide it shouldn't feel their wives have made unreasonable demands. Some couples will still decide to divorce, but at least their decisions will be based on realistic expectations.

In these times of resurgent ethnic conflicts, the world desperately needs cross-cultural understanding. Like charity, successful cross-cultural communication should begin at home.

Deborah Tannen, professor of linguistics at Georgetown University, is the author of You Just Don't Understand: Women and Men in Conversation, *published this month by William Morrow.*

June 24, 1990

Sexual Orientation 8

Many people continue to regard the male role of breadwinner and the female role of homemaker/caretaker as predominant in our society. As a result, there is little knowledge of gay and lesbian relationships, the subject of the articles in this chapter.

The first articles examines the military's last social taboo, that of prohibiting homnosexuals in uniform, and discharging those "found out" regardless of the length and capability of their previous service. The second article explores how vulnerable gays are to violence directed against them. As one gay person says, "If you're a perpetrator, and you want to prey on a class of citizens, lets face it, we're the best ones."

The third article discusses the efforts of Lotus, a leading software company, to extend benefits for partners of homosexual employees. The fourth article gives us insight into the private lives of a lesbian couple and their commitment to each other. The final article deals with the relationship between a young boy and his gay father who now suffers from AIDS.

Military's Last Social Taboo

13,307 Discharged Since '82 for Homosexuality

LYNNE DUKE

A 30-year military career—including a Bronze Star from Vietnam, a doctoral degree in nursing, a Meritorious Service Medal and an entry in Who's Who of American Women—began unraveling two years ago when a Defense Department investigator asked Army National Guard Col. Margarethe Cammermeyer if she was homosexual. Cammermeyer answered: "I am a lesbian."

Those words, spoken in an interview required of officers seeking top-level security clearance, closed off Cammermeyer's chance of becoming the National Guard's chief nurse. Last month, she stood before a panel of four Army colonels assembled to determine her fate. Despite her "superb leadership" that had been a "great asset" to the military, they said, the Pentagon prohibition against homosexuals in uniform left them no choice but to recommend that Cammermeyer's military career be terminated. It was, according to one of the colonels quoted in a transcript, their "sad duty."

When the final paperwork is approved by the Department of the Army, Cammermeyer will join the more than 13,000 service people who have been discharged from the military over the past decade through the enforcement of a policy that gay-rights activists and other opponents say is based on discrimination and homophobia. Pentagon officials, generally backed by the courts, defend it as necessary "to maintain discipline, good order and morale."

The Defense Department publicly defended the policy this summer when a firestorm of criticism from gay-rights advocates erupted after the honorable discharge of Air Force Capt. Greg Greeley was put on hold, and Greeley was interrogated for hours, because he marched at the helm of the annual Lesbian and Gay Pride Parade here. Reps. Gerry E. Studds and Barney Frank, Massachusetts Democrats who are homosexual and advocates for gay rights, have called along with others for the Pentagon to abandon its policy.

Early this month, the controversy swirled again when a gay-oriented magazine, the *Advocate,* published an article saying that a high-level civilian Pentagon official is gay. The article, and gay-rights organizations, charged that it was hypocritical for the Pentagon to allow the official to remain in his job while homosexual uniformed personnel are routinely discharged.

In congressional testimony and in a television interview, Defense Secretary Richard B. Cheney defended the policy, saying he did not think it "fundamentally wrong for us to make a distinction between civilian and military personnel." But he noted he had "inherited" the policy, and called the traditional Pentagon argument that homosexuals are a security risk "a bit of an old chestnut."

Gay-rights advocates and others felt Cheney was distancing himself. But Christopher Jehn, assistant defense secretary for force management and personnel, said in an interview last week that Pentagon officials are not reviewing the policy and have no plans to review it.

Jehn defended the policy more forcefully than his boss.

"The fundamental thing I think everybody needs to understand is that the military is a conservative organization" reluctant to make changes unless the outcome is assured, Jehn said. "And what people are asking now is that the military become some sort of social science laboratory, and very frankly our first and foremost job is not to advance social causes, however meritorious they may be."

Asked to describe the basis for the Pentagon's belief that homosexuals are detrimental to military order, Jehn said the evidence "is not systematic in the scientific sense, but is based on a professional judgment of military leadership."

"The classic example, of course, is an individual on a ship or in an infantry battalion who winds up deciding, for whatever motives, to proposition or come on to some of his colleagues," he said. "Those kinds of situations inevitably have led to a breakdown in discipline, often fighting or disruption of some kind. And that, while I wouldn't say it's common, is something that has happened often enough to be in the minds of senior military officials when they think through the consequences of changing this policy."

Gay-rights advocates, homosexuals who have been discharged from the service and other opponents say sexual conduct of homosexuals in the military could be governed by the same rules that govern heterosexual conduct.

But Jehn said same-sex fraternization would be more problematic than that between men and women because it would be more difficult to control.

Homosexuals who want to join the military must lie on their enlistment papers, where they are asked if they are homosexual. As part of the necessary concealment, some enter into sham marriages. If they are discovered, their military careers are over.

Cammermeyer, 49, a neuro-science specialist at the American Lake Veterans Affairs Medical Center near Seattle, knew her career was over as soon as she acknowledged her lesbianism in the 1989 interview. She said she was not a lesbian when she enlisted 30 years ago. She married, had four sons and was divorced before realizing in the early 1980s that women were her sexual preference, she said. She considered it, she said, a "very private, very personal" identity that "had no bearing on my work."

When she admitted it to the investigator, she did not consider her case a cause. Now, however, "I'm hoping that the fact that I, as a senior military person, have come out . . . that perhaps it will enable people to see that we are not out of the ordinary, that homosexuality is a part of life, it is a part of our society, and currently that homosexuals are probably the most discriminated against group here in the United States," she said.

Lawrence J. Korb, a former assistant secretary of defense in the Reagan administration who testified on Cammermeyer's behalf, said in an interview: "Here is a woman who goes to Vietnam, gets a Bronze Star, gets thrown out for violating a policy enforced by people who skipped Vietnam. The ironies are incredible." Korb said he was referring to Cheney, who was of draft-eligible age during the Vietnam War but received numerous deferments and did not serve in the military.

Homosexuality in uniform may be the last social taboo facing the military. Blacks were integrated into the armed forces in the 1940s. Women were admitted in large numbers in the 1970s and '80s, and given limited combat roles in the '90s. Gay-rights advocates say they believe that the taboos surrounding homosexuals within the military also will fall.

Jehn said, however, that "opening the military to homosexuals would represent a more radical, a bigger change, a more momentous change in policy than the racial-integrating the military did in 1948."

But, he said, comparing the homosexual policy to past policies on blacks is "misleading." Blacks were treated differently because of what they were; homosexuals are treated differently because of what they do, he said.

"This is a situation where their behavior, the behavior of homosexuals, the behavior that they do not deny, contradict or argue with in any way, is viewed by a large segment of the population as not just distasteful but immoral, sinful. The Old Testament refers to it as an 'abomination,'" said Jehn, citing a verse out of Leviticus. He said the fact that homosexual activity is outlawed in more than half the states supports his characterization of American popular opinion.

To a lot of people, homosexuality is a "personal bother. . . . It's a personal, inner kind of negative feeling," said Army Col. Michael E. McAleer, who sat on the panel that recommended Cammermeyer's removal. "I know that there are great Americans who are homosexuals or lesbians and I do not dispute that."

But, he said, "We all take an oath to obey and fight and defend the Constitution and defend the beliefs of Americans." Part of what Americans believe, he said, is that homosexuality is "against Christian ideals."

Major, nationwide public opinion polls, however, have shown consistently over the past decade that slightly more than half of those surveyed said homosexuals should be allowed into the military and should not be discharged for their sexual preference.

The military prohibition against homosexuals states that their presence "seriously impairs the accomplishments of the military mission," and "affects the ability of the military services to maintain discipline, good order and morale . . . and to prevent breaches of security."

An internal Pentagon study, concluded two years ago but criticized internally as technically flawed and never officially released, discounted the theory that homosexuals are more apt to fall victim to blackmail.

That internal report, called "Nonconforming Sexual Orientations and Military Suitability," said it is a "reasonable assumption" that the number of homosexuals in uniform "may be as high as 10 percent," mirroring estimates of their numbers in the general population. Jehn said estimating the number was impossible because those in the military must hide their orientation.

The study concluded, "The military cannot indefinitely isolate itself from the changes occurring in the wider society of which it is an integral part."

But from 1982 through this past June, 13,307 men and women in all branches had been discharged for violating the policy, according to the Defense Department. Their discharges can be honorable, other than honorable, or dishonorable, depending on the circumstances of their cases.

Among those discharged in the past decade was Donald O'Higgins, 27, until 1986 a senior airman, son of an Army master sergeant who died in Vietnam. While stationed at Minot Air Force Base in North Dakota, O'Higgins lived two lives.

According to an Airman Performance Report dated April 15, 1985, his performance was "superb." "His potential at this point remains virtually limitless," Maj. John B. Mallory wrote. "I strongly recommend his retention and continued progression in the Air Force. Promote."

In off-duty hours, however, O'Higgins lived as a homosexual, and perhaps too much so, he said in retrospect. "There didn't seem to be a threat to us for being discharged because it didn't seem to us that they were actively pursuing the witch hunts that we had heard about. We let our guards down. We went to the NCO [noncommissioned officer] clubs on base and we danced together . . . and that was a big flaw."

When rumors of an investigation circulated, he attempted to hide his homosexuality behind the camouflage of marriage, he said in an interview. His bride was a good friend.

"We'd known each other for years," he said. "We suspected that there was some sort of a witch hunt happening. It scared us a lot and we got married as a way of covering up."

O'Higgins said he was caught in an investigation that netted 35 homosexual suspects. A sergeant claimed in an affidavit that O'Higgins had taken advantage of him at a party. O'Higgins said that although he had dated the sergeant, that specific allegation was untrue.

After O'Higgins was targeted for discharge, he said, he was transferred to Fairford Air Base in England, where upon his arrival "my new sergeant said, 'I'd like to show you around the base. I think the first place we'll start is the Office of Special Investigations,' " where O'Higgins said he was read his rights. He said he was segregated from other airmen, placed under guard, and eventually discharged with honors.

"I just think it's basic discrimination," said O'Higgins, now an events planner with the Human Rights Campaign Fund, which lobbies on behalf of gay rights.

Homosexuals are not among the classes of people protected from discrimination by the Civil Rights Act of 1964. Gay-rights legislation has been proposed in Congress for the past several years.

While it is against civil service regulations to fire someone merely because of sexual orientation, the military has been allowed to retain its absolute prohibition on homosexuality.

Until 1982, the policy prohibited homosexual acts, not homosexual orientation, but it was applied differently from branch to branch of the military services and some exceptions were allowed.

The courts, however, challenged the application of that policy in the case of Air Force Sgt. Leonard Matlovich, who was discharged in 1975. An appeals court ruled that the Air Force had not clarified possible exceptions that would have allowed Matlovich to remain in the service. Matlovich eventually settled his case out of court. Later, he died of complications of AIDS.

In 1982, the Pentagon adjusted the policy and made homosexuality, whether acted out or admitted, grounds for discharge, with no exceptions.

Since then, the courts generally have not tampered with the policy.

In the case of Army Sgt. Perry Watkins, who was denied permission to reenlist in 1982 on the grounds of his sexual orientation, the Supreme Court last year refused to hear an appeal of a ruling that favored his reenlistment. Watkins disclosed his homosexuality to the Army when he was drafted, but an examining psychiatrist apparently did not believe him, according to the court. The narrow ruling in the case did not examine the constitutionality of the Pentagon policy.

Also last year, the high court refused to hear the appeal of Miriam Ben-Shalom, an Army sergeant who argued that the efforts to bar her from reenlisting after she announced she was a lesbian violated her rights to equal protection and free speech.

The court last year also declined the case of James M. Woodward, a discharged Navy airman. A federal appeals court had rejected his request for reinstatement, saying the military policy "serves legitimate state interests."

As those cases went to the Supreme Court, Pentagon officials had braced themselves for a possible challenge, said Air Force Lt. Col. Doug Hart, a Pentagon spokesman. An internal memorandum prepared by the Headquarters Office of the Department of the Army proposed a revised policy that would have allowed homosexuals to join and remain in the military so long as they exercised "restraint and discretion." Because the court did not challenge the policy, the memo, prepared 18 months ago, "just didn't go any further than that," said Hart.

Because homosexuals are not afforded strict judicial scrutiny given groups protected under the Civil Rights Act, lawyers for discharged homosexuals say they have been hamstrung.

"What the courts have not allowed us to do is to look at and examine the basis of the policy," said Mary Newcomb of the Lambda Legal Defense and Education Fund. "What they have done is deferred to the military's judgment."

The policy can be changed by an act of Congress, an executive order of the president or by the secretary of defense.

Pressure for change is not likely to come from within the uniformed ranks, said Korb, who described the military's self-image as "a macho male occupation."

"The only way it's going to change is civilians have to do something about it just as they have to do everything," Korb said. "If you left it up to the military . . . it would be composed of white, single, heterosexual males . . . because then they wouldn't have all these quote-unquote other problems."

But Charles Moskos, a military sociologist and professor at Northwestern University, supports the policy as a necessity. If any change is to occur, it should be limited, he said, such as a return to the old policy of prohibiting homosexual acts. McAleer, the colonel from the panel that recommended Cammermeyer's removal, also has thought about this distinction and said, "The homosexual tendency that's not acted on is something that needs to be addressed."

Moskos said that because of the close and constant contact between members of the armed forces—in trenches, on ships, in barracks—the debate hinges on a question that heterosexuals should ask themselves:

"If you were compelled to live with a homosexual, what would you think? That's the question people have to answer," Moskos said.

August 19, 1991

Gay Groups Mount Offensive as Assaults Increase

GABRIEL ESCOBAR

The window at Remingtons—a bar with a predominantly gay crowd and a recent history of anti-gay violence—had no sooner been punched out by an angry Marine than the first call was made.

By 5:30 a.m. last Sunday, about two hours after the incident, the officer of the day at the Marine barracks had made the short trip to the bar in Southeast. Within hours, a Marine had confessed in writing and he and his two companions had replaced the glass.

On Wednesday, justice was meted out. Jason Lucas, 21, underwent a summary court-martial after pleading guilty to three charges stemming from the incident. His punishment includes 30 days in the brig, and commanders also are seeking his discharge because they say Lucas has been in trouble before. His two companions, whose names were not released, were reduced in rank, restricted to barracks, given additional duties and fined about $800 each.

In the community of gay activists in the District, the Resingtons episode was well known by Monday. Members of the different groups, from the controversial ACT-UP, which focuses on AIDS issues, to the National Gay & Lesbian Task Force to the local Gay & Lesbian Activists Alliance, learned of it through word-of-mouth or from eyewitnesses.

But beyond that, the incident itself illustrated a significant change in the way some gay and lesbian groups in the District are reacting to what they say are an increasing number of violent incidents. With greater frequency and some success, they are protesting and pressing for punishment, insisting that these incidents be recorded, and encouraging often hesitant members of the community to speak out when abused.

A telephone hot line established by the local alliance, for example, has recorded 15 physical assaults and 20 incidents of verbal harassment this year.

The incidents are only a fraction of the actual cases that occur because victims are still reluctant to come forward, gay activists say. In areas where gay people socialize—bars in Southeast, Northwest and Dupont Circle, the gay cruising area at Rock Creek Park known as P Street Beach—activists say gay men and women are being abused as never before.

"We believe it's worse, primarily because the community, on a daily basis, is getting more visible, more active and more out," said Tom Swift, chairman of the

D.C. Lesbian and Gay Anti-Violence Task Force, a coalition of gay groups. "And as that happens, people who hate us are doing something about it."

The most serious incident this year occurred in January in front of the Brass Rail, a popular black gay bar in Northwest. Michael Warren, 27, who activists said came to the aid of a transvestite being harassed by a group of young men, was shot and killed outside the club. Police, who said the shooting stemmed from an argument, later arrested an 18-year-old man and charged him with first-degree murder.

More recently—in the Dupont Circle area on Aug. 6—two juveniles driving on P Street NW verbally abused two gay men, apparently drove around the block and on the second encounter beat them with a club. The two juveniles were held by several witnesses and later charged with assault with a deadly weapon.

The beating, one of at least three in the neighborhood recorded during the last few months by ACT-UP, was an exception because it led to an arrest. What is more common, activists say, are the abuses that go unrecorded—because victims remain fearful and silent, the abuse is limited to a verbal attack or the assailant proves too elusive.

"If you're a perpetrator, and you want to prey on a class of citizens, let's face it, we're the best ones," said Mindi A. Daniels, president of the Gay & Lesbian Activists Alliance.

In the black gay community, which is less active than the white community, activists say abuses occur weekly and almost all go unreported. The extent of violence is not known—particularly against black lesbians—and no statistics are maintained.

The reasons for this are varied, but one of the main causes is the stigma many in the black community still place on gay men, said Philip E. Pannell, a longtime activist and member of the D.C. Council of Black Gay Men and Women.

The coalition has met with bar owners and asked for more security. But the greatest obstacle is still the reluctance among gay blacks to report these crimes—a reluctance gay blacks say runs much deeper than in the white gay community.

"If they are victims of things like harassment, victims of things like assault and robberies, they are more apt to not pursue matters for fear of having to come out," said Thomas Gleaton, president of the black coalition. "I think we could all recount a story of ourselves or of our friends who were either assaulted or robbed coming from a club."

As a result of the fear of reporting anti-gay crimes, statistics are not seen as a reliable gauge of the violence in the community. For example, U.S. Park Police have recorded three robberies, two attempted robberies and six assaults so far this year in the P Street Beach area, a slight increase over 1989. Gay activists insist those reports understate the extent of the problem.

The statistics do not say whether they were bias-related, and activists say victims are very reluctant to come forward because the area is known for gay cruising. The police department, whose cooperation with gay and lesbian groups is generally praised, records all sex-bias incidents in compliance with a new federal law, but a computer breakdown is not yet available, a spokesman said.

The increase in anti-gay violence locally is following a national pattern. Among the reasons cited are the increased visibility on the part of gay people, a better accounting of the violence, AIDS-related retribution and opposition from ultra-right conservatives. Entertainers such as Andrew Dice Clay and Public Enemy are also seen as contributors because of anti-gay sentiments expressed in their acts.

"The bottom line," says Robert Bray, spokesman for the National Gay Lesbian Task Force, "is that violence against gays and lesbians is increasing. We are a community under siege."

In response, the largest and most vocal local groups are fighting back. ACT-UP has been distributing whistles and pamphlets on weekends, urging gay people to protect themselves. There are plans to form a D.C. chapter of the Pink Panthers, a gay security patrol system that has been successful in parts of New York, where activists say anti-gay violence increased 110 percent in the first half of this year, as compared with 1989.

"Increasingly, it is very difficult to know anyone" who has not been abused, said Peter Thompson of the local chapter of ACT-UP. "That's what prompted us to start hitting the streets."

If there is some consolation, it has been the response gay activists have gotten for their protests. After a brawl involving Marines at Remingtons in June, activists insisted on a meeting with the commander of the barracks, Col. Peter Pace. Although there have been other clashes between Marines and gay people in Southeast, the last one on record at the barracks occurred eight years earlier, pointing to what Pace called a communication problem.

"We went out and we got to call all the leaders in the business community, and asked them to call us immediately if there was any incident involving the Marines," Pace said. "That's exactly what happened early Sunday morning. The message is out that we will not tolerate this."

Gay activists used the same tactic in June, when a group of gay people was harassed at Union Station by other patrons.

These advances aside, it is the increase in violence that preoccupies the gay community. Many still remember the 1988 beating of Rod Johnson, whose case led to the conviction last year of two men. Activists point to the lasting effects suffered by the abused, arguing they remain victims long after the court cases—if it gets that far—are settled.

"It can happen to anybody at any time," Johnson, who is 38 and still recovering, said last week. "It took a long time to come back to where I am today, a lot of frustrations and a lot of pent-up emotions. I just couldn't understand why someone could walk down the street with a baseball bat and beat somebody."

September 2, 1990

Firm Widens Benefits for Gay Employees

Lotus is Largest Company to
Make Workers' Partners Eligible

SANDRA SUGAWARA

Lotus Development Corp., one of the nation's leading computer software companies, is offering partners of homosexual employees the same benefits that are available to the spouses of its married workers making it the largest private company in the country to take this step.

"I think it's a fairness issue and an equity issue," said Russ Campanello, Lotus vice president of human resources. He added that Lotus hopes the new policy will help the Cambridge, Mass.-based company, best known for its 1-2-3 computer spreadsheet program, to attract and retain the best employees. "As it gets more and more competitive to hire the best employees, we want to be seen as the employer of choice," Campanello said.

Lotus estimates that about 10 percent of its 3,879 employees are homosexual, but said it does not expect all of them to have eligible partners. To become eligible for benefits, partners of homosexual employees and the employees themselves must sign an affidavit saying they intend to live together permanently. Company officials said they will view the affidavits just as they would a certificate of marriage.

Lotus said it is not extending the coverage to unmarried heterosexual couples because they have the option of marrying, while homosexual couples do not.

Eligible partners can then receive the entire range of employee benefits at Lotus, including medical and dental coverage, life insurance, relocation help, bereavement leave and overseas assignment benefits.

Lotus's new policy represents a radical change from the traditional view that employers are only responsible for an employee, the worker's legally wedded spouse and their children. It also reflects concerted efforts by gay and lesbian rights groups to force companies and the government to provide the same rights and benefits for gay couples that they provide for married couples.

"I think it's a breakthrough that a corporation as large as Lotus would extend benefits like this," said Ivy Young, an official of the National Gay and Lesbian Task Force. "It's not the first private-sector company to do this, but they are the largest, so it breaks a logjam."

Campanello said he has been swamped this week with calls from human resources executives across the nation wanting to know more about how the program would work. "It's something that employers are going to have to think about, whether a lot of them do it or not," said Nancy Jones, an employee benefit expert with A. Foster-Higgins & Co., a benefits consulting firm based in New York.

However, at least one employee benefits consultant said he did not foresee any other companies moving in the same direction. "It flies in the face of what most employers are concerned with today, which is the galloping increase in the costs in health care," said John Hoos, a partner at Hewitt Associates, an employee benefit consulting firm in Lincolnshire, Ill.

In particular, Hoos said, Lotus is extending coverage to a group that has a significantly higher risk of AIDS, which makes the action even more of a financial risk.

Campanello, however, said that Lotus talked to the handful of municipalities that have extended benefits to homosexual employees and to the Vermont-based Ben & Jerry's Homemade Inc., which made similar changes two years ago.

"What they told us was [that] the expense issue was not something to be concerned with," Campanello said. He said a typical AIDS case costs a company about $50,000 in medical benefits, a typical heart attack costs $45,000 and cancer treatment can cost in the hundreds of thousands of dollars.

Nancy Edler, a benefits specialist with the city of Berkeley, Calif., which extended employee benefits to both homosexual partners and unmarried heterosexual partners in 1985, said the city's health insurance rates have not been affected by the move. Berkeley was the first municipality to offer benefits for homosexual partners. Likewise Carol Hickman, a benefits specialist at Ben & Jerry's, said the benefits change did not have any adverse effect on the company's financial health.

Lotus began considering the new policy, which was disclosed this week in the Boston Globe, two years ago after a group of gay and lesbian employees requested the change. Anne Canavan, one of those employees, said she was aware that no other large company had taken such a step, but she was hopeful that Lotus would agree with the employees' contention that it was an issue of fairness. "I'm extremely satisfied with the outcome," she said.

Campanello said Lotus's insurance company originally feared that the change would cost it more money. But he said the company was satisfied with Lotus's research showing that the risk would be minimal.

About a dozen municipalities, including Takoma Park and the District of Columbia, have extended some benefits to nontraditional families, although many of them do not involve payments of money. In the District, homosexuals are covered by the D.C. Family and Medical Leave Act, which entitles employees to as many as 16 weeks of unpaid leave every two years to care for a child or seriously ill family member. Takoma Park extends sick leave and bereavement leave to domestic partners.

Only a scattering of companies have extended such benefits to the partners of homosexual employees, and most are small or nonprofit organizations, such as Greenpeace, The Village Voice newspaper, the American Psychological

Association and the American Friends Service Committee. Before the Lotus announcement, the largest company to provide benefits to partners of homosexual employees was Montefiore Medical Center in New York City.

A group of gay and lesbian teachers in New York has filed a suit against New York City to force the city to permit them to register their partners for health and other benefits, and a lesbian has sued American Telephone & Telegraph Co. over the company's decision not to pay death benefits to her when her partner died, according to Lambda Legal Defense and Education Fund, which is involved in both lawsuits.

September 7, 1991

Private Lives

Ellen and Debbie—A Lesbian
Couple and Their Commitment

PATRICIA F. SINGER

When the invitation came, some of the recipients recognized the inverted lambda symbol and some did not. Ellen and Debbie "invite you to participate in a ceremony of our commitment to each other," it read.

Debbie, who is my husband's niece, had announced her lesbianism to her parents eight years earlier, as a freshman at Brown University. She had "come out" by calling home with the news that she had joined the campus gay and lesbian club.

Now 25, Debbie works as a sex-equity counselor for the state of Rhode Island, helping high-school teachers and guidance counselors avoid steering girls into stereotypical careers such as nursing or teaching.

Since 1986, she has been living with Ellen, who is 24 and also a graduate of Brown. Sometime last year, the two decided they wanted to confirm and celebrate their relationship in a public ceremony.

Who in the extended family would be invited? Who would come? These quickly became political questions in Debbie's large, close, but rather proper family.

One uncle declined to bring his wife and 5-year-old daughter because, he explained, the child would be confused seeing two women get married. One grandfather said he would not be "comfortable" attending, then sent a sizable check. One grandmother, in her nineties, maintains official ignorance of her granddaughter's homosexuality; she was spared an invitation.

In the end, about a dozen family members drove to Providence for the occasion, including both Debbie's and Ellen's parents. My husband and I had been informed by our 20-year-old daughter that we were going. We set out from Silver Spring on I-95, stopping to pick her up at the University of Delaware. The weather cooperated with dazzling October sunshine all along the East Coast.

Guests arriving late Friday from out of town were invited to dine on Chinese carryout at a Brown professor's house. The professor, a fortyish woman who looked a little like Linda Evans, shared a big old house with her lesbian companion and her teenage son from a former marriage.

About 35 guests stood and spooned the Chinese food from paper plates, eyeing each other curiously. Which ones are lesbians? I found myself thinking. Her? Her?

Introductions and small talk smoothed over the initial awkwardness of the evening. Yet after the meal the guests drifted into three clumps, each talking in a separate room: relatives, lesbians, and old friends from high school.

One small gift caused an appreciative stir in all three groups: an autographed picture of Rep. Barney Frank, for whom I worked as a legislative assistant.

Frank (D-Mass.) is one of the two acknowledged homosexuals in Congress. (The other is Democratic Rep. Gerry Studds, also of Massachusetts.) Usually Frank avoids writing dedications on photos, but this time he had obligingly inscribed, "To Debbie & Ellen, Mazel Tov and Bon Chance."

Lifetime Event

The ceremony was scheduled for Saturday night at the Brown chapel. Ellen, who works as the university's AIDS information coordinator, had been able to rent the chapel and a reception room without paying the usual fee for damage insurance. The reason: The Brown administration had just decreed that homosexual commitment ceremonies qualify as "lifetime events," which receive insurance waivers.

However, Debbie said that when she talked with the florist and other suppliers for the occasion, she had pretended it was a standard heterosexual marriage. "We didn't register at the department store bridal registry," she said. "Too much of a hassle."

Of the 120 guests who filed into the chapel, about half were straight and half lesbian. Male and female high-school friends, mostly heterosexual, had come from Idaho, Maine and Montreal. One lesbian couple had flown in from California.

An artist/cousin arrived with her lesbian partner at the last minute. They had driven from New York City. "I'm awfully glad I made it on time," she whispered, sliding into a pew. "You know, this is new to me, too."

Ellen is Catholic and Debbie is Jewish, so originally they hadn't planned to have any members of the clergy in the ceremony. Then they decided to ask a sympathetic Unitarian minister, a woman, to officiate. Her role was mainly to make a few supportive remarks and stand on the altar in clerical robes as a benevolent visual anchor.

Debbie wore a black, off-the-shoulder cocktail dress, diamond earrings and a long braid laced with beads. Ellen, without jewelry or makeup, had chosen a white suit and black pumps.

The formalities started with a video showing the two in parallel shots at different ages: as toddlers, as snaggletoothed 6-year-olds, as adolescents. Then today, pictured together.

Next, a series of friends, gay and straight, approached the altar one by one and recited prayers or made statements of encouragement. Debbie's brother sang a song.

One woman guest delivered a short history of the risks earlier gays had taken to make it possible for today's generation to come out openly.

Like many couples, Ellen and Debbie had written their own vows. Ellen promised "communication, honesty, trust and laughter," adding, "We have fun in so many ways." Debbie said she has "a sense of happiness and rightness each day" with Ellen. Then they put on matching gold rings.

Breaking a Glass

To conclude the ritual, the two simultaneously stamped on a glass wrapped in tissue—the traditional end of a Jewish wedding—and hugged. ("I think we were concerned about kissing in front of other people," Debbie said later. "We didn't want to make people uncomfortable.") When the glass shattered, the audience broke into applause and rose for a standing ovation.

The reception featured a DJ and a supper orchestrated by Franco. When he heard about plans for the ceremony, he had volunteered his skills as a low-budget party-planner, borrowing tablecloths and concocting pasta salads.

As the music picked up, the atmosphere in the reception room became more and more joyous. Cameras flashed. Hugs and laughter alternated with exuberant dancing. For the lesbians present, it was a rare chance to celebrate who they were, and to have straight friends and family celebrate with them.

The sight of women dancing with women—mostly to rock music, but sometimes to slow, romantic numbers—appeared to leave the straight guests unperturbed. I danced with my daughter until I was breathless. Then three of us danced together—she, her father and I.

Finally my husband's mother, a formal woman of 74 who recently had a hip replaced, accepted my invitation and began to bob around the floor with me. Onlookers circled us and clapped in time.

Various Kinds of Distance

During the ceremony, Debbie had pointedly thanked "people who've traveled various kinds of distances to be here." Her father had perhaps traveled farthest.

For months before the ceremony, he vacillated about attending. His struggle to reconcile himself to Debbie's sexual orientation had been more difficult than his wife's. Held even seen a psychologist about it for a while.

But he had never seriously contemplated reacting as some parents do—by disowning his child. At family get-togethers, he welcomed Ellen and treated her warmly. And he had proudly related the news when she was elected to Phi Beta Kappa her senior year at Brown.

Still, the prospect of a lesbian wedding was too much. Too painful a contrast to the kind of marriage (Jewish husband-and-children) he had once visualized for his only daughter. Ultimately he compromised, saying he'd come to Providence for the weekend but he wouldn't attend the ceremony itself.

Nevertheless, just before the ceremony began, he appeared and sat down alone in the last pew. And then he observed what all the straight audience observed: rows of happy, well-educated, lively lesbian women; affection radiating between Debbie and Ellen; reminders of the obstacles and rejection they faced every day.

Sometime during the ceremony, he moved up among Debbie's friends. And when the time came for microphone thank-you's during the party, he took the mike. The room went silent.

"I wanted to be able to toast you, Debbie and Ellen," he started. "But I realized I couldn't do it without being at the ceremony. You have a hard road ahead of you. I wish it were easier. But I want you to know I think you're both fantastic, and you will have all my love and support."

Later a young lawyer from Providence, Gretchen, told him wistfully, "I wish all 100 parents represented here could hear you say that." The reception drew to a close. Franco appeared from the kitchen and urged departing revelers to take the leftover cakes home. Ellen walked into the hall to look for a water fountain. A security guard sat against the wall in a folding chair, looking bored. "Are you the bride?" he asked, brightening. "Well," she answered, "I'm one of the brides."

Ritual Resources

There are more than 20 predominantly gay religious groups in the Washington area, thus giving homosexual couples several options if they want a commitment ceremony.

Many of the congregations meet in buildings belonging to larger straight churches. Bet Mishpachah, a gay Jewish congregation, holds its services at Christ United Methodist Church in the District, for example.

Some gay churches are completely independent. One denomination, the Metropolitan Community Church, was formed in 1970 in Washington especially for homosexual men and women. It has two branches in the District and one each in Northern Virginia and suburban Maryland. The church has developed a special rite, called a "holy union," for same-sex ceremonies.

"We probably get at least one call a day asking for a holy union," says the Rev. Larry J. Uhrig, head minister of the MCC congregation on M Street NW.

Some congregations impose conditions on couples who want a ceremony performed under the their auspices. MCC requires that applicants for a holy union live together at least a year, and stresses in required meetings with the couple that the ceremony is a religious rite, not a legal one.

Bet Mishpachah hands out a formal "policy statement:" Couples must "have basic knowledge of Jewish law and tradition regarding marriage, commit to keeping a Jewish home," and provide for each other financially through wills, powers of attorney and beneficiary designations.

A number of straight congregations in the Washington area also invite homosexual members, and most of these welcome commitment ceremonies in their facilities.

Some Protestant denominations use special terms for these congregations: The United Church of Christ calls them "Open and Affirming" churches, the Presbyterians' designation is "More Light," the united Methodists' "Reconciling."

The Washington Blade, a weekly newspaper aimed at a homosexual audience, started a new column last August, partly to cover commitment ceremonies. "It was also an attempt to balance all the obituaries in the paper for people dying of AIDS," says assistant editor Colleen Marzek.

Marzek says the commitment ceremonies "are new to us in terms of how to cover them. We don't want to simply mimic what's done in a heterosexual wedding announcement. So, we try to look for the things that are unique to gay culture."

Last June, during the D.C. mayoral campaign, candidates Sharon Pratt Dixon and Charlene Drew Jarvis attended the commitment ceremony of Christopher Echols and Mauro Montoya at the Friends Meeting House on Florida Avenue NW. Echols, 34, is now a member of Dixon's staff. Montoya, 32, heads the Gertrude Stein Democratic Club, a gay political group with considerable clout in the District.

How much should a homosexual ceremony borrow from heterosexual wedding symbols and rites? Each gay couple debates the question and comes up with the degree of tradition that feels meaningful but not servile, according to Montoya. "There's no gay Miss Manners who's written a book on this yet," he says.

Beth Goodman, a Bet Mishpachah member, closely followed Jewish wedding tradition when she and her partner held their ceremony at the Washington Plaza Hotel in October.

Goodman, 41, works as a medical office assistant in Washington and also presides over the Fairfax Gay and Lesbian Citizens Association. Her 46-year-old companion keeps her own identity guarded because her job requires security clearance. They live in Arlington.

The couple stood under the Jewish wedding canopy for the service and read portions of their ketuba, or traditional marriage contract.

For couples just starting to plan their ceremony, two books offer advice and sample services: "The Two of Us," by Larry J. Uhrig (Boston, Alyson Publications, 1984, $6.95) and "Ceremonies of the Heart: Celebrating Lesbian Unions," edited by Becky Butler (Seattle, The Seal Press, 1990, $14.95).

Some homosexuals find commitment ceremonies unappealing. Joe Martin, a congressional aide who has lived with his partner for more than a decade, notes wryly, "I'm not the marrying kind."

One writer who often chronicles the gay community in Washington says she is "baffled" by the union phenomenon. "I have no desire to have a commitment ceremony with my lover; it wouldn't mean anything to me," she says.

For many other couples, though, the ceremonies are a step toward the fuller life they crave. Fred Strassburger, former president of the D.C. Psychological

Association, says his work with homosexual patients has led him to believe that "a public commitment is especially important to some gay people. They feel a symbolic statement strengthens their relationship, just like a heterosexual couple."

Beth Goodman explains that she and her partner "decided to do this just for ourselves. We have a very happy married life."

May 27, 1991

A Parent-Child Bond Faces a Final Test

Sorrow of AIDS Hits Home for
Virginia Teen with Gay Father

SUE ANNE PRESSLEY

Growing up for Kris Shelley meant Thanksgiving dinners where 14 men were the guests and his dad presided over a feast table of elaborate dishes, each cook trying to outdo the other. It meant talking to his father's gay partner about his career plans, then going to school and hearing his classmates laugh about "fag" jokes. It meant walking away when neighborhood kids would call his dad "a queer."

And now it means knowing that his father has AIDS and will probably die.

A long time ago, Kris, now a college freshman, realized what an unconventional—and in many ways, he believes, special—upbringing he had. After his parents' divorce when he was 9, he went to live with his father, Robert Shelley, of Alexandria, a chef who had decided he would no longer deny his homosexuality.

It was a household unlike any of his classmates' homes, and it taught him a lot, he said, about "accepting people the way they are." It's true there were times, when he was 13 or 14, that he would hesitate to invite his friends over. Suddenly, he could see things through their eyes—the calendars with the pictures of the male models, the two men lounging on the living room couch together watching TV—and he was afraid they wouldn't understand.

But there were also times when his father would say to him: "Is there anything in my life that has caused you pain? Do you wish things had been different?" And he would answer: "No, Dad, you're the best. I wouldn't trade you for anything." And the fact was, no one else was as much fun to be around.

It is sad for them to think that after all their years together—after proving, they say, that it makes no difference that a parent is gay—this disease would come and especially strike men of his father's lifestyle. The son is beginning his adult life at a time when the father, at 45, is preparing to lose his.

Many of their friends already have died, and for someone who just turned 19, Kris has had to say many good-byes. He still can't believe that Billy Hayes is dead, the man he jokingly called Mama Billy, who lived with them for three years in the mid-1980s, an overgrown child who preferred to stay home and play games rather than go to his messenger's job. Another dozen friends have died, men who spent holidays at Kris's house, played hours of Monopoly with him and gave him, a young heterosexual coming of age, new and varied definitions of what a man is.

Sometimes, late at night, in his dorm room at James Madison University, he worries about his father and what he too is going to have to go through. Robert Shelley has Kaposi's sarcoma, an AIDS-related skin cancer, and he has tested positive for a virus that causes blindness. In that way of parents, he already has tried to shield his child from his worst moments.

"My dad just told me that there was a time last September when he actually thought he was going to die," Kris said. "That really struck me, like, wow, so you tell me now. You didn't tell me then. Thanks a lot."

In a world where being different is both celebrated and reviled, Kris Shelley and his father are a rare duo. It is rare for openly gay men to have custody of their children, according to gay-rights groups. In all their years together, Kris and his father ran into only one other father-son team like theirs.

In fact, Shelley shared custody with Kris's mother—his homosexuality was not spelled out to the courts—but it became obvious soon after their 1982 divorce that Kris was out of control and needed a firmer hand. He recalls missing 80 days of school in the fourth grade, just sitting around his mother's house watching television, and then he went to live with his father, who ruled with an easygoing but strict style.

By the time Kris graduated from T.C. Williams High School last year, he was in the top 10 percent of his class, and now the fourth-grade burnout talks of becoming a pediatrician. He has continued to see his mother often, and he loves her very much, he said, but the central influence in his turnaround was his dad.

Robert Shelley says that he would have liked to have had six children and that he always enjoyed being a father and watching his small son's mind at work. He is a slight, mustachioed man who points to his graying hair and laments that it "used to be a beautiful head of red hair," and Kris says with a laugh that the only thing that ever embarrasses him about his father is his corny expressions. Talking about how he contracted AIDS, for example, Shelley said with an elaborate shrug, "You can drag a rabbit through a briar patch, but you can't say which briar stuck the deepest." That kind of thing makes Kris roll his eyes.

When Robert Shelley was 11 years old, he had his first sexual experience with a neighborhood boy in rural Pennsylvania. But, like many gay men of his time, he thought that his impulses were wrong and that he should marry and live a traditional life. His 1969 marriage to a woman he met at a Lutheran church was a full-blown ceremony with numerous attendants and ringing bells.

But six months after Kris's birth in 1973, he began a relationship with a male waiter at the Metropolitan Club, where he worked as a chef, and for the next several years, he said, he led a double life of great guilt. After the split, he was determined to live the way he had always secretly wanted; it was a misfortune he shared with many gay men to come out at a time when a strange virus was beginning its deadly course.

Although neither Kris nor his father went around advertising that Shelley is gay, other people would sometimes pick up on it and criticize the arrangement.

"I've been told by some good, strong, Christian people," Shelley said, "that I had no business raising a son."

And it is true that once in a while, especially during his early teenage years, Kris would find himself wishing he had brothers and sisters and a rollicking family "like the Brady bunch." Sometimes it struck him as odd to be grocery shopping with his dad and his dad's boyfriend, or riding with members of his dad's gay motorcycle club, all of them clad in black leather.

But most of the time, it didn't feel weird at all. It was just his life. "Being young and exposed so early, I didn't have any preconceived ideas about homosexuality, or about what makes a man a man," he said. "Other people might have told me it was wrong, but I didn't see anything bad. My dad was very good to me. He took care of me. I wanted him to be happy.

"I figured, well, everybody has their little differences."

Kris first noticed their friends getting sick three or four years ago. John-John or Sid would come over to visit, looking weaker and more shrunken each time. His father would get emergency phone calls and rush out to drive someone to the hospital. The lighthearted days of the elaborate feasts had come to an end.

"It hits me a lot more, the whole AIDS thing," Kris said. "In school, we read about things, and people come in who are infected and tell their stories. That's the closest most people would come to knowing a sick person. But I think living through it and watching people you like gradually getting worse, that's something that can really haunt you." One day a year ago, Robert Shelley noticed a purplish bruise on his leg, the first sign that his illness, diagnosed in 1986, had taken a grave turn. He talks about "not giving in to negatives" and makes an adventure out of his visits to the National Institutes of Health for treatment. "You know how it is, 'Everybody wants to go to heaven, but nobody wants to die,' " he said, breaking into song in a way that undoubtedly would make his son wince.

But, of course, Robert Shelley wants to see Kris graduate from college. He wants to be there for his wedding, and he would love to be a grandfather someday. The odds are that he won't live to witness any of those milestones in his son's life.

It is an ending that both are thinking about more and more now, the father as he feels himself getting weaker, the son as he tries to distract himself with rugby games and freshman chemistry labs. They both know that these are the last days of their life together.

"I dearly love my dad," Kris said quietly, his head bowed. He is not much of a crier.

March 24, 1992

Family 9

The traditional notion of marriage and family is a far cry from the realities of today, where family life is fraught with a variety of problems.

The first article explores an increasingly common phenomenon, that of multiple generations of a family living in the same household. This is brought out in part by prolonged life spans (due to advances in medical technology), and the tendency among couples to delay marriage and childbirth into their thirties (due in part to social and economic changes). Homelife in the United States is increasingly an experience that one sociologist calls "interwoven biographies", resulting in a variety of stressful pressures.

The second article discusses the effect of divorce on parents and children, and the effects this has throughout their lives. The third article explores one rarely reported aspect of spousal abuse, wife battering.

The final article deals with a relatively new alternative family form, the single-parent family.

Caring for Three Generations

Families Juggle Needs of Elderly, Young

BARBARA VOBEJDA

Jim McEuen was home sick the day his father died. He could have reached the hospital in a few minutes, but he first had to drive downtown to get his wife at work, then back to a Bethesda day-care center to pick up their son.

By the time he arrived at Holy Cross Hospital in Silver Spring, his father was in surgery.

"Shortly after I got there, they told me he was dead," McEuen said. "It was that delay that prevented me from saying goodbye to him."

McEuen tells this story often, matter-of-factly and without rancor, when he is asked about the simultaneous and often competing pressures he has faced as the son of elderly parents and the father of young children. The conflicting demands of that day, he said, epitomize what he calls "the new family dynamic."

McEuen, like many of his Baby Boom peers, is facing the new reality of dual responsibility—struggling to meet the needs of aging parents who have, in some cases unexpectedly, become less self-sufficient just as his family gears up to meet the demands of young sons.

Unlike families in the past, in which children were often into adulthood by the time their grandparents needed help, today's Baby Boomers are ever more likely to find themselves caring for both generations at once.

The growth of the so-called "sandwich generation" is the coincidental result of two demographic trends: prolonged life span, largely due to advances in medical technology, and the tendency among couples to delay marriage and childbirth into their thirties.

In the past, couples typically began having children in their twenties, and so when their parents became frail, at the age of 70, for example, the youngest generation was already into its twenties and less likely to be dependent.

But at the same time that social and economic changes have led couples to delay childbirth, life expectancy has increased. Men and women today will spend about twice as many adult years with a surviving parent than they would have in 1900.

Thus, despite the lingering expectation that generational dependencies should unfold in well-timed sequence, American home life is increasingly an experience that one sociologist calls "interwoven biographies." While this can mean a graceful

186

blending of young and old, the reality is often one of daily pressure in managing logistics, overwhelming responsibility and guilt over unmet expectations.

Families already frustrated in their search for the right day care for their toddlers may find themselves looking at the same time for a good "elder care" program for their parents. Weekend time must be parceled out between trips to the mall for school clothes and grocery shopping for grandparents.

There are medical bills for three generations. And the trauma of watching parents decline may only be heightened by the stress of dividing precious time among family members.

"The constant feeling is one of being stretched thin," McEuen said.

Jim and Caroline McEuen, both 42, waited until they were in their thirties to have their two sons, 9-year-old Jonathan and 3-year-old Ian. Jim McEuen's mother, Estelle, 72, is debilitated by a central nervous system disorder.

The demands of this demographic puzzle hit McEuen abruptly upon the death of his father three years ago. His mother needed full-time care immediately, his parents' home needed to be renovated and sold and, on the day of his father's funeral, the McEuens discovered they were going to have their second child.

Two weeks later, Estelle McEuen entered a nursing home in Olney. Two months later, Caroline McEuen's mother died of cancer. Later that year, Ian was born.

It was a period of turmoil and change that "we still haven't gotten over," McEuen said.

Today, family life has fallen into a more settled pattern, but one still fraught with the realities of constant duty.

McEuen, an editor at the International Monetary Fund, must take time from work to take his mother to the doctor. He prepares her taxes, shops for her and visits her on Sundays. It is a long drive, and by the time he gets home, it is often dark.

Jonathan regularly asks why his father must go, insisting instead that he stay home and play, or take him to a birthday party or Cub Scouts.

"He's a very understanding kid. He doesn't hold grudges," McEuen said. But he makes straightforward judgments, "and his judgment is that my mother makes too many demands.'

"That's the cost of being in the 'sandwich.' You try to balance, but sometimes you can't. . . . Where do the loyalties lie? They have to lie with the future and not with the past. It's not triage; we've been able to do both." But then he laughs: "Look at the metaphor. 'Sandwich generation.' What's in the middle? Chopped meat." Sociologists agree that the number of families with such dual responsibilities is greater than ever before, but estimates vary widely.

The Agency for Health Care Policy and Research, an arm of the Public Health Service, estimated last year that there are 3.6 million men and women with children under 15 who also take care of a disabled parent. That number represents 7.4 percent of parents with children in that age group.

The study counted only those people whose parents needed help with basic, daily activities, such as eating or dressing, and did not include families who provide less critical assistance, such as taking their parents shopping, or visiting regularly.

The Older Women's League estimates that nearly a third of women will give care to both elderly parents and children, and argues that women can expect to spend 18 years of their lives helping an aging parent and 17 years caring for children.

"The dependency burden has increased," said Jane A. Menken, a sociologist and demographer at the University of Pennsylvania, in a 1987 paper written with two colleagues. "Not only has time spent with old and young dependents increased, but so has the number of years with simultaneous obligations to both groups."

Another set of trends—the entry of women into the labor force and more single-parent families—have complicated the pressures, meaning there are fewer caretakers at home. Taken together, the demographics paint a chaotic family portrait.

Diane Krevolin lives in West Haven, Conn., with her husband, three children ranging in age from 11 to 5, and her 80-year-old mother, Evelyn Skornik, who suffers from what her daughter describes as dementia.

The household scene on weekday mornings is frenetic: Krevolin is up before 6 a.m., then wakes her mother, who must get ready for an adult day-care program.

Krevolin gets herself ready for her job as a supervisor in the state unemployment office, at the same time checking in often—as many as a dozen times a morning—to push her mother along. She wakes up the three children by 7 a.m., helps them get dressed and fed, makes their lunches, signs notes for school and is out the door by 7:45 a.m.

Her mother is picked up by a bus at about 8:20. And her husband, Daniel, a city planner in an anti-poverty agency, drops the children at their bus stop at 8:25.

After work, Diane Krevolin usually takes a child or her mother to an appointment, gets home by 5 p.m., makes dinner, helps with homework, gives baths and puts the children to bed.

"Then I do the dinner dishes and collapse, hopefully, by 11," she said.

Krevolin said the crush of family and work is complicated by her mother's disability—she barely communicates and is unable to care for herself. But Krevolin promised her father at his death that she would not put her mother in a nursing home.

"You have to do a lot of planning to pull it off," said Krevolin, who is 42. "It doesn't leave any time for spontaneity. It affects career decisions. my husband was out of work, and it meant we couldn't up and move" to follow his career, she said. "Sometimes, it's overwhelming."

Barbara Kane is co-founder of Aging Network Services in Bethesda, which helps families in which parents and children do not live near one another find appropriate care for elderly parents. She said those in the middle "feel like they have to be all things to both generations." But the solutions, including the option of having a parent move in, often are difficult.

Kane said families are grappling not only with the logistics of managing three generations but with the guilt of divided loyalties. "Sometimes my clients feel if they didn't have children, they could be more available" to their parents, "or if they didn't have elder care, they could be more available for the children."

November 24, 1990

Broken Children, Broken Homes

MEGAN ROSENFELD

You may remember the old joke about the elderly couple who come into a lawyer's office to arrange their divorce after 60-plus years of marriage. After learning that the aged duo are indeed serious and want only to be rid of each other, the lawyer says, "Pardon my asking, but if you guys are so unhappy with each other, why didn't you come to see me sooner?"

Their reply: "We wanted to wait until the children died."

Despite its gruesomeness, this gag usually gets a good laugh. But for some—the children of divorce—the laugh is bittersweet. The unhappy truth that emerges from the latest research is that in the long run, divorce is beneficial for the mismatched spouses, but intensely disturbing to the kids. For them, our soaring divorce rates are little comfort. In 1960, the number of marriages in the U.S. outnumbered divorces by nearly four to one; by 1970 it was three to one, by 1980 only two to one. The persistence of the divorce boom has enabled scientists to complete a substantial volume of research on the effects of divorce on children, including several long-term projects tracking their subjects into adulthood. Results vary by group, sex and age. But it now seems clear that:

The effects of divorce on kids, ranging from the mild to the disabling, last much longer than psychologists anticipated; and

Negative effects can be muted, and children can survive with healthier psyches, if the parents keep their hostilities under control, pay attention to their kids, and generally refrain from behaving like jerks.

Researchers have ceased to study divorce as a discrete event but see it rather as a complex process that starts before the actual separation and continues through successive disruptions: changes in residence and economic status; loss of the nonresident parent; adjustment to parental dating; remarriage and the introduction of stepfamilies and sometimes half-siblings.

Meanwhile, access to the custodial parent—usually the mother—is curtailed as she goes back to school or to work, is disabled by her own depression, alcohol use or despair, and reactivates (in many cases frenetically) her social life.

"For kids, the misery their parents may feel in an unhappy marriage is usually less significant than the changes [the children] have to go through after a divorce," says Neil Kalter, a psychologist at the University of Michigan who has spent several years developing support groups in public schools for children of divorce. "They'd rather their parents keep fighting and not get divorced."

The first two years following separation are generally considered the crisis period. Unfortunately, this is often the time at which the parents, preoccupied and consumed with their own life changes, are least able to help their children. These effects go on for years as the child continues to react, his family circumstances combining with the normal difficulties of growing up.

Judith Wallerstein and Joan Berlin Kelly, authors of the seminal work "Surviving the Break Up: How Parents and Children Cope with Divorce," found that few of the kids in their follow-up survey agreed with their parents' decision to divorce—even five years after the parents separated. (These results are part of the researchers' continuing study of 144 middle- and upper-middle class California children of divorce.) In a 10-year follow-up, published last month in the American Journal of Psychiatry, Wallerstein reported that among the 38 young people in the original study who were between 6 and 8 at the time their parents split, over half later viewed the divorce as "the central experience in their lives." A majority expressed "feelings of sadness or neediness, of a sense of their vulnerability," and were "burdened by intense worries about failure in present and future relationships . . . and by an overall sense of their own powerlessness."

As the Twig Is Bent

Several researchers have found that although divorce has no discernible influence on a child's academic achievement, it does affect his social and mental health. In a national survey of 699 children, John Guidobaldi of Kent State University and Joseph D. Perry of Tod Babies' and Children's Hospital (Youngstown, Ohio) found that children of divorced parents performed worse than children of intact families on 9 of 30 mental-health measures, showing more dependency, more irrelevant talk, withdrawal, blaming, inattention, decreased work effort and unhappiness. Several researchers have observed that children of divorce are over-represented among patients at mental health clinics.

Boys and girls, it seems, react to divorce in significantly different ways.

Mavis Hetherington of the University of Virginia, who surveyed 144 middle-class white children over a six-year period, found that in general divorce has more long-term effects on boys than girls, although girls have more problems with a mother's remarriage. She also found, in a study of girls between 13 and 17, that they sought attention from males more often than girls from intact or widowed families, had less self-esteem, and were more likely to be sexually active. Guidobaldi and Perry found that boys fared somewhat less well than girls in the mental-health measures.

Wallerstein and Kelly also noted a variety of sex differences. Girls whose mothers took the initiative in getting divorced coped better than their brothers. Eighteen months after the separation, they found that more boys than girls were still opposed to the divorce, more longed for their father, more felt rejected by him, and more were depressed. Boys between 9 and 12 at the time of the divorce were more likely to be angry (as opposed to depressed or withdrawn) and to retain that anger.

Girls, however, were more likely to be concerned about the family's economic situation, and were more likely to do well in school if they felt financially secure. Boys whose mothers did not work full-time were more likely to do well in school. However, girls often had delayed reactions to the divorce; these appeared when they hit the mine-field of adolescence. In her 10-year follow-up study, Wallerstein found that out of 38 subjects, five had dropped out of high school—all of them girls. Of the 24 young women in the sample, 8 (33 percent) had gotten pregnant out of wedlock and four had had at least one abortion; two had second abortions. Sixteen had a history of mild delinquency (usually drinking or drug use). Male misbehavior, however, was more serious: Four of 14 boys had been arrested more than once and two had served time in jail.

A "significant minority" of the girls expressed their insecurity, anger or lack of self-esteem in promiscuous sexual behavior, some deliberately gravitating to older men or a series of aimless relationships. One 20-year-old said, "I've had no limits and no control. I'm prepared for anything. I don't expect a lot. I just want to stay alive. Love is a strange idea to me. Life is a chess game. I've always been a pawn."

Kalter also found a higher rate of sexual activity, substance abuse and running away among adolescent girls, especially when the divorce occurred before elementary school and the father had departed. Other studies show that female children of divorced parents are more likely to have marital problems of their own, more likely to choose "inadequate husbands" and to be pregnant at their weddings.

Their Fathers' Daughters

Another survey of 40 white, middle-class midwestern girls in third and sixth grades found few academic differences between those whose parents had been divorced and those from intact families. But third graders scored distinctly lower than their intact-family counterparts on social and physical competence scales. These differences were not found among the sixth graders, however—perhaps, the researchers speculate, because the divorce is a relatively more recent event in the lives of the younger group.

A study of 84 women—half of them children of divorce—at an exclusive private college found that there was no dissimilarity in the two groups' academic achievements. The main difference was in their perception of masculinity and femininity: The 'D' group girls were more prone to see men as unfeeling and weak, and women as insensitive and immature, than were the 'I' (for intact) group. The D group members also felt less certain about their own chances of having a lasting marriage.

One theme that consistently and strikingly emerges from research on divorce and children is the significance of the father. Historically fathers have tended to downgrade their importance in their child's development, especially during the early years, but research into the effects of divorce shows this notion to be a myth. Whether the child be girl or boy, preschooler or adolescent or pre-pubescent, Dad's present behavior or absent neglect produces enduring psychic ramifications.

Even when a father has been undeniably rotten, children long for his presence and attention. The disruption of the relationship with a loving, attentive father is brutal, as the child perceives that the man who adored him has now left him flat. A good father can ameliorate the effects of a dysfunctioning custodial mother and augment the impact of a good one; even a less competent father provides a link that children seem desperately to need.

Wallerstein and Kelly describe a "passionate, persistent yearning of the children" for the father, especially in those 8 years old and younger. Although children will sometimes say they don't want to visit their father (in order to avoid fights between their parents), only 11 percent of the children in the study were either genuinely reluctant to see him or relieved that the presence of an overbearing, cruel or domineering father was removed from their lives.

Eighteen months after the divorce, children perceive the father with less respect; and half of the 9-to-12-year-old boys openly rejected him as role model. But by the five-year mark, there was a clear correlation between the health of the relationship with the father and the child's attitude toward the divorce: Those who still felt the divorce had been a mistake (approximately 28 percent) had a bad relationship with the custodial mother or yearned for their father. Boys between 9 and 13 expressed particular longing for their fathers and worried that their own masculinity was in jeopardy without a role model. However, the survey also found that while the children who were still depressed five years after the divorce generally had neglectful fathers, a caring and involved father was no talisman against gloom, especially if the mother was inadequate.

(Although 85 percent of the fathers in Wallerstein's study of relatively affluent professionals paid child support, a surprising number refused to help pay for college. Partly as a result, only 66 percent of the eligible children in the study were attending or had graduated from college at the time of the 10-year follow-up, although 85 percent of the high-school graduates in the community went on to a higher education.)

Feeling and Failure

Inevitably, the conduct of the parents is crucial to the outcome. If a separated couple maintains "mutual respect and minimal hostility, empathetic awareness of children's needs to feel loved and valued, and 'the' father's continued involvement," then children can emerge from the divorce without major psychic damage. They may even demonstrate greater maturity, independence and empathy for others as a result of their own experiences. Unfortunately this situation is all too rare.

Most parents forget, or are unaware, that children often interpret parental trauma as rejection. And as Wallerstein and Kelly note, "children cannot mark time for an extended period while parents integrate their own lives."

January 3, 1992

Battered Wives

Centuries of Silence

SANDY ROVNER

Until five years ago when she shot and killed her husband after years of enduring his physical abuse, Mytokia Friend was a Baltimore policewoman by day, a battered wife by night.

Friend never consulted a doctor for treatment of the wounds, mostly punches and bites, inflicted by her husband, a Baltimore corrections officer. She was "just too ashamed," she said.

But even if she had, a group of about 250 health care workers were told recently, she might well have received little or no help beyond treatment of her immediate injuries.

Friend is one of eight women whose sentences for killing their abusive spouses have been commuted this year by Maryland Gov. William Donald Schaefer. She was one of the featured speakers at a recent day-long conference on domestic violence and the medical profession sponsored by the National Women's Health Resource Center, a nonprofit educational organization affiliated with Columbia Hospital for Women.

Although precise statistics are impossible to obtain, health officials estimate that each year more than 4 million women are battered by their husbands or lovers and more than 4,000 women are beaten to death.

A 1987 surgeon general's report found that "battery results in more injury to women than rape, auto accidents and muggings combined."

In many cases, the first people who encounter these women are health care workers—doctors, nurses, paramedics and others who fail to identify or assist them beyond immediate treatment of their injuries.

Spousal abuse has remained an unrecognized crime for centuries. Although health care workers now are required to report incidents of suspected child abuse, no such imperative exists in cases of wife-beating. Moreover, the widely held societal view that the woman has probably brought the abuse on herself is often shared by the victim, who may be driven by the severity of her injuries to seek medical help but who is too humiliated or too terrified to say how she got them.

"We as physicians are just not as sensitized to spouse abuse as we are, for example, to child abuse," said Constance Bohon, a Washington obstetrician-gynecologist who chaired the conference. "If a woman comes in with a sprained ankle and says she fell when she was running, we're inclined to believe her."

Leslye Orloff, a Washington attorney who represents battered women, said that "one of the reasons women get to the point where they kill is that they don't get any assistance before they get there."

There is a direct correlation between increased shelter services and a reduction in the number of homicides committed by women against abusive partners, said Orloff, citing statistics compiled by the National Coalition Against Domestic Violence, an advocacy group based in Washington. Orloff said that she gets virtually no cooperation from the medical community when she is trying to arrange assistance for battered women, such as protective court orders. "I can get medical records that are usually illegible, but I can't get a doctor or nurse or any health provider who saw the woman to come testify," she said.

Bohon said she believes this is largely due to physician reluctance to become involved with the legal system, linked in many doctors' minds with malpractice suits. "You say 'court' to a physician and he'll shudder," she said. "They'd rather be spending spare time volunteering in a clinic than testifying."

The problem, Orloff said, is compounded because lawyers who can't obtain witnesses "stop trying" and are reluctant to pursue cases. "If there were people in the medical field who were sensitive to this and would work with us the way social workers do—they'll call and say, 'I think I've got a battered woman here'—at least that would help," she added. Orloff said she doesn't expect doctors to call a lawyer for their battered patients. "Whenever there is independent corroboration of the wife's accusation of battering, the case is usually won. It's as simple as that."

A 1989 bulletin published by the American College of Obstetrics and Gynecology for its members, notes that in one study in an unidentified city "only 5 percent of 107 victims of domestic violence seen in a metropolitan emergency department were identified as such by physicians on the emergency room report."

"As a general rule," said Beverly Coleman-Miller, an internist who is deputy D.C. Health Commissioner for medical Affairs, la woman visits an emergency room in a hospital two or three times in a lifetime. A battered women goes to an E.R. two or three times a year. Some 40 percent of women who (seek treatment) at emergency rooms are battered," she said, citing statistics developed by domestic violence protection groups.

Other women visit a family doctor "with all sorts of vague complaints." Too often, she said, physicians fail to detect the true problem because many women are reluctant to report they are being beaten.

"Battered women don't report abuse for a variety of reasons," said Leslie Wolfe, executive director of the Center for Women Policy Studies, a feminist think tank. "Women face the very legitimate fear that their partners will carry out those threats of retaliatory violence, not only against themselves but against the children and other family members."

Coleman-Miller said that detecting abuse is not difficult, even when a woman denies it. Multiple injuries at different stages of healing—a black eye, a sprained wrist, a bruised hip, for example—or something as specific as a knife wound are "sure signs of battering," she said. That is also true of women who arrive with severe injuries that are a week old or who have problems with their necks, heads or faces. Other injuries, such as burns, may be less clear-cut. "Sometimes, the woman will say something like 'I burned my hand cooking dinner,'" she added.

Coleman-Miller and Orloff urged that health care workers who suspect abuse never question women in the presence of a husband or boyfriend who accompanies her to the hospital. "Often the batterer accompanies the woman on such visits and stays close at hand so as to monitor what she says to the physician," the ACOG bulletin cautions.

Coleman-Miller told the group that sometimes men who are overly solicitous should raise suspicions. Recently, she said, she went out with a D.C. ambulance crew and "There was a woman brought down to the ambulance; sitting there holding ice to her jaw. Her husband was hovering, 'Honey, should I call the doctor? Want me to go with you?' And she said, 'No, nothing,' and I looked and there was blood on his knuckles.'"

Orloff, who runs a legal aid program for Spanish-speaking battered women— Clinica Legal Latina, AYUDA—based in the District, said that a 1989 study conducted by the D.C. Coalition Against Domestic Violence found that only 5 percent of domestic violence calls ended in arrest by the police. "What is most important for this audience is of that entire survey (that included) every woman who was injured sufficiently to be hospitalized more than five days, there were no arrests and no reports." Hospital personnel did not question the source of the injuries and police were not informed, she said.

Said psychiatrist Raymond Patterson, administrator of forensic services for the District, "Until society sees the same imperative in stopping spousal abuse that it is beginning to see in child abuse, it will continue to go unremarked. No matter what kinds of jargon we get into to explain it away, when someone is being beaten, the first step is to stop the beating."

August 20, 1991

When Baby Makes Two

Deciding to Have a Child Without a Husband

DAVID STREITFELD

Every year, there's an increasing number of children for whom Father's Day is just another Sunday. Dad, in their case, was something out of a sperm bank. New technology and loosening social mores have made this form of single motherhood possible, not always to universal approval.

The method involved was previously called "artificial insemination," but that phrase is quickly becoming taboo. "Donor insemination" is now the wording of choice. The children that result, point out the women that have used this method, are just as bouncy and cute as those created the old-fashioned way. There's nothing artificial about them.

Births out of wedlock are nothing new. About 300,000 teenage girls do it every year, as do nearly as many in the 20-24 age group. What's surprising is the increasing number of single women over 30 who are getting pregnant on purpose.

Between 1970 and '87, births to unmarried women between 30 and 34 more than quadrupled, while the number for those 35 to 39 almost tripled. The '87 total for both groups was 120,000. Not all of these women, obviously, have been to a sperm bank or even are going it alone: Some are having babies with a man but aren't married to him, just like Mia Farrow and Woody Allen.

A more precise accounting of the truly single is difficult to come by. One local donor insemination specialist estimated that, at the most, 175 such women in the Washington area use the process each year. They generally are college-educated. They have careers, or at least jobs that bring in enough to support a family of two. They don't hate men; they still believe that the nuclear family of mother, father and child is the most desirable. It just doesn't seem to be happening that way for them.

Another quality they share is a heaping quantity of self-esteem. If women who have children without a man no longer are forced to wear a scarlet letter, they still have to explain the situation to friends and family, to the child, to themselves. It begins with pregnancy—Are you nuts? friends sometimes blurt out. From casual acquaintances, there can even be: Are you planning to keep it? These women say they feel good about themselves and their children. In interviews with a reporter they were frank about why they were without a husband, the travails they underwent before they finally held their child in their arms, whether they considered their situation second-best. However, all but two were unwilling to have their names published.

198

They didn't care if their friends could identify them. It was everyone else they were concerned about, for what they said were pragmatic reasons. One was worried that her child's friends' parents would read the story and it would be used as a playground weapon against him. "I'm not in this to defend my position to strangers," said another. Said a third: "It's none of their business. Plus, there are just too many nutty people out there."

Society, somehow, doesn't quite know where to place these women. After Jane Fowler filled out the information for her son's birth certificate, it was handed right back to her. "You forgot the most important thing," the hospital clerk said.

"To sign my name?" Fowler asked.

"No, the name of the father."

"There isn't any," Fowler said.

The clerk insisted there had to be a name on the sheet. Fowler offered to write "Not Applicable." The matter was referred to her obstetrician. He took the humorous approach. "Put in John Doe," he suggested. "Or Art Sperm."

Fowler finally printed donor inseminated in the appropriate box. The clerk was satisfied. A couple of weeks later, she received the official birth certificate in the mail. Under "Father's Name," it was blank.

"I Didn't Want to Keep Waiting"

A child with a divorced mother might look and act the same as one who never had a father, but there are plenty of differences beneath the surface. The divorced mother has, or can get, financial support. She has another authority for that child—a male parental figure. In a crisis, there is someone who cares as much as she.

"As a single mother by choice, the one thing I can counsel others is there will be no one who is as invested in that child as you are," says a 43-year-old health-care professional with a 6-year-old. "When push comes to shove on difficult decisions, you are alone. You have to know you have the strength, the stamina, to do it."

Stamina often is required just for the pregnancy. One woman interviewed, a 40-year-old House of Representatives staffer who gave birth last year, needed $15,000 in operations and fertility treatments, hardly any of it covered by insurance. Jane Fowler, a medical librarian who lives in Wheaton, lost her first baby to sudden infant death syndrome while her third pregnancy ended in a miscarriage. A 37-year-old researcher for a D.C. magazine had an ectopic pregnancy; on her second, ultimately successful, attempt two years ago, she spent three months in the hospital.

If the pregnancies aren't easy, neither are the decisions to start inevitable. "As the years went on and I got older, I knew it was important for me to have a child," says Barbara Davis, a Richmond nurse with 6-year-old twin boys. "But I never even imagined I would be sitting here as a single mother. I imagined a marriage and family and white picket fence and dog."

Davis set out on this path earlier than most. She was a little under 30 when she decided, and got pregnant 15 months later. "A lot of my friends say, "If I'm not married at 35, I'll consider it." But I didn't want to keep waiting and waiting and waiting to find someone to marry or to have a child."

All the mothers interviewed say a support group was crucial. This prevents single parenthood from becoming overwhelming or lonely at the most vulnerable moments—when they're sick, or during childbirth classes.

"Of course, there are ups and downs," says the House staffer. "I went into this knowing it was all me, knowing this is the way it was going to be: my son and myself. I would have liked to have a husband around at the birth but I didn't, so I guess I don't regret it."

The child, she adds, compensates for not having a partner. "We are a package. If and when I meet a man and have a relationship with him, my son will be first. I'm looking at his picture now. I can't fathom my life without him."

The mothers say that, with only a few exceptions, those around them were understanding when they got the news. But every now and again they also feel some hostility from the culture as a whole. Many families don't have fathers, but to do it deliberately offends some souls, as if this were a form of child abuse.

Kids who never had a father, a disapproving Ellen Goodman asserted in 1983 at the start of the trend, "are likely to grow up with a built-in longing in their lives." On her CNN talk show two months ago, Sonya Friedman declared "I'm sure that there are a lot of people who are uncomfortable with the fact that medical technology makes it possible, but this is our reality." Her interviews with four mothers could best be described as hostile.

"Some people," says Fowler, "will come up and say, 'Poor Pernell, he's from a broken home.' And I'll say, 'No, he isn't, his home has never been broken.'"

She doesn't let it bother her. "I've been on cloud nine ever since Day One. I just can't get off it, and I'm not willing to."

One Mother's Lament

Without Dad, armchair psychologists say, boys won't learn anything about masculinity and consequently will grow up to have trouble with the opposite sex, while girls will turn into insecure, skittish women.

"I've heard two people say, 'Your son doesn't have a father, he's going to be homosexual,' " says Fowler, who seems to have encountered more insensitive statements than any of the other women interviewed.

A 1988 UCLA study compared 50 two-parent families with others that were unconventional, including 50 single mothers. "At age 8, no significant differences in school adjustment were attributable to single-parent status," the authors said. "And such children were no more apt to be described as disturbed than were children from two-parent families."

A 10-year study of 156 single mothers and their children began last year. Coauthor Paul Ciborowski, a professor at Long Island University, has already noted one effect: "Years of dreams, hopes, aspirations and energy went into having these children. They're seen as something extremely precious. If single mothers are going to err, it's toward being overly anxious, overly protective."

He stresses that this may only be a temporary phenomenon. "We'll have to see how it's going to play out in five or 10 years." It's way too early, in other words, to assume these kids will one day be members of Adult Children of Mothers Without Men, sitting around in a circle and complaining, "Mom never let me do anything. She smothered me!"

Says a prospective Washington single mother: "It seems to me that children who are raised without one parent don't have a perfect environment. They have an obstacle before them. But that obstacle is no greater than it is for many other children—such as kids raised in single-parent families that are not that way by choice."

A 49-year-old government administrator with a 15-year-old doesn't agree. "I don't feel this should be encouraged," she says. "If a woman wakes up when she's 35 and says, "My God, Prince Charming is never going to come along, what am I going to do?," I would say adopt. Don't grow your own from the selfish perspective that you want this. The cost to the child is high."

This woman is different from the other mothers interviewed: She became pregnant by accident, and decided then to keep the child. "He feels incomplete," she says. "In retrospect, I would have made an effort to establish paternity just so [my son] would be told, 'This is the individual who is your biological father.'"

Her son knows he's different. Still, "It must be uncomfortable for him every time people say, 'What does your father do?' and he says, 'I don't know.' I did him a disservice. People talk about the father figure. Well, it's one thing to have a lot of men friends around so the boy knows how to throw a ball, and another to have a stable family relationship."

She wouldn't do it the same way again. Oh, she has no regrets having had her son. It's doing it alone that was the problem. "I would have glommed onto the first man to come along who looked even remotely likely."

In Need of a Father Figure

The mothers say they plan to avoid trouble by exposing their children to lots of male friends and relatives. Sometimes, this is easier said than done. If there were that many men interested in children, there probably wouldn't be any single mothers in the first place.

"This is a problem with all families headed by a mother, whether or not they were ever married," says Davis, the mother of the twin boys. "It's very hard to find that male influence, someone who's willing to be a role model."

She tried to sign up her boys for the Indian Guides program—where fathers and sons or daughters do outdoorsy things together—but was told she needed to supply an adult male. Catch-22: That's why she was coming to the program in the first place.

Then there's the explanation issue. All children want to know where they came from and why. With single mothers, there's an extra burden.

"I talk about how there are different kinds of families," says Davis. "There are so many single parents out there that I don't think we're that much of an oddity."

Adds the House staffer: "Basically I came to the conclusion that I'm going to be honest—'I wanted you so badly I went to a doctor who helped me have you.' Other single mothers tell me their children take it less seriously than they had feared."

Which is not to say it doesn't cause awkwardness. How do you convince the child he isn't somehow inferior?

"That's the bittersweetness," says the health-care professional. "My son has expressed a very natural yearning—a yearning for a dad . . . Parents want to respond, to give children what they want—when it's reasonable."

Which in this case, it isn't.

The Husband Gap

These single mothers stress that they've got nothing against men. If they did, they'd be in trouble at home: Every one of them had boys.

"I would have liked nothing better than to have a child 'conventionally'—to have a child with my husband," says the House staffer. "But that wasn't coming about, and I was dealing with a biological clock."

Says the health-care professional: "The reality is, when we get to a certain stage in life, the nice stories we had as children don't always pan out." Starting with, there's a handsome, successful, interesting man out there who loves children and wants to have them with you.

One advantage of having a child alone is that it puts all your cards on the table: There's no semi-panicky search for someone to have kids with while there's still time. When you've already had the child, the pressure is off.

On the other hand, says the health-care professional, her boy "has decreased my ability to connect with men. When they see me, they assume I'm married. And there are many men who don't want to take on what they see as a significant responsibility that they didn't have anything to do with."

What about the argument that, for the sake of the child, it's better for the mother to be married to someone, anyone? "If you're settling for something less than what you want, you're not going to have a good marriage," says the magazine researcher, "and a mediocre marriage isn't better for a child."

On the Way "Now's the time," the 38-year-old newsletter editor realized this summer. She had been thinking for several years about making a major change—perhaps leaving Washington and starting her own business elsewhere. Then, after the breakup of her last relationship, she concluded she had had it wrong: What she really wanted was a family.

She drew up a budget and did some research. Did she really want to change diapers 10 times a day? Yes, she realized. Like the other women interviewed, she would rather be doing this with a man. But then, "Life doesn't give you what you want when you want it all the time."

In any case, she decided, "It's much more important to raise a child in an environment of love and contentedness than to simply have two parents. I had a mother and father present when I was growing up, and it didn't give me a strong, stable upbringing to fall back on. It gave me a background of strife and competition and fighting."

Five weeks ago, she was inseminated for the first time. This week is Round Two. She's hopeful and expectant in the larger sense, if not yet the specific one.

"Someone said to me the other day, 'Do you realize how much your life is going to change?' I said, 'Isn't that the point?' "

Support Group

Most of the women interviewed for this story belong to Single Mothers by Choice (SMC), a 10-year-old organization with 1,200 members. New York therapist Jane Mattes started it as a support group for herself when she had her son.

SMC (P.O. Box 1642, Gracie Square Station, New York, N.Y., 10028) produces a newsletter on a regular basis, holds workshops and helps put single mothers in a particular area or city in touch with each other.

Not all members choose the donor insemination route. "Sometimes," says Mattes, "there are accidents, and sometimes there are accidents on purpose." Then there are women who have adopted and women who have gotten pregnant through a male friend. In years past, the weekend fling was also used as a pregnancy device. AIDS has put a major dent in this.

Women who have accidents on purpose may hope to trap the guy into marriage. When it doesn't work out, there's bitterness. "They're more like a divorced woman than a single mother by choice," says Mattes. "They can have trouble fitting into our group."

There's another group of members: those who neither have a child nor are pregnant. These are the so-called "Thinkers." There is a drop-out rate for them of more than 50 percent. The biggest stumbling block: how to present the lack of father both to the child and the rest of the world.

"I'm a therapist," says Mattes, "and every single person who comes to my office had two parents. Having two bodies there doesn't guarantee anything. But the one body in our families really wanted and loves and is thrilled they have this child."

November 12, 1991

10 *Aging*

The articles in this chapter explore various aspects of the discrimination faced by the elderly in our society today.

The first article discusses how the cost of living is rising faster for the elderly than for the rest of the population, as higher proportions of their budgets go for medical care and shelter. The next article discusses how poverty among elderly Americans is found predominantly among women. This poverty gap could be closed by relatively modest increases in federal spending, in the form of welfare and Supplemental Security Income. Another problem faced by the elderly is that of abuse, be it verbal abuse, neglect, or physical violence.

The following article discusses some of the ways seniors are beating the odds to get work in a limited market, as more and more employers are starting to realize that seniors can make terrific employees.

Cost of Living Rising Faster for Elderly

Retirement Payouts Lag, New U.S. Study Finds

SPENCER RICH

The cost of living is rising faster for the elderly than for the rest of the population, according to a study by the Labor Department's Bureau of Labor Statistics.

The study found that from December 1982 to December 1987, a special experimental consumer price index for households headed by a person 62 or over rose 19.5 percent.

That compared with an increase of 18.2 percent for the basic consumer price index (CPI-U), which measures price increases experienced by Americans living in urban areas.

The "seniors' index" also exceeded the 16.5 percent, five-year increase in another price index, called the CPI-W, which is based on spending patterns of urban wage and clerical workers. The CPI-W, which represents the spending habits of one-third of the national population, is used to calculate annual Social Security benefit increases.

The study, released last week, also found that Social Security recipients would have received an annual benefit increase averaging 3.7 percent per year if the seniors' experimental index had been used for cost-of-living adjustments from 1984 through 1987.

Instead, Social Security beneficiaries received increases averaging 3 percent a year, the study found.

The study appeared to bear out what Senate Committee on Aging Chairman John Melcher (D-Mont.) and some spokesmen for the aging have been arguing for years: that the costs of the "market basket" of goods and services that older people typically purchase—especially for medical care and shelter—have been rising faster than prices for the selection of goods purchased by the population as a whole.

Melcher said the survey strongly suggests that Social Security benefit increases are not keeping up with the actual rate of inflation for the goods and services seniors buy.

However, Commissioner of Labor Statistics Janet L. Norwood cautioned that the study, mandated by a Melcher-sponsored amendment to the Older Americans Act of 1987, was only a "first approximation" of a reliable special inflation measure for the aged. She said considerably more work is needed to develop an index that can accurately be used to make pension adjustments.

The experimental index was developed by revising the relative weight given to such items as fuel, medical care and food to take into account the special consumer spending patterns of the elderly. The calculations were based on the BLS's Consumer Expenditure Surveys of 1972-73 and 1982-84.

The study found that the elderly spent a higher proportion of their budgets on medical care and shelter, items that increased rapidly in price from 1982 to 1987. That is why the experimental index for the elderly rose faster than either of the two official price indexes, both of which cover people of all ages.

For example, medical care costs over the five-year period rose over 37 percent, the largest increase of seven major consumer expenditure categories. Surveys have found that the elderly spend close to twice as much on medical care (more than 9 percent of their budgets) than does the broader population covered by the CPI-W.

"Virtually all of the difference between the experimental index and the two official measures during the five-year period can be explained by the differential effects of the shelter and medical care components," the BLS study said. "The shelter component accounted for about 40 percent of the difference between the CPI-U and the experimental index. Almost all of the remaining difference was accounted for by the medical care component."

John Rother, legislative director of the American Association of Retired Persons, said that the solution might be "to use the CPI-U instead of the CPI-W to increase Social Security." The BLS study found that using the CPI-U would have granted benefit increases of 3.4 percent a year, less than the experimental index but more than seniors actually received.

Enid Kassner of the National Council of Senior Citizens said, "For the lowest-income senior citizens particularly, it is especially important that we have an accurate measure of the real increase in their cost of living."

July 6, 1988

The Woes of Widows in America

Being Old and Alone Equals Poverty for Women

DON COLBURN

In an bitter parody of lifeboat protocol, poverty in America often comes to women and children first.

That demographic fact, fraught with social, health, political and budgetary implications, is highlighted by two reports this month on poverty among the nation's young and old.

One study, issued by the Commonwealth Fund, a not-for-profit foundation specializing in health issues, found that two thirds of the elderly poor are widows and predicted the figure would rise to three quarters by the year 2020. Old people who live alone are five times as likely as couples to be poor, and four out of five people 65 and older who live alone are women.

"By the year 2020, poverty among elderly Americans will be confined primarily to women living alone," concluded the report, titled "Old, Alone and Poor," by the fund's 19-member Commission on Elderly People Living Alone.

The other study, by the House Select Committee on Children, Youth and Families, reported that nearly 13 million American children under 18 are living in poverty. The children's poverty rate in 1985 was 20.1 percent, down from 26.9 percent in 1959, the first year such figures were tallied, but up from 14.9 percent in 1970. The government defines the poverty level for a family of four as an annual income of less than $10,989.

While the American family remains a powerful institution, said Rep. George Miller (D-Calif.), chairman of the committee, it is "under enormous economic stress."

Among the fast-growing older population, recent overall gains in income mask sharp distinctions by sex, race and family status.

Increasingly, to be old and female in the United States is to live alone, often in poverty or near-poverty.

"Elderly poverty in the past will rapidly become widows' poverty in the future," said Thomas W. Moloney, senior vice president of the Commonwealth Fund.

Of the 27 million noninstitutionalized Americans 65 or older, 8.8 million, or about one third, live alone. But among the most striking findings of the Commonwealth Fund report is the preponderance of women in this group. more than 80 percent of the elderly who live alone are women. Two out of three—67 percent—are widows.

According to the report, the number of elderly widows is expected to quintuple from 1.5 million to about 7.5 million by the year 2020.

Elderly women who live alone are twice as likely to be poor as the average elderly person living alone, and five times as likely to be poor as elderly couples.

"More than any other group, [elderly widows] exemplify the trend toward two very different worlds of aging," Moloney said.

The first world includes older couples in good health who are active, mobile and relatively affluent. They see retirement and old age as a kind of "second adolescence," a long sabbatical from employment and child raising—the time of their lives.

But the second world is inhabited mainly by women who live alone. Many are in mediocre or poor health. "Their conversation is not about golf," Moloney said, "but about a series of health problems such as osteoporosis and urinary incontinence."

Elderly people who live alone "often lack the essential economic, physical and emotional support that can mean the difference between a happy retirement and a spiraling deterioration," the Commonwealth Fund report concluded.

The report, the first in a planned series on problems of elderly Americans who live alone, is based on 1985 Census Bureau data adjusted for more recent changes in income, benefits, prices, employment and demographic trends. Technical analyses for the report were prepared by ICF, a Washington consulting firm.

"Why is poverty the genetic penalty of older women?" said Moloney. "Simply because they outlive men."

Not only do women outlive men in the United States by an average of seven years. But many of them have reduced or wiped out life savings to pay for a husband's care, and only 15 percent of elderly widows have home equity at $25,000 or more, Moloney said.

"The death of the husband often induces poverty—just the fact that the husband dies," said David A. Wise, professor of political economics at Harvard's Kennedy School of Government.

In a study of elderly couples, less than 10 percent of whom were poor, Wise found that when the husband died, 40 percent of the surviving widows fell below the poverty line within a year.

All this is taking place while there is growing evidence that the over-65 generation of Americans as a whole is doing better financially. Between 1980 and 1985, the largest gains in median household income occurred among those 65 or older, *American Demographics* magazine reported in an analysis of Census Bureau data last month. Overall, the poverty rate for the elderly has dropped from 35 percent in 1959 to 13 percent today.

But the gains are primarily enjoyed by men and by couples, not women who live alone. Rising Social Security benefits and improvements in pensions will help men more than women in the next generation, the Commonwealth Fund report concluded, because men are more likely to have had higher earnings over a long period of time. Men are also much more likely than women to be part of a couple or to remarry in old age.

"A widow's poverty is a life sentence," Moloney said, because traditional escape routes out of poverty—such as employment and remarriage—are "simply not available" to most elderly widows. Less than 1 percent of their income comes from employment, and there are about five elderly widows for every widower, Moloney notes.

For poverty in old age, Moloney said, "we have a self-correcting situation for males and a perpetuating situation for widows."

Race is a big factor in poverty rates. At both ends of the age cycle—in children under 5 and in adults over 65—poverty rates are dramatically higher in minority families.

Among the elderly who live alone, the Commonwealth Fund study found that the rate of poverty is 16 percent for whites, 35 percent for Hispanics and 43 percent for blacks.

Similarly, the congressional report found a poverty rate among children was 15.6 percent for whites, 39.6 percent for Hispanics and 43.1 percent for blacks.

A report last month by the Children's Defense Fund painted an even bleaker picture of the state of the American child. in children under 5, the group estimated in a document called "A Children's Defense Budget," the poverty rate in 1985 was 23 percent, or exactly double the poverty rate in adults.

Of today's 4- and 5-year-olds, CDF estimated, one in four is poor, one in five is at risk of becoming a teen parent, one in six has no health insurance and one in six lives in a family where both parents are unemployed.

And of every 100 new babies, the report said, 20 will be born out of wedlock, 13 will have a teen-age mother, 15 will be born into a household without an employed parent, 25 will be on welfare at some point before reaching adulthood.

"The most important step the nation can take to solve the welfare problem is to prevent it in the first place," said Marian Wright Edelman, president of the Children's Defense Fund. "This is the critical domestic task facing our nation over the next decade."

The growing numbers of elderly women who are below the poverty line and young women—including teen-age mothers—who are unemployed and dependent on welfare have given added weight to the phrase "feminization of poverty."

Political debate on poverty in America and what to do about it is hardly new. Twenty-two years ago this month, Daniel P. Moynihan, then a Harvard professor, wrote a landmark study, "The Negro Family—The Case for National Action." The controversial study argued that instability in black families—measured by poverty, out-of-wedlock births and single-parent households—would result in increased welfare dependency.

Moynihan, now a Democratic senator from New York, returned to Harvard 20 years later to deliver a series of lectures in which he repeated the theme of his original report and again argued for adoption of a national policy on strengthening the American family.

"I do not know more than I knew then," Moynihan told his Harvard audience. "It is simply that I feel more strongly about it."

In the past 20 years, overall poverty rates among the elderly have fallen faster than they have among children. The critical factor in poverty today is no longer race but age, Moynihan said.

"The United States in the 1980s," he said, "may be the first society in history in which the children are distinctly worse off than adults." But if adults as a group are better off than children, there are large segments of the older population—particularly minorities and older women who live alone—who have been bypassed by the general prosperity.

Both the Commonwealth Fund and the Children's Defense Fund reports said that in both the young and the elderly, the poverty gap—the amount of money needed to bring income up to the poverty level—could be closed by relatively modest increases in federal spending.

Without governmental initiatives, poverty among the elderly who live alone will not decline by the year 2000 and will increase among those 75 and older, said Karen Davis, a health economist who chairs the Department of Health Policy and Management at Johns Hopkins University and directed the Commonwealth Fund commission.

The main source of welfare for the elderly poor is a federal program called Supplemental Security Income, or SSI. But the maximum federal SSI benefit does not even bring recipients up to the poverty level. The current SSI benefit is $340 per month for a person living alone (76 percent of the poverty level) and $510 for a couple (90 percent of the poverty level).

States can supplement SSI federal benefits, but only five states—Alaska, California, Connecticut, Massachusetts and Wisconsin—bring total SSI benefits up to the poverty level.

Only one third of the elderly poor who live alone receive SSI benefits, Davis said.

One reason is that the eligibility cutoff point is below the poverty line of about $5,400 for individuals and $6,800 for couples. Others are excluded because their financial assets, not counting homes or automobiles, exceed $1,800 for an individual or $2,700 for couple. Still others, Davis said, simply aren't aware of the SSI program or erroneously believe that they are ineligible.

Increasing the federal SSI benefit to the poverty level—at a cost of about $4 billion or a little more than I percent of current federal spending on the elderly—would be "an extraordinarily effective measure," Davis said. But congressional sources said passage of such a program in the current term is out of the question because Congress, preoccupied with Medicare reform and the trade and budget deficits, is leery of any additions to federal spending.

Even hearings on the issue are doubtful this year, said M. Kenneth Bowler, deputy chief of staff of the House Ways and Means Committee.

"Raising SSI to the poverty level is on its face a necessary thing to do," said Larry Atkins, a staff member of the Senate Special Committee on Aging. "The problem is the $4 billion."

April 28, 1987

Abuse of the Elderly—Often It's the Spouse

DAVID STREITFELD

When noninstitutionalized elderly people are abused, the explanation often runs something like this: The son or daughter who is taking care of the elderly person becomes exhausted, and unthinkingly lashes out.

A new study by the Family Research Laboratory at the University of New Hampshire, however, suggests this stereotype may be largely inaccurate. For one thing, only 23 percent of the abused elderly in the study had been maltreated by their children, while 58 percent had been abused by their spouses.

Secondly, the mistreated elderly were far more likely to describe their abuser as relying on them for assistance in a number of areas, including finances, housing, transportation, cooking and cleaning.

This dependency, according to the study of 2,020 Boston-area people age 65 or older, appeared to be related to mental or emotional problems. The abusers were also likely to have experienced stressful life events, such as an illness or the death of a loved one.

"The prevailing image of elder abuse is that an old person has become a burden to his overstressed relatives," says sociologist Karl Pillemer, who conducted the study with sociologist David Finkelhor. "In a way, that blames the victim—it says these otherwise well-meaning caretakers just can't handle it anymore. That scenario is true in some cases, but our study indicates that these situations are in a minority."

Says Linda Harootyan of the Gerontological Society of America: "It's a significant study because we now have a better sense of who is abusing whom, and that has important implications for how we address the problem."

Overall, 3.2 percent of the elderly surveyed had been abused in one of the following ways since they turned 65: verbal aggression (insults or threats that were repeated at least 10 times in the preceding year); physical violence (ranging from a shove, push or grab to having something thrown at them, being slapped or beaten up); or neglect (the regular failure of a caregiver to provide what was needed). On a national basis, that translates into 700,000 to 1.1 million abused elderly, but Pillemer says the figures could easily be higher.

"This study was done in the Northeast, and since that region ranks lower on most rates of violence, it may be that there is less elder abuse as well," he says. "Our study underrepresented blacks and other minorities, which some studies have shown to have higher rates of intrafamily violence. Thirdly, surely people underreport this phenomena. And finally, our rates of elder abuse don't include some kinds of maltreatment, such as financial exploitation."

With regard to the higher rates of abuse by spouses, the underlying cause seems to stem from the fact that most elder abuse occurs in a shared living situation. "Nearly 40 percent of the elderly in the U.S. live with their spouses, and about 10 percent live with children," says Pillemer. "More spouses live with each other, so there's simply more opportunity."

Moreover, since spouse abuse of all ages has generally been ignored until recently, the actual rate may be even higher, he says, citing studies that "a fairly large proportion of the American population see spouses hitting one another as normal."

These results suggest, says Harootyan of the Gerontological Society, that more retired people need to be prepared for the difficulties of constant companionship. "We need to look at preretirement counseling for the husband and wife who are going to be living together on a 24-hour basis, and preparing them for some of the stresses they might encounter. We also need to start thinking of shelters for this sort of abuse. It's not as if the abuser was a daughter or son whom you could stop from coming into the home. The abuser is often already in the home." The New Hampshire study, which was financed by the National Institute on Aging, is billed as the first reliable estimate of the extent of elder abuse in the general population. Earlier researchers, Pillemer says, had obtained their data from agencies that serve the elderly.

"We know from all forms of family violence that the cases that come to an agency's attention are the most extreme," he says. "The people who wind up in an elder abuse program are only a small minority of the abused."

Follow-up interviews were done on 46 of the abuse cases discovered by the New Hampshire study. Only two had been seen by the Massachusetts protective services agency—less than 5 percent.

November 26, 1986

Seniors

Seeking Work in a Limited Market—There are Numerous Ways to Beat the Odds

DEBORAH CHURCHMAN

You're over 40. You're out of work.

Maybe you were riffed. Maybe your company was bought out. Maybe your spouse died or left. Maybe it's the recession. And maybe it's been 10 or 15 or even 20 years since you've looked for a job.

So . . . how do people of a certain age go about getting work?

"Very carefully," says Sally Kera of the Jewish Council for the Aging.

There's a widely held, almost mythical belief that the possibilities for employment over age 40 are far fewer than those for the under-40 crowd.

"The field is narrower," admits Crane Miller of Forty Plus, a support group for professionals age 40 and older. "But that's because of your expertise, not your age," he feels. "There are simply fewer jobs near the top than near the bottom."

Maybe. Or maybe most employers just aren't as willing to hire folks over 40. "In most cases it's an advantage to hire a senior," says Mel Radowitz of the American Association of Retired Persons (AARP). "But employers with certain types of benefits plans do find it cheaper to hire younger people. If a company invests retirement money in a 35-year-old," he explains, "and the person quits at age 45, they have 20 years to accrue interest on that money before paying it out. With a 55-year-old who retires at 65, they have to pay out right away."

And a 35-year-old, he points out, "actually has a better chance of dying before he retires than someone who's already passed the 50-year mark."

There also are strong psychological factors working against the older person, says Jack Everett, also of AARP. "There's a big intimidation factor," he says. "Say you're supposed to interview a guy whose resume says his last job was CEO of Exxon. What kind of job are you going to give him?" In many cases, he believes, "the interviewer thinks, 'This person's much more qualified than I am, he or she's going to try to get my job.'"

Everett thinks such prejudice is best met head-on. "Tell them frankly that you're not on a career track—that you just want to work, and are looking for a place where you can use your experience and expertise to benefit others." He also believes that the older worker's resume should be underwritten rather than overwritten. "There's too much information on these resumes—they look intimidating. Just list the skills you have that will get this particular job done."

Then there's the perception that "you can't teach an old dog new tricks," as Radowitz puts it—an idea that he feels becomes "a self-fulfilling prophecy. Companies invest a certain amount in teaching new technologies and decide not to offer the training to their older workers. Then they complain that those workers are out-of-date."

Radowitz says he thinks that older workers may be at fault in this as well: "You've got to keep up, to take extra courses, to insist on access to these training sessions. Technology's changing so fast that even if you only have five more years to work, you've got to learn new skills."

Behind all these negative stereotypes, say senior employment counselors, stands a large group of highly employable people. Studies and actual experience of hiring seniors have proven that older workers are: Better people managers. "Long experience has taught them not just their field of expertise, but how to get along with people in an office," says Kera. "Plus they already know basic things—to not make a lot of personal calls or wear inappropriate clothes, for example. You don't have to train them in how to hold a job—just how to do this particular job." more loyal and committed to the job. "Seniors are painfully aware of just how few other jobs there are out there," says Radowitz. Everett echoes this: "Younger workers are trying out a job to see what they want," he says. "Older workers want this job." The result: a lower turnover rate among seniors.

More likely to work hard. "These people are old-fashioned enough to still have the work ethic," says Kera. "They'll give you a full eight-hour day."

Less likely to have accidents on the job, according to a new study of workers age 50 and higher by the American Management Association.

"We have to educate employers about the advantages of hiring seniors every day," says Rob Walker of ElderTemps, a senior temporary employment agency. Walker advises job applicants to do the same.

What else can help people over 40 to land a job? "There are probably a dozen different techniques," says Forty Plus's Miller, "and they all work in some situations."

The first step, most counselors agree, is identifying all your job skills. Al Akers of Senior Employment Resources, a nonprofit senior job bank, says they dig these out with a 10-page questionnaire that covers everything from paid to volunteer work.

Forty Plus uses a different technique to get at those job skills.

"We ask people to think of all the times when they've faced and overcome a problem," says Miller. Then they have to describe the problem and what they did to successfully solve it—something they dub a PRS (Problem-Result-Success). "People are generally elated when they finish making this list," he says. "They can clearly see what sort of problem-solving skills they can bring to an employer."

Then, like all people looking for a job, seniors are advised to network. "Tell everyone you know that you're looking for a job," says Miller. But he warns the senior job-seeker about talking to employed friends. "It just makes them depressed to hear from you," he says. "Those calls should be informational only."

Far better, say most counselors, is to find a peer group of job seekers. "Looking for a job can be a brutal, devastating process," says Kera. "It's easier and less lonely to face it in a group."

"Your mood swings up and down during the job search," says Miller—a process that the rule of thumb says takes about one month per $10,000 you want to earn. Being with a group can keep the lows from getting too low, he suggests. "We don't coddle people. We sympathize with their feelings and urge them to keep going."

Perhaps the hardest thing to face is the possibility that your job search may not take you up the career ladder—but sideways, or even down instead. "I just got back from a meeting in North Carolina," says AARP's Monica Brown, "where a big company had let go of a lot of mid-level managers. They all thought they were going to find another job exactly like the one they left. But those jobs just aren't there anymore."

Now is the time, Brown says, to look at "what you really want from a job. What's most important to you? Do you need to work with people? Travel? Work close to home? Don't look for the next step up the career ladder—look for a job where you'll be the happiest."

Regardless of what kind of job you're looking for, you should "try everything," says Kera. "You need to dress well for your interview, learn everything you can about the job beforehand, memorize your resume. You need to stay optimistic, and keep going," she says—something she admits is painfully hard to do sometimes.

"And don't be desperate," adds Everett. "We're getting more and more people who don't know how they're going to keep their house or pay for their groceries. And, of course, that's the kiss of death at an interview."

But take heart: According to Marion Jacknow of Fairfax County's Program for Mature Workers, "There's never been a better time than this to be an older worker. More and more employers are starting to realize that seniors make terrific employees."

June 17, 1991

Illness and Health Care 11

Issues of health care in the United States and around the world have been the subject of much controversy in recent years.

The first article explores the results of a World Health Organization report that estimates more than 20% of the people in the world are seriously malnourished. Many of these people are in Asia and sub-Saharan Africa, where malnutrition and disease, including AIDS are believed to affect 30 percent of the population. Many of the diseases could be prevented by drugs readily available in developed countries.

Tuberculosis rates are on the rise in the United States. It is a prime public health problem, considered to be out of control in homeless shelters, and among drug users and the HIV-infected. The next article explores some of the needless deaths from treatable diseases, and a study that points to the lack of access to basic medical care as the main cause. The next article confirms the differential availability of health care—organ transplants are far less likely to be performed on people without insurance.

The final two articles deal with other problems of the medical system, one of which is medical fraud by doctors, clinics, and other health care providers. The final article deals with national health insurance as a possible remedy for a health care system that most experts agree is riddled with problems and out of control.

Health Crisis Confronts 1.3 Billion

U.N. Reports 20% of World Population
Sick or Malnourished

SUSAN OKIE

About 1.3 billion people, or more than 20 percent of the world's population, are seriously sick or malnourished, according to a World Health Organization report that provides the first comprehensive estimates of the global toll of disease.

Most affected are south and east Asia, where an estimated 500 million people, or about 40 percent of the population, suffer from malnutrition or diseases such as malaria, measles, diarrhea and respiratory illness. Health problems are also severe in sub-Saharan Africa, where malnutrition and disease, including AIDS, are believed to affect 30 percent of the population, or 160 million people.

Much of the toll is caused by contagious diseases that can be prevented by vaccines or treated with drugs that are readily available in developed countries. "The missing ingredient is the will to help the developing countries," said Hiroshi Nakajima, director-general of WHO, which released the report yesterday.

Increasing annual health spending in developing countries by 75 cents per person would provide enough money to immunize all children in those countries, eradicate polio worldwide, and buy the drugs needed to treat all cases in those countries of childhood diarrhea, tuberculosis, bacterial pneumonia, malaria, schistosomiasis and venereal disease, said Jack Woodall, a WHO epidemiologist who compiled the figures in the report. The total cost of such a program would be about $2.8 billion a year.

Money could be most effectively used to attack diseases that are already preventable, such as polio, tetanus, measles, diphtheria, pertussis and tuberculosis, which each year kill about 2.8 million children, Woodall said. Currently, about 60 percent of children in developing countries receive vaccines for these diseases. The report estimated that it would cost less than $1 billion a year to vaccinate all children in these countries.

The report predicts that by the year 2000, a global WHO vaccination campaign already under way will eradicate polio, which currently strikes about 208,000 children each year. "It has already been almost eradicated from the Americas," Woodall said. A similar WHO campaign resulted in the global eradication of smallpox in 1979.

218

Diarrhea caused by viruses, bacteria and parasites is a major killer in developing countries, causing an estimated 4 million deaths from dehydration each year in children under 5. Two-thirds of such deaths can be prevented by treating children with a solution made by mixing sugar and salts with boiled water.

Although the cost of the treatment is about 20 cents, less than a third of children in developing countries who suffer from diarrhea receive it. The report estimated that for $50 million a year, 2 million lives could be saved annually.

For some diseases, the outlook has improved dramatically, according to the report. Tuberculosis rates in developing countries have been declining between 2 percent and 4 percent per year for the last decade, chiefly because of the development of better drugs and of aggressive public health programs. There are about 10 million new cases each year, compared with 20 million to 30 million annually in the 1950s.

A new drug, praziquantel, has provided the first cheap and effective treatment for schistosomiasis, a disease caused by a water-borne parasite that affects 200 million people annually. The parasites, which pass to humans from fresh-water snails that live in streams, ponds and irrigation ditches, can damage organs such as the liver, spleen and bladder. With the new treatment, schistosomiasis can be cured for less than $1 a case.

Another new remedy, ivermectin, became available in 1987 to treat river blindness or onchocerciasis, a tropical disease carried by black flies. The report estimated that 4 million cases of blindness have been prevented since 1974, when the WHO began a program to spray insecticide in areas where the insects breed.

The situation is grimmer for malaria and sexually transmitted diseases, including AIDS, according to the report. There are about 100 million new cases of malaria annually—and about 2 million deaths—with little change in the figures over the last 15 years. In many parts of the world, the parasite that causes the disease has become resistant to drugs commonly used to treat it, and mosquitoes that carry the parasite have developed resistance to insecticides.

The report said that global rates of sexually transmitted diseases such as gonorrhea, herpes and AIDS are increasing as populations become more mobile and traditional values in many cultures break down. It estimated that for teenagers and young adults, the annual risk of contracting such a disease is about one in 20. Between 5 million and 10 million people in the world are infected with the virus that causes AIDS, according to the WHO.

Woodall said the estimates in the report came from statistics from member countries, which are compiled annually, and from house-to-house surveys done in several regions of the world in which residents were questioned about their health.

September 25, 1989

Tuberculosis Rates Increase Nationwide

Early Warnings Went Unheeded—Problem
Now is Far More Costly

MALCOLM GLADWELL

When tuberculosis rates in central Harlem jumped 50 percent from 1979 to 1980, the physicians who work here in some of the nation's most blighted neighborhoods immediately sounded the alarm.

New York's TB control efforts are "so grievously inadequate as nearly to amount to dereliction and default," a citywide task force concluded in 1980. The group warned that unless the city dramatically expanded its anti-tuberculosis program it would face a public health disaster.

The report, TB experts say today, was ignored.

Today, TB rates in central Harlem are about five times higher than they were a decade ago. In homeless shelters, and among drug users and the HIV-infected, the disease is out of control, with new strains of TB proving difficult if not impossible to treat using conventional drug therapy, health officials here said last week.

"All of us involved were saying, 'Listen, we still have a significant problem in this city and you'd better pay attention because it may get out of control,'" said Charles Felton, head of the tuberculosis program at Harlem Hospital and the chairman of the 1980 task force.

"Unfortunately, we were right."

After decades of steady decline, TB cases in the United States are now on the increase, rising last year by 10 percent. In urban centers, where high-risk conditions are most prevalent, TB has reached epidemic status. New York City cases increased 38 percent last year. Miami's incidence rate is higher today than that of the entire country in the early 1950s, when tuberculosis was considered one of the nation's most pressing public health problems.

Although the rate of tuberculosis is lower in Washington than in many other major cities, the disease is spreading here too. From 1986 to 1990, for example, the number of cases in the District rose from 169 to 190, while in Montgomery Country they rose from 70 to 97 and in Prince George's County from 49 to 84. In Fairfax County the number of cases rose from 36 to 65; in Alexandria the number rose from 13 to 17 and in Arlington from 15 to 20.

Unlike AIDS, which appeared suddenly and mysteriously, the tuberculosis epidemic sweeping through inner cities caught no one who works on the front lines of public health by surprise. Throughout the late 1970s and 1980s, as state and federal governments cut back or eliminated TB control programs, one group after another warned publicly—and fruitlessly—that unless funding was restored, the disease could come roaring back.

In 1981, the House Energy and Commerce subcommittee on health and the environment said that the United States had "significant tuberculosis control problems" and restored the federal TB program canceled by the Reagan administration. But Congress gave the program no money.

The following year the American Lung Association testified with alarm before Congress that some states had stopped all spending on TB control, and called for $15 million in federal funding. The Centers for Disease Control were given $1 million. In 1988, CDC estimated that $154 million was necessary to rein in the mounting national problem over the next five years. Congress gave the centers $73 million for that period.

To those fighting the TB epidemic, the decade of unheeded warnings serves as a lesson in how public health problems are addressed in the United States. For want of adequate action during the 1980s, they say, the country is facing a vastly more serious and costly problem today. Thousands who once could have been treated easily now die or require repeated hospitalizations lasting months; and thousands more who never would have contracted the disease are becoming infected.

"This has become a standard feature of the American health care system," said Jay Dobkin, professor of medicine at the Columbia Medical School. "We take public health progress for granted and abandon necessary programs either because they don't seem necessary anymore or it looks like a way to save a few bucks."

"I put the blame right at the top," Dobkin said. "This is a disaster, and we will be paying the price for this for years to come."

The inability of the United States to contain tuberculosis over the past 10 years has very little to do with the nature of the disease itself, which, since the 1950s, has been about 98 percent curable by a simple regimen of drug therapy.

Instead, the difficulty lies almost entirely in the amount of time, personnel and effort required to find and follow those spreading the disease.

"You cannot do TB control on a shoestring," said Lee Reichman, president of the American Lung Association and a TB specialist at the University of Medicine and Dentistry of New Jersey. "The only TB control that works is labor intensive."

The reasons are twofold. First, tuberculosis is caused by a bacterial infection that can be dormant for years. It only progresses to an infectious disease state in a small percentage of infected persons, principally those who live in unhealthy conditions or who, like AIDS patients, have compromised immune systems. Ideally, public health officials prefer to find and treat TB before it progresses to the infectious stage. But because people infected with TB very often do not know they carry the bacteria, health care workers have to go out into the community and find the carriers.

Second, although there are drugs that are highly effective against TB, the medicines have to be taken regularly at precise intervals for months or even years. Failure to follow that regimen means that the bacterium, instead of being wiped out, simply goes into remission, emerging at a later state in a much more virulent form that is harder to treat.

Noncompliance is such a huge problem among TB patients—particularly the homeless or drug abusers—that for years the standard way to control TB was to have individual caseworkers go out into the community every day, identify patients who have difficulty sticking to their treatment, hand them their medicine and watch them take it.

By the early 1970s, federal, state and local health officials working together had built a network of clinics, outreach workers and screening programs that was highly successful in steadily lowering the spread of the disease. But as TB cases dropped to record lows, the program became a victim of its own success and public health workers' annual requests for money were taken less seriously.

New York City, for example, went from spending $40 million on TB control in 1969 to $2 million 10 years later. Many states eliminated spending altogether. Between 1982 and 1989, the yearly funding allocated by Congress to the CDC to help fund TB programs in problem areas never exceeded $6 million a year and dipped as low as $1 million. By comparison, the CDC was distributing about $20 million a year in grants in the late 1960s, approximately $70 million in current dollars.

Meanwhile, public health experts say, the AIDS epidemic created a large pool of people whose immune systems were so damaged that they were highly susceptible to TB. Homeless shelters that sprang up in the 1980s became breeding grounds for the disease. Immigrants from Southeast Asia and Latin American brought the disease to the United States in increasing numbers. Of the 26,000 cases reported nationally in 1990, a quarter occurred among foreign-born Americans, the majority of whom had been in the country less than five years.

"This is another legacy of the mindless budget-cutting of 1980s," said Jeff Levy, director of government affairs for AIDS Action Council, which last month held a TB summit in Washington. "Policymakers just didn't understand the importance of prevention."

Federal health officials say they are now trying to correct the decade of TB underfunding. For fiscal 1993 the CDC asked Congress for $66 million, which is an increase of more than $50 million over what the federal government is spending this fiscal year. To make the request more compelling to Congress, federal health officials broke tuberculosis out of the broad budget for infectious diseases for the first time and gave it its own separate authorization.

"We're trying to give it more exposure," said Donald Kopanoff, CDC's associate director of tuberculosis evaluation.

But even if that request is granted, Kopanoff said, it may not be enough. Treating the new drug-resistant strains of TB is much more expensive than traditional cases, with long hospitalizations that can cost $10,000 to $20,000 per patient. Federal money also makes up less than 20 percent of the total TB control money spent in the United States with the rest coming from state and city governments. Whether those two groups, which are in increasing financial straits, will find the money to attack TB effectively is unclear.

A recent study at Harlem Hospital, for example, estimated that 89 percent of its TB patients were not taking their medicine. The hospital, the report noted, did not have the resources to track down even half of those people and ensure that they begin taking their pills again.

Felton said that to begin to address the problem, the hospital would need to triple the number of outreach workers, add substantially to the staff of its clinic, and put together a citywide database to make treatment and tracking of TB cases easier.

Those are exactly the same three requests he made unsuccessfully 12 years ago as head of the New York City TB task force.

March 9, 1992

Needless Deaths from Treatable Diseases

Study Points To Lack of Access to Basic Care as the Main Cause

DON COLBURN

Every year, thousands of Americans in what should be the prime of life die from a dozen illnesses that can be treated or prevented by routine medical care, a study by District health officials shows.

The victims of these needless deaths are much more likely to be black than white, the study found. Blacks had higher death rates than whites for 11 of the 12 illnesses, and the overall black mortality rate was 4.5 times the white rate.

The study is important, researchers said, because it shows that lack of access to basic care not only worsens illness and increases hospital spending but also can be lethal.

"People should not be dying of these diseases in these age groups," said Eugene Schwartz, chief of the bureau of cancer control in the District Commission of Public Health and a co-author of the study.

The 12 medical conditions the study looked at are appendicitis, influenza, asthma, gallbladder infection, pneumonia and bronchitis, Hodgkin's disease, cervical cancer, hypertensive heart disease, tuberculosis, abdominal hernia, acute respiratory disease and rheumatic heart disease. They are called "sentinels" because they are rarely fatal in people ages 15 to 64 if treated promptly. Deaths from such diseases are a sign of gaps in health care.

"People are dying from 12 medical conditions that can be cured or treated if (the patients) only had access to basic medical care that a family physician can provide," said Marc Rivo, a co-author and deputy administrator of the District public health commission. "We're not talking about new drugs or new technology or sophisticated care in a major medical center."

Nearly 122,000 Americans died of those conditions between 1980 and 1986, the study found. more than 80 percent of them were black, even though only 12 percent of the population is black.

The biggest killer among the 12 treatable conditions studied was hypertensive heart disease—damage to the heart and arteries caused by abnormally high blood pressure—followed by pneumonia and bronchitis, cervical cancer and asthma.

Most of those deaths were preventable. Risk of hypertensive heart disease is dramatically reduced when blood pressure is kept under control. Similarly, if pneumonia and bronchitis are promptly diagnosed and treated, they are rarely fatal in this age group unless related to AIDS. With early detection by a Pap test, cervical cancer is much less likely to be fatal.

The study was conducted by four officials from the District health commission: Reed V. Tuckson, who resigned as health commissioner last year to become senior vice president of the national March of Dimes Birth Defects Foundation; Vincent Y. Kofie, an epidemiologist with the cancer bureau; Schwartz and Rivo. Findings were reported in the September issue of the International Journal of Epidemiology.

While the study cannot specify why so many people died of these treatable illnesses, poverty and lack of health insurance are seen as prime suspects because they keep patients from getting basic care. Uninsured patients are more likely than insured patients to die in the hospital from the same disease, a national study led by researchers at Georgetown University School of Medicine reported this month.

"It is said that we have the best health care system in the world," Schwartz said. "Maybe it's more correct to say we have the best health care money can buy."

A study sponsored by the D.C. Hospital Association in 1988 found that about one third of the uninsured patients admitted to District hospitals had medical conditions that could have been treated or prevented with timely care in a clinic or doctor's office. The new study takes those findings one step further, said Rivo, who is president of the District of Columbia Academy of Family Physicians.

"Not only are patients getting admitted to the hospital unnecessarily," he said, "but they are dying."

While blacks are four times more likely to rely on emergency rooms and hospital clinics for health care, low-income people of all ethnic groups "must postpone seeking primary care until their need for treatment becomes urgent and . . . then turn to hospital emergency rooms," the study concluded.

"It's not that you're black, it's that you don't have health insurance," Rivo said. "It's not that you're black, it's that you're poor." Sorting out exactly why people don't get the health care they need is complicated, the study noted. Designing solutions is even more so. But they begin with what doctors call primary care—a doctor's office or clinic where patients can go on a regular basis for checkups, routine care and follow-ups.

The entire health care system tends to give short shrift to primary care, Rivo said. Medical schools train more specialists than family physicians. Health insurance policies are more likely to pay in full for elective surgery than routine physicals, cancer detection, counseling of patients who smoke or drugs for controlling blood pressure.

Family physicians, as a group, are the lowest paid among medical specialties, according to the American medical Association. The average doctor's income reached $155,000 in 1989. Surgeons were the highest paid specialists, averaging $221,000, and family physicians the lowest, at $96,000.

More than 30 million Americans—including an estimated 110,000 District residents—have no health insurance at all. The public clinics on which these people rely are underfunded, poorly staffed and rarely open during off-hours when the working poor can visit them. "The system for low-income people discourages them from using primary care," Rivo said. "The poor delay seeking care until it's absolutely necessary, and then they seek it in hospital emergency rooms when it's often too late."

Broadening health insurance coverage is a key first step but not enough by itself, he said. A comprehensive approach to boosting primary care would include educating the public about preventable health problems, extending clinic hours and improving public transportation.

For many poor residents of the District, Rivo said, "it's a bus ride or two to the clinic. And when they get there, the pharmacy may be closed."

When budget cuts necessitated closing the District's Congress Heights health clinic during the evening, physicians at the District Commission on Public Health pitched in to staff it voluntarily on Wednesday nights.

Tuckson recalled a 40-year-old woman who showed up one evening at the clinic with dangerously high blood pressure. She was out of medication and said she couldn't afford to buy more. She worked at a marginal job with no health insurance and had young children at home.

"Let's say we weren't open," Tuckson said. "She'd walk around for maybe another year and get really sick with congestive heart failure and she'd go to the emergency room and sit there till midnight and they'd have no choice but to admit her even though she had no insurance.

"That lady is classic," Tuckson remembered. Unless she gets basic care, she has "shortened her life." Nor is she the only victim. "What we don't see [right away] is that she's not feeling well all this time and she's not taking good care of those kids," Tuckson said.

Rebuilding the health care system involves two monumental efforts, Tuckson said. The first begins with an attitude, one that tells a patient: "You are important. Your life has value. Don't disrespect it. "Second, you give people access to care— the full range of health services to help them act in their own best self-interest." That means health insurance, primary care, transportation, clinics in the neighborhoods where people live and open during hours when they aren't at work.

"What else in the world is more important than this?" Tuckson said. "What other thing on the public agenda matters more than whether the citizenry survives?"

Blacks More Likely to Die of Preventable Illness

A recent study looked at death rates from 12 conditions that are largely preventable or easily controlled when patients have access to prompt and regular medical care. In both the District and the nation as a whole, blacks were more likely than whites to die of most of those illnesses.

The following table shows how black death rates compare with those of whites:

Table 11–1 • Black Death Rates Compared to those of Whites

	In the U.S..		In the District	
Tuberculosis	8.9	times higher	23	times higher
Cervical Cancer	2.6	times higher	3.5	times higher
Hodgkin's disease.	20	percent lower	70	percent lower
Rheumatic heart disease.	2.8	times higher	*	
Hypertensive heart disease	6.5	times higher	3.4	times higher
Acute respiratory disease.	2	times higher	*	
Pneumonia and bronchitis..	3.8	times higher	3.5	times higher
Influenza	1.3	times higher	*	
Asthma	4.4	times higher	2.7	times higher
Appendicitis	3.2	times higher	1.04	times higher
Hernias..	2.4	times higher	3	times higher
Gall bladder infection..	1.6	times higher	*	

* (For these conditions, there were no reported deaths among whites in the District)

January 29, 1991

Organ Transplants

Rationing by Wallet? Uninsured are Unlikely Recipients, Raising Questions of Fairness

SPENCER RICH

Over the past decade or so, deciding who gets organ transplants has become a mostly formal process, based on complicated medical judgments rather than the social value or talents of a transplant candidate.

But there is one nonmedical characteristic almost all who get transplants share: They have a way to pay for the operation.

Beyond the 34 million Americans who have no public or private insurance, there is an untold number whose insurance does not cover transplants. For almost all, this means they are not considered for the often-lifesaving operations. Experts say these gaps constitute a de facto form of rationing medical care—by wallet—that undermines attempts at fairness and universality in the organ-allocation system.

William Dobbs of Upper Marlboro knows both sides of the issue.

Last January, Dobbs was bleeding internally and in need of a liver transplant, a $200,000 operation he could not pay for. At 65, he no longer qualified for his former insurance. With assets of more than $3,000 and income exceeding $495 a month, he was ineligible for Maryland's Medicaid program for the poor.

But on April 12, a decision from Washington dramatically changed Dobbs's life. Years after many insurance companies and state Medicaid programs made the move, Medicare announced it would start paying for some adult liver transplants. Dobbs got his new liver three months later, at Pittsburgh Presbyterian Hospital.

By 1994, Medicare estimates, it will be paying for several hundred transplants each year, at an annual cost of about $120 million.

But beyond the immediate impact, Medicare's decision raised again the question of which costly new forms of medical care are worth paying for at a time when health care costs are soaring and insurance companies and governments are embracing rationing.

There is no single system or national agency authorized to make the decisions for all insurers about which medical services to pay for, or, for example, whether $150,000 is best spent putting a new heart into a 60-year-old or immunizing low-income children.

Instead, there is a web of conflicting rules for hundreds of different insurers.

Medicare covers the cost of a new health procedure if it considers it medically necessary and if the Public Health Service concludes it is medically established, safe and effective. Medicare in theory does not take into account how much the procedure costs, but some in the system say price inevitably creeps into the decision.

A regulation proposed by Medicare officials would explicitly authorize that cost-effectiveness be considered in coverage decisions. Some fear this could lead to rationing by allowing program officials to rule out any new procedure that is very costly, but Medicare chief Gail R. Wilensky said the proposal is not meant to block "something that's a great advance just because it costs a lot." Rather, she said, it would merely allow Medicare to compare costs of alternative treatments for a given illness, then pay no more for a new one than for an equally effective older one.

Medicare is just one insurance system, albeit an influential one. Some insurers simply adopt Medicare's decisions, while others use the same general criteria but make their own decisions. Cost is often a consideration. Payment is often limited.

Medicare now covers heart, kidney and liver transplants (and some others), and Blue Cross says virtually all its plans cover the major transplants. State Medicaid systems make their own decisions; in 1990, 50 Medicaid programs covered kidney transplants, but only 40 paid for heart transplants and 38 paid for liver transplants for adults. About two-thirds of the larger commercial group insurers covered these three transplants as a standard practice. Information on small-insurer coverage was not available, but such insurers probably cover less than bigger companies.

As a result, others have been less lucky than Dobbs. When Oregon cut off Medicaid transplants for the poor several years ago to save money, 7-year-old Coby Howard and 2-year-old David Holladay were unable to get bone marrow transplants and died. (The state has since changed its policy on some transplants.) When Arizona's Medicaid program dropped liver transplants in 1987, 43-year-old Dianna Brown died because she had no way to pay for the operation.

Such cases are dangerous examples of how to limit medical coverage, say some medical ethicists. "If there is to be rationing, it should not be on the basis of ability to pay," said Joshua M. Wiener, senior fellow at the Brookings Institution.

The system for deciding who gets a scarce organ is in many ways more coherent. Roger Evans of the Battelle-Seattle Research Center estimates that in 1990, there were 96,000 Americans who could have benefited from major organ transplants, making the first form of "rationing" self-evident: About 12,000 people die each year under conditions that make use of their organs possible, and only a limited number of those organs are "harvested."

As a result, slightly more than 2,000 Americans received heart transplants in 1990. The figure was higher for liver transplants, and nearly 10,000 people received kidney transplants, according to the United Network for Organ Sharing.

There were nearly 24,000 people on the organ network's waiting list in 1990— people found medically suited for a transplant and with a potential source of funding. Another 2,000 who had been on the list "died waiting for organs" in 1990, Surgeon General Antonia Novello said July 10.

The first step in allocating the organs is determining who is a good candidate for a transplant, a decision that is based on widely accepted medical criteria but allows transplant surgeons great discretion.

From there, allocating available organs is based on formal rules, which are nationally binding and are intended to screen out decisions based on the "social value," talents or age of a transplant candidate.

There is, however, a strong medical bias in favor of the young. It is based on the fact that older people are more likely to have diseases and debilities that make them poor transplant candidates, with less chance of survival for a reasonable number of years after the transplant.

Thus, in a 1987 regulation, Medicare advised doctors that heart candidates beyond 55 should be viewed with extreme caution because they often have "coexisting disease" or "impaired capacity to withstand post-operative and immunosuppressive complications."

Paul Corso, a heart surgeon at Washington Hospital Center, said the patient should be one whom the transplant would enable "to get back to an active form of life . . . to go back to work, recreational activities, sports. . . . If you can only get them back to a barely viable condition, then the answer may be no."

Corso said he makes a medical judgment as to whether the patient can live some substantial amount of time after a heart transplant—at least two to five years and possibly more. But he does not automatically favor younger patients on the moral grounds that they have not yet had their shot at life or that, for example, a 30-year-old patient might have decades of life expectancy while a 55-year-old might have only a decade or so.

A successful candidate's name is put on a national computerized priority list maintained by the United Network for Organ Sharing to guide who will get the organs. All organs available in the nation are distributed through the list.

For a heart, liver or kidney, the organ network generally dictates that priority be given to a patient based on closeness of blood and tissue match, length of time on the waiting list and urgency, all rated by scoring systems. In many cases, it is permissible to use organs in the locality or region where obtained even if the recipient has a lower priority score than someone elsewhere.

Even though the allocation system is designed to eliminate preferences based on race, sex, social value and nonmedical age distinctions, studies by Philip J. Held of the Urban Institute and others suggest that more whites than blacks, more men than women and more high-income than low-income candidates succeed in obtaining kidney transplants.

The reasons are unclear, but the Institute of Medicine said some observers believe "subconscious bias" and the difficulties low-income people often have in finding their way around the health system are factors, even though Medicare, under a special law, pays most kidney transplant costs for nearly everyone getting them, including children.

Others believe that in transplant decisions in general, some surgeons have an ethical bias against approving for a scarce organ an older person who has lived out most of his or her life.

Even if allocation problems were solved, however, there would still be a debate over transplants—and other expensive medical procedures—and whether their costs can be justified in terms of the relatively few who benefit.

Daniel Callahan, director of the Hastings Center, which considers ethical issues, favors guaranteeing basic health care to everyone and putting limits on highly expensive procedures that extend life for a relatively brief period, particularly for the elderly, and on procedures such as organ transplants that provide "expensive and individual cures for relatively few people."

Others say that if some choices must eventually be made, there should be some bias toward the young, on the grounds that they are entitled to a fair shot at a life of normal length. Wiener said that if the only choice was between a heart for a 60-year-old and immunizing thousands of children, "I'd do the inoculations."

Robert Veatch, director of Georgetown University's Kennedy Institute of Ethics, said some favor giving preference to the most "socially useful," but, "Suppose you had to choose between a corporate executive and a great poet? It would require society to rank all roles in life as to value. It's too hard and too divisive."

Veatch said he sees no reason to deny a 65-year-old a transplant so that children could be inoculated against a non-life-threatening disease such as the common cold. But for "diphtheria, whooping cough or polio . . . it's quite plausible to favor this over 65-year-old [patient] transplants." Veatch said that in making allocation decisions for scarce organs, he favors giving children a few extra points.

Evans, looking at social value theories, said, "It's not unlike sitting around trying to decide who's of value to society."

Said Wiener: "All this seems to say: So far, we haven't yet figured out how to play God."

September 1, 1991

Diagnosing Medical Fraud

Cheaters are Increasingly Doctor, Clinics, Other 'Providers'

ALBERT B. CRENSHAW

In California, it's "rolling labs." In South Carolina, it's weight loss centers. In New York, it's "TENS." The names and schemes are different, but all across the country, medical insurers say, new and more imaginative abuses and outright frauds are cropping up every day.

And unlike a few years ago, when most cheaters were patients trying to collect a few extra bucks, today's scam artists are more likely to be doctors, clinics and other "providers."

In many cases, the schemes are little more than padding bills or prescribing unnecessary treatments. But in others, like the California rolling labs, it appears that the practice of medicine has become incidental to the practice of insurance fraud, according to insurers.

The result is hundreds of millions of dollars in higher costs to a health care system that already takes 12 cents out of every dollar spent in this country. A survey earlier this year by the Health Insurance Association of America, a trade association here, concluded that commercial insurers could save $350 million annually by adopting anti-fraud programs.

Anti-fraud programs used by Blue Cross and Blue Shield plans across the country netted $43.7 million in recoveries and savings last year, up 15 percent in just two years. In California alone, recoveries last year topped $9 million—a 600 percent rise from the year before.

Overall, fraud adds an estimated $60 billion to $80 billion to the cost of the U.S. health care system, said James L. Garcia, an Aetna Insurance Co. expert on fraud. That is a "staggering figure," Garcia said, but every industry has 10 percent or so built into its prices to make up for theft and other illegalities.

"When you go in to buy a shirt, there's a 10 percent markup for shoplifting," he said, and in health care, just as in shirt-buying, "we [the consumers] are paying for it."

Health care fraud has been changing, too. In years past, it was often the consumer who was trying to get a little something extra out of his or her insurance company. Today the thieves are primarily providers—doctors, clinics, laboratories and the like—sometimes in cahoots with the consumer, but more often taking advantage of the consumer's ignorance or lack of attention.

In some cases, milking the insurance company is the provider's main business.

The California rolling labs—so named because they rarely stay in the same place very long—offer "free" medical checkups to consumers. Potential customers are reached through telemarketing programs and sometimes through health clubs. They are subjected to a battery of routine "noninvasive" tests, such as electrocardiograms and blood pressure checks, and sometimes blood tests.

The patient is asked to sign a blank insurance form, which the lab then submits to the patient's insurer. A creative lab can rack up $10,000 worth of charges from a single visit, and by promising to waive co-payments and deductibles—the patient's share of the charges, which most insurers require the patient to pay—the lab sends the patient on his or her way unconcerned about the cost.

Blue Cross and Blue Shield of California have brought a number of lawsuits, and last week a federal grand jury in Los Angeles indicted six people—including two physicians and Michael Smushkevich, the alleged mastermind—on charges of operating a $1 billion rolling lab scam.

"This is the biggest health insurance fraud case we have ever prosecuted," an assistant U.S. attorney told the Los Angeles Times.

In New York, officials of a Bronx company pleaded guilty last month to charges of submitting $3.7 million in false claims to Medicare. The firm supplied transcutaneous electrical nerve stimulators—TENS units—which are used to treat chronic pain. Medicare pays for these devices and accessory kits only under certain circumstances, and the officials pleaded guilty to altering claims to get Medicare to pay for them.

Tom Ward, director of Empire Blue Cross and Blue Shield's program security department, said his unit has found cases in which TENS units were prescribed for patients who didn't need them, didn't get them and didn't even know about the prescription. One group altered the addresses on claim forms so that patients did not get the routine acknowledgments from their insurers—which might have alerted them to the scam.

There is a growing move among insurers to educate consumers. They are not suggesting that you distrust your physician—the vast majority, they emphasize, are honest and competent. But simple precautions, if taken by everyone, could save the system colossal amounts of money.

Garcia outlined five points for consumers to bear in mind:

Be aware that fraud does exist. If something looks funny, don't simply assume that doctor knows best.

Don't be afraid to ask questions. Following on the first point, Garcia said, if you don't understand something, ask. Is this procedure necessary? Why? How much is it going to cost? Also, the most common fraud is billing for services not delivered. Make sure you got what you and your insurer are paying for.

Sign only one claim form per visit, and date it. This will make it easier for the insurer to match bills with services and harder for cheaters.

When the insurance company sends you a notice that they paid a claim, read the notice. If there seems to be something you don't remember getting or don't understand, ask about it. Also, let your insurer or employer know of any discrepancy. A discrepancy doesn't necessarily mean fraud, but it doesn't hurt to check.

Garcia noted that in addition to the cost, fraud has other dangers. Cheaters "are the real bad apples of the profession," he said, and they are definitely "not the ones you want to trust your life to."

The rolling labs and other wholesalers of fraud "are the ones that frighten me the most," he said. "You as a consumer are a dollar sign to them. They don't care what your health is. You might have something seriously wrong with you and they'll tell you you're healthy."

June 16, 1991

National Health Insurance

Is it the Cure for America's Ailing Medical Care System?

SANDRA G. BOODMAN

Proposals for universal health insurance, which would have been denounced as "socialized medicine" several years ago, are being studied carefully as possible remedies for a health care system that most experts agree is riddled with problems and fiscally out of control.

Fueling the demand for national health coverage is the plight of the estimated 37 million Americans who have no insurance—one-third of them children—and an additional 15 million who have inadequate insurance. Their ranks are expected to swell in the 1990s as employers struggle to curb skyrocketing medical costs by reducing staff and cutting benefits.

"Our health insurance system looks a little bit like I-880 [the California freeway] after the earthquake," said Robert Hunter, the former federal insurance administrator who directs the National Insurance Consumers Organization, an Alexandria-based group sponsored by Ralph Nader. "The onramps—youth—are a mess, the offramps—Medicare—are a mess and a major portion of the bridge—the uninsured—has collapsed."

In the next few weeks, a presidential commission headed by Sen. John D. Rockefeller IV (D-W.Va.) is expected to announce its support of universal health insurance, a proposal both the Bush and Reagan administrations have long opposed on the grounds that it is too expensive.

The Rockefeller proposal is similar to a plan adopted by Massachusetts, one of the first states to devise a health insurance program for the uninsured. Several other proposals are currently circulating in Congress and academia, among them one modeled on Canada's national health program.

The Canadian program, regarded as one of the best in the world, is essentially a taxpayer-financed insurance system that is far less costly than the American system, with its welter of 1,500 insurance companies as well as state, federal and local programs. Most Canadians never see a hospital bill; they choose their own doctors whose bills are paid by the government. The government limits the amount it will spend on health care, thereby exerting enormous leverage on hospital costs and doctors' fees.

"Doctors are looking around and seeing that our Canadian colleagues have much more clinical freedom than we do," said David U. Himmelstein, co-founder of Physicians for National Health Insurance, which is based in Cambridge, Mass.

The latest push for national health insurance reflects the convergence of several factors, including the burgeoning number of poor people whose ranks rose sharply in the Reagan era, increasing the burden on public hospitals and denying all but the most basic medical services to a growing number of Americans. Meanwhile, the cost of health care, which consumed $600 billion last year—11 percent of the gross national product—continues to rise three times as fast as the consumer price index. This has led to a major shift in attitude among influential corporate chieftains, including Chrysler Corp. Chairman Lee Iacocca, who are championing national health insurance as an antidote to rising medical costs that threaten to erode profits and America's ability to remain competitive with the Japanese.

Growing dissatisfaction by doctors also has helped place national health insurance on the political agenda.

"I think there's been a real sea change on the part of the medical profession," said Himmelstein. "It's ironic that while people were worrying about the bogeyman of government control, the worst excesses have crept in through the back door."

For many physicians, the problems are not just interference from insurance companies questioning clinical judgments, but the fact that increasing numbers of sick people are not getting treated at all. "Over the past 10 years, access to health care has steadily deteriorated," said Himmelstein, an internist.

No one knows precisely how many people lack health insurance: the best estimates fluctuate between 31 million and 37 million, figures derived from Census Bureau data and interviews with a random sample of residents of 60,000 households.

While nearly all of the uninsured are poor, they are not poor enough to qualify for Medicaid, the state and federal program for the poor. Today Medicaid covers only 45 percent of those below the poverty line compared with 66 percent a decade ago. Eligibility requirements vary widely from state to state. In Alabama, for example, a family of three had to earn less than $1,146 a year to qualify for Medicaid in 1988; in Virginia the cutoff was $3,492, far below the federal poverty line of $9,300.

Various studies show that the majority of the uninsured—and the underinsured—are the working poor and their families. More than 60 percent have full-time jobs or are members of families headed by someone who does.

They are more likely to be self-employed or to work in the fastest growing sector of the economy at low-paying service jobs—as babysitters, fast-food employees, sales clerks or construction workers. And they are more likely to live in the South or West and to be black or Hispanic. They tend to be sicker than those with insurance because they receive less or inferior care and often delay seeking attention for life-threatening illnesses such as cancer until the disease is advanced.

Their numbers will continue to grow; 1 million Americans annually lose their health insurance, according to the Bureau of Labor Statistics.

"I really am quite confident that in the next two or three years we'll see some kind of comprehensive national health plan," said Melvin A. Glasser, director of the Committee for National Health Insurance, a 23-year-old organization funded by 40 labor unions that supports adoption of the Canadian model.

Not everyone is as sanguine about the prospects for national health insurance as Glasser. Jimmy Carter promised his support for it in 1976 during his presidential campaign and legislation sponsored by influential lawmakers including Sen. Edward M. Kennedy (D-Mass.) has, so far, met with little success.

Part of the reason lies in the considerable power of the opposition, which includes the American Medical Association, and the hospital, insurance and pharmaceutical industries. Opponents argue that national health insurance is a simplistic and unworkable solution that overlooks the heterogeneous nature of the uninsured, tramples on the time-honored American tradition of free enterprise and would result in the rationing of care.

But there are signs that the traditionally fierce opposition on the part of the insurance industry, under escalating pressure to do something, might be moderating. In recent testimony before Congress, Carl Schramm, president of the Health Insurance Industry Association, presented his trade association's own plan to cover the uninsured, a proposal that largely relies on expanding Medicaid and state high risk pools.

But for many health economists, the debate and sense of urgency are all too familiar. In a recent article in the New England Journal of Medicine, Samuel Levey and James Hill warn, "We have come this way many times before."

They argue that the power of special interests, the lack of resolve by politicians, the absence of widespread discontent by many Americans about their health care and the 1980s obsession with good health may signal a continuation of the status quo, which would leave the uninsured just as they are.

For major reform to occur, Levey and Hill write, "either an upwelling of popular discontent or strong, active leadership is necessary. . . . Without such ferment and leadership, the best we can hope for in the direction of universal health care is a series of half measures and fragmented financing mechanisms—more equivocation."

January 30, 1990

12 *Mental Disorders*

The first article in this chapter explores the rise in mental health costs. A study finds that across the board cuts in mental health spending are unfair since most of the increase in spiraling costs comes from substance abuse treatment. In general, mental health benefits have been shrinking. As businesses are faced with unabated health care cost increases, they look to managed care for solutions, and insurance companies feel their dollars are better spent where effectiveness can be clearly quantified.

The final article discusses a study by the Task Force on Women and Depression that points to a whole range of social conditions that denigrate and victimize, leading to depression. From being underpaid in the workplace, to being beaten up at home, to being raped on campus, it is clear that our culture plays a major role in depression, especially among women.

Rise in Mental Health Costs
is Unequally Distributed

SANDY ROVNER

Across-the-board cuts in mental health services to control spiraling costs are inappropriate because most of the increase comes from substance abuse treatment, a study prepared by Johns Hopkins University economists for the American Psychiatric Association concludes.

Officials of the Washington-based APA, which represents about 37,000 psychiatrists nationwide, have long been concerned that sharp cuts or the elimination of mental health services by insurance companies have occurred at a time when studies show that many Americans with treatable mental disorders are not getting appropriate care.

The new unpublished study concludes that the cost of treating mental illness among adults has been exaggerated and that the demand for psychiatric services has been moderate compared with increases for other kinds of medical care. But the study showed that the cost of treating children and adolescents has risen, as has the cost of substance abuse treatment.

The study, conducted by Richard Frank and David Salkever of the Hopkins School of Hygiene and Public Health, surveyed information from MEDSTAT Systems, Inc. a processor of health insurance claims data for major industries, as well as from hospital discharge records from the states of Maryland and Washington.

They also found that the use of inpatient care for adult psychiatric disorders has grown at a slower rate than inpatient care for all medical conditions. But the use of inpatient treatment for substance abuse "has grown at exceptional rates," as has the cost of such treatment.

According to the study, the average charge per insured person for treating an adult substance abuse patient rose 31 percent between 1986 and 1988, from $29 to $38. The charge for treating other mental disorders increased 20 percent, from $85 to $102. Charges for treating children and adolescents with mental disorders rose 68.7 percent, from $16 to $27. Steven S. Sharfstein, chairman of the APA's Committee on Managed Care and medical director of Sheppard and Enoch Pratt Hospital in Towson, said that "financing psychiatric care has been a saga of cost shifting, of trying to get someone else to pay the bill."

When insurance companies cut the benefits, then somebody else has to pay—either families, the criminal justice system, or taxpayers, he said.

"We need more flexibility to provide the most cost-effective programs," Sharfstein said. For example, he said, there is good evidence from scientific studies that intensive outpatient or day programs are as effective in treating drug or alcohol problems as are 28-day inpatient programs tailored to match the standard requirements of many insurance programs. Extending benefits to cover less expensive outpatient programs would "make a big economic difference," he said.

January 22, 1991

Shrinkage of Mental Health Benefits

SANDY ROVNER

Kit Erskine has been treated for bouts of deep depression for years. He is self-employed, and his wife's group health insurance covers them both. Her group policy, with the Maryland school system in which she teaches, had covered Erskine's outpatient therapy without question. The policy hasn't changed, but two years ago Erskine's coverage essentially disappeared.

What he calls his "insurance nightmare" began when the school and employees renegotiated their contract and in an effort to keep costs down agreed to have a so-called "utilization and review board" oversee the mental health expenditures and limit some coverage. Following that, Erskine's five-day-a-week therapy was rejected because, the management company said in a letter, it was "not medically necessary." Today, he is forced to pick up the cost of his $14,000-a-year therapy, deemed essential by his psychiatrist.

Nancy Poster's story is different but no less harrowing. Poster is a Virginia attorney who was covered by her husband's policy until her marriage broke up. Poster applied for health coverage for herself and her daughter from a group plan offered by the Virginia State Bar Association, of which she is a member.

But three years previously, her daughter had been hospitalized for about a month in a psychiatric hospital for treatment of depression. The hospitalization was covered without question as were other hospitalizations for the daughter's serious heart condition that had been rectified by surgery.

Although the state bar association policy was with the same company that had covered the daughter's previous problems, Poster's application was rejected late last month. Her daughter's hospitalization for depression was cited as the reason for denial of coverage. The daughter would only be eligible seven years after treatment. The program for the Virginia lawyers was, the letter said, "established as an opportunity for applicants who are considered low risk for incurring claims ..."

Such stories are all too common, according to mental health professionals. "Mental health is the orphan of health coverage in this country," said Alvin Golub, executive director of the Washington Psychiatric Society, the local chapter of the American Psychiatric Association.

The situation is especially frustrating to the psychiatric community because in recent years diagnosis and drug treatment of many mental disorders, such as depression, have become highly successful, and for many people the stigma once attached to mental illness is fading. Yet only a fraction of those afflicted are receiving help.

Insurance companies increasingly are demanding therapists prove that any given treatment in individual cases is effective, but mental health professionals argue that review boards authorizing insurance coverage often do not include specialists who are in a position to judge.

The situation is complicated. While mental health specialists point to improvements in current therapies, insurance companies struggling with higher costs in all aspects of medical care argue that their dollars are better spent where effectiveness can be clearly quantified to them.

"Faced with unabated health care cost increases over the past 15 years, businesses look more and more to managed care for solutions," health policy specialists Mary Jane England and Veronica A. Vaccaro wrote last year in Health Affairs magazine. "The debate over managed care in mental health practice has been particularly bitter and controversial."

Leaders of the mental health community are upset over the failure of federal lawmakers to address mental health coverage as the debate begins on general health care reform. American Psychiatric Association president Melvin Sabshin last month bitterly criticized President Bush's health plan, saying: "The president wants his administration to be a thousand points of light, but his health care plan leaves 23 million Americans [with mental illness] in total darkness."

Even some officials in the insurance industry echo this point, including England, a former vice president for group medical services at Prudential Insurance Co. and now president of the Washington Business Group on Health, a nonprofit association of business leaders that studies health policy. She noted that none of the health proposals on Capitol Hill calls for mental health coverage of more than 45 days for hospital care and 20 outpatient sessions.

Mental illness and drug abuse costs for 1989, the most recent year for which figures are available, were estimated at about $106 billion by the Health Insurance Association of America, about 17 percent of the total national health expenditure. Substance abuse treatment accounted for about one third of that and is seen as the principal reason for the explosive rise in mental health costs—up to 23 percent a year over the past five years.

Faced with that increase, insurance companies began sharply cutting back on benefits and instituting lifetime limits. As a result, some patients find themselves without coverage.

According to England, insurance companies generally set up mental health coverage to favor hospitalized care, covering up to 90 or 100 percent, although many policies also limit the total amount any patient can spend on hospitalized mental treatment.

In addition, she said, most companies cover only up to 50 percent of outpatient care. This was based on older experience, she said, and does not take into account today's immensely successful psychoactive drugs and the increased understanding about the different forms of mental illness and their biological roots.

Psychiatric hospitalization can cost up to $500 a day, while outpatient treatments often run around $100 per session, industry officials said.

Mental health care providers say that review boards and other forms of managed care to cut costs frequently work against the patients' best interests. They complain that because mental health care is such an individualized treatment, management boards that may be staffed by specialists in other fields or by nonprofessionals make arbitrary decisions from afar that can have devastating impacts on individuals' lives.

One of the most controversial aspects of insurance coverage is the frequent use of lifetime limits on mental health coverage. England, who also serves as treasurer of the American Psychiatric Association, often disagrees with her colleagues on ways to provide mental health coverage and control costs at the same time, but she agrees that lifetime limits on coverage are unrealistic.

"Heavy-duty mental illness [depression and schizophrenia, for example] is a chronic illness like heart disease or diabetes and should have the same lifetime limits," she said.

According to Golub, virtually all insurance policies and health maintenance organizations in the area have lifetime caps no higher than about $50,000; most of them are lower. Comparable lifetime limits for other major illnesses in some policies can run up to $1 million.

Limiting lifetime treatment by numbers of days or hours is "like ruling that all surgery shall stop after one hour," said Lawrence Sack, consultant to the D.C. Commission on mental Health who was speaking at a recent Capitol Hill forum on behalf of the American Psychoanalytic Association.

Accountability is a major factor in the frustration of the mental health community. Carol Kleinman, who will later this year become president of the Washington Psychiatric Society, said that managed care should be held to the same standards "as the rest of us. If we abandon patients because they have no insurance, we are held accountable. If a hospital discharges a patient because his insurance runs out and that patient runs out and commits suicide, the hospital is accountable."

Meanwhile, Erskine continues to pay for his therapy out of pocket and Poster is seeking a health plan. The problem is, said Harold I. Eist, president of the American Association of Private Practice Psychiatrists, should Poster or her daughter need care, the lack of insurance would drop them to the level "where many of our citizens, . . . because they cannot afford to pay for mental health care, are increases in the last two years."

The company recently put a cap of 60 days on the amount of time it will cover inpatient care. The company's health plan formerly had no limits on inpatient psychiatric stays.

"This helped control costs somewhat, but they are still out of sight," Horning said, adding that prescription drugs, psychiatric care and substance abuse treatment account for 20 percent of health benefit costs.

Employee health benefit experts say inpatient treatment has become more popular for several reasons. There are many empty general care hospital beds that are now being used for psychiatric treatment, and psychiatrists who are affiliated with hospitals increasingly are recommending extended stays for their patients who otherwise might simply come in for outpatient visits.

"It's been destigmatized," said James M. Oher, a psychologist in New York who is a consultant for Towers Perrin Co., a benefits consulting firm.

Also adding to the growth in claims is the treatment of adolescents for "conduct disorders" and other problems. Horning said Gannett has seen an "alarming increase" in the use of psychiatric facilities for dependents or the children of employees. "It makes us wonder if employees have the resources to identify appropriate levels of care," she said.

Part of the increased spending on mental health costs stems from the employers themselves, many of whom have initiated employee assistance programs that help identify workers with substance abuse and other problems. Courses of treatment, such as residential treatment programs, then may be suggested.

Now employers like Gannett have begun to clamp down. A recent nationwide survey by the benefits consulting firm A. Foster Higgins & Co. in New York found that 87 percent of employers in 1989 limited benefits for inpatient treatment of mental disorders and substance abuse, up from 75 percent in 1988. More than half were limiting the amount that could be spent on inpatient care over a lifetime—a $50,000 cap is the most common. Others are limiting the number of days of inpatient treatment that will be paid for in any given year—often 30 days, which takes in the average stay for most acute mental illnesses or the most common substance abuse treatment programs. Smaller firms are even less comprehensive in their coverage, the survey found, many setting dollar limits of $10,000 a year.

John Erb, a managing consultant in Foster Higgins's New York office, said some employers are setting up networks of mental health care providers that employees are encouraged to use. Providers, who are encouraged to recommend outpatient treatment, are paid a set amount under the terms of a contract with the company. Limiting the number of providers employees can use is supposed to reduce the cost of mental health care benefits.

Gannett is encouraging its employees to seek help under its own employee assistance programs first. It also has a case management program where employees can volunteer to have their physicians work with the company's insurance carrier to find the best course of treatment.

The benefit to the employee is lower co-payment insurance costs if inpatient treatment can be avoided.

Limiting benefits does lower costs, the survey showed. Companies that had no special limitations on inpatient costs spent an average of $282 per employee on mental health and substance abuse claims, or 23 percent more than those that had limits.

Oher said employers are paying increased attention to the cost of inpatient treatment because the fees charged by providers are unregulated and before now there was little drive to contain costs.

Faulty diagnosis and treatment also can play a role in increasing costs. "There is some need for inpatient care, but it's not needed in many cases," Oher said.

March 3, 1992

Our Culture as a Cause of Depression

JUDY MANN

The American Psychological Association has issued a report sharply challenging the comfortable old assumptions about why twice as many women suffer from major depressions as men. Turns out it isn't all hormones, after all.

Quite the contrary. After a three-year study, the Task Force on Women and Depression has pointed the finger at a whole range of social conditions that denigrate and victimize women as being substantial contributors to women's depression.

On one level, one could say that you don't have to be a psychologist to figure out that a class of people who are underpaid in the workplace, beaten up at home and raped almost routinely on college campuses are going to suffer much more from depression than people who aren't victimized. What is important about the study, however, is that it bears the stamp of authority of the APA and marks the first time it has linked cultural causes to depression in a formal task force report.

While it does not discount biological causes of depression, the panel said that mental health professionals need to "develop ways of thinking about women's depression in a biopsychological context. Understanding the complexities of women's higher risk for depression requires understanding the interaction of women's biology with their environment. It requires clear definitions of depression and of the biological, psychological and social variables used to predict it."

The panel recommended that a great deal more research be done in the whole area of women and depression and how they differ from men in causes and treatment. The panel also found that depression was misdiagnosed in women 30 to 50 percent of the time. It cautioned that anti-depressant drugs, 70 percent of which are prescribed for women, are often misprescribed and improperly monitored. "Prescription drug misuse is a very real danger for women," the report warned.

About 7 million women suffer from diagnosable depression, and the researchers put the overall cost to society at $16 billion a year. They were particularly concerned about the lack of access to mental health care by the 37 million people who have no health insurance, as well as those whose policies don't cover mental health care. Sixty-seven percent of employer policies don't have mental health benefits. Fully 8.5 million American women—15 percent of the female population—live in poverty, and the numbers are increasing yearly. "The hopelessness and crisis-oriented nature of living in poverty not only contribute to depression and related responses, but also provide significant barriers to receiving appropriate mental health treatment and care," the panel advised.

One of its most striking findings had to do with violence against women. "The rate of sexual and physical abuse of females is much higher than previously suspected and is a major factor in women's depression. One study estimated that 37 percent of women have a significant experience of physical or sexual abuse before the age of 21. Several task force members felt . . . the real numbers may be as high as 50 percent," according to the report. The panel suggested that for those women depression may be the result of post-traumatic stress syndrome.

Sexual harassment at work, which one study found could happen to as many as 71 percent of all working women, often results in job loss and other traumas, and the panel suggested that because of the high incidence of sexual harassment it should be considered as a possible trigger for depression in women.

Women's experiences in trying to balance work and family life, and the support they get from their husbands, affect depression. One study found that mothers who had no trouble finding child care, and whose husbands shared child-care responsibilities, had low rates of depression, as low as husbands and employed women with no children. The employed mothers who shouldered all of the child-care responsibilities had high rates of depression. Higher rates were found among women caring for aging parents.

And the panel cited other studies that found an elevated rate of suicide among women professionals who are in fields traditionally dominated by men. Another study found an elevated rate of suicide among male nurses, who are operating in an environment dominated traditionally by women.

The workplace and home clearly have an impact on women's mental health, as well as physical health. Those concerned with rising health care costs ought to ponder the implications of the task force report very carefully. It has debunked the notion that women's mental health is an immutable product of hormones. The culture is leading to depression, too—and that can be changed.

December 17, 1990

13 *Education*

Several factors work against the educational system's goal of fostering equal opportunity, from costs of education, to testing and tracking policies, to curriculum content.

The first article explores the results of a new national study of math skills, which shows that U.S. students on average fall below their grade level, a problem in an age when computers and advanced technology will demand much more sophisticated knowledge in the workplace. The second article discusses the pressure on African-American students in particular to perform well on achievement and SAT tests, defying an often heard stereotype that minority students are unable to perform as well as others on standardized tests. The next article explores possible discrimination by colleges and universities, exploring why African-Americans and Native Americans often have to go into debt to finish their doctorate degrees, while foreign students are able to get financial aid.

Another component of the problems in education is that of teacher competency. Quality concerns remain even after higher pay, wider competency testing, and tougher certification standards have been enacted.

Head Start has come to be regarded as an essential component of any strategy for upgrading U.S. education. Designed for poor, pre-school children, it builds a foundation of self esteem, social skills, and basic lessons to get them ready for school. The next article explores a family literacy program, Even Start, where illiterate parents actually go to school with their child to take their own classes. The final article discusses the concept of bringing social services into the schools, a holistic approach which offers health and child care, and family counseling.

U.S. Youth Fail Math Test
District Eighth-Graders Rank Near Bottom

KENNETH J. COOPER

A new national study of mathematics skills shows that most students have not mastered more than basic arithmetic in an age when computers and advanced technology will demand much more sophisticated knowledge in the workplace.

The study—the first valid comparison of student achievement in different states—showed no state's students performed at their grade level. Students in some states scored much lower than others.

Eighth-graders in the District of Columbia ranked next to last among the 37 states and three territories that participated in the study—only the Virgin Islands did worse—and the impact was immediate. District school officials ordered a "total and sweeping reform" in the way math is taught.

Virginia and Maryland students ranked in the middle of the survey.

The math tests, administered to representative samples of students last year, showed that most high school seniors perform below the eighth-grade level and only 5 percent of them are prepared for college math, federal officials said.

The tests reinforced educators' worries about the mathematical abilities of the nation's students, but the study's biggest impact is expected to be felt at the state level. States at the bottom will likely reconsider their approaches to math instruction; California officials reacted to the scores by revamping high school classes. State officials were briefed on their students' performances on Monday.

Eighth-graders in public schools were the only students directly compared, and four rural states in the heartland—North Dakota, Montana, Iowa and Nebraska—performed best in the National Assessment of Educational Progress, a congressionally mandated series of tests.

Federal officials said that the national results could not be compared with previous ones dating back to 1973 because the contents of the tests were different. The 1990 results, they said, provide a basis for tracking U.S. progress toward becoming the best in the world in math and science by the year 2000, one of six educational goals that President Bush and the nation's governors adopted last year.

"We had better fire up our engines because we have an enormous challenge ahead of us," said Education Secretary Lamar Alexander.

Bush, remarking generally on the math results Monday, said that they showed "we are not measuring up."

The national sample included 26,000 students in grades four, eight and 12 who attend both public and private schools.

Scores were reported on a scale of 0 to 500, with 300 representing what eighth-graders ought to be able to do, according to Alexander. The report describes that level of math as solving problems that involve fractions, decimals, percents, basic geometry and simple algebra.

Examples of 300-level problems that many eighth-graders did not answer correctly include computing the combined weight of 50 tomatoes that averaged 2.36 pounds; identifying a decimal between .07 and .08; and converting 3 3/10s, expressed as a fraction, into a decimal.

Nationwide, the average score was 295 for 12th-graders, and 54 percent of them scored below 300. Only 5 percent scored 350 or better.

Gary W. Phillips, acting associate commissioner for education assessments, described the top-scorers as "equipped to do college work" in advanced algebra and geometry, but not necessarily calculus.

In keeping with longstanding patterns, Asians scored highest, followed by whites. Poor students in big cities were outperformed by "advantaged" students in the suburbs. Students in private schools did slightly better than those in public schools.

The average score nationwide was 265 for eighth-graders and 216 for fourth-graders. The top state score, 281, went to eighth-graders in North Dakota, although Montana, Iowa and Nebraska trailed by a statistically insignificant 1 to 5 points.

Wayne G. Sanstead, superintendent of public instruction in North Dakota, attributed his state's performance in part to what he called "the rural verities. . . . The work ethic would be number one—whatever you do, you work at it, including school."

Sanstead also acknowledged that North Dakota students were not as distracted by the entertainment and recreation opportunities available to youngsters in metropolitan areas. "Somebody said to me, humorously, 'No mountains and no beaches,'" he said.

North Dakota also ranked high on several factors that tended to correlate with higher scores: low student absenteeism, less television viewing, two-parent families, college-educated parents and more reading material in the home. The state's schools also do not group eighth-graders according to their math ability.

Federal officials said the 13 states that did not participate generally could not get the funding or legislative approvals to conduct the tests, or attached a higher priority to their own testing programs. Those states were: Alaska, Kansas, Maine, Massachusetts, Mississippi, Missouri, Nevada, South Carolina, South Dakota, Tennessee, Utah, Vermont and Washington.

When Congress funded the National Assessment in the 1960s, it prohibited state-level comparisons because of fears of federal intrusion into state or local educational issues such as curriculum.

Comparing states by other means is difficult, because college placement examinations are not taken by representative groups of high school students, and various standardized achievement tests are administered to younger students at different times of the year.

49% Can Solve this Problem

Mathematics Question Posed to Eight-Graders The weight of an object on the Moon is 1/6 the weight of that object on the Earth. An object that weighs 30 pound on Earth would weigh how many pounds on the Moon?

Answer: 5

The Test Results

This chart shows the results of the National Assessment of Educational Progress math test given to eighth grade public school students in 37 states, the District of Columbia, the Virgin Islands and Guam last year.

The states are ranked according to their students' average score on a scale of 0 to 500: students in North Dakota earned the highest marks, while students in the Virgin Islands and the District of Columbia received the lowest marks.

Table 13–1 • Average State Test Scores

A test score of 300 was considered appropriate for this age group.

Rank	State	Test Score
1.	North Dakota	281
2.	Montana	280
3.	Iowa	278
4.	Nebraska	276
5.	Minnesota	276
6.	Wisconsin	274
7.	New Hampshire	273
8.	Wyoming	272
9.	Idaho	272
10.	Oregon	271
11.	Connecticut	270
12.	New Jersey	269

continued

table 13–1 continued

Rank	State	Test Score
13.	Colorado	267
14.	Indiana	267
15.	Pennsylvania	266
16.	Michigan	264
17.	Virginia	264
18.	Ohio	264
19.	Oklahoma	263
20.	New York	261
21.	Delaware	261
22.	Maryland	260
23.	Illinois	260
24.	Rhode Island	260
25.	Arizona	259
26.	Georgia	258
27.	Texas	258
28.	Kentucky	256
29.	California	256
30.	New Mexico	256
31.	Arkansas	256
32.	West Virginia	256
33.	Florida	255
34.	Alabama	252
35.	Hawaii	251
36.	North Carolina	250
37.	Louisiana	246
38.	Guam	231
39.	District of Columbia	231
40.	Virgin Islands	218

Note: Experts explain that slight differences in test scores that affect ranking are not statistically significant.

June 7, 1991

A Test of Character

Minorities Strive to Crush SAT Stereotypes

DeNeen L. Brown

When Chris Williams sits down to take the College Board achievement tests today, his goal will be much more lofty than just getting into college. He wants respect.

He says he will be on a mission to make a lie out of an often-heard stereotype that minority students are unable to perform as well as others on standardized tests.

"It's kind of like a pressure to get respect, not just from people at your school but from the general public," said Williams, a top student at Langley High School in Fairfax County and one of about 44,000 students in Maryland, Virginia and the District expected to take the Scholastic Aptitude and achievement tests this weekend.

The achievement tests and the SAT, which he plans to take in December, are "proof that I am serious, I work hard and I plan to be successful," Williams said.

Many black students say they constantly are aware of the need to prove themselves by doing well on college entrance tests such as the SAT. Counselors and educators say that is an unfair burden for these students, many of whom do extremely well on the tests.

"It bothers me," said Tamara Carrington, a 17-year-old senior at Woodrow Wilson High School in the District who scored more than 1,300 out of a possible 1,600 on the SAT. "I think people, they try to prove racist theories like blacks are less intelligent, which I don't believe."

Kihlon Golden, 17, a senior at T.C. Williams High School in Alexandria, said: "I think if you hear something enough you start to believe it. It makes me want to work harder to prove to myself and others that I'm not just average."

Georgia Booker, the guidance director at Wilson, said: "It's a stigma. When you read that [black students, on average, score lower than whites on the SAT] in the paper, you don't stop to say that's an average. You feel all scores are low. I have white students who don't do as well as some black students on tests."

Some students said that in addition to feeling a responsibility to prove themselves, they often must deal with subtle pressure not to achieve. Some say they are accused by peers of "acting white" if they buckle down academically. Some say they have encountered teachers who don't seem to expect as much of them because they are black.

Damon Tweedy, 17, a senior in the college preparatory program at Eleanor Roosevelt High School in Prince George's County, said people often don't expect him to be smart because he is black and plays basketball. He scored 1,280 on the SAT.

"They are always kind of surprised I could do as well. . . . If another person did well it wasn't as much of a big deal," Tweedy said. He recalled an incident in the ninth grade when he received a 98 on a mathematics test and although other students did well, his teacher singled him for praise. "It was like, 'Great job, Damon.' I was wondering why she singled me out."

"Anyone who has been in education knows about the self-fulfilling prophecy that messages send out," said Carol Gray, director of guidance at Eleanor Roosevelt High School. "If I don't have a real strong sense of purpose and I'm confronted with, 'You as a minority are not going to do well,' I would tend to think that would erode my confidence."

Counselors and educators say that the lack of encouragement many black students get to take more difficult courses also may contribute to the lack of success at testing some minorities have.

Fred Moreno, director of public affairs for the College Board, which sponsors the SAT and achievement tests, said that most theories about the performance of minority students on the SAT have focused on socioeconomic background. Many minority students, for example, have fewer opportunities to travel or have access to cultural experiences that often translate into higher verbal scores on the test. These theories emphasize that scores are a reflection of exposure rather than lack of ability.

Since 1976 the average SAT score of black students has risen 19 points on the verbal portion of the test and 31 points on the math portion, Moreno said.

"No other group has that kind of an increase by far," Moreno said. "Actually, whites have dropped 10 points in verbal." Moreno said.

During this period the proportion of blacks among the test takers also has risen, from 8.2 percent in 1976 to 10 percent nationally in 1991.

The average scores for whites in 1990 were 441 in verbal, 589 in math; for blacks 351 in verbal, 385 in math; and for Asians, 411 in verbal, 530 in math. The College Board does not publish a cumulative score for Hispanics.

The College Board considers a score higher than 600 on the math or verbal sections of the test to be high. Of the 94,311 blacks who took the SAT in 1990, 1 percent scored above 600 on the verbal section, and 3 percent scored above 600 on the mathematics section.

Nine percent of Asian students scored above 600 on verbal and 34 percent scored above 600 on math. Among whites, about 8 percent scored above 600 on verbal and 19 percent on mathematics.

"The fact is there are minority kids who do well," Moreno said. "But there are not enough of those kids doing well."

As part of a well-publicized national debate on how best to reform public education, many local school systems are trying to raise minority achievement. One tack is to reduce the number of lower-level math and science courses to force students to take more challenging courses. Some local school systems also have begun to address teacher expectations by training teachers to expect that all students have a capacity to learn.

"Any average teacher can be successful with motivated kids," said Fairfax school Superintendent Robert R. Spillane, "but the real pros can teach the unmotivated, the angry and the ill-prepared."

Several black students interviewed for this article said they have seen many of their peers who lack the drive to do well, and whose parents are not involved in their education, sit on the academic sidelines.

"It seems to me like they don't try hard enough," said Golden, who hopes to be a surgeon. He said what drives him is the desire not to turn out like some of the people he sees around his who graduate from high school and do nothing. "For one thing, my mom, she gives me a lot of inspiration. . . . She keeps on me . . . 'You have plenty of time to go out and do all that other stuff. Your education is important.'"

At Eleanor Roosevelt, five minority students who each scored higher than 1,200 on the SAT sat around a table recently and talked about the test and what they did to prepare themselves and why they did well.

Their backgrounds varied widely. Some had highly educated parents with professional careers, while others did not. A few took SAT preparatory courses.

Every one said their parents supported them. They all were avid readers, highly motivated and all had taken challenging math and science courses that they said had helped them do well.

Nicole Aqui, 17, a senior, said that her first gift from her parents was not a teddy bear but a book, "Charlotte's Web."

Tweedy said that in his neighborhood education doesn't seem to be important to many youths. Instead, his family has been his primary motivator.

"In my neighborhood, they try to distract you from going to school. I heard the phrase, 'You are acting white,' " Tweedy said. "I didn't really care much. It didn't matter to me."

Some minority students said they encounter another kind of pressure from whites who say they don't have to work as hard because they are minorities.

Tania Sibila, a 17-year-old whose parents are Cuban, said: "They say you're going to get in college because you're a 'Spic.' I hate that. My grades are good because I worked hard. . . . The fact that I'm Hispanic has nothing to do with it."

Aqui said: "People will tell me, first of all because you're black and second of all because you're a female you have a better chance of getting into college. If that's really going to help me get into college of my choice, I'm going to utilize that. But I think people who think that are wrong."

"They're living proof minority students can do well," Gray said. "It's a combination of home support, motivation and a good education, and it works."

November 2, 1991

Graduate School Mystery

Why Must Black Americans and Native Americans Go into Debt to Finish Their Doctorates, While Foreign Students Get Financial Aid?

WILLIAM RASPBERRY

Just over a year ago, when the proposal first surfaced, and again last month when Secretary of Education Lamar Alexander announced the department's new rules on race-specific scholarships, a lot of us wondered about the insistence on fixing something that wasn't broken.

Even those who (like myself) believe it is generally better to seek racial justice through laws and policies that are, on their face, race-neutral wondered at the out-of-the-blue decision to tell universities how to distribute their scholarships. There had been no complaint of bias in favor of black students, no allegation that deserving white students were being discriminated against. (The scholarships at issue do not involve government money but come from private sources or the universities' own funds.)

As I wrote in December 1990, "America's racial problem is not that black people have too much opportunity, but too little."

I'd have said that a lot more forcefully had I known what Frank L. Morris knows.

Morris has completed a study that shows American universities discriminating against black American doctoral students (particularly black males) in favor of foreign students.

The dean of graduate studies and research at Morgan State University isn't just playing the numbers game, though the numbers are bad enough: In all of 1990, only four American blacks (and five Puerto Ricans and Mexican Americans) received doctorates in math from U.S. universities; 413 foreigners did. The numbers are similar across a range of math and science specialties.

Between 1975 and 1990, said Morris in a recent speech to the Council of Graduate Schools, the number of foreigners receiving doctoral degrees in this country rose from 5,870 to 9,398, while "the group which suffered the greatest decline during this period was black males . . . from 650 in 1975 to 320 in 1990, a decline of more than 50 percent."

According to Morris, the black-male decline tracks the decline in federal assistance. "Once American black doctoral students had to depend upon American universities as the prime source of funding to finance their studies, they became much worse off, because American universities have chosen to allocate more of their resources to fields where they have admitted and supported foreign students."

How solid a case does Morris make? The most obvious objections to his claim that universities are preferring foreign students are (1) that there is a dearth of black Americans qualified for (or interested in pursuing) terminal degrees, and (2) that the fields in which blacks are most likely to seek doctorates (education, for instance) are those that bring least prestige to the universities and therefore the least proffer of scholarship assistance.

The best test of Morris's thesis is not what universities might do given some theoretical confluence of applicant eligibility and interest but what the universities actually do.

A 1990 National Research Council review of scholars who had succeeded in earning a PhD found that the universities themselves were the chief funding source for 68.8 percent of the foreign candidates, but less than 25 percent of the African-American doctorates. "For more than 60 percent of African Americans (and Native Americans) the primary source of support for their doctoral education was their own personal funds, such as loans. In contrast, only 13.8 percent of international students primarily depended on personal funds to finance their doctoral education."

As for the "wrong fields" argument, 81 percent of black Americans who earned doctorates in education (where a high proportion of minorities earn their terminal degrees) had to rely on personal resources to finance their study; only 12 percent got the bulk of their funding from their universities. For foreign students earning doctorates in education, only 41 percent depended primarily on personal resources, and 28 percent were funded primarily by the universities—more than twice the rate for blacks. Similar patterns held for the social sciences and the humanities.

What's going on, and why? Even Morris isn't sure, except that he thinks it may have something to do with the "irrational fears" that can make life difficult for black men in general.

In point of fact, it may not even be necessary to figure out why universities are preferring foreigners to fully qualified U.S. citizens. What is wanted is not some fruitless argument over who caused the problem but a determination to fix it.

Frank Morris's paper is an excellent place to start.

January 6, 1991

Seeking Better Teachers

Ferment over Status, Competence Continues

KENNETH J. COOPER

After nearly a decade of trying to attract better teachers to U.S. classrooms with higher pay, wider competency testing and tougher certification standards, educators remain concerned about the quality of the nation's teaching force.

There is a widespread sense of disappointment in how little those measures and other education reforms of the 1980s, most of which affected teachers in some way, have changed education's bottom line—student achievement. Expressions of dismay have come from Education Secretary Lauro F. Cavazos, teachers themselves and, most recently, some of the state officials responsible for implementing legislative mandates designed to improve public schools.

"Over 1,000 pieces of legislation regarding teachers were developed during the 1980s, and many of these policy proposals are now being implemented. Yet, studies indicate that the policies developed during the recent 'wave' of educational reform, which mandate improvement in teacher and student performance, have actually had only a marginal impact on the quality of classroom instruction," a study group of the National Association of State Boards of Education observed last month.

"Thus, it would appear that the majority of strategies incorporated thus far have been inadequate and perhaps even inappropriate tools for improving education," the panel concluded.

The study group, led by Thomas Howerton, chairman of the Colorado State Board of Education, cited the same test data that Cavazos had earlier this year. The 1988 results of the National Assessment of Education Progress, a congressionally mandated series of tests, showed almost no improvement in writing skills among U.S. students since 1971 and found most advancement in basic reading skills occurred in the 1970s—before the education reform movement.

Teachers also appear to be disappointed in this outcome. A survey of 21,389 teachers conducted for the Carnegie Foundation for the Advancement of Teaching found that four out of five teachers graded the 1980s reforms as deserving a grade of "C" or lower. Most teachers surveyed said the biggest change since 1983 had come in their salaries, which have outpaced inflation in recent years and now average about $31,000, according to the National Education Association, the nation's largest teachers union.

As a result, teacher pay no longer dominates the education agenda, although there have been some proposals for salary differentials to reward master teachers or to ease shortages of mathematics, science and minority teachers. The emerging issue of the 1990s, giving teachers more authority and flexibility, is meant in part to address a longstanding view among the 2.3 million public school teachers that they are not treated as professionals.

There are some observers who see signs of improvement—or prospects for it—in the teaching force. David Imig, executive director of the American Association of Colleges for Teacher Education, said enrollments in teacher-training programs have increased 65 percent in the last five years even as colleges were raising the grade-point averages required to declare an education major. "I think this suggests we're having some success," he said.

Driving the enrollment growth, Imig said, is an increase in older students who have entered graduate programs to prepare for a second career. Like the existing teaching force, which is 72 percent female, many of these older students are women. "They're saying they always wanted to teach and now they're going to do it," he said.

Though teacher advocates like Sharon Robinson, director of the NEA's National Center for Innovation, argue that successful teachers need "a passion for learning," in addition to a love of children, the main reason students choose education careers has not changed. Most still enter teaching for the love of children, not for the love of learning. In a recent Lou Harris survey, 71 percent of the beginning teachers interviewed cited a stronger interest in young people than in a particular academic subject.

This basic motivation may be one reason that teachers' intellectual rigor remains in question even though they seem to be generally well-educated on paper. Slightly more than half of all public school teachers held a master's degree in 1986, according to the NEA. But their strongest motivation for obtaining advanced degrees may not be a love of learning: Collective bargaining agreements commonly pay teachers more if they accumulate graduate credits.

Fitful moves have been made to deepen the intellectual content of teacher training programs. A few states, including Virginia, Texas and New Jersey, have limited the number of education courses that can count towards the academic requirements for a teaching certificate. A handful of colleges have converted to five-year programs that require an undergraduate major in a subject other than education and conclude with a master's degree.

Supporters of such moves argue that prospective teachers spend too much time learning how to teach, and not enough studying what they will teach. This criticism has been lodged in particular against elementary school teachers, who take a smattering of courses because they will teach several subjects.

Despite the unflattering appraisals that some college students give education courses, education practitioners say knowledge of subject matter is not enough. Robert S. Peterkin, superintendent of the Milwaukee schools, said inability to control a classroom was the most frequent reason that beginning teachers fail in his district, followed by an inadequate command of academic subjects.

The NEA's Robinson agreed on the importance of what is known as "classroom management" in the teaching trade. "If you can't get them [students] organized to learn, I don't care how much you know. You can't get them to learn," she said.

Both the Reagan and Bush administrations have advocated that states authorize nontraditional routes to a teaching certificate as a way to bolster the academic strength of the teaching force. Generally, these new procedures allow college graduates trained in other fields to begin teaching without first taking standard education courses. So far these paths to "alternative certification" have attracted relatively few new teachers.

C. Emily Feistritzer, director of the National Center for Education Information, reported earlier this year that since 1985 only 12,000 new teachers had taken various alternative routes, out of a million who were hired nationwide. About 30 states have provisions for alternative certification.

Imig, whose organization represents traditional education colleges and departments, said attracting better teaching candidates means realizing a long-held goal of making the career "valued and honored" and well-paid. Though teacher salaries have increased, Imig argues that they have only gone "back to where they were in 19721 in terms of purchasing power. "Those strides haven't been all that great," he said.

Ideally, Imig said, salaries for experienced master teachers would approach the $70,000 a year they receive in Rochester, N.Y. He also endorsed higher pay for scarce math and science teachers as well as for minority teachers, whose numbers are expected to dwindle as the percentage of minority students increases. Currently, minority teachers are projected to decline from 10 percent to 5 percent of the profession as the proportion of minority students reaches 30 percent in the year 2000.

"There are going to have to be salary differentials for minority teachers that are going to cause some tensions in the (education) system," he said.

Such pay differentials would represent a major change, because standard teacher salary scales are now based on seniority and education. Moreover, racial tensions have divided teachers in a number of cities where federal courts mandated hiring preferences for minority teachers to remedy segregation. Salary differentials for minority teachers could create similar disputes.

A recent report for Imig's organization concluded that the economics of choosing a teaching career are different for minorities. Mary Dilworth, the author of the report, said minorities were dissuaded from teaching because they carry higher college loan debts, rely on women to produce a greater share of household income and find testing requirements "present a greater challenge to them."

Dilworth concluded: "The educational community has not offered individuals of color compelling reasons to join its ranks. The often cited reward of being a 'positive role model' is inadequate for most . . . If black, Hispanic, Asian and Native Americans have reasonable assurance that they will be trained, employed and compensated well, consulted with and promoted for their unique contributions, the field will certainly be more attractive."

Those issues fall into the broad category of professionalization and could apply to any prospective teacher, Robinson said. About 45 percent of teachers in the Carnegie survey, up from 25 percent in 1987, said they were dissatisfied with their degree of control over their professional lives. One high school teacher from Connecticut expressed a common sense of lack of respect: "I would like my words to make a difference, but I have learned from experience that the public, boards of education and superintendents will not listen . . . "

Robinson predicted that the situation may change with "the creation of a new professional ethic" that will see teachers more involved in school improvement, curriculum, research and their own continuing education. A small number of districts have experimented with "school-based management," which gives teachers more decision-making authority.

Robinson said that pressure from teachers would spawn more experiments of that kind: "If policymakers weren't serious when they started talking about professionalization of teachers in the mid-'80s, it's too late now."

Imig was more skeptical. "Every time we've had a teacher shortage, we talk about getting more professional teachers," he said.

One professionalization effort widely supported by teachers is the issuance of a voluntary teaching credential from an independent national board, much as the American Medical Association and American Bar Association certify doctors and lawyers. The National Board for Professional Teaching Standards, created in 1987, has launched such a project and expects to issue the first national certificates in 1993. States would retain the right to set their own certification requirements.

The Carnegie survey found that 64 percent of teachers supported the concept of a national teaching certificate. The board's own survey of the National Education Association and American Federation of Teachers found 85 percent of their members backed the idea. Nearly equal percentages said their main motives for seeking such a national certificate would be professional recognition from the public or the possibility of higher salaries.

November 11, 1990

Head Start Endures, Making a Difference

Support for Program is Wide but Funding Accord Elusive

KENNETH J. COOPER

There was no running water, indoor toilet or kitchen, and the homemade playground was so spare that she often climbed the trees. But the substandard facilities of the church near here are not what Angela Moore remembers most about being one of the first children in Head Start 25 years ago.

Moore, then 5, recalls sensing the personal warmth of her teacher, being around children her own age and learning things for the first time—among them that she was a good student. Those experiences provided an edge when Moore, who is black, integrated a Catholic kindergarten in Holly Springs that fall of 1965.

"I had to wait for the other kids to catch up," said Moore, now a medical doctor living in Texas. "I already knew my ABCs. I already knew how to count. I knew my colors and different shapes. . . . Head Start prepared me to be able to interact with other kids regardless of their race—how to share, how to be part of a group."

Moore described almost exactly what its founders in the Great Society intended Head Start to do for poor preschool children: Build a foundation of self-esteem, social skills and basic lessons to get then ready for school. Unlike some other social programs of that era, Head Start has endured, evolved and attracted bipartisan support, largely because of evidence that it works.

Child advocates and business leaders have come to regard Head Start as an essential component of any strategy for upgrading U.S. education. They have repeatedly called for giving the preschool program enough money to enroll all of the estimated 2.5 million children age 3 to 5 who are eligible for it. Currently, 488,470 poor children—about 20 percent of those eligible—are in Head Start.

But so far the consensus on Head Start's educational value has yielded no political agreement on full funding, or on how large an increase over the current budget of nearly $1.4 billion is eventually needed. The administration says about $1 billion; congressional Democrats say more than $6 billion. The disagreement involves what age children to serve, for how many years and whether to increase teacher salaries and benefits. In 1988, teachers' pay averaged $12,074.

Congress is expected to debate those issues when it reauthorizes Head Start this year and considers President Bush's request to increase its budget by $500 million in fiscal 1991. A reauthorization bill could reach the House floor next month, which marks the 25th anniversary of what began as an experimental summer program in President Lyndon B. Johnson's War on Poverty.

Since its inception, Head Start has served 11 million children and become an institution, particularly in Mississippi, a state that has received a larger share of funds because of a high poverty rate and lack of public kindergartens until 1987. It is also a state where officials resisted Head Start's arrival, because the federal government insisted that students and staffs be racially integrated.

That resistance inspired fears of racial violence in places such as Holly Springs, a town of 7,000 about 35 miles southeast of Memphis.

Nola Robinson recalled that parishioners of Newell Chapel, the black Methodist church in nearby Victoria where Moore climbed trees, were afraid it would be bombed if a Head Start center opened there.

Robinson's father, a church elder and former teacher, finally persuaded the congregation to agree.

Moore was one of the first students. Robinson was her teacher. Today, Moore chairs the natural sciences department at Wiley College, a small black school in Marshall, Tex. Robinson directs the same Head Start center, now housed in a modular classroom building a few miles away in Byhalia.

They have strong memories of each other.

"I just remember how nice she was, how friendly she was, how warm she was. . . . I guess I just bonded to that," said Moore, 29.

"She was smart . . . very neat with her work," Robinson said of Moore. "We had trees on the playground, and I had to get her out of the trees quite a bit."

The Head Start program that Robinson runs, called the Whitaker Center—one of 21 in nine counties that the Institute for Community Services (ICS), a nonprofit organization in Holly Springs, oversees—has much better facilities than its forerunner had in 1965. But it retains the personal touch that left such an impression on Moore.

The modular building, which has aluminum siding outside and wood paneling inside, holds six classrooms for 120 children—about 85 percent of them black—who are 4 or 5 years old. There is also an assembly room, separate bathrooms for boys and girls, and a full kitchen to prepare breakfast and lunch. The grassy playground is fenced, treeless and full of modern playground equipment, including two "circle-cycles," which are a sort of stationary tricycle for five.

One recent morning the six-hour day began with a teacher and an aide leading 19 children in prayer before a breakfast of link sausage, toast, orange juice and milk. They prayed: "God is good, God is grace, and we thank you for our food. Bow our head, must be fed, give us Lord our daily bread. Amen."

After the meal, the teacher and aide cleared the dishes, wiped the two tables and escorted the children to bathrooms to brush their teeth. Then the teacher, Gloria Moore, no relation to Angela, assigned each child to one of six activities around the room. About half stayed at the tables and practiced printing their names, while others played with blocks, painted at an easel, read books, tied the laces of wooden sneakers or did "housekeeping" with a small bed.

The assignments, Moore explained to a visitor, were tailored to help each child sharpen specific skills, based on regular assessment of their strengths and weaknesses. She and aide Lula Hardaway moved about the room, stopping to talk quietly with a child or reassign one who seemed bored or frustrated.

The flexibility and individual attention appeared quite different from the common pattern in public schools, where a single teacher typically stands in front of a class and administers the same lesson to every student at the same time.

"They have more structured material, more ditto sheets and like that," said Katherine Culp, another teacher at Whitaker. "They do everything in a structured way, and we help the child get where we want him to go. . . . We try not to get any child upset because he can't master a task."

Research on Head Start has generally shown that its graduates are more likely to do better in school than other poor children. Head Start graduates have been found to have better attendance, miss fewer tests, need special education less and drop out less often.

The program's supporters say those are the results of avoiding an initial failure that can alienate students from school and lower teachers' expectations of them. Once those attitudes develop, disadvantaged children tend to fall further behind the longer they stay in school. That is why Head Start supporters see intervention in early childhood as the most effective strategy.

But Head Start advocates warn that the program may not be the only intervention poor children need. "You cannot inoculate them from all the perils of poverty," said Helen Blank of the Children's Defense Fund. In fact, teachers at the Whitaker Center said the structured classrooms in area public schools have caused problems for students used to Head Start's flexibility.

The six teachers at the center are experienced, averaging more than 10 years of work in Head Start. Culp has taught in Head Start since 1966. But while an entry-level kindergarten teacher in the state is paid about $18,000, a Head Start teacher working for ICS makes an average of $8,000, below the federal poverty line for a family of two. None of Whitaker's teachers makes more than $8,900 a year.

"The majority of our teachers are living in poverty," said Arvern Moore, executive director of ICS since 1967. "Most of those who are single parents are eligible for all the public assistance programs." Moore, a former science teacher who is Angela's father, complained that the $5 million in federal funds ICS receives leaves no room for higher pay or expanded benefits. About 80 percent of the agency's 367 employees cannot afford to pay premiums for private health insurance, which cost $645 for a teacher earning $8,500 last year, he said.

Whether to improve teacher pay and benefits is an issue in the debate over full funding of the program. The Bush administration has opposed increases in compensation, preferring instead to expand the number of slots for children.

"If we have to choose, it's more important to get more children into it. . . . The children who are left out are the real losers," Health and Human Secretary Louis W. Sullivan said in an interview last month.

Legislation sponsored by Sen. Christopher J. Dodd (D-Conn.), Sen. Edward M. Kennedy (D-Mass.) and Rep. Dale E. Kildee (D-Mich.) would authorize increasing Head Start funds to $7.7 billion in 1994 and reserving 12 percent of annual appropriations for program improvements, including teacher raises and benefits.

Head Start teachers need not be college graduates. But Kildee said those who have the same academic credentials as public school teachers should earn comparable pay.

Arvern Moore said, "It just infuriates me that the secretary or anybody else would . . . disregard the people who made this program what it is today."

But Moore partially agreed with the Bush administration on another funding issue. He said Head Start need not serve 5-year-olds who can enroll in kindergartens. In 1965, kindergartens were not available in every state, but they are now.

The Bush administration has focused on enrolling all eligible 4-year-olds, citing a study that showed a second year of preschool for poor children is less cost-effective than the first.

The Democrats' bill would authorize funds to serve all 3- and 4-year-olds as well as 30 percent of 5-year-olds, a total of 1.9 million children.

If Head Start were fully funded in that way, Arvern Moore believes the program would improve the life prospects of more poor people in the Holly Springs area, which has never completely recovered from the devastation brought to this onetime cotton capital by the Civil War.

It is not that Head Start would inspire every child to become a doctor like his daughter, Moore said, but it could interest more families in education as a route to a better life. He spoke of two parents who, after enrolling four daughters in Head Start, completed General Educational Development certificates, got better jobs and were able to buy a home. All four daughters finished college.

"It's happened time and time again," Moore said.

April 22, 1990

A Chance at Starting Even

Family Literacy Program Blossoms in Virginia

MARYLOU TOUSIGNANT

Every morning, 4-year-old Lizzie Cobb awakens her mother with the same question: "Are we going to school today?"

It's the same story at Melody Parker's house a few blocks away. "She's dragging me to the bus every morning," Parker says of daughter DeShay, who will turn 4 in a week.

Christina Beruete hasn't missed a day of school with 3-year-old Joshua, the mother of seven says proudly. "If I did, I'd feel like I was cheating myself. . . . For once I'm doing something for me."

Since November, the three women and their preschoolers have been going to school together four mornings a week, as part of a special federally funded program called Even Start Family Literacy at two elementary schools in Prince William County.

Thirty-three families are enrolled in the program, which teaches mothers and fathers parenting skills and basic academic subjects while it gives their youngsters a preschool education.

On a typical day, the parents—mostly mothers, although a few fathers participate—and children arrive at school on the bus about 8:45, eat breakfast together and then have shared music, story and writing time. After that, the mothers go off together for language, math and science instruction, while the children roll up their sleeves and dig into the sandbox, or shaving cream, or whatever else is planned for the day.

After lunch and more shared story time, the children select books to take home for reading aloud that night. The program's four teachers make home visits in the afternoon.

By including parent education as well as preschooling, Even Start takes a broader approach than its big brother, Head Start, which yesterday got President Bush's promise of more funding during a presidential visit to a Catonsville, Md., Head Start center.

A multimillion-dollar federal effort begun in 1989, Even Start is one in a host of family literacy programs that have mushroomed nationwide, from an estimated 300 five years ago to about 3,000 today, according to Meta Potts, who directs adult learning services for the National Center for Family Literacy, a nonprofit research and training center in Louisville.

An estimated 25 million adults in the United States are functionally illiterate, meaning they cannot perform everyday tasks such as balancing a checkbook. Estimates of the number of adults who read with only minimal comprehension are as high as 45 million.

Not surprisingly, one effect has been a legacy of illiteracy, handed down from one generation to the next.

"If parents don't know how to read, they're going to pass that on to their children. We've got to break that cycle," said Letitia Rennings, the U.S. Department of Education's national coordinator for Even Start, which targets children from birth to age 7 in 233 projects around the country, including one each in Prince George's County and the District, which together serve about 150 families.

"The parent is the critical teacher' for a child, said Potts. "If they've dropped out or lost their excitement for learning . . . then they won't transmit that value to their children."

The parents in the Even Start program at Dumfries Elementary School, one of the two schools participating in Prince William, can read and write, with varying degrees of proficiency. Two of the mothers have a high school diploma or its equivalent. For those women, the program offers an educational boost for their youngsters—the Prince William program targets 3- and 4-year-olds—and a chance to hone their own skills for a better job and some financial and personal independence.

"The reason we're here is to better ourselves. . . . None of us has to be here; this is something we want to do," said Valerie Bollen, who completed high school and now wants to learn computers.

"My husband's been taking care of me, and I've been taking care of the kids" since she married 12 years ago, said Beruete, 28.

With seven children to raise, she had little time or thought for education. "My mind was turning to Jell-O. I never got out of the house. I never got away from the kids."

Her husband, Jose, would tell her, "You have to start somewhere. You can't just sit here and wish it to happen," but until Even Start came along, she didn't know where to begin. Now she is working toward her General Educational Development certificate and hopes to attend college someday. "I'd like to be able to choose what I want to do," Beruete said. "To me, it's like I'm starting right from the beginning."

Diane Cobb, 33, explains her presence in the program by saying "I'm doing this mostly for Lizzie. I want for her what I didn't get," including a high school diploma, which Cobb has set as one of her goals.

The women say their children have become increasingly independent and outgoing since starting school. "And I'll bet every one of them knows their ABCs now," said Pam Zahm, who attends with Jennifer, 3.

Nonetheless, coming to class has not been easy for some of the women, even though organizers removed two major hurdles by providing school buses—essential because Prince William has no public transportation and many of the mothers do not have cars—and day care for children under 3.

"I'd say 'I don't have the time, I don't have a sitter, I don't have a car,' and (the teacher recruiters} would say 'We take care of that.' I was running out of excuses" not to come, said Beruete.

Several of the mothers said they were initially apprehensive about what the other women would think of them. "I felt ashamed at first that I was so old" and hadn't completed school, said Cuca Khaef, 33, who dropped out after the 11th grade to get a job.

Cobb lost her nerve the first day and turned around at the schoolhouse door without going in. "I didn't know how the other mothers were going to treat me," she said. "I thought they'd laugh." But she changed her mind and returned a week later "because Lizzie really wanted to go to school and I felt I was depriving her."

The mothers say they've become friends, like family, in what they describe as a nonthreatening, no-pressure atmosphere where they can set their own goals and work at their own pace. They help one another with everything from solving math problems to sharing tips on discipline and homework for their older children.

Dumfries Principal Paul R. Rodericks said his school, which sits within dodgeball distance of Interstate 95 in southeastern Prince William County near Quantico Marine Base, has more than its share of educationally disadvantaged children. He sees the Even Start program, funded largely by a four-year renewable federal grant with some county money tossed in, as the first rung on a "big-time, language-rich" preschool ladder that he hopes will take children as young as 3 and help them each step of the way up to kindergarten and first grade.

Studies have shown that family literacy programs, which received an economic shot in the arm last July when Bush signed the National Literacy Act, doubling the funding authorizations for Even Start and workplace literacy programs, remove much of the risk from so-called at-risk children.

In a study last year of 14 such programs in Indiana, West Virginia and Kentucky, the National Center for Family Literacy found that children who participated as preschoolers were less likely to need special education services later on and were overwhelmingly rated by their elementary school teachers as eager to learn. Typically, 25 percent of at-risk children fail at least one grade before fourth grade, but none of the children in the study had been held back.

The benefits of family literacy efforts often go well beyond the classroom. "We're doing a little bit of everything," said Howard Miller, Even Start coordinator in Prince George's County, which serves about 75 families at five locations and had to turn some applicants away this year. "We've interceded on evictions. We provide emergency food and clothing. We're advocates and sit in with parents at school conferences," Miller said, and help with jobs, immigration and health problems. One staff member was even in the delivery room when a mother gave birth.

The mothers at Dumfries say the Prince William program has fired up not only their educational interest, but their older children's as well. Patricia Saldana said her fourth-grader, Martin, tells her "Mom, I want to come to class with you and see what you're doing in school."

Violet Carter said her 8-year-old, Sequyoah, tells friends that "my mom's going to school, after all these years."

And Christina Beruete tells the story of the night her fifth-grader brought home the same math homework she had.

As the two sat working on their fractions, Beruete said, her daughter looked over and said, "Mom, you're not doing it right."

"And I said, 'Casey, my teacher, told me to do it this way. So you do it your way and I'll do it my way.' "

January 22, 1992

Bringing Social Services into Schools

Holistic Approach Offers Health and Child Care, Family Counseling

PAUL TAYLOR

Here at Plainfield High School, a student can get help for just about any of life's woes: geometry, grammar, toothaches, child care, drug addiction, depression and parents who just don't understand.

It's known as a "one-stop-shopping" school, a place where a broad range of social, health and counseling services are gathered under the same roof. Lots of educators think it's the school of the future.

"The concept couldn't be simpler," said Ed Tetelman, a New Jersey Department of Human Services official who has built the nation's most extensive network of multi-service schools in 29 communities, both urban and suburban. "Kids are a lot like adults. If you want them to take advantage of something, convenience makes all the difference."

The movement toward bringing services into the schools—which got a glancing nod of approval in the education plan President Bush unveiled last month—is popping up all over the country as educators frustrated by the failures of earlier rounds of education reform are concluding that the way to students' minds is through their whole selves.

The District's Ballou High School was the first school in the Washington area to offer a comprehensive health clinic to its students, and Northwestern High School in Hyattsville would become the second under a proposal being drafted by the Prince George's County Commission on Families and Youth. In Alexandria, a teen clinic has been located a few blocks from T.C. Williams High School.

"There was a time not too long ago when schools wanted to be islands unto themselves, which said to communities and parents, "Leave your kids at the schoolhouse door and we'll give them back to you at the end of the day a little bit smarter," said Michael Casserly, associate director of the Council of Great City Schools, which represents the nation's 50 largest school districts. "But nowadays, kids are arriving at the schoolhouse door with so many problems, coming from families and communities in such disarray, schools have to do more for them or they won't have much chance of educating them."

If schools have been islands, social service agencies have Often been ships passing in the night—scattering programs at dispersed locations and rarely exchanging information with one another.

"Children and their families bounce like pinballs from problem to problem, from one agency to the next," said a recent report issued by the Education and Human Services Consortium, a coalition of 22 national organizations that is trying to encourage interagency collaborations at the local level.

Plainfield High School serves an inner-city community about 25 miles from Manhattan plagued by the familiar grim tableau of drugs, violence and high rates of teenage pregnancy.

Before the school-based youth services program was established here two years ago, teenage mothers had little choice but to drop out. Now there's a room for infants and toddlers 15 yards down the hall from the main office. The young mothers drop off their babies at 7:30 a.m., return at lunch and during free periods throughout the day for play and parenting lessons, and are guaranteed a job at AT&T headquarters nearby.

The dropout rate among teenage mothers is down, and so is what Teen Parent Program director Diane DesPlantes calls "recidivism"—the rate of second pregnancies. Of 48 young mothers who have taken part in the program in the first two years, some of whom are not students, only one has become pregnant a second time.

In another wing of the school, a fourth-floor storage area has been converted into a lounge, where students hang out after school, shooting pool or playing computer games. Two mental health counselors hang out with them, available for counseling in a setting free of stigma.

Not long ago, one student confided to a counselor that her girlfriend was on the verge of running away from home. "The counselor approached the troubled girl and found out that she had just been raped by her sister's boyfriend, and that she was afraid to go home because her stepfather had been teasing her sexually. Her mother wasn't there to protect her anymore—she'd gotten fed up with his physical abuse and had gone to live with relatives," recalled Roberta Knowlton, director of the New Jersey School-based Youth Services Program.

"The counselor got the mother and stepfather to come in and talk," Knowlton said. "He signed a contract promising to stop the abuse, the mother returned home and she and the daughter agreed to come in for regular counseling."

"If I had to live the lives some of these kids are living, without any outside support, I'm not sure I would have made it," said Fred Brown Jr., principal of New Brunswick High School, which is located about 15 miles south of Plainfield, serves a similar population and also started a school-based youth services program two years ago.

Brown is the first to admit he was initially wary of ceding his turf to outside bureaucrats. Though housed in schools, the social services programs are typically run by local hospitals, mental health clinics, nonprofit community groups or city agencies.

"I made it clear from the start that if I didn't have input as to who the director was, I wasn't interested," said Brown, a former police officer who has a sign on his desk that reads: "Unless you're the lead dog, the view never changes."

The University of Medicine and Dentistry of New Jersey is the "lead dog" at the New Brunswick school-based program, but Brown was allowed to choose the director. He's delighted with the way it has worked out.

"I've had parents come into my office and say they're ready to give up on their child. They're frustrated, their kids are involved in drugs, and they don't know what to do. I know as principal I don't have the time or resources to deal with these problems. A lot of my teachers are older, most of them are white, and when it's dismissal time, they're gone. They're out of Dodge City long before the sun sets. What these kids need are adults they can trust and talk to."

Many also have more basic needs—help with math, advice when they are applying for a first job, care when they are sick. "I have a theory that the first time a kid has a bad toothache and nothing is done about it, he discovers that the adult world is against him," said Knowlton.

While most of the programs have been established in urban schools, one of the most successful is at South Brunswick High School, which draws students from 43 square miles of suburban sprawl and semi-rural stretches north of Princeton. It is an area made up of small hamlets, a few trailer parks, lots of dual-earner suburban families—and no sense of community or central gathering place. "There is really no other place to hang out," said Elizabeth McAllister, 17, who spends her afternoons in a teen recreation center set up in the school's two home economics rooms. The center remains open during the summer, when it takes over the school gymnasium.

Scores of students at South Brunswick also are receiving mental health counseling—for depression, drug abuse, problems at home. Dozens of family members come in regularly to participate in family counseling, sometimes to talk about parental substance abuse. "If Johnnie has so much stuff going on in his life that he can't focus, how are we going to teach him geometry?" asked Richard Kaye, principal of South Brunswick for the past 17 years and a lifelong proponent of holistic education.

His fellow principals are beginning to jump on board—partly out of enlightenment, partly self-defense. At its annual convention last month, the National Association of Secondary School Principals held a debate on the following resolution: "Schools that both attempt to teach academics and provide social services are doomed to fail." By 166 to 110, the principals rejected the proposition. "I think we are realizing that if we are going to be held more accountable for the output of education, we need to get more involved with the prerequisites for learning," said Richard Kruse, director of government relations for the association.

Educators have lined up behind a bill sponsored by Sens. Bill Bradley (D-N.J.) and Edward M. Kennedy (D-Mass.) that would provide $50 million in federal demonstration grants to school districts that find ways to coordinate a wide range of social services. But it's already happening, without the federal carrot. Iowa and

Kentucky are putting together statewide programs similar to the New Jersey model, and cities all over California are forging collaborative efforts.

Some in the vanguard of the movement say they think school should offer a broad range of services not just for students, but their whole families. "I look forward to a time when we keep schools open to 10 o'clock every night, have them going 12 months a year, make them a place where poor families can pick up Food Stamps and their food from the WIC program and their AFDC checks, and where they can sign up for job training," said Gov. Lawton Chiles (D) of Florida, which already is a leader in locating health clinics in schools.

There are inevitable controversies. In New Brunswick, a plan to locate a toddler center at the high school ran into opposition from local church groups, which worried that it would reward teenage child-bearing. (Several schools in the Washington area—including Ballou and Northwestern high schools and the District's Hart Junior High—have toddler centers). In Florida, a school-based health clinic that distributes condoms to students who have their parents' approval has drawn pickets. In Alexandria, the teen clinic was placed a few blocks away from T.C. Williams High when parents and community members objected to condom prescription and distribution on school premises.

Bush's education plan was careful to observe that while schools can sometimes house additional social services, they should not try to supplant the basic mission of families, nor should they try to "become hospitals or welfare agencies."

"The president's statement didn't give the collaboration movement the emphasis I had hoped it would," conceded Martin Blank, an author of the Education and Human Services Consortium report. Still, he said, the real force behind the movement is coming from the grass roots—and so are the most daunting challenges.

"The toughest nut to crack is to change institutional patterns of behavior—to get agencies to really collaborate," he said. He noted, for example, that the New Jersey program is funded with a special $6.5 million appropriation from the state legislature. "That means it is politically vulnerable. Now, when you get each participating agency taking money and staff out of its own budget and putting it into a collaborative model, that's when you've really broken down some barriers."

May 2, 1991

14 Work

==

There are many problems in the workplace, from crime to gender inequality, to issues of health and safety.

The first article looks at unemployment in the steel industry as an example of the current shakeout in the U.S. economy. Continued unemployment has far ranging effects, from violence, to divorce to mortgages unpaid. These former steelworkers are part of a generation of workers rendered obsolete by technology.

The second article talks about the jobless safety net falling short. Designed to help tide people over when they lose their jobs, unemployment insurance is staggering under a new wave of applicants, and actually serving a smaller percentage of the overall unemployed now than in the 1970s. The next article explores the maquiladora industry, where United States companies move operations into Mexican territory, using inexpensive Mexican labor.

The final article looks at the future of work in the year 2000, where it is estimated that 80% of all new entrants into the American workforce will be women, minorities, or immigrants; assembly line workers will be less than 5% of the workforce; and the service sector will create a greater economic gap between skilled and semiskilled worker.

Learning to Forge a New Life Beyond the Mill

DALE RUSSAKOFF

In the French pastry class at the Restaurant School, Bill and Bob Adams are alone among aspiring chefs, headwaiters and restaurant managers in believing that making profiteroles feels like making steel.

Amid aromas of rum and mocha, in perhaps the cleanest of workplaces, it is jarring to imagine parallels with one of the filthiest, a steel mill. But steel is the Adams family's point of reference. The brothers and their father made it at the Fairless Works continuously for almost 40 years. The heritage is apparent even with Bill and Bob in chef's whites from the head down, which is to say that nobody here has shoulders like the Adams brothers.

"My brother and I spent 25 years in industry and saw all the industry go overseas," Bob said. "We wanted something you couldn't send overseas. We figured: Who's going to send overseas for a hamburger or a coq au vin?"

"At least we're still making something," he said, sliding a tray of profiteroles and eclairs into an oven. "We're making food, instead of steel, but it's the same idea. With steel, you take all the elements and mix them together and put them into a furnace. Here you put them in an oven."

Across the cooking table, a young classmate named Chris looked up from under his white hat. "Ah, the mighty Fairless Works," he intoned, "reduced to the image of a kitchen."

In a world that no longer needs them as steelworkers, the Adams brothers are trying to remake themselves as restaurant managers. It is as if they are repeating the journey of their father, who left Scotland with his family in 1919 to seek opportunity in America.

He finally found it at the Fairless Works. They are not sure whether they will find it at all. Along with hundreds of others from Fairless, they are in mid-passage, emigrating from an old world where opportunity was exhausted to a new one where nothing is guaranteed.

It is a quintessentially American experience, played out for centuries by immigrants, by farmers who left the land during the Industrial Revolution, by generations of workers rendered obsolete by technology. Now it is repeating itself, not only for workers in basic industries but also in services, which boomed in the last decade only to founder in this one. The uncertainty so common to life at Fairless has invaded law, finance, journalism, defense contracting and other once-insulated worlds.

The men and women of the Fairless Works have shown an overwhelming impulse to remake themselves. From past mass layoffs, government officials expected, at most, 400 of about 2,000 laid-off workers to seek training in new fields. But as the national recession deepened and so many Fairless workers found so little opportunity, more than 1,000 expressed interest in training for careers from physical therapy to truck driving.

The government had not counted on so many voyagers. The Labor Department granted $1.6 million from a fund for "catastrophic" layoffs. The money was expected to cover tuition and expenses for retraining workers. But even with a second federal training program for which many workers qualified, hundreds were left at the docks.

For those making it, the journey has required enormous personal sacrifice. Bob Adams and his wife, Arlene, had to sell their house to keep their daughters in college while he spends as many as 70 hours a week at the Restaurant School. That bought some peace of mind, he said. Then, on the first day of class, an instructor warned that only I percent of new restaurants survive for five years.

One place where Fairless workers start remaking themselves is a center for dislocated workers in a steel-walled building alongside their rusting, abandoned furnaces. Run by four laid-off steelworkers, it sometimes seems like a naturalization center, an Ellis Island of the economy, because the world in which former Fairless workers find themselves might as well be a foreign country.

Those who cannot pay the mortgage or buy food and clothing find help from counselor Janice Heck at the center, but the most popular offering has been a coping class that could be called "Getting Up the Creek Without a Paddle."

The four-day class starts with Joe Vandegrift, 46, a gruff-voiced veteran of 25 years in the Fairless open hearth, standing beside an American flag in front of a roomful of steelworkers and giving it to them as bluntly as he can:

"We were all making a pretty good living here," Vandegrift told one group of 14. "That's not where you're going to be able to start. You're not going to find jobs in that $9- to $15-an-hour range. You're going to have to adjust."

Electricians, bulldozer operators, riggers, welders, laborers listened stoically. All were out of work or working part time, sliding more deeply into debt. None had health insurance. None knew how to conduct a methodical job search, write a resume or sell themselves to an employer in an interview.

"Nobody in this room did anything wrong," Vandegrift continued. "They made money. You made money. You cannot be embarrassed. You have to tell everyone you know what your situation is. You have to ask them to help you."

You have to call everyone on your Christmas card list, he said, everyone you remember from high school. Anyone working could know something that can help you. You go to the bank? Ask your branch manager for leads. Church? Ask your minister. Do not stop with the classified ads. Get there before the ads. Go to industrial parks. Knock on every door. Then go back. Knock again.

The classes turn very basic when Vandegrift and Beverly D'Ambrosio, another former Fairless worker, try to teach men and women who have rarely had a job interview how to survive one.

"Okay, you guys," said D'Ambrosio, who spent 23 years in the man's world of Fairless. "If you're sitting across from a woman interviewer, I don't care how tight your pants feel, how much your underpants are riding up, don't start adjusting yourselves." A formidable presence, D'Ambrosio rocked her hips Elvis-style as the class roared with laughter. "A woman interviewer is not going to like that," she said.

Vandegrift reviewed the dress code: no Hawaiian shirts, no gold chains, definitely no earrings. "A guy who's an interviewer, he might have a thing about earrings," he said. "Why have him eliminate you because you're wearing one?" If you like to hunt, do not say so; the interviewer might be into animal rights.

D'Ambrosio, 48, talked about stress, which she knows well. She is divorced, with an $1,100 monthly mortgage and two grown children and a granddaughter living with her. D'Ambrosio herself has returned to school to learn word processing, hoping to start a new career when the dislocated workers center closes, perhaps as early as next month. But she fears that she will fare poorly against workers half her age seeking the same job.

"You're dealing with a lack of control," she told one class. "You had a structure, a place to go to every day. All of a sudden, you have no place to go."

Toward the end of each class, Vandegrift plays the role of job interviewer. One day, he turned to a man who had been a welder for 25 years. "How long will you stay with us if we hire you?" he asked.

"Till whenever," the welder said, shoulders hunched, head hanging.

Vandegrift wrinkled his brow, stood tall to demonstrate appropriate posture and set the welder straight: "How about: 'As long as you're satisfied with my work and as long as I feel I'm treated fairly.' You want this job, but you want respect too."

He turned to a man who cannot read and write and for 17 years repaired tracks for trains carrying raw materials to the furnaces. "What are your special skills?" Vandegrift asked.

The only answer was a shrug.

"I know something you can do that a lot of people can't," Vandegrift said. "You can work outside in all kinds of elements—hot, cold, rain, sun, you could work in all of 'em. Some people don't like that. Some people can't do that. You can. You tell 'em you can do that."

"Look," he said to the whole class, pacing the room as if trying to walk his determination into them, "you are the product you are selling. You gotta try to get that person inside you out."

For six months, Vandegrift ended most of his days at the center by getting into his aging white Plymouth and heading for his own new world. On a typical night, he drove through the plant gates, under a huge safety sign about eye protection that was blinking "FOCUS ON YOUR FUTURE," across the Delaware River, past the Trenton, N.J., bridge with its anachronistic boast, "Trenton Makes The World Takes."

Then he boarded a train to downtown Philadelphia for a class on becoming a travel agent. The textbook in his briefcase was "The Travel Agent—Dealer in Dreams."

When he reached class, Vandegrift heard a lecture that sounded strikingly like one he gives at the steel mill: It's a jungle out there, but there's meat for the hustlers.

"If you're waiting for one person to walk through the door, you're desperate," Domenic Gallo Jr., reservations manager for a package tour company, was saying that night. "You'll sell them anything. It's the same thing that's happening with car salesmen, with insurance salesmen. That's what's wrong with this business. You have to be out canvassing, literally knocking on doors through your telephone. There's a lot of affluence in our society. Right now, luxury travel is up. You can have a piece of that."

Vandegrift, ever a step ahead, already had eyes on his piece. "Only 1 percent of people who travel have been on a cruise, and cruises sound fantastic," he said. "I think there's a real opportunity there."

For all his fervor about moving on, Vandegrift remains a steelworker. The union contract forces him to be. It guarantees anyone his age with 25 years in the mill health insurance and a lifetime pension starting two years after a shutdown. In return for that security, USX Corp., owner of Fairless, can call him to another mill within the two years—in his case, by March 1993. He must answer that call and then finish his 30th year before earning the pension, providing the next mill lasts that long.

He said he cannot afford to walk away. Not many travel agencies offer new employees pensions and health coverage.

"If it wasn't for my pension, I'd walk out the door and say, 'Goodbye, it's over,' " he said. "It's like a bad marriage, I guess. When it's over, it's over. But it can take a long time to end."

For Rochelle Conners, 32, and Paul Edelkamp, 40, it ended a lot faster. Steelworkers of their generation did not have the "whiskers," as seniority is known in the mill, to gain lifetime benefits. Both married, with children, they felt middle-class security slipping away after losing their jobs. They realized that they were as obsolete as their steel mill and would have to start from the bottom again.

Edelkamp discovered this through trial and error. An electrician in the mill, he started applying daily for electricians, jobs after the shutdown. He found sporadic work but not enough to pay the bills. During one telephone conversation, he put a reporter on hold to answer call-waiting—only to find a bill collector on the other line.

In November, Edelkamp went to the dislocated workers class. At one point, he heard the beep of a truck backing up outside and for an instant thought it was the whistle that used to blow in the open-hearth furnace when white-hot liquid steel was about to be released.

"I felt like something was going on with my mind," he said. "I almost felt sick. I found myself thinking: I'm never going to work with those people again, make that kind of money again, get those kind of benefits again."

But the class helped him. He did everything Vandegrift said, called everyone he knew, knocked on every door in every industrial park. He said he found new confidence. The resume he wrote in the class reflected it. "Works well with others under minimal supervision" was his favorite line.

Applying for the same jobs as before, but with a new resume, he started receiving calls for interviews. Within a few weeks, he got a job—not the answer, just a job. He works six days a week as an electrician for a printing company here. He brings home about $100 a week more than he could draw on unemployment, less than half of the $48,000 he made in his best year at the mill. But at least he has family health insurance. A few days into the job, he said: "I'm tickled to death to be working."

He tried but had no luck finding something better and concluded that a mere electrician has few options outside a large factory. "I'm always going to be one in 75 or 100," he said. The future seemed to him to lie with office buildings or small companies. "But they want someone to fix all the systems in the building," he said, not just electrical ones.

So last month he returned to school in air conditioning, heating, ventilation and refrigeration. For 18 months, he will go to class three nights a week while working six days.

He opted for this grueling schedule despite being offered $19 an hour as a steelworker in January. The call came from CITI Steel USA Inc., a steel mill in Claymont, Del., owned by a Chinese government corporation. During his interview, the plant manager took him to see the blast furnace, to see if he could take the heat, Edelkamp assumed.

"I said, 'If you want to, we can go a little closer,'" Edelkamp recalled. "But I told him the worst thing he could've done if he wanted me to take the job was to walk me by that furnace. When I left the steel mill, I swore I'd never come back to that environment. I did that 18 years. I'm not sure I want to do that again."

Edelkamp's wife, Maria, who runs a home-based video production business, said she was "scared stiff" when he went for the interview. "It's high wages, great benefits, good retirement, but to me that's not reality," she said. "To go back to steel, it's prehistoric. In five years, he'll be back in the same situation, and so will our family. I'd rather see him get training in another field, start off with less pay and maybe be more in tune with the economy."

Those words could have come from Rochelle Conners. Sitting in her Levittown house not far from the Edelkamps, wearing hospital blues required in the training program where she was learning to take electrocardiograms and draw blood, she said, "I have to admit I have a better future because the open hearth shut down."

Her awakening came at the dislocated workers class, during a cigarette break. She walked outside, leaned against the steel wall of the training center, lit a cigarette and found herself staring at the cold, rusting open-hearth furnace where only months earlier she was laying brick with 3,000 degrees of heat burning under her, surrounded by men who called her "Blondie."

"All I could think was: It's never going to be," she said. "God, it's never going to be again. All these he-men. The mill ran on manpower. They did it. They made steel. It was part of what made the country run. You felt real American going in those furnaces, making steel."

She went back into the center and decided to register for schooling as a medical technician. She figured the medical world was where the money was. She said she was petrified. She had been out of school for 13 years, never liked school much anyway. But just taking the class at the center taught her something valuable. "Everyone was petrified," she said.

She began classes in October. She could not afford hospital-blue uniforms, but a friend secured hand-me-downs from an acquaintance. She felt differently about herself than when she went to a filthy mill in jeans and old shirts. She began to think that maybe she had been interested in medicine all along.

After classes, she came home in the afternoon and played with her daughter, Kelly, 5, before hitting the books. She finished the course this month with a 4.0 average and is job hunting.

"I wish I could say to all those people who are scared like I was: GO!" she said.

While her future has promise, she cannot say much for the present. With only one income—her husband, Frank, is a truck driver—there are weeks when they must choose between paying bills and buying food. Her mother brings groceries, and, at Thanksgiving, the dislocated workers center arranged for a turkey from the Salvation Army. In the meantime, she said, she uses spices and cooks pasta.

"We've decided we will not skip a meal," she said. "I mean, for God's sake, this is America. We used to think we had the American dream. Now you go in the hole just striving for it."

At age 62, Olgar Watson had made one migration when steel making died at the Fairless Works. He was raised in rural South Carolina, one of 10 sons and three daughters of his farmer parents, who grew cotton and tobacco on federal allotments. His father took him out of school in the 10th grade to start work.

"It was South Carolina," he recalled. "Things were different. He thought I'd get nowhere, being black, no matter how much education I got."

But Watson's older brothers found work in Trenton after World War II, and he followed them there. "Trenton was nothing but factories," he said. "It was all work and no recreation. But I wanted to work, so it was okay with me."

He went to work in a rubber plant, served with the Army in Korea, raised six children and logged 27 years with Acme Rubber Co. before his plant closed in the 1970s. Later, he was hired at Fairless to rebuild massive steel-making equipment whenever it broke. He had been there 13 years when the end came.

Watson said he had little success job hunting and thought of training in another trade before deciding to get on with a deferred dream. For 48 years, he had wanted his high school diploma. He said he had never stopped studying math, learning more about it as a machinist. He said he had come to see math, like English, as a language with rules to be mastered.

So while his younger co-workers went to school to be truck drivers, nurses and travel agents, Watson went after his General Equivalency Diploma (GED). He took classes in writing, social studies, science, literature, art and math. "I always liked studying and learning," he said. "I still do."

He took his final exam in February and received his diploma April 2. He is training as a part-time school bus driver. He has begun drawing Social Security, and his wife, Katie, is a housekeeper in Trenton, but they need money for health insurance, which he lost along with his job. His old policy costs $514 a month, about what he receives from Social Security, and he said he must pay it until Medicare covers him at age 65.

Watson said he is daunted by the cost of getting by, but that has not stopped him. With his GED and part-time job, he said, he plans to study computers and perhaps go to college. It would be fun, he said, because he could team with his youngest child, a sophomore at Rutgers University.

"He's doing well," Watson said. "He's into it like I would've been."

At the restaurant school, Bill and Bob Adams appear comfortable in the ambiance of a kitchen full of students. The brothers are obvious favorites, known to classmates half their age as "the Adams family." At 42 and 45, respectively, they are the oldest in their group of 25, but that is hardly obvious when everyone wears white sous-chef hats, white shirts, white aprons.

As always, they are a team. They drive to school together, just as they drove to the mill together. In a recent pastry class, Bill made the cream, Bob made the dough. When a batch of eclairs burned as they talked to a reporter, Bob cracked: "French pastry is supposed to be crisp. But I think we've gone straight to incinerated."

As much fun as the brothers are having, Bill pointedly said, "I would have preferred to stay in an industrial job. Everyone hates change."

"There was just no living wage out there," Bob said. "So we decided to take advantage of the training. Now that we've tried this, it's like the momentum is shifting. We want to try our hands at it."

They said they would like to open an informal French restaurant, appealing to working families like theirs. They want to call it "The French Peasant—French Food Without the Attitude."

Any doubts about whether steelworkers belonged at the Restaurant School vanished quickly, when Bob saved the day at a buffet dinner for 150 people at the school's in-house restaurant. Both water heaters inexplicably went down, and dirty dishes piled up as students desperately boiled water.

Amid the chaos, Bob, a mechanic at Fairless, disappeared into the boiler room. When he returned, the hot water was on. The kitchen staff burst into applause. Even months later, everyone tells the story.

"It was just the pilot," Bob said. "But nobody else knew what to do." The cheer the brothers exuded in pastry class faded when they sat down in the restaurant for a soda.

They said they cannot stop thinking about people they know who are unemployed or fear for their jobs. They and their families have stopped eating out; they wonder whether others will do the same, dooming The French Peasant.

"There are nights it's hard to sleep," Bob said. "I've got two daughters, so I've got two weddings. I've got student loans, two college educations. I have a lot of money I have to make in the future."

"It's definitely going to be tough," Bill said. "This business is built on discretionary funds. People don't have money to throw around like they did in the 1980s."

Bob, whose house is already invested in this venture, tried to be more positive. "If we can find the right location, the right amount of money," he said.

"If the economy turns around," Bill said.

The brothers looked at each other as if they had replayed this conversation many times. Bill delivered the bottom line:

"There's a lot of ifs."

April 14, 1992

Jobless Safety Net Falls Short

Unemployment Benefits Being Taxed to the Full

ALBERT B. CRENSHAW

Now that official Washington has recognized what much of the country has long known—that we are in a recession—attention is again being focused on an often misunderstood part of the social safety net, unemployment insurance.

Designed to help tide people over when they lose their jobs, unemployment insurance is a joint state-federal program under which employers pay taxes into a group of trust funds. When a worker is laid off, he or she can claim benefits that are paid out of the funds.

But like a lot of other parts of the safety net, unemployment insurance has problems. At the same time that the system is staggering under a wave of new applicants, it is actually serving a smaller percentage of the overall unemployed than it did during the 1970s.

The system remains financially sound overall, and eligible workers eventually do get their checks. But its problems are another example of how disruptive the budget deficit and the fiscal games that both Congress and the White House play to minimize it are to the workings of government.

A major issue involves assistance that the federal government is supposed to provide states in the processing of claims.

When employers pay their unemployment taxes, all of the money goes into the U.S. Treasury. But there it is divided into several trust accounts. Some goes into an account specifically for the employer's state. That money is used to pay the actual benefits to the jobless. Some $40 billion is now piled up in those accounts, enough, Labor Department officials believe, to cover expected costs of benefits during the recession.

The rest of the employer tax money goes into three other trusts. One makes loans available to states that overdraw their state accounts. Another provides money for extended benefits if the economic situation becomes bad enough to trigger them. The third contains money to help states pay for administrative costs of the program.

But the administrative assistance payouts are not automatic. They require an appropriation from Congress. For the past several fiscal years, the Bush administration has underestimated the demand for unemployment insurance and Congress has gone along, even though both presumably could see that the estimates were out of date. As a result, inadequate assistance has been forthcoming.

The shortfall currently is estimated at about $200 million, and the administration has said it will ask for a supplemental appropriation of $100 million.

Labor, states and some employer groups are pressing for a reserve fund that could be used during sudden economic downturns, avoiding the delay inherent in the appropriation process.

Further inhibiting the appropriation process is the fact that spending the money counts against the federal budget ceiling and adds to the federal deficit. Holding on to it, however, works real hardship in many states.

Rep. Sander Levin (D-Mich.) told a House Ways and Means subcommittee hearing last week that it took him four hours just to get through on the phone to a state unemployment office in his district and that people there are having to wait five to six weeks for their first benefit check.

Closer to home, the District's benefits office has recently been so overwhelmed that some would-be applicants were forced to come back a second time when the office closed while they were in line. City officials said last week, though, that by pulling clerks from other duties they are currently able to avoid sending anyone away. "We're doing pretty well now," a spokesman said.

Ron Montgomery of the Virginia Employment Commission noted that his agency is unable to staff some offices fully even though Virginia has one of the fastest-growing workloads in the nation.

According to the Interstate Conference of Employment Security Agencies here, problems have also surfaced in Arizona, Arkansas, Connecticut, Iowa, Kansas, Maine, Montana, Minnesota, Nevada, New Mexico, New York, Ohio, Tennessee, Texas, Washington and West Virginia.

At the same time, a smaller portion of all unemployed workers are drawing benefits than was the case 20 years ago. At one point, more than half of all jobless workers got unemployment benefits. By the early 1980s, though, states and the federal government had substantially tightened the rules. "There seemed to be a perception that the program was too liberal" and benefits too easy to get, said Cheryl Templeman of the interstate conference.

During the '80s, the number receiving benefits fell off sharply, dipping to below one-third of all jobless workers for most of the decade.

Part of the drop stems from the way the program works. Meant as temporary aid to people who have lost their jobs, the program excludes new entrants to the work force as well as people who have left the work force and are returning. In non-recessionary times, these people make up a higher proportion of the jobless.

Some studies suggest that the entrance into the work force of a large number of young people during the '80s accounted for much of the gap, but others also indicate that a large number of jobless people don't apply for benefits because they believe they are not eligible. It is not clear, however, whether they are really ineligible.

Table 14–1 • Unemployment Insurance

Percentage of Jobless People with Coverage has Slipped

Year	Jobless Covered (in thousands)	Total Jobless (in thousands)	Percent Covered
1973	1,745	4,365	40.0
1974	2,382	5,156	46.2
1975	4,174	7,929	52.6
1976	3,148	7,406	42.5
1977	2,852	6,991	40.8
1978	2,463	6,202	39.7
1979	2,483	6,137	40.5
1980	3,414	7,637	44.7
1981	3,110	8,273	37.6
1982	4,"30	10,678	38.7
1983	3,487	10,717	32.5
1984	2,472	8,539	28.9
1985	2,604	8,312	31.3
1986	2,648	8,237	32.1
1987	2,327	7,425	31.3
1988	2,118	6,701	31.6
1989	2,151	6,528	32.9
1990	2,525	6,874	36.7
Jan. 1991	3,969	8,595	46.2
Jan. 1990	2,863	7,256	39.5

Note: Figures on who is covered by unemployment insurance do not include Puerto Rico or the Virgin Islands. Extended benefit and supplemental benefit programs also are not included. Latest monthly figures are not seasonally adjusted.

Source: Bureau of Labor Statistics

Labor Department officials noted that the number of eligible applicants is rising again as more "job losers" seek benefits.

Failing to apply if you are eligible can be costly. While the benefits won't put you on easy street, they help put food on the table. Locally, benefits range up to $293 a week in the District, $215 in Maryland and $198 in Virginia, according to officials of those jurisdictions. The exact weekly amount and duration is determined by a formula related to recent earnings. Those eligible can receive benefit checks for 12 to 26 weeks.

Eligibility requirements vary by state, but in general, workers must have earned a minimum amount in the past year or so—a total of at least $3,000 in two recent quarters in Virginia, for example—and they must be unemployed through no fault of their own. Workers also must be willing and able to work and actively seeking work.

February 10, 1991

The Assembly Lines South of the Border

'Maquiladoras' Thrive on Cheap Labor

WILLIAM BRANIGIN

Wearing a white smock designating him as a company executive, Jesus Luis Zuniga padded down the Sony television assembly line and pointed out the huge 46-inch stereo TVs being assembled here from Japanese and U.S. components.

"There are a lot of myths about the maquiladora industry," he said.

Instead of taking jobs away from Americans, he argued, "we're really creating jobs in Mexico and the United States that would have gone to the Orient."

Zuniga, senior vice president of the Sony Corp. plant here called Video Tec de Mexico, was referring to the assembly operations, known as maquiladoras, that set up shop on Mexican territory, import materials from the United States, assemble them with cheap Mexican labor and export the finished products back across the border. Under Mexican law, the components come in duty free, while under U.S. customs regulations the finished products are taxed only on the "value added" in Mexico.

For several years, the maquiladora industry has been the bright spot in an otherwise stagnant Mexican economy. According to Alejandro Bustamante, the Tijuana-based president of the National Maquiladora Association, annual growth in the industry has been 17 percent to 19 percent for the last six years, "and we feel it's going to increase in the future."

There are more than 1,800 plants throughout Mexico, but most are concentrated along the 2,000-mile border with the United States. Last year, the maquiladora industry employed nearly 500,000 workers, 17 percent of total manufacturing employment in Mexico and earned the country nearly $3 billion. Those earnings made the maquiladora sector the second-largest source of foreign exchange for Mexico after oil exports.

Now, as the United States and Mexico move toward talks on a free-trade agreement, the maquiladora industry hopes to benefit from its position on the cutting edge of bilateral trade between the two countries. Industry officials say it stands to attract increased foreign investment, notably from Japanese and other Asian companies eager to cash in on greater access to the U.S. market.

U.S. maquiladora activities range from stuffing junk mail in envelopes and processing American supermarkets' discount coupons to building yachts and home appliances. Toy makers such as Mattel Inc., Fisher-Price and Tonka Corp. operate

286

maquiladoras in Mexico, as do defense contractors such as Hughes Aircraft Co. and Rockwell International Corp.

There now are even maquiladora farms, which bring U.S. seeds and agricultural equipment into the Mexican interior and produce frozen vegetables for such firms as General Foods Corp., parent of Birds Eye; Green Giant Co.; and Campbell Soup Co.

Mexican officials say interest in maquiladoras is increasing, especially among investors from Japan, South Korea, Hong Kong and Taiwan.

Already there has been significant Japanese investment in Tijuana, a popular site with Japanese executives for its proximity to the "golf course heaven" of Southern California. Although Japanese firms account for fewer than 60 of the 1,800 maquiladoras, they rank as some of the biggest. Of the five largest maquiladoras in Tijuana, three are Japanese. They are led by Sanyo Electric Co., which has invested $300 million in six plants employing 2,800 workers.

Thanks to companies like Sanyo, Sony, Hitachi Ltd., Matsushita Electric Industrial Co. and the South Korean firm Samsung Electronics Co., Tijuana has quietly become the TV assembly capital of the world. According to U.S. government estimates, 70 percent of all televisions sold in the United States are now made here.

At the three-year-old Sony plant, which employs 1,700 workers and produces 100,000 sets a month, Zuniga said he sees the maquiladora industry as "a natural progression in the world economy" that has "helped the United States as much as Mexico."

Although U.S. labor unions have opposed the plants on grounds that they take away American jobs, Zuniga and other proponents argue that they preserve "high end" U.S. jobs making components, jobs that might otherwise have gone overseas.

"U.S. business is using the maquiladoras to go head to head with Japan, Korea and the other dragons," said an American official who monitors the industry. "To meet the competition, a company has two choices: Reduce wage costs or take the whole operation to the Orient."

In the maquiladoras, Mexican workers typically earn in a day what U.S. workers make in an hour. The maquiladoras have succeeded in holding wages down to about $1.25 an hour, which is still about 20 percent above the Mexican minimum wage. The relatively low wages (compared with the United States) and the heavy competition for workers has led to monthly employee turnover rates of 10 percent to 20 percent—and sometimes as high as 50 percent.

Labor relations have grown uneasy, however, with union leaders complaining of unfair salaries and mistreatment of women, who make up the majority of the industry's employees. One group, the Association of People's Committees, recently protested the maquiladoras' policy of firing pregnant women and described as "degrading" a medical examination that female job applicants were required to take to prove they were not pregnant.

Maquiladoras also have come under criticism on environmental grounds. According to a recent U.S. government report on the industry, despite "much talk" about cleaning up pollution and toxic wastes produced by border maquiladoras, "little has been done to implement and enforce stricter environmental regulations." of particular concern have been woodworking firms that have left the Los Angeles area to avoid environmental restrictions, only to set up on the Mexican side of the border and spew air and water pollution back into the United States.

Among the newcomers to Tijuana is General Dynamics Corp., which announced plans earlier this year to open a plant employing 200 workers to make electrical components for its defense contracts.

One of the latest Far Eastern investors is the giant South Korean firm Hyundai Motor Co., which plans to build 3,000 shipboard containers a month on a 28-acre site now under development outside Tijuana. The plant, the first heavy manufacturing industry in Baja California, is to employ about 1,500 workers at an average wage of $1.30 an hour, compared with the average of $12.60 an hour that Hyundai paid about 300 employees at a plant in Long Beach, Calif. The company had been cutting operations at the U.S. plant for the last few years and finally closed it in October.

July 31, 1990

Altering the Face of Work

New Skills, Retraining Required for 2000 A.D., Secretary Brock Asserts

As the nation approaches the end of the 20th century, federal policy makers have begun to turn their attention to what the American work place will look like in the year 2000 and the skills that will be required.

By the year 2000, 80 percent of all new entrants into the American work force will be women, minorities or immigrants.

The number of people working on assembly lines will be less than 5 percent of the American work force.

And the service sector threatens to create a greater economic gap between the skilled and semi-skilled worker.

The fastest growing occupations are expected to be in such areas as paralegals, computer programmers and analysts and medical technicians, all requiring high skill levels.

In absolute terms, however, government job projections show the service economy producing the biggest growth in lower paying semi-skilled work.

Last week, Labor Secretary William Brock met with several reporters from The Washington Post to discuss the American work place in the year 2000.

In his interview, the Labor secretary talked of the changes taking place in the work place and expressed concern that unless the business and education communities changed their ways the United States could evolve into an economic class society. An edited transcript of the interview follows.

Q What does the term "service economy" imply for the American work force in the year 2000?

A It implies a lot of different things. It implies a whole different range of skills that are going to be necessary to hold jobs. The skill base that we've developed in the last 200 years related to agricultural skills or manual skills, craft type skills that came from vocational or apprenticeship type of programs; and skills that are going to be required in the next, basically thinking, reasoning, communicating skills that are in a whole different order than those we have thought about and worried about, certainly in the early part of this century, implies a need for much more effective educational system, much more emphasis on flexible training that allows people to adapt to technologies as they constantly change around them in the work place.

It implies that the jobs of the next 15 years are going to be much more interesting: cleaner, safer, healthier, more productive and, I think, more rewarding jobs.

And it's a very nice prospect for those people who are given the opportunity to develop their talents in a fashion that would meet that job requirement.

Q What do you do for the 18-year-old who graduates from high school and who might not have the technical skills or even the intellectual capacity to compete for these jobs?

A Well, the work place of the year 2000 is going to be sufficiently diverse that there will be employment for everyone that wants it and has developed their talents to the degree they can. People talk about the informatics age as if everybody is going to be punching into a computer. Services implies a lot more than that, it implies much more personalized skills, much more individualized skills.

The danger is that, given the present methodologies applied in our educational system and in the post-formal education system of training, most of those skills are related to our perceptions of an industrial work place. And we do not have in this system enough emphasis upon the ability to reason, to think, to constantly upgrade your skills by being flexible.

The danger really comes to the individual you mention who may or may not have finished high school but even if he or she finished high school they may be functionally illiterate in the true sense of the word. We're still graduating hundreds of thousands of young people with diplomas that they can't read. It is a consummate national shame that we do so. But it's true that we do. And there is just no excuse for that.

But the portent of that is a disaster because you then can end up with a bifurcated work force, half or more of whom are employed productively in challenging, good jobs. And the remainder of whom are not just unemployed but they are unemployable, because they were not given tools by us.

Q What are the demographics of the work force by the year 2000?

A Well, the demographics are in place so you don't have to engage in some esoteric prophecy. Those people have been born. Eighty percent of the new entrants in the work force by the year 2000 are going to be basically from three categories: They're going to be women or minorities or immigrants. They're people that have traditionally been disadvantaged. And in too many cases uneducated, or improperly educated.

From the positive side, the job creation capability of this country is so awesome that we have in the next seven or eight years a chance to deal with societal problems, such as youth unemployment, minority unemployment, that we have failed to deal with in the last 50 years. The job demand is going to be enormous. The demand for people with skills is going to be huge.

And the question is, do we have in place the systems, the processes, to provide those skills? And the answer is really no. We're changing, we're changing pretty dramatically in a lot of states. The states have done, I think, a remarkably good job in the last three years to shape up their school systems, to put competency testing into the teachers' evaluating process, to deal with some of the issues like pay and discipline. But we have a long way yet to go. And the concern that you have is that you're going to end up 12 or 13 years from now with a group of people that just sort of got left off to the side.

Q That's been the tradition. We're not a country that has specialized in retraining. We've never had to do that. At a time when you're cutting back on all sorts of spending programs, who will pay for it?

A Oh, we're going to pay for it one way or another. The question is, do we pay for it in a fashion that yields a result that's affirmative.

One of the strangest things about the American economic-educational system is that it's been like two ships passing in the night. There's business on one side and educators on the other. They have very little contact or communication. Each seems to be shy of dealing with the other. Each seems to be somewhat intimidated by the other almost. Business has an enormous vested interest in seeing a much more effective public education system in place in this country quickly, and education, obviously, has an interest in finding out what the demands of the work place are going to be and how they can more effectively respond to them, because in that process they'll gain more support.

The question is, will we make the investment at every possible level. Business has to assume a major role. Now today business is spending already over $40 billion a year on training and retraining. A lot of that is in remediation. But it is described and designed within a particular plant, within a particular company within a particular industry; that isn't going to do it. As we begin to run into skill shortages—which we will in the next three, four or five years—the amount of money being spent by businesses is going to have to increase substantially to develop in house some of those skills.

Q Beyond working with the school systems, what else would you do?

A The first step, I think, has to be to evaluate your own existing personnel in terms of their capacity for skills, and put in place the skill development programs that allow you to stay ahead of the technology changes. It's hard because technology's changing fast.

But if what you put in place as a system in the process is reasonably well managed it becomes an automatic and I think we could demonstrate in most cases that it's very cost-effective, that you can stay ahead of your competition more effectively this way than almost any other.

We're really talking about an entirely different atmosphere of labor-management relationships. We're talking about people development in the larger sense of the word. And there are a lot of examples of this being done and being done very nicely and of the consequences of it being done well. And the one that is to me most dramatic and most exciting is the Fremont, California, example.

If you take a look at that auto assembly operation you find that skill development has a different connotation in that plant. They've revised all their job classifications. Every worker in a team has to do everybody else's job on that team in order to be on a team.

Q If that is a model, what's the role for unions in this year 2000? The essence of unionization in an industry such as the automobile industry has been rigid job classifications, to increase the number of potential jobs which you could get away with when you didn't have the kind of competitive structure we have today. What is the role of the union in that kind of future?

A The role of the union has to change and to reflect the true interests of the worker, which is not in a job classification but job security and job growth. The union in that particular facility before the GM plant closed was one of the most adversarial unions in the United States and management was one of the most adversarial managements in the United States.

What the Japanese management did when they came in was to say, let's abolish all of the barriers to communication. Let's put managers on the shop floors, let's put people into teams, let's abolish the job classifications, let's abolish the executive washrooms and the management dining rooms and all this. And let's deal with each other as human beings. You have a collective stake in the success of the other fellow. And it really encouraged people to contribute to its consequent well-being. And they succeeded in a phenomenal fashion.

And there are other companies doing the same sorts of things, maybe different styles. The question is, does labor have to change? You bet your life they have to change. Does management have to change? Maybe sometimes even more than labor, because you're dealing with attitudes that were put into place back in the '30s in the days of industrial strife where it was a confrontation, almost certainly for survival in some cases.

Now that isn't going to hack it anymore. And I think labor is moving pretty much to modify to that changing economic role. I'm worried that I sometimes see labor indicate more self-evaluation than I do some in management.

Q Where do you come down on the criticism of management that we've been reading from inside the administration? You've got a union perspective on that, seeing the relationships on the labor side and then having worried about how well they were competing in the international side. What kind of grades do you give American management?

A Oh, it is so unfair to grade management or labor across the board. Overall, in the larger firms in the United States, I think it's pretty charitable to give a C. There are plenty of exceptions above and below that. Most of the really good management in the United States has been management in new firms, younger firms, smaller firms, more aggressive, more creative, more people-oriented types developing new companies. That's where all of the employment growth has come, that's where all the employment growth is going to come.

The trouble is that you remember in the '50s we talked about "the man in the gray flannel suit?" Well, he's still got the same suit, he's just got a lot of gray hair and precious few new ideas.

We lived in a fool's paradise, particularly in the 1970s. Inflation hid a lot of sins from us. And we found out that the price of ignoring the change is disastrous.

That's why I'm so worried about the next 15 years because I think we've got this opportunity to change now. The fact is that in the '70s, we got fat and sloppy and nonproductive. We forgot about quality, we hired people in the upper echelons or we evolved people in the upper echelons who were mathematicians and who dealt with quarterly statements with great effectiveness, and we have the bureaucratization in too many of our big firms. It's phenomenal that there are industries in the United States where we've produced high tonnage with less manpower per ton than our competitors overseas and we're still noncompetitive. I mean it doesn't make sense. Until you look at the management overhead, until you look at the lack of creativity, until you look at zero investment in R&D, new techniques, new technology. You look at the fact that we seem more interested in servicing those who are speculating on stocks on Wall Street than our customers.

Q What are the unacceptable consequences you see if we don't do it right in the next 15 years?

A Something we fought a revolutionary war to get away from, and a civil war, and that is a class society. In this case not based on race but on ability to be productive as human beings. A noncompetitive economy that is based on services which still have to serve some industrial base, with a reduced industrial base, if we allow that to happen. All of which implies a stable if not declining standard of living.

None of that's necessary, but I think those are things that you have to be concerned about.

Q Some would argue it's begun to happen already.

A In some sectors it may have.

Q And what do you do? Since the end of World War II we've built an economic middle class out of semi-skilled blue-collar workers; does that have to change to emerge the way you want by the year 2000?

A Let me ask you this, what would your question have been if we were living in 1900, 1910 or 1920, and a third of our work force was on the farm and the secretary of Labor was making all these awesome statements to you in 1920 about what was going to happen to the farm. What would you have said?

Q But the farm work force shrank as agriculture became more productive. Is the manufacturing sector headed that way?

A Yes it is. And look at what a fabulous opportunity that reflects for us. Because what happened, when we went from a third of the American work force to 3 percent directly on the farm economy, we increased the quality of farm products, markedly reduced its cost.

Q In a very rapidly growing consumer market.

A And we added an enormous consumer base to the economy. We took the amount of money we were spending on food and allowed it to be spent on automobiles and televisions and new homes and things that made it a much nicer world in which to live. And you know, granted there are some problems we've had with that 3 percent.

There are going to be people working in steel mills in the United States because we're going to have a steel industry 10, 15, 20 years from now. But it's going to be an industry that's very different from what it is today. You can make your estimates, you say 20 percent of the American work force is in manufacturing. But in truth, maybe slightly more than half of that is on the scene. By the turn of the century the amount of people on assembly lines is going to be under 5 percent. Now, that doesn't mean you're going to be producing less steel or less cars, or less product, you'll probably be producing more and you'll be producing with less people in less hazardous occupations. And you'll have a lot more people keeping those plants operating from small firms outside of it, which means you've got a more flexible, more creative, more dynamic economy, much more people-oriented. In other words, it can be a much better world.

Q You used an example I'd like to go back to if I may and that is in Japan, you talk about the base industries serviced by the small industries. They treat their labor force quite differently. If you're in those small industries, you're not counted when you're laid off, you're not counted as unemployed. You have no lifetime employment. You have none of the benefits of mainstream society. Is that the fate of the manufacturing worker who is employed by for these small firms?

A It's possible. It isn't necessary. And, you know, Japan gets far more credit than it deserves. All this garbage about lifetime employment only applies to a few large firms. It certainly does not apply to those small businesses that service the large firms. And that's how they handle their surges in economic activity. What's happening in the United States is a little different. We do have the small firms and they, some of them, are wedded to one job, but very, very few are. Most of them have been smart enough to diversify their market base so that if one industry is sliding and something else is coming up, they can maintain their growth pattern. But something else is lying on top of that, now, that's interesting. Of some concern, but also of some opportunity, and that's part-time work. We didn't talk much earlier about what's happened to change the work force by the advent of women in the work place. Women are now 44 percent of our work force. They will by the turn of the century be at 47 percent. Way over half of those women are going to have babies while they are in the work force. And most of them will have, or at least a large number of them will have, more than one. What that says is important in a couple of respects. One, we haven't begun to change our mentality about the nature of work to reflect that half the women will comprise almost half of our work force, and the special needs that they bring to the work force.

Some businesses are providing a smorgasbord or a cafeteria plan of benefits so that women who work could choose one range of benefits, elderly workers could choose another range and the young something else. That's good. Now, we're going to need those women because we're going to need their skills. They are an enormous economic asset to the United States. But we do have to understand that we cannot build our economy and destroy the family in the process. And we haven't paid attention to that recently.

Now, if by the combination of all of these things—the differing work schedules, the part-time work, the small business development—if we create a kind of diversity of economic opportunity that I think is possible, then we've maximized our productivity opportunity, our growth opportunity.

November 30, 1986

15 *Crime*

This chapter deals with problems of the criminal justice system, and crime-related issues in the United States and around the world.

The first article talks about an increasingly common reaction to crime, that of victims turning on their attackers in a search for private justice. Public fears have intensified with the surge in violent, drug-related crime.

The second article discusses the problem of prison overcrowding. There are too many inmates, and no money for new cells or new programs. The following article deals with differential prison sentencing, and how facts beyond the case at hand can lengthen a prison term. The next article talks about the changing face of organized crime, where emerging New York gangs profit by preying on their ethnic communities.

The final article deals with Mafia-like crime in Japan. This country adopted the core idea of organized crime syndicates from the West. The "yazuka" who have been highly visible in Japanese society, now threaten to move underground as police are determined to shut them down.

New York's Public Fear, Private Justice

As Violent Crime Surges, More
Victims are Turning on Attackers

HOWARD KURTZ

When Kenny Mendoza heard the screams from his East Harlem tenement, he clambered up the fire escape and into a fifth-floor apartment, where a knife-wielding intruder was threatening his pregnant neighbor, Nydia Albaladejo.

After the intruder, Ronald Ford, ran into the bathroom, Mendoza allegedly was handed a .38-caliber pistol by another neighbor and fired once, hitting the 30-year-old man in the chest. Ford, a convicted robber, died after jumping from the bathroom window to a litter-strewn alley.

"A lot of people wrote me letters saying I did the right thing," Mendoza, 19, said last week, nervously smoking a cigarette and wearing an ill-fitting suit while awaiting a court hearing. "They said they wish there were more people like me."

Despite being hailed as a hero after the April 4 incident, Mendoza has been charged with intentional murder and criminal possession of a weapon. He wants to testify before a Manhattan grand jury in an effort to avoid indictment.

As violent crime becomes an increasingly commonplace fact of New York life, people such as Mendoza are fighting back, cheered by an angry public that seems to relish the sight of victims turning on their attackers. Although many of these episodes involve unlicensed guns and clouded circumstances, the protagonists generally are portrayed in the news media as avenging angels.

The debate about citizen justice has swirled with particular force here since 1984, when a white electronics engineer named Bernhard Goetz shot four black youths who asked him for $5 on a Manhattan subway car. But after a rash of "self-defense" shootings and stabbings, sentiment is growing that citizens are justified in taking the law into their own hands.

"A lot of people are saying I'm going to be my own policeman," said Thomas Reppetto, president of the Citizens Crime Commission of New York. Ordinary citizens are fast losing faith in the criminal-justice system. They say, "I'll carry a gun, and if the police catch me with it, it's better than some criminal catching me without it."

But Ronald Kuby, who represents one of Goetz's victims, insisted that a vigilante-type shooting "is no less murder simply because a lot of people agree with it. It's Charles Bronson stuff.

"You're always going to find people to applaud a white man for shooting down a black man," he said. "If he's young and had a prior brush with the law, he's deemed to be a criminal and scum and someone who is eligible for summary execution."

The trend toward vigilante-type justice is highlighted by these recent cases in which those killed, like Ford, have been black: on April 12, a gray-haired man in his late forties was accosted on a Brooklyn train by several young men from Brownsville smoking marijuana and drinking brandy while traveling to a Times Square disco. Police said the razor-wielding assailants took the victim's wallet and watch and were beating and kicking him when he pulled a gun from his waistband and fired, killing Ricky Pickett, 25, a career criminal. The shooter calmly left the train and disappeared into the night. He has ignored all calls to surrender. On Jan. 21, Rodney Sumter, an unemployed Harlem plumber traveling with his son, 3, was punched and spat upon by a screaming homeless man at the Columbus Circle subway station. Sumter knocked the man down and slammed his head against the concrete platform, killing him. After being charged with manslaughter, Sumter, 39, voluntarily testified before a grand jury, which refused to indict him. The homeless man, in his sixties, was never identified.

"I shielded my son," Sumter told reporters. "He was coming right at me. . . . I still think I did the right thing." On Dec. 9, two knife-wielding muggers approached straphanger Jean-Claude Vincent on a Harlem train, demanding his money. Another passenger suddenly declared, "We're not going to have any more of this," and fatally stabbed Jamal Johns, 23, of the Bronx. The so-called Subway Samaritan, hailed by Vincent as a "saint," never surrendered to police, despite a front-page offer by the *New York Post* to pay his legal costs.

"These incidents feed upon one another," said George Sternlieb, professor of urban affairs at Rutgers University. "It's becoming increasingly respectable to be armed. Once this attains a critical mass of public acceptance, it takes on a life force of its own. The wild, wild West will be a deadly reality."

Sternlieb said he was stunned when a liberal, middle-aged schoolteacher who works in a high-crime area told him that she carries a "Saturday night special." "We have a new definition of a security blanket—it's not soft and fuzzy, it's small and hard," he said.

Public fears have intensified along with the surge in drug-related crime. There were 93,377 robberies here last year, or one stickup every six minutes, making New York the nation's robbery capital. The city also had 1,905 homicides, breaking its previous record for the second consecutive year. Courts have been reduced to plea-bargain factories, while city jails are jammed with more than 20,000 inmates.

Almost no sector of society has been untouched. Assaults against teachers rose by nearly 25 percent in the first half of this school year. Cabdrivers have demanded more protection since six radio-dispatched drivers were killed in the Bronx within several weeks. Ministers in poor neighborhoods have applied for gun permits and armed themselves with baseball bats after a rash of church burglaries and assaults, including the murder of a priest in a Bedford-Stuyvesant church last fall.

"We're tired of people breaking into our churches," said the Rev. Charles Nesbitt, pastor of Bethesda Baptist Church in Brooklyn. "Some ministers have tried to get gun permits. . . . A lot of people have guns out here. You'd better fight back, otherwise you'll be dead."

Crime on subways and buses recently jumped 27 percent, fueled by an increase in robberies by youth gangs. Officials have identified about 40 such gangs, with names such as Sudden Impact and Partners In Crime. Transit police arrested 150 teenagers in 50 gang incidents from January to mid-March.

For growing numbers of New Yorkers, crime no longer is an abstract problem. Pete Hamill, a *New York Post* columnist, said his elderly mother has been mugged four times. Brooklyn District Attorney Charles J. Hynes talks about how his Flatbush home has been burglarized repeatedly. Actress Viveca Lindfors was slashed on the face on a Greenwich Village street in January by marauding youths.

The days when the wealthy could insulate themselves from such unpleasantries are gone. Elizabeth Rohatyn, wife of financier Felix Rohatyn, recently complained to a *New York Times* columnist that her purse had been snatched on the street for the third time in recent years. "I said to my daughter, who's going to dinner two blocks from her apartment, 'Get the doorman to take you there and the butler who serves dinner to take you home,' " she said.

Those without recourse to butlers have had to make other arrangements. Many elderly people shun the subways or no longer travel to Manhattan. Corporations and community groups are chipping in to hire private security forces. Despite the city's stringent gun-control laws—only 15,300 private citizens, not counting retired police officers, have permits to carry guns—experts say hundreds of thousands of others have acquired black-market weapons for protection.

"We're heading back to an era of private justice, which was rejected in the 19th century because it didn't work," Reppetto said. "If everyone's going to be carrying a gun, it's anarchy. If you and I have a collision—instead of just exchanging harsh words—if I know you have a gun, I'd better get mine out first."

Others applaud the trend toward aggressive self-defense. David Cornstein, a Manhattan businessman, recently donated $25,000 to start a fund for victims charged with crimes. "I get up in the morning and read the paper, and the stories of people being robbed and beaten start to blend together after a while," he said. "If people defend themselves and are successful, they face a terrible, long legal struggle."

That is the predicament of Kenny Mendoza, a high school dropout and part-time mechanic who shot the intruder in his neighbor's East 107th Street apartment. "It was a courageous act," said Mendoza's lawyer, Mel Sachs, who also represented Sumter. "He put his life in jeopardy, and he saved two lives—this young woman and her unborn child."

Sachs said grand juries can serve as "the conscience of the community," as in the case of Sumter and the homeless attacker. "A citizen is entitled under certain circumstances to use deadly physical force," he said. "But people are being re-victimized. First, they're the victims of other people's crimes, and then they're prosecuted."

Prosecutors say they are only following the rules. After a grand jury cleared Sumter last month, Manhattan District Attorney Robert Morgenthau praised its "open-minded investigation."

"We have unilateral discretion as to whether to prosecute a case, but it's routine to take all homicides to the grand jury," Morgenthau spokesman Gerald McKelvey said.

The case of Goetz, once lionized as the man who stood up to four young punks, looks very different from the perspective of Darrell Cabey, 24. Cabey's spine was severed when Goetz, saying, "You don't look so bad, here's another," shot him in the back as Cabey lay sprawled on a subway seat.

Cabey is paralyzed below the waist and has suffered permanent brain damage, which has left him with the intelligence of an 8-year-old. His attorneys have filed a $50 million civil suit against Goetz.

Goetz, 42, said he feared that Cabey and his friends would rob and beat him, but the teenagers said they were just panhandling. In a videotaped confession, Goetz admitted that he "turned into a monster. . . . I decided I was gonna kill 'em all, murder 'em all, do anything." Goetz was acquitted in 1987 of attempted murder and assault but convicted of illegal weapons possession, for which he served eight months in jail.

Kuby, Cabey's lawyer, said there is a strong racial element to the public support for Goetz and the more recent vigilante types, most of whose victims have been black.

"I'm a licensed handgun owner," Kuby said. "I'm not a pacifist. I believe everyone has the right of self-defense. I've been robbed at gunpoint, and it's a very degrading, humiliating experience.

"But the right of self-defense is not the right to commit murder. You can't shoot someone in the back and claim self-defense."

May 5, 1990

In Maine, Prison Crowding Leaves Grisly Legacy

SHARON LAFRANIERE

It's business as usual in the Maine state prison system these days—too many inmates, no money for new cells, no money for programs. Were Larry Richardson still there, he'd recognize it all too well.

Richardson was serving eight years for child molestation at the Maine State Prison when his body was found against the bars of his cell, hanging by a twisted sheet. He had been tortured for four nights by his cellmate, who pounded out one of his teeth against a toilet bowl and kicked him in the groin until the bruises reached from Richardson's thighs to his waistline.

Prisoners up and down a dark corridor orchestrated Richardson's punishment, but although they shouted and sang and acted out a kangaroo court at the top of their lungs, the guards insist they heard nothing, according to police interviews, court records and prison reports.

The Maine correctional system still reverberates from what inmates termed their weekend-long "party" in March 1990. The state will try one of the alleged instigators for murder in April; last month, it settled a civil suit filed by Richardson's mother for $400,000.

Attorney General William P. Barr last month said the Justice Department would try to aid states that want to get out from under court-ordered caps on inmate populations, saying some orders "have wreaked havoc with states' efforts to get criminals off the street." But to Maine officials, Richardson's death stands as a grisly testament to the dangers of pushing prisons past their limits.

Other states have their own reminders. Pennsylvania's is the charred ruins at a prison outside Harrisburg that was designed for 1,800 inmates but packed with 2,600. Nearly 400 inmates set it ablaze during a two-night rampage in 1989 that left 146 people injured.

New Hampshire's is the August burial of two inmates slain in a maximum-security unit that was meant for 93 prisoners but held 160.

On Richardson's corridor, the Maine State Prison's most volatile inmates were doubled up in 6-by-7-foot cells—the size of a walk-in closet—for 23 hours a day, with only an hour break to shower and walk the corridor. Prison officials typically go to great lengths not to double-cell inmates in segregation wings like Richardson's, because the units are meant to isolate troublesome inmates. "But our system was jammed to the rafters and we didn't have any place else to put them," said Maine Correctional Commissioner Donald Allen.

Maine stopped double-celling the unit after Richardson's killing, but only by shipping some inmates to a different crowded prison.

Like about 22 other states, Maine continues to operate its prisons well above capacity, locking up 44 percent more inmates than the institutions were designed to hold. The latest survey in January 1991 found only eight states more desperate for space. "We have no elbow room and no activities," Allen said. "Anybody who works in corrections will tell you that's a recipe for a . . . disaster."

Maine boosted its corrections budget by an average of 9 percent during the past two years, but voters drew the line at building more prisons: They've rejected prison construction bonds three years in a row. Nationally, state corrections budgets grew an average of 12 percent during the past two years, making prisons the second-fastest growing segment of state spending after Medicaid. This year the growth in state corrections spending is expected to slow to 8 percent.

Barr said last month that not every state can operate its prisons far above capacity levels, but he reversed a policy under which the Justice Department had argued for court orders to cap inmate populations, saying "many courts went beyond what the Constitution required."

Instead, Barr said, the department would be sympathetic to states seeking to lift population caps. Court orders now limit the inmate populations at one or more prisons in 33 states. Barr's offer brought him at least one early taker. Officials from Texas met with Justice Department lawyers earlier this month to discuss the chances of ending a seven-year-old consent decree governing that state's entire prison population.

The day after Barr gave states hope that the department would help them out of population caps, the Supreme Court made it easier for state and local officials to challenge such court orders. The justices said a federal judge in Massachusetts applied too strict a standard in refusing to lift a 10-year-old prohibition against double-celling in a local jail.

Barr cited the federal prison system as an example to states, noting it operated at 166 percent of capacity last year and yet is free of court orders or consent decrees. "If states could operate at the level of the federal prison system, that would mean an additional 286,000 inmate beds," Barr said.

To some state prison officials and activists, though, the federal system is a poor comparison because it has more programs and better-trained guards than many state systems. For example, 22 percent of federal inmates make goods for sale to the federal government in a prison industries program, while similar programs reach only 7 percent of state inmates.

Federal prison officials also have the advantage of size: If they need to transfer an inmate such as Richardson, they have a wealth of institutions to choose from, while a small state like Maine has only one or two.

"Federal prisons are well-funded and well-programmed," said Allen. "We're underfunded and have too much idleness. . . . We don't have the flexibility to move people or to keep them occupied."

"The state can't afford these programs and they don't do it," said Mark Lopez, a National Prison Project attorney who has twice sued the state of Maine over prison conditions. "The federal system is infinitely better funded and more professional."

According to inmates' accounts, Richardson's torture became a source of entertainment in the Maine State Prison's segregation unit, where even television and radios are denied as a disciplinary measure. One inmate described the nightly drama as "suspenseful . . . like a movie." Thomas J. Connolly, a Portland attorney who represents an inmate charged with Richardson's killing, said, "It was a form of passing the time."

As a child molester—or "skinner," in prison parlance—Richardson ranked at the very bottom of the inmate hierarchy. He became an instant lightning rod for the hostility pent up in the aged, red-brick prison on Maine's craggy coast.

A slight man of 31, Richardson entered the prison in late 1989—frightened, submissive and "at risk for abuse and exploitation and self-injurious behavior," a psychological report said. He attempted suicide, was deemed unable to adjust, and finally transferred to the segregation unit to share a cell with Roger Smith.

Smith, 21, and 202 pounds, was serving three years for assaulting his retarded girlfriend with a hammer. His psychological report warned he could become aggressive if frustrated, and he was quickly irritated with his new cellmate.

He shouted out to the 16 other inmates on the corridor: "We got us another skinner in here. We're going to party tonight."

The inmates could not see one another, but they could communicate by yelling through the small windows in the solid steel doors of their cells. They assumed the roles of prosecutor, judge and jury in what they called "the court of the north side."

They demanded that Richardson describe his crimes, then beg for beatings and cups of his cellmate's urine to drink, among other punishments. Smith's kicks to Richardson's groin ruptured one of Richardson's testicles; deep grooves in the porcelain of the toilet marked where Smith smashed out Richardson's tooth.

Prisoners told police they kept up a steady clamor, hollering "pound him. . . . Give him one for me." They joined to sing a "skinner" song about the abuse of a young girl.

Inmates in the next corridor told investigators they heard the commotion through the weekend, but the two guards on duty each night reported no unusual noises. "There is no possible way the guards couldn't hear all this," one inmate told police.

On Richardson's last night, Smith told a nurse on a "pill run" that Richardson had blackened his eye and bruised his groin falling out of the bunk. Smith also showed the nurse his own bruised knuckles. But the nurse testified she did not examine Richardson or question his at any length because "if you stopped and examined every complaint . . . you would never be able to deliver your medication on time."

The inmates urged Richardson to hang himself and advised Smith how to help. Smith said Richardson was "scared" and "didn't want to do it," but eventually tied his sheet to the bars. Smith kicked Richardson's legs out from under him.

Smith was sentenced in November to 70 years for Richardson's killing. A second inmate, Randall Tenggren, is scheduled to be tried for murder in April. Tenggren was eight cells down from Richardson, but he mailed Richardson's tooth to the warden with a note that read: "This is what happens to" child molesters.

Despite questions about the guards' behavior, state police and prison investigators did not interview the guards for at least 1 1/2 years after Richardson's death. Instead, the guards provided short written statements. One guard on duty when Richardson died wrote two lines, saying he "saw or heard nothing."

The state attorney general's office has now begun an investigation that may lead to disciplinary action against some guards, but the inquiry appears to provide small comfort to Maine Superior Court Judge Margaret J. Kravchuk, who presided over Smith's trial. At one sentencing last year, Kravchuk cited the revelations in Smith's trial and announced from the bench: "I . . . don't have much faith in warehousing people at the Maine State Prison."

Tom Connolly, Tenggren's defense attorney, wants to put the state's whole prison system on trial in April. "The only difference between this and what happens all the time is the poor guy died," he said.

Table 15–1 • Overcrowded Prisons

Growth in the Number of Inmates, as of Jan. 1, 1991
Entire Prison System Operating Under Court Order or Consent Decree (Nine States)

State	Rated Capacity	Number of Inmates	Percentage Over
Alaska	2,808	2,427	-13.6%
Florida	50,645	43,920	-13.3
Kansas	6014	5,635	-6.3
Louisiana	15,006	13,849	-7.7
Mississippi	8,125	6,724	-17.2
Rhode Island	2,876	2,377	-17.4
South Carolina	15,238	15,529	1.9
Tennessee	8,700	8,380	-3.7
Texas	49,333	49,316	0.0

One or More Prisons Operating Under Court Order or Consent Decree (30 states and the District of Columbia)

State	Rated Capacity	Number of Inmates	Percentage Over
Arizona	13,884	14,115	-1.7
California	52,698	94,050	78.5
Colorado	6,120	6,057	1.0
Connecticut	9,820	10,101	2.9
Delaware	2,514	3,474	38.2
District of Columbia	8,253	9,121	10.5
Georgia	19,121	22,302	16.6
Hawaii	2,401	2,370	-1.3
Idaho	1,828	1,857	1.6
Illinois	22,419	27,516	22.7
Indiana	10,951	12,736	16.3
Iowa	3,694	4,307	16.6
Kentucky	7,866	7,705	-2.0
Maryland	11,467	16,899	47.4
Massachusetts	4,983	9,183	84.3
Michigan	26,790	31,240	16.6
Missouri	15,296	14,946	-2.3
Nevada	5,406	5,640	4.3
New Hampshire	1,366	1,407	3.0
New Mexico	3,225	3,195	-0.9
New York	45,163	54,895	21.5
North Carolina	15,942	18,605	16.7
Ohio	20,598	31,501	52.9
Oklahoma	8,088	10,502	29.8
Pennsylvania	14,338	21,399	49.2
South Dakota	1,110	1,360	22.5
Utah	3,087	2,459	-20.3
Virginia	13,537	14,507	7.2
Washington	6,262	7,995	27.7
West Virginia	1,565	1,504	-3.9
Wisconsin	5,081	7,247	42.6

Major prisons not under court order or consent decree. (11 states and the federal system)

State	Rated Capacity	Number of Inmates	Percentage Over
Alabama	13,782	13,142	-4.6%
Arkansas	6,535	6,533	0.0
Maine	1,193	1,548	29.8

Continued

Table 15–1 continued

State	Rated Capacity	Number of Inmates	Percentage Over
Minnesota	3,251	3,179	-2.2
Montana	1,442	1,393	-3.4
Nebraska	1,666	2,382	43.0
New Jersey	17,848	16,743	-6.2
North Dakota	597	542	-9.2
Oregon	6,166	6,120	-0.7
Vermont	647	787	21.6
Wyoming	794	796	0.3
Federal System	36,624	60,734	65.8

Sources: Criminal Justice Institute Inc., National Prison Project of the American Civil Liberties Union, American Correctional Association and individual states

February 21, 1992

Supreme Court Eases Rules on Prisons

Federal Judge's Standard on
Overcrowding Said to be Too Strict

RUTH MARCUS

The Supreme Court yesterday made it easier for state and local officials to challenge court settlements requiring them to improve conditions at prisons and other public institutions.

The court ruled that a federal judge in Massachusetts had applied too strict a standard in refusing to change a prohibition against putting two convicts in each cell at the Suffolk County [Boston] jail.

Local officials had agreed to stop double-bunking in 1979, as part of a settlement with inmates who challenged jail conditions. Ten years later, pointing to a dramatic increase in the number of those being held before trial, the officials unsuccessfully asked the judge to release them from that agreement.

Yesterday, in an opinion written by Justice Byron R. White, the justices told the judge to reconsider the case and decide whether a "significant change" in the factual circumstances or interpretation of the law justified altering terms of the settlement.

The ruling came a day after Attorney General William P. Barr reversed Justice Department policy and said his office would aid some states seeking to change consent decrees on prison overcrowding.

Two justices, John Paul Stevens and Harry Blackmun, dissented. They agreed with the standard used by the majority but said it would not justify lifting the double-celling prohibition. Justice Clarence Thomas did not participate because he was not on the bench when the case was argued. Both sides in the case, *Rufo* v. *Inmates of Suffolk County Jail,* found something to cheer about in yesterday's ruling.

Solicitor General Kenneth W. Starr, whose office had entered the case on the side of government officials, described the ruling as a "highly significant opinion" with implications not only for prison crowding cases but also for other public institutions, such as schools, mental hospitals and facilities for mentally retarded people.

"I think this sends a very powerful message . . . ."

January 16, 1992

Facts Beyond Case at Hand Can Lengthen Prison Term

Some Call Sentencing Just a Computation

TRACY THOMPSON

D.C. police had no search warrant when they broke down Keith McCrory's apartment door in February 1989 and seized 3.3 pounds of cocaine. As it turned out, that didn't matter when it came time to sentence him.

Officers later acknowledged that their search was illegal, and prosecutors didn't try to introduce evidence at McCrory's trial about the 3.3 pounds. He was convicted of selling an undercover officer less than one gram of crack (there are about 453 grams in a pound), and that carries a maximum sentence of 33 months. But he was sentenced to 19.5 years, as if evidence about the 3.3 pounds had been introduced after all.

"McCrory claims, understandably, that a more patent end run around the exclusionary rule is hard to imagine," D.C. Circuit Court of Appeals Judge Laurence Silberman wrote in April, referring to the constitutional doctrine that requires judges to exclude illegally obtained evidence from presentation at trials.

But the appeals court upheld McCrory's sentence.

The court wasn't setting legal precedent. Across the country, drug defendants are discovering that federal sentencing guidelines now hold them responsible not just for the drugs they are convicted of possessing or selling, but also for drugs that were seized illegally, drugs they may have talked about selling, or even drugs they were acquitted of possessing.

Prosecutors, and the authors of the guidelines, say such "conduct-based" sentencing is realistic, that it simply makes clear what judges have been doing all along, and that it makes it all but impossible for wily criminals to evade punishment through clever plea-bargaining.

"I think you have to look at (society's) interest in having the defendant punished for what he actually did," said Paul Martin, deputy staff director of the U.S. Sentencing Commission, which drew up the guidelines.

The guidelines are based on the mandatory minimum prison terms set by federal statutes and are used to fine-tune penalties for individual defendants.

Judges always have considered a host of factors not in evidence, including a defendant's demeanor, a juvenile record the jury can't be told about, or drugs not included in evidence that the judge concludes the defendant possessed.

But now the sentencing guidelines precisely list those extra factors and translate drug quantities into months in prison, the same way the Internal Revenue Service calibrates tax brackets.

Defense lawyers and civil libertarians worry that such formulaic attention to quantity, instead of to proof of guilt, means that bedrock guarantees—such as the Fourth Amendment's ban on unreasonable searches and seizures, and the requirement that guilt be proved beyond a reasonable doubt—are rendered obsolete.

"There's a great deal of angst about this," said San Diego public defender Judy Clark, who publishes the "Guidelines Grapevine' to keep defense lawyers across the country up to date on the latest interpretations of the guidelines, which federal courts began to use two years ago. "That's probably the biggest rub in the guidelines right now—the consideration of unconvicted conduct."

Before the guidelines, a judge also could consider several factors in a defendant's background, such as whether the person was a Harvard law student or a welfare mother. But the guidelines ban the use of "socioeconomic" information at sentencing. The aim was to eliminate disparate treatment along lines of wealth or race, but the effect is to exclude most defense character witnesses and pleas for leniency.

By restricting mitigating evidence and quantifying aggravating evidence, critics said, the guidelines have yielded an unexpected result in the last two years: Defendants get extra months in prison, established by formula, for offenses they were never convicted of.

For example:

In addition to the D.C. Circuit, the Philadelphia-based 3rd Circuit and the Atlanta-based 11th Circuit have held recently that illegally seized evidence can be used to calculate a sentence under the guidelines' formula, even if it is excluded at trial.

All three courts added a caveat: Police cannot conduct illegal searches just in the hopes of finding more drugs and adding to a defendant's prison time.

But, as Silberman noted in the McCrory case, "I cannot imagine how a defendant could ever show that the police illegally broke in to search his house for the very . . . purpose of enhancing his sentence." At least two federal appeals courts—the New Orleans-based 5th Circuit and the Cincinnati-based 6th Circuit—have ruled that judges may include in the guidelines' formula the amount of illegal drugs the defendant agreed to sell an undercover agent, even if the drugs were never produced. In the 5th Circuit case, the defendant agreed to sell an undercover agent 2,000 pounds of marijuana, but only produced 500. He was sentenced as if he had sold all 2,000 pounds.

Several appeals courts have ruled that judges can calculate sentences based on a quantity of drugs a defendant was acquitted of possessing, as long as prosecutors can convince a judge by a "preponderance of the evidence" that the defendant had the drugs. Jurors cannot convict someone unless they are convinced of guilt under a much tougher standard—"beyond a reasonable doubt."

Though not all 12 federal appeals courts have ruled on this precise issue, Clark said, "I can't think of a circuit that has said anything contrary."

Perhaps the best-publicized example of this rule was the six-month prison sentence given last year to D.C. Mayor Marion Barry on a single count of cocaine possession. (Barry's case recently was sent back for resentencing on technical grounds.)

Absent the new guidelines, most first-time offenders convicted on that charge could expect to be sentenced to probation. At last October's sentencing, U.S. District Judge Thomas Penfield Jackson said he was basing his sentence on his belief that Barry was guilty of some if not all of the other counts in the indictment—one drug possession charge of which he was acquitted, as well as nine cocaine possession counts and three perjury counts on which the jury could not reach a verdict.

The guidelines are producing a body of law in which legal concepts can come second to arithmetic, critics say. As Washington defense lawyer Mary Davis put it, instead of law books, "now you use an adding machine."

In LSD cases, do courts weigh the drug plus the blotter paper the drug is stored on? Yes, courts have said. In the old days, drug statutes said nothing about amounts and judges considered quantity informally at sentencing, on a case-by-case basis. Now the precise weight ratchets up the sentence on the calibrated scale.

That's what happened in a case involving Dilaudid pills, even though only a fraction of the pills contained the federally controlled drug hydromorphone, according to a D.C. Circuit opinion written last May by Judge Clarence Thomas. Counting just the hydromorphone, one defendant would have gotten about 21 months and the other 16. Weighing all the ingredients of the Dilaudid pills—even those ingredients that are not controlled substances—bumped the sentences up to 51 months and 27 months.

The new rules for plea bargaining have tripped up some defendants.

In U.S. District Court here last week, the rules created an unpleasant surprise for Miguel Profeta, the leader of a cocaine ring who had been persuaded to plead guilty and testify against his former comrades. The guidelines say a defendant such as Profeta can avoid a life sentence only if he provides "substantial assistance" to the government.

The prosecutor, not the judge, decides whether a defendant has cooperated enough, and the U.S. Attorney's Office decided not to give Profeta credit for his help because he had changed parts of his story on the witness stand.

Changes in the plea bargain guidelines surprise many defense lawyers who don't practice regularly in federal court. That was illustrated in a ruling from the D.C. Circuit last month on Perry Dukes, indicted on a charge of possessing with intent to distribute five to 50 grams of crack.

That charge carries a mandatory sentence of at least five years, so Dukes probably thought he was getting a break when a prosecutor let him plead guilty to the less serious offense of possession with intent to distribute only a "detectable" amount of crack. That was before U.S. District Judge Gerhard Gesell computed his sentence.

Taking into account the exact amount of crack Dukes was caught with, 11.02 grams, and the fact that he had some prior convictions, Gesell came up with a sentence of 63 months—or five years and three months.

As the D.C. Circuit noted, "Dukes did not negotiate much of a deal." It upheld his sentence.

July 22, 1991

The Changing Face of Organized Crime

'Emerging' New York Gangs Profit By Preying on Their Ethnic Communities

LAURIE GOODSTEIN

The new face of organized crime in this city does not grin like John Gotti or eat fettucini with pomodoro sauce.

He showed up one day amid the squid and the bok choy at the Tinjun Food Market in Brooklyn. Demanding to see the proprietor, he told her he expected a regular monthly payment of $100. Cooperate, and she'd be left alone. Refuse, and one day she'd find her well-scrubbed new store burned to the ground.

When the thug from the Gum Sing gang returned to collect his money, Sgt. Pat Russo was waiting with handcuffs. It was a rare arrest of a Chinese mobster on Brooklyn's 8th Avenue, where gangs extort with impunity and run gambling rings out of storefronts stocked with only laundry detergent. Rare because the market proprietor, a young woman wearing hoop earrings who asked not to be identified, collaborated with the police.

"She's gutsy," Russo explained. "A lot of the owners say they'd rather pay. They consider it like a business expense."

Mob king John Gotti traded his Italian suits for an orange prison uniform on Thursday, but the murder and racketeering conviction of the boss of the Gambino crime family brings no relief to those who combat the criminal underworld. The Gambinos—the nation's largest crime family, with 400 inducted members—are expected by police to regenerate and reorganize, although their new leaders may operate less ostentatiously than the "the Dapper Don."

But investigators are just beginning to focus on what they call "the emerging groups" of organized criminals now in the same nascent stages of development that the traditional mob families were 60 years ago.

Among the newcomers are Colombian cartels, Chinese triads, Jamaican posses, Dominican drug gangs and Vietnamese squads with names such as "Born to Kill."

Each has its own territory and means of making money. The Colombians and Jamaicans deal in cocaine, the Chinese in heroin and petty extortion, said William Doran, the special agent supervising the criminal division of New York's FBI office. But, he said, they operate more in the margins of the netherworld than the entrenched mob families, and are harder to crack.

The Latin and Caribbean-based gangs "are, to a large extent, products of and controlled out of their own countries," Doran said. "They come into this country and they do a tour. They don't stay. They're very mobile and they don't have established routes."

Like the Mafia in its early days, many of these novice street gangs profit by preying on their own communities. Four members of the "Green Dragon" gang, an Asian-American ring based in Queens, were being tried this week in a nearly empty Brooklyn courtroom two floors below the standing-room-only Gotti trial. The Green Dragons are charged with kidnapping members of rival gangs, murdering seven people and extorting money from Chinese restaurants in Queens.

"The Asians really have a limited portfolio," said Howard Abadinsky, professor of criminology at St. Xavier College in Chicago and the author of three books on organized crime. "They are not even close to the stage of the traditional crime families in New York that thrive on labor and business racketeering. They haven't been Americanized enough to involve themselves in that.

By infiltrating nearly every blue-collar industry in New York City—construction, trucking, sanitation, shipping, garment making, concrete and even gas stations—mob families here have grown rich by skimming a significant portion off the local tax base. That is not likely to change, according to experts, even with the leadership of four of the five New York crime families currently in prison or under indictment.

"The Mafia almost immediately got a foothold into the unions," said James Fox, who heads the FBI office here. "The Asian gangs will not have that advantage."

They may never get the opportunity, because the traditional mob networks are highly sophisticated and still intact, said several organized crime experts. Business owners accustomed to paying off the mobs' agents in return for guarantees of no competition tend to see the relationship as mutually beneficial, Abadinsky said, and they are reluctant to break it.

With the choke hold that old world crime families still have on many industries and unions, the new gangs occupy niches hidden from the glare of the news media, and often the police.

Task forces secretly videotaped Gotti and his associates as they strolled the sidewalks of Little Italy in Manhattan. They planted listening devices in his clubhouses and meeting rooms and transcribed hours of tapes that became highly damaging evidence at his trial.

But members of many Chinese gangs can rest secure that they are safe from surveillance because the police have no teams who can understand their dialects. Few New York police officers qualify to infiltrate the violent Vietnamese gangs.

In addition, the gangs who victimize their own people know they are targeting the segment of society least likely to inform or cooperate with the police. In some cases, the victims are new to this country, don't speak English or fear contact with authorities because their immigration status is unresolved. Sometimes they distrust uniformed officials because they come from a homeland where the police are brutal or repressive.

Back at the Tinjun Market, the young owner tells police in broken English that she is nervous because the extortionist from the Gum Sing gang recently phoned her from jail and made threats.

"The bad guy, he's in jail?" she asks.

Pained to explain the complexities of bail bonds and jury trials, Sgt. Russo answers simply, "We'll keep him in as long as we can."

April 5, 1992

Japan Sets Organized Crime Crackdown

Mafia-Like Yakuza Vows to Fight Back, Take Operations Underground

T.R. REID

After decades of open and predominantly peaceful coexistence, Japan's National Police Agency has finally declared war on the mob.

The battle officially begins Sunday, when the first comprehensive anti-gang law in Japanese history takes effect, authorizing police to create what amounts to a national blacklist of designated gang members and to crack down hard on their activities.

The yakuza, Japan's version of the Mafia, has mounted vigorous protests, including a downtown Tokyo demonstration last month in which tattooed mobsters and their wives paraded with signs saying "Lay Off Our Gangs." Critics in and out of the mobs warn that the tough new law may backfire by driving Japan's highly visible organized crime families underground.

As with many other aspects of Japanese life, this country adopted the core idea of organized crime syndicates from the West—and then gave the concept a completely original twist.

In many ways, the yakuza operates like every other big business organization here. Members proudly wear yakuza lapel badges and pass out business cards—complete with phone and fax numbers—identifying their gang affiliation.

Gang leaders hold press conferences. Gang members have titles such as "trainee" and "section chief." They work their way up through the organizational chart, moving from small district offices to headquarters. The biggest yakuza groups flaunt their famous corporate logos on the front door of their office buildings.

Even without badges and business cards, the roughly 80,000 yakuza members are easy to spot in Japan. They generally wear their hair in a tight, curly crew-cut style known as a "punch perm." Their arms and chests are generally covered with elaborate tattoos. And they tend to have stubs where their little fingers could be, because chopping off fingers is a traditional form of punishment within the yakuza clans.

The yakuza are also noticeable because they tend to drive big imported cars. The Yamaguchi-gumi, Japan's largest gang, has a famous preference for Cadillacs.

Its chief rival, the Inagawa-kai, leans instead to Mercedes-Benz, or just plain "Benz" in the gangster's argot.

The gangs' high visibility has been possible because most yakuza clans—like American mobs who dabble in various front businesses -have just enough legitimate business endeavors to give themselves a veneer of legality. The gangs here operate real estate and finance businesses, and several run wholesale and distribution operations.

But the mainstays of the yakuza's income, according to police, are traditional gang enterprises: drugs, prostitution and, particularly, extortion.

In a country where lawyers are scarce and hardly anybody goes to court, the gangs provide a sort of forced "mediation, service in many disputes that would prompt law suits in the United States.

The most common instance of extortion involves the aftermath of auto accidents.

After an accident, one party frequently will hire a gang member to visit the other party. With missing fingers and yakuza lapel badge clearly evident, the gang member rarely has to make a specific threat. Rather, he "suggests" that the person make a specified payment to settle the damages.

The frightened victim generally pays up, regardless of his actual responsibility in the accident. The mobster takes a cut and delivers the rest to his client. This kind of thing happens tens of thousands of times per year, police say.

Still, Japanese society generally has been tolerant of the mobsters in its midst. For one thing, the yakuza has something of a Robin Hood image, dating back to the years just after World War II, when the gangs organized roughly on the Mafia model and got heavily involved in black-market trading. They were sometimes the only source of food for starving families.

As the yakuza groups expanded into prostitution, loan-sharking and the sale of illegal commodities such as drugs and guns, their size and wealth increased. By the mid-1980s, as Japan's economic growth was reaching its peak, the mobs took their stores of cash and moved into such legal businesses as real estate and stock speculation to launder their growing profits.

In last summer's securities-trading scandals here, several cases were revealed in which gang members had close financial ties with blue-chip banks and brokerage houses. A prominent American investor, Prescott Bush—President Bush's older brother—was hired as a consultant by a yakuza-controlled firm, although the elder Bush apparently had no idea that he was dealing with the mob.

"In the last 10 years or so, the gangs have completely changed in nature and spirit," said Takaji Kunimatsu, director of criminal investigation for the National Police Agency, Japan's version of the FBI. "They have abundant funds—enough to influence the stock or real estate markets. They have more guns. They used to leave ordinary people alone, but now they are a threat to civil order."

Accordingly, the National Police last year won approval in the national parliament for a strong, intrusive new law that should give police the power to stop yakuza extortion and other activities that were hard to prosecute until now.

The gangs, of course, are reacting in their own way. With the local police now not so much a neighbor as a threat, the yakuza leaders say they will completely change their modus operandi. The badges, business cards and corporate logos will go; clandestine underground operations will take their place.

"Up to now, people have known us," said Tokutaro Takayama, the leader of a mid-sized yakuza clan called the Aizu Kotetsu, in a television interview. "We were part of our community, we had our buildings, we were open. Of course the police could see what we were doing.

"But now the police are determined to shut us down, because they don't like us," he added.

"And our response must be to go underground. Ten years from now, we will still be here. But nobody will know who or where we are. How does that help the police?"

February 29, 1992

16 *Drugs*

Drug use and abuse is pervasive in U.S. society. The first article deals with the heavy use of alcohol among teenagers. The role of parents, and tobacco and alcohol companies promoting sales to minors play a significant part in this increase. The second article finds cocaine use on the upswing, per a survey by the National Institute on Drug Abuse. This is a major setback to government programs intended to curtail its usage.

The third article deals with crack babies, and drug addicted mothers who find treatment increasingly hard to find, and difficult to stick with. Women are deterred by social and legal barriers such as child-care quandaries, fear of prosecution, uncooperative spouses, and the lengthy admitting process. The next article talks about the problems drug-induced disabilities in children will cause in the school system, especially the taxing on teaching and financial resources. Budget cuts undermine efforts on the 'war" against drug abuse. The same recession that produced the cuts also seems to be creating an increased demand for services since hard times tend to drive more people to drugs and alcohol.

Teen Alcohol Use Heavy, Survey Finds

Surgeon General Calls Report 'Shocking'

MICHAEL ISIKOFF

About 8 million American junior and senior high school students are weekly users of alcohol, including 454,000 "binge" drinkers who consume an average of 15 drinks each week, according to a new nationwide survey of teenage alcohol use that Surgeon General Antonia C. Novello called "shocking."

All 50 states now prohibit sale of alcohol to anyone under 21. Yet the survey by the Department of Health and Human Services's inspector general's office found that an estimated 6.9 million teenagers, including some as young as 13, have no problem obtaining alcohol with false identification or from liquor stores that do not check ages.

In addition, about one-third of the nationwide sample of 956 students reported having accepted rides from persons who had been drinking. Of those students who drink, 31 percent reported drinking alone, 41 percent said they drink when they were upset because it makes them feel better and 25 percent said they drink to "get high." According to the study, a total of 20.7 million students attend seventh through 12th grades.

The survey, the first such detailed study on patterns of teenage alcohol use, underscored a point that many educators and researchers have been making with increasing frequency: while annual federal surveys have shown sharply decreasing numbers of young people using marijuana, cocaine and other illegal drugs, alcohol use and heavy drinking remain high.

Novello said she was "flabbergasted" by some of the findings, adding that they emphasize the need for parents to play a greater role in educating youngsters about dangers of alcohol. "I've even had many parents telling me, 'Thank God, my kids drink, they don't use drugs,' " Novello said.

While the new survey did not ask about illegal drug use, HHS's most recent annual survey of high school seniors found that about 14 percent acknowledged using marijuana in the past month and less than 2 percent used cocaine, while 57 percent reported drinking alcohol. But some critics have charged that the Bush administration consistently has deemphasized alcohol abuse treatment, in part to fund large increases in the fight against illegal drugs.

This year, for example, the administration has proposed cutting the budget for the National Institute on Alcohol Abuse and Alcoholism from $171 million to

$166.7 million, while proposing a $30 million increase for the National Institute on Drug Abuse. It has directed that all of a proposed $99 million increase in substance treatment funding for the states be spent on illegal drugs, as recommended by the Office of National Drug Control Policy.

A separate survey also released yesterday said the problem of youthful drinking has been compounded by the alcoholic beverage industry, which has introduced an array of new products, such as fruit-flavored wine coolers, that are packaged as fruit drinks and contain little or no alcoholic taste even though they have high alcoholic content.

Nearly two of every three teenagers surveyed were unable to distinguish these products—with names such as Tropical Passion, Purple Passion or Cisco—from non-alcoholic drinks on store shelves.

Novello said she wants improved labeling on all such products, including listings of alcoholic content on beer and malt liquors, and was commissioning an interagency task force to make recommendations.

Beer and wine industry officials consistently have argued that they have no interest in selling products to teenagers. But the survey indicated that teenage drinking has become a significant portion of the market for many products. It calculated that junior and senior high school students account for 35 percent of all sales of wine coolers.

Officials yesterday said that among the most alarming findings was the prevalence of binge drinking—defined as taking five or more drinks in a row. The survey projected that 5.4 million students have "binged" at least once and more than 3 million have done so in the past month. The average "binger" is a 16-year-old white male in 10th grade who took his first drink when he was 12.

June 7, 1992

Cocaine Use on the Upswing

Survey Results a Setback for Administration

MICHAEL ISIKOFF

The number of Americans using cocaine at least once a month rose to an estimated 1.9 million this year, an 18 percent jump over last year caused by substantial increases in drug use among blacks, the unemployed and persons over 35, according to results of an annual federal survey.

The National Institute on Drug Abuse (NIDA) household survey, based on a sample of more than 32,000 people, reverses a five-year downward trend in cocaine use and represents an unexpected setback for the Bush administration's anti-drug effort.

Two years ago, White House drug policy officials declared the household survey one of their principal benchmarks for measuring progress and set as one of their goals a 50 percent drop in habitual cocaine use—defined as people who use the drug once a week or more—by the 1991 survey.

But this year's survey, due to be officially released today, reports the number of weekly cocaine users actually increased 29 percent this year. This resulted in an estimated 855,000 habitual cocaine users, virtually identical to the figure reported by the survey for 1988.

Even more disturbing, officials said, is a separate report showing dramatic increases in cocaine—and heroin-related visits to hospital emergency rooms. The number of cocaine-related emergencies recorded by the government's Drug Abuse Warning Network—considered by many experts the best yardstick for measuring the consequences of hard-core abuse—reached 25,370 from April to June of this year, a 30 percent increase over the comparable period a year ago.

In a statement prepared for a news conference today, national drug control director Bob Martinez argues that continued sharp declines in cocaine and marijuana use among the middle-class, suburban residents and teenagers illustrate that "we are continuing to make progress" and that "overall, most of the trend lines are going in the right direction."

But Martinez acknowledges that the new figures show that the effort to curb hard-core abuse has slowed and will likely become more difficult as increasing numbers of long-time users lapse into addiction.

"The problem seems to be collapsing into groups within our society who can least afford the problems caused by their addiction: older and inner city addicts," he said. "As the great middle class cures itself of this epidemic, there is the danger that the media, the Congress and others will walk away from this problem."

Numerous drug abuse experts have long cautioned against putting too much stock in the household survey because most people are unlikely to acknowledge illegal drug use even when promised anonymity. But NIDA officials have contended that while the absolute numbers may be subject to question, the overall trends are reliable and usually consistent with other indicators.

William J. Bennett, the former drug policy director who repeatedly cited earlier surveys as evidence of administration progress, said yesterday the new results were not a surprise. "We said a number of times we'd see declines followed by plateaus," Bennett said in a telephone interview. Bennett also said there was substantial "good news" in the survey, adding that lone has to question what would have happened without the effort we made."

The new survey, combined with the hospital emergency room figures, indicates that current trends on the drug front are mixed. An estimated 12.6 million Americans used an illegal drug once a month or more in 1991, down from 12.9 million in 1990 and 14.5 million in 1988, the survey estimates. As reported by all previous household surveys, the bulk of that drug use remains marijuana, which was used by an estimated 9.7 million Americans this year, down from 10.2 million the previous year.

The most encouraging signs, officials said, were among young people. The estimated number of users 12- to 17-years-old dropped to 1.4 million, 25 percent below the 1988 estimate.

But the survey shows a substantial increase in reported drug use among blacks. An internal White House analysis of the results shows that 9.3 percent of blacks questioned in the survey acknowledged using illegal drugs in the past month, up from 7.8 percent in 1988. In addition, the analysis says, "cocaine use increased dramatically among black men over the age of 35."

At least one explanation for the increases, some experts said, is the presence of more cocaine at cheaper prices on the streets. Last year, federal officials reported shortages of cocaine in some cities and higher prices, a development attributed to the Colombian government's crackdown on the Medellin cartel.

But this year, officials said, a rival drug group, the Cali cartel, has taken over much of the U.S. market and street cocaine again is plentiful, leading to the surge in cocaine-related hospital visits, said Mark Kleiman, a Harvard University drug researcher.

December 19, 1991

Cries in the Dark Often Go Unanswered

For Drug-Addicted Mothers, Treatment is Hard to Find, Even Harder to Stick With

MICHELE L. NORRIS

Behind every child exposed to crack in the womb is a mother who used drugs during her pregnancy.

Motherhood takes a back seat to the desire for drugs in the world of crack addiction. The women in this world come in all colors, from all walks of life, and they turn to drugs for all kinds of reasons. Their drug use frequently is only one strand in a web of problems that defy simple solutions. And there is no simple solution to crack addiction. Even intensive drug treatment seems to help relatively few crack addicts, and treatment is rarely available to mothers of young children.

Katy, a 29-year-old resident of Washington's Trinidad neighborhood, tried to fight her way out of addiction. Desperate for help late one Friday evening last September, Katy called her obstetrician from a pay phone on the street, high on crack and visibly pregnant.

Katy, who asked that her last name be withheld, had overcome several obstacles before making that call: the worry that her companion of nine years would leave her while she was in treatment, the fear of being charged with child abuse, and the thought that her future child and her son, Kevin, 2, might be removed from her care by city social workers.

Tom Raskauskas, who had been her obstetrician while she was pregnant with her first child, was used to Katy's late-night phone calls. "She was an addict, but she gets her kids in here every week for their appointments, so I knew that somewhere inside her there was some untapped strength," Raskauskas said. "I told her to call me whenever she needed help."

Up to that point, Katy had thought of going through treatment on several occasions, but each time the urge to seek help was overcome by her craving for drugs.

A small woman with a wide smile and a rapid-fire way of speaking that belies her lethargy, Katy describes herself as an "A-one addict." She began using drugs as a teenager, she said, to escape the pain of a life that included parental neglect, academic failure and the poor self-esteem that so often accompanies persistent poverty. In one conversation with a reporter, Katy said, "I don't get high, I get numb."

She began shooting speed when she was 17 and later moved on to heroin, powdered cocaine and eventually crack—the drug that she says amplified her addiction to the point where she began exchanging sex for drugs on the streets and alleys of Trinidad, near Gallaudet University in Northeast Washington. Often unable to find a sitter, she would carry her child in her arms, setting him on the ground when she found a willing customer.

Katy's addiction was so strong that she sometimes would trade her child's food for money to buy crack. Once she sold a case of baby formula provided to her by the government to a neighborhood grocer and used the money to buy crack outside the store.

"I knew my life was going nowhere, but the word around here was if you're pregnant and you want to get into treatment, forget it," Katy said. "Everybody knows that trying to get in treatment is worse than trying to get on public aid. It's paperwork and more paperwork, and then maybe you can get into a program."

Katy had heard Raskauskas's warnings about what drugs could do to her fetus. She had seen the ads and watched the television shows about how drugs dash a child's potential before birth. But all around her in her neighborhood were adorable babies born to women who, as Katy says, "lived for the pipe."

"The problem we have in telling women not to use drugs while they are pregnant is that they look around and see other women who have beautiful, bouncy babies even though they smoked crack throughout the pregnancy," Raskauskas said. "They think, 'Well, it didn't affect her baby, so mine will be just fine.' If only that were true.

"When the babies start to walk and talk and try to coordinate their thoughts and actions, that is when the mothers come back and say, 'Hey, something is wrong with my child. He can't sit still. He's uncoordinated and he stumbles all the time. He can't put his words together,' " Raskauskas said.

Trying to Help

Katy's companion, Jack, who said he does not drink or use drugs, stayed by her side as she sank deeper into addiction, all the time urging her to seek help and warning her about what drugs would do to her baby. Jack is a Mack truck of a man with a balding crown and a sprinkling of gray in his beard. He says he stays with Katy out of love. "Without me, she'd be lost," he said.

But Katy says Jack is equally dependent on her. "He puts me out, but he always takes me back because, whether he wants to admit it or not, he needs me as much as I need him."

When Katy became pregnant with their son Kevin, Jack took to locking Katy in their apartment when he went to work to keep her off the streets and away from drugs. Most of the time it worked. On at least one occasion, though, she pulled the air conditioner out of the bedroom window when she was eight months pregnant and climbed down from the second story to slip away and find crack.

It was on a night when Katy had escaped to smoke crack that she called Raskauskas, tired of the roller-coaster life of drug addiction and eager to give her second child a better start in life. But Katy's call came hours after the admissions office closed at the Seneca Melwood Treatment Center in Olney, a program that accepts pregnant women on Medicaid and where Raskauskas had admitting privileges. Raskauskas could have asked Katy to come back in the morning and hoped that the desire to go straight would see her through the night. Instead, he admitted her to Washington Hospital Center's psychiatric unit overnight and started the drug treatment admissions process in the morning.

"You can't do it for everyone, but sometimes you have to play hardball to get these women into treatment; otherwise they just go back to the streets," Raskauskas said.

Pregnant women often are the pariahs of drug treatment, routinely turned away by programs or forced to choose between seeking help or abandoning their children to relatives or child protective services.

Less than 20 percent of the drug treatment programs in the Washington area admit pregnant women, regardless of whether they are rich or poor, carry insurance or depend on Medicaid. And less than 5 percent help women find temporary placement for their children while they seek help, or allow mothers to keep their children with them during treatment.

With scant exceptions, private drug treatment centers refuse to accept expectant women, citing inadequate staffing, facilities or insurance to cover special needs or complications posed by pregnancy, said Diane Canova, of the National Association of State Alcohol and Drug Addiction Directors.

"Pregnant substance abusers have the least access to treatment," Canova said.

In the public sector, the District, Maryland and Virginia all have expanded treatment space for pregnant women in the last year and have pledged to give expectant women priority in securing spaces in residential treatment facilities. But those efforts have had limited effect because the number of spaces is small and the admissions process for publicly financed programs is so protracted that many women never make it past the red tape.

System a 'Roadblock'

"Right now the system . . . is a roadblock to treatment," said J. Harold Nickens, a District obstetrician who works with pregnant substance abusers. "When someone comes to you and asks for help for substance abuse, you have to be prepared to face them. You can't say fill out papers for a week and come back and be interviewed two or three times and then we will try and place you within a week to 10 days."

Officials in the District have discovered that expanding the availability of drug treatment for pregnant women is only the first step toward increasing the number of women who get help. Health officials estimate that thousands of women in Washington are abusing drugs. And yet it is a rare occurrence when all 18 treatment beds that the District has set aside for pregnant women are in use, said John Jackson, director of the District's Office of Alcohol and Drug Abuse Services

Administration. Jackson and others interpret this to mean that women are deterred by social and legal barriers such as child-care quandaries, fear of prosecution, uncooperative spouses and the lengthy admitting process, not to mention their own weaknesses.

Even when a program is available, other obstacles can keep women out of treatment. The lack of child care was identified as the No. 1 barrier to women seeking drug treatment in a study of treatment programs in 34 cities conducted by the National Association of Junior Leagues in 1986.

Beyond arranging child care, women seeking treatment also must overcome the stigma of being labeled as "bad mothers" and losing their children. They sometimes must fight objections from spouses or lovers. Often, a spouse resents having to assume housekeeping and child-care responsibilities while a woman is in drug treatment. A spouse also may fear that the woman will change during the course of treatment and want to end the relationship when she emerges, said Lynn Christopher, director of the women's program at the Mountain Manor drug treatment center in Emmitsburg, Md.

And many community-based drug counseling programs do not allow adults to bring their children to meetings. Some of those that do are not convenient to public transportation. Criminal Matters

Some argue that efforts to criminalize maternal drug use have created another roadblock to treatment. Since 1988, there have been several well-publicized cases in which legal action was taken against pregnant substance abusers. Women from Alaska to Wyoming to Florida have been charged, and in a handful of cases convicted, of delivering controlled substances to their fetuses.

Prosecutors, law enforcement officials and children's advocates argue that such cases will force women to think twice about using drugs while they are pregnant and prompt more women to seek help with their addictions. But several medical and women's groups, including the American Medical Association and the American Public Health Association, attack what they call the "pregnancy police' movement. According to critics, prosecutors tend to single out poor minority women. They argue that charging a few pregnant substance abusers will keep many more from seeking treatment or prenatal care.

"Women are afraid they are going to lose their kids," said mountain Manor's Christopher. "We have created a whole new barrier for women who need treatment by forcing them to choose between keeping their children and seeking help for their addictions."

Even if a woman can enter a program, treatment provides no guarantee of a drug-free life. Female substance abusers usually return to drug-infested environments after treatment. And no widely successful method has been found for helping addicts overcome the intense cravings produced by crack cocaine.

"Treatment provides people with a chance to start again, but there are no guarantees, no money-back warranties," Jackson said. "Especially since crack showed up."

Richard Rawson, an addiction researcher affiliated with the University of California at Los Angeles, said: "We have never seen anything like the intensity of cravings we see with crack cocaine. . . . Treating crack is difficult because there is nothing out there that can effectively blunt the severity of that craving."

Prenatal substance abuse is an age-old phenomenon. Anthropologists have uncovered ancient documents that describe how Inca women inured to chewing coca leaves maintained the habit while pregnant.

Eighteenth-century British newspapers detailed a marked increase in miscarriages and birth defects among poor white women who drank heavily while pregnant during that country's "Gin Epidemic." And modern society has seen the unfortunate increase in the number of babies exposed to all manner of drugs in the womb, including heroin, PCP, marijuana, powdered cocaine and prescription drugs.

"Everyone is acting like the problem of maternal substance abuse began with crack," Christopher said. "This problem has been around for a long, long time.

"If there is one thing that makes me sad, it is the effects of my addiction on my children," said Christopher, a recovering addict now working with women at Mountain Manor. She wonders whether her 18-year-old son's academic and emotional problems are rooted in her use of drugs and alcohol during her pregnancy. "People think that women who use drugs while they are pregnant are evil. They forget that addiction is a disease. You would never show that lack of compassion for someone who has cancer or another disease."

Christopher now counsels other women, many of them mothers, at Mountain Manor, the primary treatment center in the area that allows Medicaid patients to keep their children throughout treatment. The former roadside motel includes quarters for as many as eight children and a four-crib nursery with a round-the-clock nursing staff.

"For pregnant women or women with kids, we are often their last chance for hope," Christopher said.

Taking the Chance

One woman trying to seize that last chance came to Mountain Manor last year after several other facilities turned her away. The 25-year-old secretary from Western Maryland became addicted to cocaine, marijuana and methamphetamine after her husband started giving her the drugs to ease the discomfort of pregnancy. The woman, who asked that her name be withheld, looks at her flaxen-haired daughter and wonders whether her drug use has marred the 8-year-old's future. When she became pregnant a second time nearly two years ago, she decided to seek help.

"It is easy to call up sympathy for a cute little child," she said. "But people have to remember that that child came from someone, a woman. And unless there are programs to help those women, those cute little children could be doomed."

But even the best programs can't address the whole problem. Katy went through a 28-day program in September at the facility in Olney, at first experiencing the intense pain of withdrawal while undergoing therapy sunup to sundown.

But abstinence was not easy when she returned to Trinidad. On some nights, people she used to smoke crack with would call her name from the streets, urging her to come down from her apartment and join them. She found it hard to attend therapy groups because many would not permit children to attend, and those that did were not always accessible by public transportation. For Katy, who can read only the simplest words, the literature designed to guide her through her recovery was nearly useless. And she often would experience vomiting and diarrhea because her cravings for crack went unanswered.

In December, Katy returned to the pipe. Mostly she blames herself for slipping. But she also blames a treatment system that is poorly suited to women with children.

"I know it's my fault that I can't stay [straight]," Katy said. "But the system doesn't make it any easier, though. There are lots of women like me who need help, but they have given up on the system."

July 2, 1991

And the Children Shall Need

Drug-Induced Disabilities Will Tax School Resources

MICHELE L. NORRIS

The kindergartners spill into their East Harlem elementary school each morning bubbling with enthusiasm, but for some enthusiasm is not enough.

There is the little girl who is almost 6 but has the language skills of a child half her age. She repeats what sounds like "Kiyeh da boo" over and over until a baffled aide discovers that the child is trying to say, "Can I have the book?"

Then there is the little boy who is unable to sit still for more than a few minutes. He fidgets in his seat so feverishly that his desk is out of position with his row. Another child has such problems controlling his hands that he sometimes drops his face into his plate to eat lunch; picking up a spoon or a fork is too taxing.

Their problems seem disparate, but these students all have something in common: Their bodies and brains developed in wombs contaminated by crack.

As the smokable form of cocaine known as crack marked its fifth year as a popular street drug last year, so too did the first generation of children born to women who smoked crack while they were pregnant.

Those 5-year-olds entered kindergarten last fall in New York, Los Angeles and Miami, cities where the crack epidemic first took root. Schools in those cities have been hit with a crush of troubled students who frazzle teachers who often are untrained or simply too burdened to meet their extraordinary needs.

"It is not like there are one or two special cases where the children exhibit bizarre behavior," said Hattye Brown, a kindergarten teacher at PS 146 in the East Harlem section of New York. "I am talking about a whole lot of children who are not functioning where they should be. We all better put our seat belts on, because in five years it is going to be real bad."

The crack market in Washington and its suburbs began to flourish about a year behind New York's. So this fall the first sizable number of local children exposed to crack in the womb will enter city and suburban schools. And crack's soaring popularity since the mid-1980s indicates that the pool of crack-affected youngsters will grow dramatically each year until at least 1995.

Compounding the problem for local schools is that the vast majority of these children will not be in special programs geared to their needs. They will share desks, textbooks and lunchrooms with other students. And all the children who were not exposed to crack in the womb will suffer as their teachers become preoccupied with the crack-affected youngsters' overwhelming problems.

"We are going to have to do something to save these other children," Brown said. "Because the crack kids are going to take up all their teachers' energy."

Concerned about the future expenses facing the state, New York State Comptroller Edward Regan estimated that in nine years there will be about 72,000 children in New York City who were exposed to crack in the womb.

Officials in the District and its suburbs have declined to offer such an estimate. But local hospitals, using sporadic drug testing, found that more than 2,000 drug-affected babies were born in 1990, enough to fill about 80 kindergarten classes. The total number is certainly much larger.

Exactly how many children have been exposed to crack in the womb is unknown because maternal drug testing by hospitals is sporadic. Studies in Florida, Tennessee and Philadelphia show little disparity in the rate of prenatal drug use between poor women seeking care at public health clinics and more affluent women who see private doctors.

"Don't be fooled into thinking that these children only reside in the ghetto," said Ira Chasnoff, president and founder of the National Association for Prenatal Research and Education, the preeminent research facility on maternal substance abuse. "They are everywhere. They are in rural America. They are in the suburbs. They come in all colors and creeds."

The Problem Explodes

Drug-affected children are not new to school systems. Brown, who has taught in New York's most blighted neighborhoods, has worked with children exposed in the womb to heroin, alcohol, powdered cocaine and other drugs since she began teaching in 1969. But before this school year, Brown said, she had never witnessed so many children with such short attention spans, children who seem to have no control over their actions and who are so inconsistent in their behavior and abilities.

At an age when most youngsters are losing their teeth and learning the alphabet, many crack-affected children show Alzheimer's-like symptoms, beginning a task only to stop moments later, unable to recall what they were working on. Poor coordination also is common. Preschoolers have trouble picking up everyday objects such as building blocks, crayons and eating utensils. They bump into walls, trip over nothing and fall to the floor when they try to sit down.

There is no typical profile for a crack-affected child. Their problems can include extreme hyperactivity, uncontrollable mood swings, language delays, disorganized thinking, lapses in short-term memory, poor coordination and difficulty with fine motor skills.

"Teachers are out there on their own because the collective education community has been so slow in responding to this problem," said Valerie Wallace, a school psychologist who works with the Los Angeles school system's program for drug-affected children. "They are on the front lines and they often don't know how to even identify the children, let alone deal with their special needs."

Trying to identify crack-affected children through behavior alone is tricky. Their problems are easily confused with or compounded by other factors common to children of poverty, including lead poisoning, a lack of prenatal care, abuse, neglect or poor diet and rest habits.

Studies in Los Angeles, Chicago, Philadelphia and Miami have shown that a majority of crack-affected children suffer from problems that will make it difficult for them to flourish in a traditional classroom setting.

Most schools subscribe to a code of behavior that is difficult, even impossible, for some crack-affected children to follow. Sitting at a desk for hours on end is an onerous task for an extremely hyperactive child. And quietly reading a book can seem impossible for students with attention deficit disorder—a condition in which children cannot screen out unimportant sights and sounds.

The sounds that serve as background noise in most school buildings—slamming doors, screeching chairs, coughing and playground noise—present constant interruptions that can't be disregarded by crack-affected children.

Old Ways Don't Apply

"I don't think the old methods are going to work with these children," said Maria Isabel Villanueva, a kindergarten teacher at PS 146 whose class of 25 students includes three who have been identified by parents or guardians as children exposed to crack and other drugs in the womb.

One of Villanueva's students, a spry little boy with a gap-toothed grin, is so antsy on some days that she helps him hold his pencil so he can write his name at the top of the page. On his own, the student uses both his tiny hands to grip his pencils or crayons to help keep the instruments steady.

The student, whose name is being withheld at his guardian's request, can't concentrate for more than a few minutes at a time. Picking up small objects such as chalk or puzzle pieces requires formidable effort. The student also has problems gauging spatial relationships. He attempts to sit down at his seat and misses his chair altogether. Likewise, he moves a fish sandwich toward his mouth but the food winds up smashing into his nose.

The child also exhibits language delays, and a seeming inability to control his emotions so that mild frustration rapidly ascends to temper tantrums and abusive behavior.

Yet aptitude tests indicate that the boy is bright, even advanced, in art and the ability to tell a story. But teachers say it will be difficult to cultivate his innate talents if they cannot control his behavior or meet his special needs.

With the oldest crack-affected children only 7 or 8, it is too early to know for sure how the drug affects their long-term prospects. Some doctors and educators have put a hopeful spin on the problem, pointing to research that indicates that crack-affected children can succeed in school with ample doses of patience, understanding and individual attention.

"These children are salvageable," said Mary Jones, a teacher at the Salvin Special Education Center in Los Angeles, which houses the program aimed at developing teaching strategies for drug-affected students. "We want to do everything possible to avoid putting children in the human scrap heap. We cannot give them new nerve endings. We cannot replace dead brain tissue. But we can give them nurturing and love and patience. Often these are the things that they are not getting at home."

New Programs

Several school systems, including the District's, have established programs to observe crack-affected youngsters and develop new methods for teaching them.

The District's Daisy Program, loosely modeled on a program in Los Angeles, has two classes of 15 students in two elementary schools, where crack-affected children are grouped with youngsters with no known drug exposure. The rooms have play areas, complete with jungle gym-like apparatus, to allow hyperactive children to unleash surplus energy. In some rooms, the traditional rows of desks have been replaced with pillow-filled areas where children can move about easily without being confined behind desks. Instructors in the Daisy program hope that some of their strategies can be adapted for use in regular classrooms as early as this fall. Concerned about protecting the children's privacy, District officials would not allow reporters to visit the classes.

The Prince George's County school system intends to hire doctors and child development specialists to conduct seminars for teachers. The seminars for elementary school and Head Start teachers are designed to help them handle problems such as extreme hyperactivity, emotional outbursts and other symptoms relatively common to children prenatally exposed to drugs.

But such efforts are rare, and little is being done in college education programs to prepare future teachers for students with such staggering needs.

Jones and others in the Los Angeles program recommend a highly structured program for teachers working with crack-affected students. The children may need to be walked through transitions from one task to another. Shorter assignments help students who have trouble paying attention for more than a few moments. A method called "learning through play," which uses puppets and toys to teach more formal subjects such as math, reading and science, can help put restive energy to good use.

Mamie Johnson, principal of New York's PS 146, said computers could help students who lack the dexterity to write clearly. Similarly, workbooks with large print and only a few problems on each page can help students who have trouble concentrating.

And smaller classrooms would allow teachers to spend more time with individual students. Since that's hard to do in austere economic times, schools across the country, including PS 146, have placed teachers' helpers in kindergarten classrooms to provide an additional authority figure to help cope with disruptive or otherwise needy students. Other schools are recruiting parents, retirees and grandparents to volunteer as teachers' aides.

Increasing Demands

So far, efforts to develop teaching strategies for crack-affected youngsters have taken place in specialized classrooms and pilot programs restricted to a small number of students. The vast majority of crack-affected children will begin school in normal classes, where overwhelmed teachers will have no special assistance to cope with their needs.

As the children get older and as the demands of school are increasingly beyond their reach, schools are likely to move many of them into special education, where instruction and therapy can drive the annual cost of educating a student to $10,000 or more than in a regular classroom. Los Angeles, for example, spends $15,000 a student each year in its special program for drug-affected children, compared with just more than $3,000 a year in a regular classroom, said Carol Cole, a special education specialist who helped design the Los Angeles pilot program.

"As kindergarten and first-grade and other teachers see that the problems are more than just immaturity, that is when we are probably going to see these children go to special placement," Cole said.

Already, the influx of crack-exposed children is swelling the demand for special education services in New York and Los Angeles. More than 1,600 students were referred for special education evaluations in New York City during the school year just ended, compared with 1,071 referrals last year. New York State Comptroller Regan said the annual cost of providing special care for crack-affected infants will peak in the late 1990s at more than $176 million. Officials have not estimated the cost in the Washington area.

Maurice Sykes, director of early childhood education in the District, said the city will try to keep drug-affected children out of special education by providing teachers with training and written materials to help them deal with troublesome students in a normal classroom setting, regardless of the cause of their problems.

Such an approach assumes that crack-affected children can function in a normal classroom setting despite their problems, an assertion that is still being tested.

"In spite of all their problems, the children are coping because children, as we know, are incredibly resilient," said Johnson, principal of PS 146. "Somehow I have to have the hope that given the proper nurturing, the proper care, the proper love, that the children will become productive."

July 1, 1991

Budget Cuts Undermining 'War' Against Drug Abuse

MICHAEL ISIKOFF AND MARCIA SLACUM GREENE

In recent years, Second Genesis has been a showcase in Prince George's County's "war" on drug abuse—a 70-bed residential treatment facility that has been a haven for crack-smoking mothers, heroin addicts and other substance abusers seeking to break free of their drug habits.

But last week, county officials announced that budget cuts will force then to stop funding Second Genesis, resulting in the facility closing next January. Struggling to wipe out a $450 million deficit, Maryland officials have slashed $7.2 million from the state's funding for substance abuse, leading to the shutdown of 29 treatment programs and eliminating services for more than 9,400 drug and alcohol abusers.

"I'm not ready to leave this place," said Sharon Still, 34, a recovering crack addict and mother of three, as she wiped away tears at the Second Genesis facility last week. "They are closing the doors to my second chance on life. It seems they feel that we are not worth it or we don't matter."

The cutbacks in Maryland are not isolated. More than two years after President Bush and Congress vowed to launch a renewed national attack on drug abuse, rehabilitation programs across the country are shutting down or paring back operations because of declining state and local funding.

As in the Washington area, the cuts primarily are the result of a recession that has forced state legislatures and city councils to carve deeply into a broad range of social and public health programs. But many officials say the cuts in drug treatment also illustrate the rapidly waning commitment to an issue that until recently was at the forefront of the nation's domestic agenda.

In part, many treatment officials say, surveys showing declines in the casual use of drugs among high school students and the middle class have eroded much of the political urgency behind the drug issue. But Herb Kleber, deputy national drug control director for treatment and prevention programs, noted that those same surveys show a continued concentration of drug abuse among the poor, the unemployed and the homeless, the groups most dependent on publicly funded treatment.

"I'm very distressed . . . we feel frustrated," said Kleber, who this month announced his resignation. "If we don't treat these people, it will be a tragedy. Our streets will not get safer . . . Law enforcement alone will not solve the drug problem."

Over the past few months, more than a dozen states—among them Florida, Massachusetts, Connecticut, Georgia, New Jersey, and Pennsylvania—have reduced funding for drug and alcohol treatment and other states are likely to follow.

Federal officials estimate that as many as 6 million Americans are heavy drug users and that about half of them could benefit from treatment programs if they were available. Kleber said the cuts announced so far likely will reduce the number of publicly funded treatment slots from about 2.2 million to less than 2 million, leaving more than 1 million addicts without access to help.

Moreover, in some inner-city communities, where the cuts have been hardest, local officials predict there could be devastating side effects: setting back efforts to reduce the number of crack-addicted babies and checking the spread of AIDS by intravenous drug users.

In New York City, where officials estimate 14,000 drug-exposed babies are born annually, plans to start a dozen new clinics to treat pregnant addicts were scrapped as a result of a $34 million cut in the city's treatment program.

In the District, where the arrival of crack four years ago ushered in a wave of violence that has given the city the highest murder rate in the nation, Mayor Sharon Pratt Dixon last summer slashed $9.2 million from the city's treatment budget.

City officials said more than 2,000 District residents are on waiting lists for treatment and new applicants are being told they may have to wait up to nine months to get into a treatment program. At D.C. General Hospital's detoxification program, 500 people are waiting for 20 slots.

Dixon said last week that she hopes to review the cuts. "Drug treatment has not fallen as a priority," said Vada Manager, Dixon's press secretary. "But in our ability to fund it, we were restricted by inheriting a deficit. She had to make cuts based on numbers and not budget priorities. Things are better now."

In Colorado, a $3 million cut in alcohol and drug abuse funding will eliminate services for more than 8,000 mostly indigent clients, state officials said. In Florida, the entry point for a large portion of the nation's cocaine supply, officials recently announced that the state's only publicly funded hospital for substance abusers will shut down and nearly 10,000 drug abusers will lose services as a result of a $19.4 million cut in treatment programs.

"It's already had a drastic impact," said Pamela Petersen, acting deputy assistant secretary for alcohol and drug abuse, who said Florida's waiting list has more than doubled. "We have citizens writing us letters saying, 'We can't get help anymore, we can't get treatment, what do you want us to do?'"

Perhaps most troubling, some treatment officials said, is that the same recession that produced the cuts also seems to be creating an increased demand for services. In part, hard times tend to drive more people to drugs and alcohol. In addition, some treatment officials said, patients who in the past might have enrolled in expensive private programs now are signing up for publicly funded clinics.

Although Virginia has increased its substance abuse budget by 3.9 percent, some jurisdictions, including Fairfax County, have experienced minor cuts. Fairfax

County officials said at least 30 people a week are being turned away from detoxification and 150 are on a five- to six-month waiting list for residential treatment.

"Our demand is increasing, and we are far below the need," said Joan N. Volpe, director of substance abuse services for the community services board.

Treatment officials said the cutbacks are especially jarring when contrasted with the highly charged political rhetoric that surrounded the drug issue only two years ago.

In his first nationwide television speech as chief executive in September 1989, President Bush declared drug abuse "the gravest domestic threat facing the nation" and called for a renewed national commitment that included a major expansion of the country's treatment programs, although congressional Democrats at the time attacked the president for failing to dedicate enough funding for such an expansion.

Since then, budget documents show federal funding for state and local treatment has increased by more than 80 percent. The administration proposed $1.65 billion for the fiscal year that began Oct. 1. Yet, there have been few presidential pronouncements on the issue lately and meeting the administration's treatment goals appears further away than ever, some anti-drug officials said.

In many states, officials said, the recent cuts in local funds have more than wiped out the benefits of increased federal funding over the past three years. "In terms of level of services, we are back to where we were five or six years ago," said Rick Samson, director of the Maryland Alcohol and Drug Abuse Administration.

Moreover, Kleber and federal officials fear that the cutbacks could be even more severe, depending on the outcome of a House-Senate conference committee meeting this week on appropriations for the departments of Labor and Health and Human Services.

Although Democrats repeatedly have attacked the Bush administration for neglecting treatment programs, the House-passed version of the bill would cut $135 million from the president's drug treatment budget. The Senate, on the other hand, proposes funding at only slightly less than was recommended by the president.

Some congressional staff workers said last week that the cuts also reflect doubts about the effectiveness of many treatment programs. Some studies have shown that anywhere from 50 to 90 percent of drug addicts who start treatment programs never finish. A recent General Accounting Office study found there was little information available on the results of increased federal spending for treatment.

"We've been spending a lot more money out there for treatment, but what are we getting for it?' asked Edward Jurith, staff director for the House Select Committee on Narcotics Abuse and Control. "There's nobody who can answer that question for you.,

But the lack of such hard data was small consolation last week at the Second Genesis facility in Prince George's County, where $500,000 a year in county funds supports 48 of the beds, and private sources, including insurance, support the remaining 22.

Michael C. Fuller, director of addiction services for the Prince George's County Health Department, said that the county will make efforts to relocate the Second Genesis clients to outpatient and other programs.

But Sidney Shankman, executive director of Second Genesis, said such alternatives are not available. "These people will have to return to the streets . . . you're assigning them to a death sentence," Shankman said.

Second Genesis, which cannot survive without the county funds, is known as "therapeutic community," an intensive year-long program that seeks to help addicts by forcing them to cope with the underlying problems in their lives that lead to their addictions.

Several residents said they had tried unsuccessfully to end their habits in short-term programs and failed. Second Genesis's approach works, they said, because it touches all aspects of their lives by including such services as family counseling, support groups and educational and vocational classes.

"I always felt I could use drugs because I had control over other areas of my life," said Maurice, 30, a college graduate who was paid $3,800 a month as a computer engineer before he became addicted to crack cocaine. After Maurice lost his job, he was arrested for selling crack on the streets to support his drug habit.

"I thought it was just poor people from dysfunctional families and who didn't have good educations who used drugs," he said. "Without programs like this, people just like me who use drugs to find their identities will have no hope."

October 27, 1991